THE ESSENTIAL
KEVIN HUNTER
COLLECTION

Spirit Guides and Angels, Soul Mates and Twin Flames, Raising Your Vibration, Divine Messages for Humanity, Connecting with the Archangels

KEVIN HUNTER

WARRIOR
OF LIGHT
PRESS
Los Angeles, California

Warrior of Light Press
www.kevin-hunter.com

Body, Mind & Spirit/Angels & Guides
Inspiration & Personal Growth
Spirit Writing. Channeling (Spiritualism). Spiritual life.

PRODUCTION CREDITS:
Project Editor: James Szopo

All rights reserved. Copyright ©2011-2014

ISBN-10: 0692700072
ISBN-13: 978-0692700075

Acknowledgements

Thank you to my spirit posse that consists of God and my personal sports team of Angels, Guides, Archangels, and Saints. Thank you also to my loyal beautiful readers for their immense support over the years.

Dedication

If you have this book in your hand, then that is because you were guided to it by your own Spirit team in Heaven. If someone recommended it to you, then it was for good reason. This is for you in order to help change humanity towards a brighter new world.

A Word

"It does not matter if you are a believer or a skeptic, because your team of Guides and Angels believe in you regardless. They are always present illuminating the path on your soul's journey. They are guiding you out of despair and towards peace, love, and joy throughout your Earthly life. All you need to do is pay attention to their messages and signs."

~ Kevin Hunter

Content

SPIRIT GUIDES AND ANGELS

SOUL MATES AND TWIN FLAMES

RAISING YOUR VIBRATION

DIVINE MESSAGES FOR HUMANITY

<u>CONNECTING WITH THE ARCHANGELS</u>

Introduction

The Essential Kevin Hunter Collection is a compilation of all the material taken from the Warrior of Light pocket book series called *Spirit Guides and Angels, Soul Mates and Twin Flames, Divine Messages for Humanity, Raising Your Vibration,* and *Connecting with the Archangels.* Those five books were from the bigger books *Warrior of Light, Empowering Spirit Wisdom,* and *Darkness of Ego.* The purpose of compiling it all in one gigantic greatest hits collection is for those who prefer not to purchase each book individually and would rather have all the key introductory spiritual empowerment information all in one gigantic book.

If you have this book in your hand and not the others listed in this introduction, then there is no reason to pick up the other books since the material is all available here in this big one, unless of course you choose to. Some people prefer specific content and not the rest. They might only pick up the pocket book on the *Connecting with the Archangels* or the one on *Soul Mates and Twin Flames.* Those who desire all five of the pocket books can find them all in this volume. This book can also be used as a spiritual encyclopedia, a coffee table book, or you may choose to allow whatever page is intended to fall open be the one you were meant to see. This is in order to deliver a specific message or guidance piece you needed to know at any particular time.

THE ESSENTIAL
KEVIN HUNTER
COLLECTION

Featuring the following books:
Warrior of Light, Empowering Spirit Wisdom, Darkness of Ego,
Spirit Guides and Angels, Soul Mates and Twin Flames, Raising
Your Vibration, Divine Messages for Humanity, and Connecting
with the Archangels.

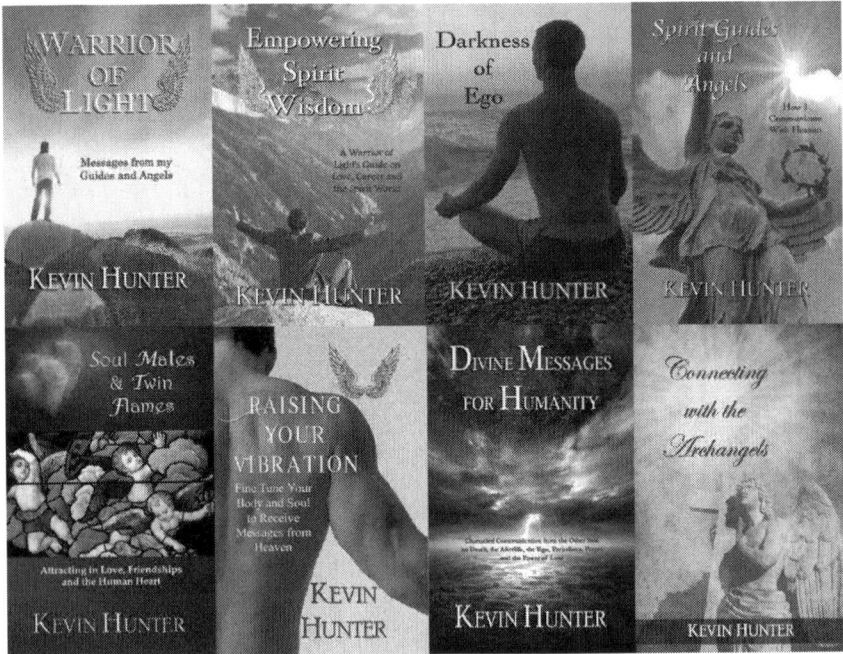

Author's Note

All of the information in this book is infused with practical messages and guidance that my Spirit team has taught and shared with me revolving around many different topics. The main goal is to fine tune your body, mind, and soul. This improves humanity one person at a time. You are a Divine communicator and perfectly adjusted and capable of receiving messages from Heaven. This is for your benefit in order to live a happier, richer life. It is your individual responsibility to respect yourself and this planet while on your journey here.

The messages and information enclosed in this and all of the *Warrior of Light* books may be in my own words, but they do not come from me. They come from God, the Holy Spirit, my Spirit team of guides, angels, and sometimes certain Archangels and Saints. I am merely the liaison or messenger in delivering and interpreting the intentions of what they wish to communicate in a practical modern way that others can easily understand. Heaven loves that I talk about them and share this stuff as it gets other people to work with them too!

There is one main hierarchy Saint who works with me leading the pack. His name is Nathaniel. He is often brutally truthful and forceful, as he does not mince words. There may be topics in this and my other books that might bother you or make you uncomfortable. He asks that you examine the underlying cause of this discomfort and come to terms with the fear attached. He cuts right to the heart of humanity without apology. I have learned quite a bit from him while adopting his ideology, which is Heaven's philosophy as a whole.

I am one with the Holy Spirit and have many Spirit Guides and Angels around me. As my connections to the other side grew to be daily over the course of my life, more of them joined in behind the others. I have often seen, sensed, heard, and been privy to the dozens of magnificent lights that crowd around me on occasion.

If I use the word "He" when pertaining to God, this does not mean that I am advocating that he is a male. Simply replace the word, "He" with one you are comfortable using to identify God for you to be. This goes for any gender I use as examples. When I say, "spirit team", I am referring to a team of 'Guides and Angels'. The purpose of the *Warrior of Light* books is to empower and help you improve yourself, your life, and humanity as a whole. It does not matter if you are a beginner or well versed in the subject matter. There may be something that reminds you of something you already know or something that you were unaware of. We all have much to share with one another, as we are all one in the end. This book and all of the *Warrior of Light* series of books contain information and directions on how to reach the place where you can be a fine tuned instrument to receive your own messages from your own Spirit team.

Some of my personal stories are infused and sprinkled in the books. This is in order for you to see how it works effectively for me. With some of my methods, I hope that you gain insight, knowledge, or inspiration. It may prompt you to recall incidents where you were receiving heavenly messages in your own life. There are helpful ways that you can improve your existence and have a connection with Heaven throughout this book. Doing so will greatly transform yourself in all ways allowing you to attract wonderful circumstances at higher levels and live a happier more content life.

~ Kevin Hunter

THE ESSENTIAL
KEVIN HUNTER
COLLECTION

SPIRIT GUIDES AND ANGELS

How I Communicate with Heaven

Chapter One

SPIRIT GUIDES AND ANGELS

How often do you find yourself thinking about nothing in particular when suddenly a jolt of clear-cut information flies through your mind? What you receive is so commanding you experience a surge of uplifting joy coursing through all of the cells in your body. The idea, key, or answer you gained was the missing piece of the puzzle to something you needed to know at that particular time. How many times have you received a nudge to do something that would positively change your life? Instead of taking action on it, you deny it chalking it off to wishful thinking. You later discover that it was indeed an answered prayer, if only you had taken notice and followed the guidance. These are some examples of how you can tell when it is your Spirit Guide or Guardian Angel communicating with you. When you get your lower self and ego out of the way, then that is when the profound answer you had been hoping for is revealed to you. The impression you acquire is so powerful that it pulls you out of the darkness you were previously stuck in. It is a bright light shining its focus directly onto the message in unadorned view. It is crystal clear as if it had been there all along and you wonder why you had not noticed it before.

There are so many joyless faces out there waiting, complaining, or praying for a miracle. Instead you choose to fill your days up partaking in activities that only erode your self-esteem and overall well-being. These activities can be something you are not aware of such as sitting in traffic completely tense. You experience another mundane routine day screaming for an escape from this prison of a life you have created. You stay unhappy in your jobs, the places you live in, and with certain friendships or relationships. You ponder over not having that home of your dreams or sharing your life with someone in a loving relationship. The days having this dull mindset turn into months and years with no miracle in sight. This disappointment grows like mold causing you to appear and feel eternally glum, negative, and bitter. The emotional traits mask your dissatisfaction and heartbreak attracting more of that stuff to you. To cope you drown those nasty emotions with addictions from drinking heavily, ingesting chemicals, doing drugs or by partaking in time wasting activities such as gossip and Internet surfing.

You choose to be disconnected living behind a wall built of your own attitude and yet it is in your basic human nature to want to connect to other human souls, to someone, or something. You want to be happy, but that state can feel so out of reach and unobtainable you drown in its thoughts. Our way of communicating today is primarily through phone, texting, email and social networking. Even if you truly wanted to sit face-to-face you are too busy or worn out to bother. You were not intended to live your life in misery and unhappiness. For some reason, you choose to fall into a pattern of suffering. Human souls as a whole are to blame for this design.

It is never too late to improve your life. What you are looking for is right in front of you and closer than you think. Strengthen your faith and believe in the power of what exists outside of your human body. This will bring you closer to the happiness that resides within. God, your angels, spirit guides and all in Heaven can and want to assist you out of this hopelessness. They are always present around you. They want to lift you out of your life of desolation. It is irrelevant what your beliefs are and whether you are religious or an atheist. It does not matter what race you were born into in this lifetime. Nor does it matter if you are rich or poor, gay or straight,

2

liberal or conservative. Whatever you agreed to come into this lifetime as, you are loved equally. No one is more special than anyone else. God and the angels see each of your inner lights, your innocence and your true purpose for being here. If you have veered long off course, they can help you get back to where you need to be. Who you are is a perfect child of God and love no matter where you are from or who you are.

A Spirit Guide once lived as a human soul, but a Guardian Angel has always been a Spirit. Every human soul has one Spirit Guide and one Guardian Angel assigned to work with them throughout their entire Earthly life. They are your immediate army that works with you daily. This is from the moment you were born until you pass on to the next life. They know everything about you, from your thoughts and feelings, to your wants and desires. Murderers, serial killers and those filled with hate towards other human souls also have one Spirit Guide and one Guardian Angel with them. Because you have free will choice, those human souls are not listening to or following the guidance that is passed onto them by their Spirit team.

Your personal Spirit team is anyone on the other side you work with regularly. Since everyone is assigned at least one Spirit Guide and one Guardian Angel from birth until death, then that is your Spirit team. Some human souls have more than one Spirit Guide and one Guardian Angel, if you have been requesting additional assistance from Heaven, or you are working with angels on a daily basis. These Guides and Angels are attracted to your light and know if you are an honorable person. They can see how bright your light shines. The brighter your light is, the more attracted they are to you and may then come to your side. They know you are one with Heaven and are excited to work with you and help you along your journey. Some may come to you simply to protect you. Others may come to you in order to assist you with an important task. Once that task has been accomplished, then that Guide or Angel leaves to help someone else. Meanwhile your one main Spirit Guide and Guardian Angel never leave until you cross over where you will come face to face with them.

Your Spirit team does not make your choices for you. They

3

work with you to help you along with your spiritual growth and to keep you on the right path. They assist in orchestrating circumstances that will improve your life when it is time. This can include coming into contact with particular people on Earth to help enhance your life in some way, or to teach you certain lessons or gain specific knowledge. You can call on your Spirit team to assist you at anytime. You do have to personally ask for their assistance because they cannot intervene with your free will. They may stand idly around while you make one mistake after another. They are unable to interfere with your poor choices unless you have asked them to or permanently invited them in. They will attempt to get your attention if you are heading off your life path, but they cannot stop you. They know that these mistakes you make are essential to your spiritual growth.

When you make mistakes and bad things continuously happen for you, then this is a wakeup call. These situations are getting you to notice the negative synchronistic pattern, and to stop the cycle and find another path. Your Guides and Angels hope that it will wake you up to say, *"Wait a minute. What am I doing? Obviously, the way I have been living has not been entirely successful. Guides and Angels, I call upon you now. Please work with me by guiding me down the right path. Help me to reach a place of peace. Thank you."*

You are always receiving Guardian Angel and Spirit Guide communication, messages, and nudges, but are you paying attention to them?

More people than not believe in angels regardless of what their spiritual beliefs are. God, Heaven, and the Angels are all non-denominational. This means that they do not belong to any religious sect. You can be a non-believer and they are still with you, working with you, and guiding you.

Your Spirit Guide and Guardian Angel are with you from the time you are born until you exit this life. Your Spirit Guide is typically a deceased relative, but not always. This deceased relative is one who has chosen to be your Spirit Guide before you were born. It can even be a relative from centuries back! This Spirit Guide has gone through formal training to be able to efficiently guide you. They know when not to interfere and to allow you free will choice. If they see that you are a danger to yourself or someone else, they will tap you on the shoulder and attempt to divert your attention.

Let's use an extreme story and say that you decide to head over to someone's house to do drugs all night. Your Spirit Guide will nudge you to head down another course. Your ego is so strong and powerful that it will convince you that you will be happier if you go into that house and get high. What might end up happening can be a circumstance that propels you into the bell jar. An array of negative activity can follow such as you experience an overdose, someone steals your wallet, something medically goes wrong, or you have an accident. Perhaps you lose your job, a friendship, relationship, or any other incident that thrusts your life into a downward spiral preceding that night. From this one incident, you attract in more of the same causing you to experience one detriment after another further delaying your life purpose. Your Spirit Guide cannot stop you, but they are communicating with you in an attempt to get you to notice a different life choice that will not have such negative repercussions. This is the extent of the intervention since they are not allowed to stop you from doing that drug unless it results in death before your time. Even then, many human souls under the influence of drugs or alcohol rarely listen to their Spirit team. There are cases where your guides did all they can do and were unable to divert you from continued bad behavior. You were not paying attention, but instead consumed in pain, greed, or rebelliousness. The end result is your early death.

Your Spirit Guide and Guardian Angel may alternate with specific roles in helping you. When you are down or depressed, your Guardian Angel may be the one that tries to get your attention to focus on the bright side of life. They will caress and soothe your heart Chakra relieving you of any heavy burdens you might be feeling. Your Guardian Angel will be the one that works with you on your feelings of well-being, prompting you to be more optimistic and joyful. Your Spirit Guide will work with you on practical matters with you that lead you to the job or career you always wanted. Your Spirit Guide may direct you to take certain classes in the area of your dream making sure you stick to it. This is followed

5

by the job that is beneficial for you at that time, even if it is not quite the job you always wanted. Sometimes you have to go through your own individual training and lessons with several different jobs before you are shown the big dream job. They do not give you anything immediately necessarily, but they gradually guide you towards your dream goal in steps.

You could be someone who has spent years looking for a job only to be met with distress that there is no work out there. There may be times where there are no jobs in your chosen area of interest. You are guided to take a particular job, but you do not notice it since it is not the job you want. You are being expected to start somewhere even in a position you do not want. You may be asked to take a position that you feel is beneath you or for less pay. I have done this myself only to find that it leads directly to the dream position I do want. I am suddenly catapulted upwards towards one of the greatest jobs I would have had to date. You need to have faith and understand that there is a divine plan for you.

All those in Heaven are present in this Earthly life to make your life easier, but the catch is that you have to ask them for help, as they cannot intervene without your consent. The only time they do intercede is when there is a life-threatening situation before it's your time to go. This is God's law as he gave you an ego and free will. Ego and free will are the biggest cause of turmoil, hate, and destruction known to man. You are given free will choice to either live in peace or live stressed out. Which one would you like to have?

You can have more peace and joy in your life when you start paying attention to your Spirit team's guidance. They do not live your life for you because you are here to learn and grow. However, they do assist you in navigating gracefully out of circumstances that consistently cause you grief, stress, and depression. They do not want you to suffer, but you must learn valuable lessons while here on Earth.

I made great strides and shifts from living under duress with a wide range of addictions to living more at peace by working with my Spirit team. Your Spirit Guide and Guardian Angel help improve your soul. They can help you have more time available, to getting more exercise, or to finding the right job. For some circumstances, the change is immediate. For bigger needs, it may take much longer. This is because there are pieces of the puzzle that they must maneuver around on your behalf. You may not be quite ready for what is to come. You have additional life lessons to learn before you graduate to the next step. Everything is all set according to divine timing, but if you do not ask your Spirit team for help, then they stand by watching you suffer. They watch you feel needlessly miserable when all you need to do is call out to them. I liken it to the mythological stories about Vampires that state that a Vampire cannot enter your house unless you invite it in. This concept is similar to asking anyone in Heaven or the Spirit world for assistance. They will stand outside your door waiting patiently for you to say the magic words and invite them into your life. It is like having a winning sports team on your side, as you cannot lose!

I have always believed in angels and have never questioned Heaven's existence. I do not falsely follow something without testing it out first. I have an analytical mind that questions everything and is suspicious of anything. When I receive proof or a response that validates what I am questioning, then I become a believer.

The reason I greatly believe in God, Heaven, the Angels and Spirit Guides is that I have been testing them my entire life. I have had immense feedback and success simply by paying attention to their Divine intervention and communication. I do not try to convince or convert anybody, but rather share information about them to those interested. I will graciously part with some of the messages that they have shared with me throughout my life.

There are those who are deeply religious who have said that you are not supposed to pray to angels or archangels. I have never seen anyone including myself urge anyone to pray to the angels. Asking your guide and Angel for assistance is not praying to them. They are the gifts from God who are available to help when you need it. They are His arms and hands that connect you to Him. When you are experiencing negative emotions, then you cut yourself off from God. The angels, guides, and archangels raise your vibration to the level of happiness so that you feel God's connection. Their role is to lift you to a happier state where you are at peace. This level is where you will feel God's presence and receive His communication. When you ask your Spirit team for help, you are essentially reaching out to God.

Asking them for help is mandatory if you desire assistance in your life. When you are upset or stressed out, not only do you not receive God's wisdom, but you forget to ask for help. All you have to do is ask, whether that be mentally, out loud or even in writing. I have even sent some of them an email. I send it to myself and then I file it away. You can write to them in a journal, notebook, or on a piece of paper. It does not matter how you ask for help, or how you word it, or how you say it, since no special invocation is needed. They will move into your vicinity before you have finished your sentence. What is important is having the intention.

For example, you can think something like this, "Okay angels, I need your help with this." The right Guide or Angel has already rushed in before you have finished your sentence. Sometimes they respond immediately, but if it is a complicated issue it may take a bit longer. It is important to have faith and trust that they are and have indeed stepped in, and they are working with you on your concern. Sometimes they may respond in ways that you may not be noticing. After it has hit you a few times you may get that moment where you say, "Okay, I thought something was going on with that." You must be open and receptive knowing that sometimes they may not answer you in the way you are expecting.

My mom taught me how to pray when I was a wee tike. Every night as I went to bed she would enter my room and say my prayers with me. We were not religious and there was not a shred of guilt, fear, or damnation surrounding our prayers. Her goal was that we all grow up to be good people helping and contributing to the world in a positive way. We said these prayers every night.

My mom was and is all compassion and love for all people regardless of their interests or lifestyle choices. Her mantra in these prayers was to practice and teach love while in this lifetime when we were young and when we grow up. She would walk me through communicating to Jesus, Mother Mary, and Joseph. I never had the fear and guilt when connecting to Jesus or Mother Mary specifically. I did grow up to notice that others did not share these same beliefs.

I had noticed that when I used the words God, Heaven, Jesus, or Mother Mary around certain people that they would fidget uncomfortably. Some of that is fear and guilt. They were raised to associate those words with those who speak of an angry, judgmental, and negative God. Even if others disagreed, I have never seen Jesus or Mother Mary in any other way than all love. It is important to not be led by human ego. They insist on creating the fear that there is a merciless Heaven that will cast you out into fire and brimstone at any moment. God will never cease to love you, but he does expect you to correct your mistakes and behavior. This is especially true if it is delaying you on your path, and you are hurting yourself or someone else.

You have a life purpose and mission to accomplish while you are here and it is your goal to discover what that is. Everyone needs to be contributing something in a positive way that is bringing love to another person. You were not born angry, bitter, and depressed. Other human souls have inflicted that belief system on you. You absorbed it and reacted to it in ways where it might have permanently damaged you. It will be reversed and undone in this life or in the next when you pray and ask for heavenly assistance to lift those burdens off your soul. Invite in Heaven to permanently work with you on improving your life. They love you and want to help you reach a state of peace and contentment in your life.

Chapter Two

How Do Guides and Angels Communicate With You

There are a plethora of spirit beings in many of the heavenly realms that exist. They include angels, guides, archangels, spirit guides, guardian angels, realm spirits, saints, ascended masters, and deceased loved ones. Since they cannot just pick up the phone and call you, they use other varying means and methods to communicate with you called *clairs*. Your senses are divine communication tools with Heaven! This is why your senses, Chakras and over all well-being needs to be kept clean of debris and trash that blocks the communication line with God. The more negative you are, then the more clogged your *clairs* get. This is why spiritual practitioners insist on living as joyful and toxic free of a life as you can manage. You are born with naturally heightened clear channels of communication to the other side.

The four basic Clair channels are:

Clairvoyance (clear seeing)
Clairaudience (clear hearing)
Clairsentience (clear feeling)
Claircognizance (clear knowing)

Others have shared stories of children talking to angels or friends that no one else can see. Unfortunately, some adults thrash and shatter that belief in those children by saying, "Oh that's just your imaginary friend." These invented friends are not always as imaginary as a jaded adult might believe.

You are born with heightened functioning clairs, but there are typically one or two clairs that are more dominant in you than others. Over time your clair channels dim and darken due to things such as: Blocks created by society, a heavy interest in the material world, domination of your ego, consumption of negative substances, and poor lifestyle choices. These are some of the predominant situations that clog your clair channels. When your clair channels are clogged, then this prevents you from communicating or even knowing that you are receiving messages from Heaven.

CLAIRAUDIENCE

Clairaudience means "clear hearing". You are hearing the voices of Heavenly messages and guidance being filtered through what is called your Ear Chakra. For as long as I can remember, I have heard voices from the spirit world in my left ear as guidance and messages. The voices of my Guides and Angels are clear as if they are standing next to me talking into an ear that has been deafer than the other since birth. When I was four years old, my Mother had taken me to the Doctor for repeated hearing checkups. She had later told me that I was not responding to any of the tests in one of my ears. Therefore, they thought I might be fully deaf in that ear. The sounds of the outside world are fainter in that ear than the other. Instead the volume is cranked up to the spirit world in the deafer ear. Every now and then I hear a ringing in that ear. This has been undetected by medical professionals to be anything of concern. This is my Spirit team downloading important and vital information for me that I would need to access at some point. I equate it to hooking up a flash drive to your computer and moving important files off it and onto your hard drive for immediate access. At times, I will hear a dial up internet sound in my inner ear as if it is trying to connect. Other times if the reception is not clear, it will sound as if I am switching the channels on a radio station until I hear a clear song.

Music is and has always been my escape. I love music as I am a rocker after all, but that is the only area I prefer it loud. As a clairaudient, I hear the heavenly inspiration and messages carried on the notes of music. This is where I hear everything clearly. All other loud sounds and noises are intrusive and strictly shunned and forbidden around me. This includes things such as crowd noise, sirens, airplanes, trashcans banging, screaming of any kind. Unpleasant noises are incredibly heightened and uncomfortable. I hear footsteps around me or someone approaching and I immediately know who is coming or what type of person they are. I figured I was odd in that I constantly fixated on what others deemed to be an unimportant sound. These are signs of someone having a higher level of clairaudience.

I put my spark and passion into my writing projects. I hear the music and the rhythms and that is how my Spirit team communicates with me. I hear it in the notes, in the music, in people's conversations, in the line at the store and it inspires me. I tap into the waves of the ocean and the voices rush over that and through the white noise. The music translates into verbal messages coming through the sounds and inspiration.

I hear everything in the sounds, from people's voices, to the patterns in people's footsteps. I can tell what people are up to from those sounds. As a child, I thought I was just a spaz having an acute hearing ability to every sound that happens around me. I did not know until adulthood that there was an actual word for it called *clairaudience*.

One afternoon I was running late and I could not find my car keys anywhere. I started throwing everything around in a panic mentally shouting, "Where are my keys!"

I huffed and puffed throwing items all over the place in a panic. I shouted again, "Angels. Where are my keys?!"

I heard a loud male voice in my left ear shout, "On your bed!!"

Without hesitating, I charged into the bedroom. There were my keys on the bed sitting all alone. I grabbed them abruptly and headed towards my car. I mentally repeated the words to my Spirit team, "Thank you. Thank you. Thank you." Heaven is unfazed by your sudden upset. All they see is the love buried inside you. This does not give one license to behave as I did, but as you work with them more, you are less hostile and more appreciative. They see the light within you and ignore the range of wasted emotions, because to them everything is all right.

As my interest in the spiritual crowd grew, I wanted to know what they were like since I never believed I fit into any group. I went to an all-day spiritually based convention to be around like-minded souls. While there, I would agree to give someone a cold reading in the audience. This was not a test, but an exercise using no divination tool such as oracle or tarot cards. I personally did not need them even though part of me enjoyed double-checking and confirming the messages through those tools. This is where the angels reminded me once again as they do repeatedly with all of us, "TRUST." Having to do a cold read in a space with hundreds of people's energies around me while on little sleep was not my cup of tea. I wanted to bolt out of there at lightning speed and crawl back into bed. I knew there was no way out. I could feel my team pushing me out of my comfort zone. I would need a volunteer to participate in this exercise.

A young girl who was sitting near me raised her hand and said she will do the read with me. She pulled her chair to face me and closed her eyes. I reached my hand out around her head to feel the air pressure energy. My Spirit team said that this was not about me. This is about this girl in front of me. I closed my eyes and took several deep breaths until I was relaxed.

I called in my Spirit team and said, "Please get my ego out of the way. This is about this girl right here. It is all about her and not me. If anyone would like to come through for her, please come forward now."

I repeated those words with my eyes closed waiting in stillness for some communication in any form. I heard a male voice speak loud and clear through my clairaudience channel. My ego was naturally trying to make me second-guess it. I opened my eyes and what I said stopped her:

"There is a pleasant man who is around you right now. He says he is always with you. He is telling me that his name is Ralph. He is your grandfather. He has been working closely with you on your education and towards your life purpose."

When I noticed the girl's eyes flooded with tears I stopped talking. She informed me that she is sixteen years old and in High School. I thought she was in her early twenties as she had a mature look to her. She carried herself confidently as if she were an adult. She was also at this conference alone. She said her Mother's Dad, her Grandfather, died when she was seven years old. She then said that his name was "RALPH".

Most of the time you are getting accurate information and messages from your own Spirit team, but you discredit it or talk yourself out of it being real. I heard a male voice clearly telling me his name for this young girl. I thought I was imagining it at first. I was thinking, "I don't know any Ralph. This is silly." My Spirit team prompted me to trust in the communication I was getting and not second guess it. It may not mean anything to me, but it might mean something to someone else. I bit the bullet and decided to tell the girl what I heard knowing that I might be wrong. This was an excellent case where I realized again that there are loved ones communicating with you in Heaven. This was a complete stranger whom I had never met. Nor had I known anything about her. Yet, I told her about her deceased grandfather. I am not a working Medium, but what I did in that instance for that girl was what one would call, *Mediumship*. This is something anyone can do if they work at it. Do not doubt or second-guess the messages you receive. Do not worry if you make a mistake. To do so is operating from your imposter lower self or ego.

All psychics read in a variety of different ways. Not everyone has the same gifts. For example, some will need to have the person in front of them to read them, while others need to have them on the phone to hear their voice vibration or to pick up on their energy. I do not need to see or hear the person. I am too sensitive to every nuance around me that I have found it to be more of a distraction at times. I am able to hear the voice of spirit without having the person present. The voices are loud when I'm in a centered state. Sometimes they chime in before someone has finished their sentence.

CLAIRCOGNIZANCE

Claircognizance means "clear knowing". This is receiving heavenly messages and guidance through your crown chakra above your head. I am profoundly claircognizant, which is similar to having a computer in the mind. I receive Divine information through my crown Chakra that later proves to be true. Having claircognizance is when you know the answer to a topic or subject matter that you are not versed in.

I have had others ask, "How did you know that was going to happen?" I would say, "I don't know. I just knew." Growing up when they would ask that question I would stare at them blankly not understanding. I did not know how I knew.

Someone with claircognizance always seems to know when someone is lying to them, even if they don't call them out on it. I would typically keep it to myself unless it is something major that needs addressing. This information proves useful on occasion, but then there are certain things you do not want to know and would prefer to be naïve to. You know this information is passed onto you for a reason. It is to protect you or someone else by saving them time and potential heartache.

A claircognizant would know if someone is cheating on them or on someone else. I have known things about someone from a first meeting and what they are like. I can tell immediately what role they would play in my life if any. Everyone I dated romantically, I knew at first glance that I would be with them soon or in the future. It would later happen and come to fruition. There was no explanation for it and I never questioned it. This is an example of what claircognizance and clear knowing is.

My mind is always on, thinking and working. Sometimes I find it difficult to shut it off when I need it to. I had asked my Doctor once if there was something I could take that would help me to stop thinking specifically at night. He laughed and said, "Unfortunately, there isn't anything like that." It was something that I had to accept as a gift and learn to use it to my advantage. Knowing things before they happened and not known how or why has saved my life in many great ways.

Information or guidance comes to you when you are not trying to get it. When you push to receive guidance or messages, then that is when you block it. Your fear is that you will not pick up on any messages, or that the messages you receive are your imagination. As a result, you hear and receive nothing. Second guessing what you're receiving is a block.

Your Spirit team is always communicating with you, but your strong will to try to receive messages can dim the connection. The underlying core reason is due to fear, or destructive and unhelpful self-talk. Negative emotions block communication with the other side. You can ask the angels to remove the blocks that cut off the communication to them. Ask them to help you clearly hear, see, know, and feel the messages they wish to relay to you.

One Summer, I was talking with a group of people standing in a circle at a beach BBQ. There were many huddles of people talking at this BBQ around my group too. As I was talking to them, I took one-step back grabbing the bottle of wine behind me to my right. I proceeded to pour it into the glass of a woman who was in another huddle near my group. She jolted in shock and laughed into a shout. "I was just going to get more wine! Wait! How did you know that? Ok that was weird." I just shrugged and said, "I don't know. I just knew." I had no idea how I knew and I was not looking at the woman or facing her. Something had prompted me to turn, grab the wine and pour. Sometimes the clear knowing is slight and can surround something as insignificant as this.

Other examples of having Claircognizance are where you know the answers to problems or topics you are not educated in, yet you had the right answer that solved it when others were perplexed. People with an analytical mind tend to be claircognizant. They are great problem solvers such as a Scientist or Teacher. Their own Spirit team filters this information through them. Ironically, those with claircognizance tend to be the ones who are skeptical of psychic phenomena. One of the reasons is due to their analytical or scientific mind. They need concrete proof of anything unseen with their physical eyes. Yet, they're receiving heavenly guidance through their claircognizance channel.

I have always been wise beyond my years. In High School, I was the guy who would sit up in the bleachers, and one by one a different student would approach me to divulge their issues as if I were their own private counselor. They were from every different clique you could imagine: the nerd, the jock, the cheerleader, the techie, the bully, and the bullied would all come up to me solo at varying intervals. I would say a sentence or two to them that assisted their situation. They would cry out in relief with something along the lines of, "God you always know just what to say!"

They would say things like, "It's as if you're this old soul who knows the answers to life and yet you're a teenager in High School. How do you know so much?"

I knew that I was different, but the majority appreciated this eccentricity. I rarely had an unsettling moment. I did not think of myself as being different just for knowing information, but it was the whole package. I did not follow the crowd and was uninterested in fads or being popular. I never thought of myself as a follower and have always been an independent leader. I am comfortable with being alone and have no desire for a constant demanding need for attention. I did not care if anybody liked or did not like me. My goal was and has always been beyond that. This is also the many marks of what some call a soul of the Indigo Generation.

I was walking past a colleague from a former job in the past. He stopped me and said, "Hey Kevin, I want to ask you a question. What do you think of bacon toothpaste?"

Without flinching or displaying shock I said, "I don't know. That sounds like something someone in Iowa would invent."

His face turned white. "How the Hell did you know that?"

I said, "I don't know."

He proceeds to inform me. "I'm talking to a friend of mine online who is in Iowa and he was just telling me that he's inventing this toothpaste with bacon in it. Okay, Kevin that was weird. How did you know that?"

"I - I don't know. It's just what I thought of."

This is an example of claircognizance in action where you know the accurate answers and do not know how you know. Because this is a regular occurrence for me, I never found it to be appropriate to get into a lengthy explanation with anyone about it. There is no efficient way of explaining how I know something. It appears as if I grabbed it out of thin air. I ignore the question or run over it with something else. As a Claircognizant, I always know just how to respond.

How often have you had the answer to something you knew nothing about? You may have had that person ask you, 'How did you know that?' You stare at them blankly. "I don't know." This is an example of messages delivered to you through your claircognizance channel.

CLAIRVOYANCE

Clairvoyance means "clear seeing". It is when someone sees moving pictures in their mind's eye. These images might be a premonition of what's to come, what's already happened or is currently happening. This is the most well-known Clair. Once in awhile I see images and moving visuals in my mind's eye or Third Eye Chakra located between your eye brows. Those that have heightened clairvoyance see spirits as if they are standing in front of them. Those spirits are not necessarily whole like you and I, but rather appear opaque or translucent. Other forms of clairvoyance can include prophetic dreams. These images can be of importance to someone's future whether it is a warning or if something good is coming into their life such as a romantic partner or a great job.

As a child, I saw images of people that sometimes appeared scary. Once I saw someone who looked very real leaving my room. My heart beat fast not knowing who or what that was. The next minute I am standing in front of my mother's bed in the dark. Dead tired she asks, "What is it?" Unable to speak, I saw another visual of someone under her bed smiling. Trying to find the right words as a child to communicate that I was pretty sure I was seeing dead people was difficult. I said, "There's someone in the house." She'd say, "There's no one here. It's just your imagination." As a Claircognizant, I did not buy this response. I chose to keep it all to myself from that point forward. I knew I would not get anywhere trying to convince an adult of something that is real and not imaginary.

Clairvoyant messages delivered can come to you in many ways including in your dreams. In a vivid dream, I was wandering through what appeared to be an upper scale mall that one might find in a fancy Las Vegas Hotel. There was a Spirit in a long black robe floating high in the air in the distance. It had a robe hoodie pulled over its skeleton head with hollow eyes. It looked like the "Day of the Dead" artwork that one would find depicted in certain Mexican art. Spotting it and knowing this was no friend, I mumbled, "uh-oh". The Spirit was alerted when I said that and looked right through me. He quickly flew in the air around the gorgeous gold fountain in the center of the mall and headed directly towards me. I turned to run, but in dreams you do not always run, move or get far when being chased. Unable to move I was paralyzed with heaviness and pain. The Spirit landed in front of me pulling out a long spear. He held it up and stabbed me in the stomach with it. The pain was sharp and I sensed every bit of it as I jolted awake. The pain continued after I awoke and then evaporated to a good degree until I felt nothing. It reminded me of the horror movie, "Nightmare on Elm Street". In the movie something bad happens to you in the dream and you take it out feeling it with you as you wake up. I lit some Sage incense leaves to clear my space. Connecting with my guides I discovered that the Spirit was not a demon spirit that I invited in. It was me! It was my fear that manifested that false entity. The Spirit stabbed me in my stomach where your Sacral Chakra is. This is where your power lies. They were explaining that I was giving my power away and needed to take it back. I had to stop with the ego infested fears and worries as they were unfounded. I invoked a white light from the other side that took over that area in my body and the pain went away.

This clairvoyant example was not showing me a crystal clear

visual of what was to come or a vision of the past. Sometimes the messages you get through your clair channels need some deciphering or decoding. You might have to do a little detective work to discover what your Spirit team is relaying to you. This is specifically with clairvoyance, since the clairvoyant images may come through as symbols or signs. With claircognizance, you would immediately know what the message was, and with clairaudience, you would hear spirit telling you.

CLAIRSENTIENCE

Clairsentience means "clear feeling". It is feeling the answers, messages and guidance from Heaven. Do you ever have a gut feeling or a hunch about something specific about to happen? You advise someone accordingly about it only to discover that it later ends up coming true. Do you get a strong feeling of joy that you or someone else is on the right path and this ends up coming true as well? Do you get a fear of dread when walking into a room that someone is not of a high integrity and that turns out to be true?

These are examples of having strong clairsentience. It is similar to being an empath, but the difference is that an empath has sympathy for those around them while a clairsentient will *feel* the guidance and messages relayed to them. An empath is likely to be able to develop their clairsentience quite easily if they choose, because half of the ingredients are already there. Earth Angels are a group aligned with having the gift of clairsentience as well. They are generally sensitive and intuitive more than any other. Earth Angels will sacrifice themselves for the well-being of another, but if you are an assertive Earth Angel, you no longer accept any form of abuse or hostile environments to be in. This is why your higher self leaves those situations. Earth Angels are incredibly strong even if they or others may not be privy to this.

I have a good degree of clairsentients. Having two to three dominate clairs is rare, but I might have gladly handed the clairsentients back. It can be draining always feeling and sensing everything and everyone around you. For me, this was not always a good thing, because I sensed all of the bad and pending dooms too. I could not stand being so sensitive that when I was old enough I began drinking and later turned to drugs and other addictions. I reached for anything that would dull and turn it off for good. My clairsentients was so highly calibrated that it bounced off the Richter scale once the violence in my childhood kicked in. I found there was nothing positive about sensing every feeling that existed. It took me a good part of my life to see it as a gift.

You know you have clairsentients if you feel and sense every little thing around you. You are not just feeling and sensing it, but these feelings are giving you a sense of what is going to happen in the future. You can work on having all four primary clair channels opened regardless of having two dominant clairs.

Chapter Three

EMPATHY AND EMOTIONAL DETACHMENT

Of you rely on your hunches and intuition when receiving accurate information, then you are feeling the answers. Not all communication is in a form you would recognize such as a voice *(clairaudience)* or in front of you like a vision *(clairvoyance)*. Some of it is through your body by feeling the guidance *(clairsentience)*. Trust these gut feelings, as they could be the answered prayer you've been hoping for. Focusing on the stillness within you is where the real truth and answers are. There are a great many souls who feel every little bit of nuances around them. They may not necessarily sense the future as a clairsentient would, but they are feeling and absorbing everyone's energy. Those people are called Empaths. As an empath myself, I used to self-medicate with anything and everything possible to turn it off. This included drugs, alcohol, and pills. You name it and I likely did it. That didn't go over quite well as you can imagine. There are pluses to knowing what someone is going through just by having them walk past you or stand next to you. You are the one that everyone feels comfortable going to when they want to dump their problems off of themselves. This is why it is absolutely vital you take care of yourself and run your life like a strict executive. Do not be afraid to say, "No, I cannot help or listen to you right now." Because you feel other's energies and sympathize you will have to work on being assertive in saying no without guilt. You need to take care of you first, before you can help someone else. As an empath, you might immediately know whether or not you can possibly help someone or if you should avoid them altogether. You soak up all of that energy including the horrible stuff.

I have to shield every day before I go outside. This is by asking Archangel Michael to surround me with a permeable white light of protection. I also had to train myself to control the flow of emotional information that people outwardly direct without realizing it. If you are sensing fear, which is a common empath trait, then mentally call out to Archangel Michael to come in and extract those fears from your body. As an empath, you are more prone to absorb negativity and/or addictions. When this happens you can invite in entities you cannot see that feed off of you. You may suddenly feel drained or reach for that addiction again. This is why as an empath you need to take excellent care of your body and your surroundings more than any other might. Treat yourself delicately and with kid gloves.

Being an empath can make it impossible to be in crowds unless without choice like a concert for example. I typically avoid places where I know it'll be taxing on my soul energetically. Standing in a grocery store line can make you susceptible to soaking up the tampering energies easily. Oblivious or innocent human souls will stand too close to you in line and the empath will absorb that person's energy. Those psychically in tune tend to have trouble with being in crowds because of this. This is because they pick up on all of those frequencies around them. Someone who is oblivious is not very much in tune or aware. Your soul is so large that it doesn't fit in your body. The light of the soul is six feet all around your human body. Someone is going to be standing in your light. If they are a negative human soul, you will latch onto their toxins while it attaches itself to you. When you arrive back home, you feel drained and crave the need for a nap and do not know why. If a stranger is standing too close to me in a grocery store line or a friend is harboring negativity, then I can feel my energy being lowered. This is an example of someone who is soaked in stress or any other negative emotion. They are called *energy feeders* because that is what they are essentially doing. They drain you of your sensitive energy leaving you worn out or agitated.

If you live in a fast-paced busy city you might notice that people mostly tend to go to the store because they have to. They feel it is a drag and as an empath you can feel all of that. They stop by the store on the way home from work when their stress level is in peak form. They may be at a job they do not like or one that is cutthroat. They take that energy out into the streets and bump into other human souls who pick it up and then pass it around to someone else and so forth.

I am currently in Los Angeles and it is busy everywhere no matter what time of day it is. Unless it is in the middle of the night, the streets are always packed. It will likely take thirty minutes to travel when it should typically take ten minutes. You are also sitting in dirty smog breathing that in along with the fumes of other people's cars. The roads were not built to handle the volume of people and cars that exist today. This only adds more stress onto everyone's shoulders even if they do not realize it. Many people pass out of this life early due to the long term effects of this stress. There are things I have to do to push the energy away such as shielding.

As an empath, you have to be careful that you do not absorb other people's energy or spend an immense amount of time worrying about them. You will need to train yourself to observe *emotional detachment*. If you have been in the military or you have had to live at the hands of someone who has abused you, then you likely had developed a good level of emotional detachment. If you are faced with hostile energies, then you might react negatively in some way. You might lash out or feel completely drained. You can work on emotional detachment by breathing in deeply and exhaling until you have calmed down and relaxed. Train your mind to take these incidents that come at you objectively. Also avoid stimulants and heavy amounts of caffeine when possible as that exasperates your nervous system prompting you to be more volatile. See the innocence and naivety in how someone else might be behaving. Showcasing emotional detachment might make you seem cold or aloof to someone. Pay no mind to any of that and do not feel guilty about it. As an empath, reaching for that place of non-guilt is where emotional detachment lives. If you are the go to person where everyone comes to you with their issues regularly, then it is essential for you to practice this emotional detachment.

If you ruminate wondering how to make the world and the people in it more compassionate, aware, and humane towards one another, then you will need to learn that these are opportunities for you to practice emotional detachment. It doesn't mean you don't care, but everyone is living out their own karma and learning their own lessons. It is not your job to learn those lessons or fix any of that for them. What you can do is BE loving and supportive, but emotionally detached enough that their stuff doesn't get to you and affect your life in a negative way.

Emotional detachment doesn't necessarily mean that you don't allow yourself to feel anything. It means that you separate your emotions from your thinking and take the broader view of a situation to assess it without feeling it. Emotional detachment takes practice, and it's more of a learned skill than an intuitive one.

I went through periods of guilt, because although I have my own neurosis I had finally reached a place in my thirties where I was doing well spiritually, emotionally, physically, and financially. I have been taken care of in all ways since then as I paid my former Karmic debts to society. I ultimately surrendered permanently to the care of the Spirit and the Creator. I eventually became a spiritual teacher and warrior living in the Light as best as I possibly can. My team showed me that I lived a tough life and came out of it unscathed. I did not back down from going after what I wanted to do. I would take on everybody else's issues as the go to person. The angels had said that would darken and drain my energy if I did not back down. It was important to take constant breaks of "me-time" to re-charge. If I didn't take my time seriously, then I would grow scattered and sloppy in my connections and choices subsequently experiencing burn out. I reached a point in my life where I had acquired enough knowledge and experience with people to understand what makes them tick. My writing turned me into a master observer and this is all emotional detachment in action.

Chapter Four

MUSINGS ABOUT CONNECTING WITH THE SPIRIT WORLD

The next dimension is closer than you think. It is the spiritual plane that is right after this one and the place your soul travels to when you're done with this Earth class. Many believe it to be far, far, away and unreachable, if it even exists as some might say. It absolutely exists even if some Earthly souls are unable to fathom it. Some have lost hope or faith due to their life choices and circumstances. This causes them to express doubt. The next spiritual plane where most departed souls move to is three feet above the earth plane. This is why many gifted Mediums and Psychics successfully communicate messages from others in the spirit world so effortlessly. This is due to the spirit world being right above this plane running parallel three feet away. Keep in mind that the Earth plane is huge rising high above the clouds and into the ethers of what you know as "space" where the planets orbit. The first etheric plane above this one runs parallel above that. Actually "they" consider us and them as all one plane. I separate them to indicate that it is an entirely different world. There are other dimensions beyond the immediate etheric plane after this one where most souls move to next.

There are many gifted Mediums who communicate with the other side professionally. You are also a gifted Medium whether you use your abilities or not. Like any muscle in your body, you need to work it and use it often. The more weights you lift at the gym with your body, the stronger your body becomes. The psychic muscle is the same concept.

When you have a psychic read, the future is always probable. What is seen coming up in your life can be altered significantly if you act on free will. For example, if you choose to deny the soul mate that is in your path repeatedly, or you choose not to take a particular job, then this will alter your path and a new path is formed. If you were meant to be in a long term soul mate relationship with someone, but the other person denied it and left, then they did so out of free will. Your spirit team will work with this soul mate's team to bring you both together again. If this is unsuccessful, due to this person denying Heavenly guidance and acting out on free will, then your Spirit team will work to bring you a higher soul mate more aligned with you.

We all have varying ways of communicating with the other side. Some may be more open to seeing other souls that have departed, while others can feel them. You have those, such as myself, who hear them, as well as those who know they are present without questioning it. I have been hearing them for as long as I can remember. Some people use divination tools for confirmation of the messages they receive from the other side. Calling someone up with your telephone is similar to a divination tool. Spirit can deliver messages to you in a variety of ways, such as through your senses, through signs, symbols, and numbers or through the use of a divination tool such as an Angel Board, Tarot or Oracle deck. The tools are used to communicate or confirm what the reader is picking up on from the other side.

It can be painfully depressing to see some human souls unaware or confused and unsure of what is going on around them outside of the material world. Much of the hesitance some human souls have with crossing over is the fear of the light. The soul associates judgment or eternal Hell with the light. This is due to false teachings during their upbringing on Earth. It is hammered into their psyches by those around them and adopted as second nature.

Your ego remains as is when you cross over. No longer stuck inside your human body, you carry the traits you had while living an Earthly life. This includes any negative traits or thought patterns. If you let go and move with the process of crossing over, you will notice any pain you were previously carrying being lifted off your soul effortlessly.

Those who pass onto the other side will at times visit their loved ones on Earth to make sure they are okay. Your departed loved ones are doing fantastic, but they know that you may not be or that you may not understand their death. My Spirit team has informed me that many of the departed souls tend to assist one or more of their grandchildren if they have any. Their own children are older than their grandchildren. Because they are older, they are likely set in their ways and do not need much guidance the way a younger person might.

It is okay if you do not know who to call when addressing an angel or guide. Simply calling out to Heaven will bring in the right guide, angel, or spirit who specializes in your specific case. You can request a Heavenly soul to assist you with something particular, but results are not always instant. You may have a soul on the other side working with you for several months. They will stay with you for however long it takes to fulfill what your request is. The spirit guide leaves when their assignment with you is complete. They move on to help other human souls requesting assistance. They often have their hands full when it comes to working with human souls, because they are dealing with souls who enjoy operating from ego or using free will, which can affect and alter their circumstances significantly.

When you struggle to receive Heavenly communication, then you block it from reaching you. The ethereal communication cord is much like a telephone wire to the other side. This dims considerably when there are blocks around you. Relax and let go of the need to receive a Heavenly message and allow it to flow into you naturally.

When you shift into a greater and more fulfilling spiritual life, you need to watch what you ingest into your body. You need to be mindful of what and whom you allow to hang around your vicinity. Your sensitivity is growing and can only absorb so much before it needs to recharge. It can no longer handle that much psychic input in one sitting. I had to make some strict lifestyle changes when my portal had cracked open again after having been bathed in addictions. There was a distinct difference in my connections when I was clear minded, as opposed to being heavily intoxicated, high, or after having consumed bad foods.

When you stop and detach from whatever emotional or stressful issue you are experiencing, then you are apt to receiving the answer needed from your Spirit team. When you are under stress or worry, then that blocks the communication lines with Heavenly helpers. Ask that your Spirit team remove and lift the stress and worry off your body so that you are more receptive to the answers and messages they are relaying to you.

Your first response as to who is communicating with you is the right answer. Second-guessing the information you receive pushes you further away from your initial hit of who or what it is. You will know who it is without a doubt in the world. Trust what you receive.

There is no greater feeling of freedom than connecting with Spirit. You can do this anywhere, but being in a nature setting or calm atmosphere brings in a clearer connection. This allows Spirit to lift the weight of your burdens off your soul. You realize that nothing else matters. Human egos force restrictions upon other human souls and have no basis in reality. The forces come from one's lower self and are typically born out of fear.

I often deliver messages I receive through Spirit to others when I'm guided to, but then I walk away from it. All I do is act as the messenger in those cases. It is up to the person on the receiving end to decide how they wish to proceed or act with this information delivered. Never volunteer the information unless you are certain your Spirit team insists it will benefit someone in a positive way. Never divulge where you are getting the accurate messages from to a skeptic. When you are a messenger of God and Spirit, you must take great responsibility in the way you relay those messages.

All human souls have psychic abilities. "Psychic" is not reserved for the John Edwards' or Sylvia Browne's out there. Famous and well-known psychic mediums are where they are at because they have chosen to devote their lives to this work. They have turned it into a winning career. The same concept applies to how you are at your own job. When you have been with a company or doing a certain type of work for a long period of time, then you get better at it. You can almost do it blindfolded. This is essentially how successful psychics have turned what they do into a lucrative profession. No human soul is more special than anybody else. Everyone has diverse gifts with varying ranges within the realm of psychic abilities. It is all a matter of tuning in to discover what your specific gifts are and then re-developing that muscle. One works out their physical body this same way. You need to work your psychic muscle out as well. When you were born your soul was 100% psychic, but you were also given the dreadful ego in order to test you. The ego creates roadblocks and barriers in all aspects of your life. You also learned negative behavior patterns from those around you. Those learned traits connect you to the material and superficial world. This is only some of a handful of things that can prevent someone from being in tune to spirit.

The ego is not a part of you to punish you, even though it seems to do a good job of it at times. Its intention is to challenge you. You must learn from your challenges. When you learn, then you grow. Growing your soul is in order to know what is right from wrong.

Since all human souls have egos this makes it difficult for the majority to believe or comprehend that they indeed are psychic. The word psychic has a negative connotation to it if one is a skeptic. They may not realize that they are picking up messages from their own Spirit Guide and Guardian Angel regularly. Everyone has at least one Spirit Guide and one Guardian Angel who is with them around the clock from birth until death. They offer guidance along your path while answering some of your prayers on divine timing. If you are not listening or following this guidance, it can make your journey on Earth a bit bumpy.

You receive messages from beyond almost effortlessly when

you are relaxed, stress free, and happy. You also receive messages and guidance when you are tired. I have talked about how I successfully conducted a particular Mediumship session with a girl's departed loved one on the other side. I did this while running on no sleep. When you are in a fatigued state, then you are too tired to let your ego get in the way. It is fascinating that the human ego has incredible power that it can block someone from receiving messages from the other side.

A good place to start is by thinking back to particular circumstances where you might have professed something that later came true. You remember how that information came to you naturally from seemingly out of nowhere. Notice the way you came to this information and if it was the same process each time. This will give you a good direction on where your specific psychic abilities lie.

You are not alone and have at least one Guardian Angel and one Spirit Guide that works with you on the other side. Yet, you become absolved in your own neurosis and problems attempting to do it all on your own without accessing them. Many souls run into roadblocks or frustrations over something they are trying to make happen. I have to stop them and say, "Have you asked for help?"

They will protest, "Oh you're right! I forgot about that."

I will get a message from them later. "I asked like you said and it worked! Wow!" They will describe the outcome of what happened after days of no movement. They asked for help and suddenly the answer they needed appeared.

You have to give your Spirit team permission to help you and intervene in your life. Let them know you want them to work with you. If you do not, then they will sit their idly watching you wiggle around in stress and annoyance. Do not just ask them for help, but then let it go and let them get to work on it. When you let go, then the resolution comes to you much more quickly.

There is one way you can tell the difference between heavenly guidance and your lower self or ego. When you receive messages from heavenly spirits, you will never experience fear, anxiety, or dread. The messages they relay are full of love even if they are warning you of something negative or challenging. There is still a sense of peace or an uplifting feeling that all is okay.

Sometimes I receive clairvoyant visions especially while experiencing a lucid dream sequence. This was the case where my Spirit team delivered a message to me when I was in a deep sleep. In this instance, they were showing me what many around the world were going through at that particular time. In the dream, they are taking me into what might appear to be a nightmare to the average person. I can handle most anything and I am used to some of the abrupt ways delivered messages reach me.

I walked into my house and a man was standing there. Naturally, as you might do, I wondered why he was in my house. He approached me and asked me for money. Without thinking twice I said, "Sure." I reached into my pocket, but then he quickly moved towards me in an uncomfortable way. I asked, "What are you doing?" Before anything else could happen, he pulled out a blade and stabbed me in the heart with force. I felt a huge sharp pain as if it was really happening and I was dying. The piercing of the stab in my heart was pulling me deeper into the other world. My eyes shot open and I realized it was no longer happening. I collected myself and then brushed it off knowing it was a divine message. I knew they would reveal additional information to the stabbing image when I would fall back asleep again for part two.

I fell into another deep sleep not long afterwards to allow my Spirit team to give me the rest of the message. I heard a loud banging like construction echo going on for minutes before it stopped. I wandered through the house in the dark at 3:00 am. I was wide-awake and noticed the tiling from some of the walls were broken and crumbled all over the floor. I could see the pipes within the walls. I saw pieces of the plaster on the floor in other rooms. I glazed over it confused and perplexed. Mind you, it was happening as if it were real time. There was no comprehension that it was a dream. My eyes shot open and I looked around noticing everything was fine. No tiling or plaster on the floor. I knew then that it never happened.

I did not have to ask my team for more clarification because I understood their language and message. They filtered the messages through my crown chakra. The stabbing in my heart was telling me that it was to deliver the message that many around the world are experiencing heartbreaks in breakups of all kinds. This was backed up by the abundant amount of messages from readers I was receiving. They were all experiencing a hard relationship break up at the same time. The deterioration and crumbling of the walls in my home in the darkness were telling me that these breakups were significantly painful and happening out of nowhere. The darkness is the heavy grieving felt. Those who were experiencing these break ups and endings were feeling as if their whole world was crumbling down. The structure and stability they had come to understand was falling apart. There was much heartbreak within the dynamic of many of the connections. This was no surprise to me because at the time we were in the midst of the Venus Retrograde transit. This causes relationships of all kinds to break apart abruptly or the connections are strained.

When you experience the kind of heartbreak where you cannot find the will to pull yourself back up, call on heavenly assistance. Archangel Raphael can help bring feelings of peace and serenity. Archangel Azrael can help make the pain and transition out of a bad relationship much easier than without heavenly assistance. Archangel Raquel can help restore balance within you and your partner, friend, or whoever you experienced an abrupt issue or ending with. Know that you are not alone or ignored. It may not seem like it when you are going through heartbreak, but it is happening for a reason that will become apparent at the right time.

The Archangels are powerful benevolent beings who can show up for anyone who asks. They are unlimited after all. Archangel Michael is with me on a daily basis and always shows up even when I do not specifically request him. This is because I made a pact with him a long time ago that he would be my protector on my journey here. In another incident, I was in a deep sleep and within another vivid dream as if it was happening in real time. There was a nasty dark ugly poltergeist throwing things at me and around me. Poltergeist or noisy ghosts exist. They are not as bad as Hollywood horror films like to portray. These spirits do not realize what they are doing. They are stuck in a limbo atmosphere similar to the Earth plane, but no place for any roaming soul. This poltergeist in the dream was intense due to its real nature and by infiltrating itself into my dream. My heart fell into my stomach and I ran out of breath. I shouted in the dream, "Archangel Michael!" A huge boom sound rang out loudly like a native drum. My surroundings lit up with super bright light. My eyes shot open as I caught my breath. An overwhelming feeling of love took over my soul.

Some have lucid or vivid dreams which evaporate upon wakening. Sometimes this is due to the use of drugs and alcohol. The effects of drugs and alcohol interrupt ones sleep cycle and diminish the amount of REM (dream state) input. This can cause you to forget your dreams upon waking. When you release the need to consume drugs and alcohol, your body will go through an automatic detox. The detox process is not always smooth as inner stuff is coming out of you. When you are no longer on negative substances, your dreams become more lucid. Your consciousness travels out of your body during your dream state. Often times when going through withdrawals or detoxing, even months after the elimination, can lead you to experience fear in your dreams. Your subconscious mind and your lower self are in a tug of war while in the sleep state.

Use of alcohol and drugs hinder the brain chemicals that transmit messages. When you no longer consume heavy amounts of negative substances, then your brain's neurotransmitters go through a process of re-alignment. Part of this causes an out of body experience. Some will experience flying dreams as well as dream situations surrounding fear. Your soul is not grounded in the physical world. This can assist you in delving deeper into working with methodologies of healing and working with your clairvoyance. Remembering your dreams and having repetitive out of body experiences are signs that your third eye and clairvoyance have opened or are in the process of opening.

As a sensitive vibrational being, you will sense things more than the average person would. You enter a store where everyone else seems okay with the energy, yet your Spirit team gives you a warning sign to leave the store. You feel it in your gut area and perhaps your heart rate accelerates. You might hear your Spirit team calmly ask you to leave the store. They ask you to purchase your items somewhere else. Some of these warnings might happen while in a metaphysical store as a reader named Karen explained to me. She believed that because psychics practice there that it must be okay. Unfortunately, that is not always the case. Someone within the store may operate heavily on ego or they are unable to reel the ego in. This can attract in negativity into these stores. Perhaps a hostile client wandered into the store that day and their energy was so intense that it stayed in the store long after they left. You will know if it's not safe if you walk into the store and suddenly you experience negative thoughts or mood.

Everyone has the ability to connect and communicate with a spirit guide or angel. Some see it, others hear it, some feel it, while others know it. Pay attention to your senses as they are communication channels with the other side.

Have it set in your mind that they communicate with you every day. The more you practice, remain aware and in tune to your senses, the easier it gets to work with them. You are always communicating with them, even if you may not realize the messages you are picking up on are indeed your Spirit team.

Sometimes someone might experience a specific health scare or near death condition that re-opens the portal to Spirit. Those situations crack it open for good. I talk about how this process happened for me in my book, *"Reaching for the Warrior Within"*. My connections have been ongoing since I was coherent, but there was a health scare in particular that cracked it wide open again. It was the turning point for me as I shifted into a higher consciousness. There was no going back to my previous life and I would not have had it any other way. Archangel Michael visibly appeared as the introduction to what the next chapter and beyond would be.

It is not always up to the angels or Heaven to do it all for you. It is up to you. When will you take action? When you take action, then Heaven meets you more than half way. They will not hand anything to a human soul who sits around doing nothing, but waiting and complaining on when life will hand them something great. Heaven waits patiently for this soul to see the blessings they have around them. They watch this soul put in the work required before they intervene.

Chapter Five

KARMIC DEBT

Every decision and choice you make daily, whether good or bad, has a consequence. As this energy is put out into the universe, you have set in motion what is to come to you in the following year. The life you're living now is a direct result of the actions you previously made often without realizing it. This action or thought energy is multiplied to the third power and beyond. This means that what is mirrored and directed back to you due to one small misguided deceptive action, decision, or thought, ends up being something that pulls you and your life down. Do the right thing and learn to make sound choices in your life. The Karmic energy associated with things such as thieving and deception is huge. Understand the repercussions that will come out of an unreliable choice in the end.

In the field of spirituality, there is the teaching of giving away your gifts with nothing in return analogy. However, there needs to be an exchange of energy. There have been some who protest why psychic readers charge for their reads. The psychic reader is working and performing a job. They have bills to pay in this current modern day age, but there is the exchange of energy factor as well. You're giving someone goods in exchange for goods. This is a balanced energy. You find other avenues and ways to give freely at the same time without monetary payment.

The human souls who have incarnated from the Realm of the Wise One are a little odd walking to the beat of their individual drum. They do not typically fall into any of the boxes that one might associate someone who is spiritual to be. There are varying levels and different degrees in so many areas within the context and area of the spirituality genre. There's room for all of it in what everyone is contributing from within it. Part of the *Warrior of Light* meaning is that you will have to go to battle at times in correcting what needs to be righted. This is what my Spirit team has been instilling in me since human birth. With that come some issues naturally. It invites in unwanted antagonism and energies. It's nothing that a warrior cannot handle or ignore. They have a job to do and anything outside of that is noise.

A woman named Beverly had told me a story of how her Guides and Angels wanted her to get involved with a soul mate to work on karma from a past life. Beverly said that she understood the lesson meant to learn already. She did not feel the need to go through with the relationship. She explained that her Guides and Angels insisted this soul mate is her life partner and that she is contracted to help this soul mate in this lifetime.

My Spirit team immediately flagged a couple of spots with this inquiry. One of them is that your Guides and Angels will not insist that you connect with a soul mate you do not want. When it is your true life partner, there will rarely be any long term resistance or doubt. Any doubts entertained come from the ego which wants to sabotage you in taking any responsibility in improving a soul mate connection. If your guides and angels ask you to work on karma with a soul mate, then trust your guidance. Regardless if you see the lesson clearly, you agreed to work this out with this person before you entered a human life. If you do not, then you'll have to do it in a later lifetime. It will not evaporate, disappear, and go away.

If the connection is abusive in some form, then that would be a reason to step away. Your Spirit team would not insist that you remain in a hostile situation. This is your ego talking as it revels in seeing you suffer. Working on your karma with a soul mate can include coming to a place of forgiveness for any slights this person or you have done to the other. If there are negative feelings you have within you about this person, then that will be applied to your karmic thread that needs to be resolved. It can also be that this particular soul mate needs to balance out karma with you. By you agreeing to the connection, you're allowing this person to have that opportunity to bring peaceful closure to your union. Peaceful closure is where you are both content and at peace with wrapping the relationship up.

When souls cross over, not all of them share the same space. Your soul travels over to the dimension and area your vibration is at. Only on Earth do you share the same space. Criminals or rulers such as Hitler and Hussein do not get a free pass in Heaven. They have to go through a rigorous review as they're crossing over. The laborious reviews occur en route through what is called the back gate. You are made to know what you had done to every single soul that you harmed. Imagine going through the feelings and thoughts of one soul you harmed. You are experiencing what that one soul went through at your hands. Now add the array of an infinite number of souls that were harmed by your hand. This is a grueling process to go through for human souls such as Hitler. You have to pay the karmic debt back, which results in more than one repeated lifetime. These are Earth lifetimes where you are put in situations that are less than stellar compared to your previous lives.

It is not difficult to see what one would incarnate back into a human life as. For example: An abusive, racist, white, slave owner in past history would incarnate for another Earth lifetime as an African American. This is in order to balance out that soul's Karma with the hopes or intention they would unite all races together since we are all one. The separation that exists is designed and ordered by human ego. It has nothing to do with the real reality in the spirit world. Someone might have distaste for homosexuals. In a past life they assaulted and caused harm to anyone considered to be homosexual. They stirred up the masses with hate words about them. This has its own karmic retribution. What do you think they incarnate back into another life as? A homosexual. God will teach you to walk in another man's shoes by putting you in those shoes if it'll get your soul to experience compassion. Of course this doesn't necessarily mean that if someone came into this life as an African American or as a homosexual that it is due to karmic debt they owe their soul. These are merely examples of the possible ways it could go and has gone for some souls.

All souls have much work to do while here. There are things you're working on within you. Perfection isn't demanded by Heaven. The anxiety of perfection comes from your ego. Heaven wants you to put in an effort and do the best you can, but to be kind and compassionate to yourself and others at the same time.

About 75% of human souls will do a repeat life. This is at least one repeat life, which will be less than the current one due to that souls' Karmic debt being so great. For example, Katherine is currently living a life that is well to do with money and abundance consistently flowing in, and yet she is horrible towards other people on a daily basis. She has built up karma due to being cruel to others around her. She will be asked to do a repeat life whereby the money she has in this life will be taken away. In the next life, she may live in squalor and poverty in a third world country. This is why it's important to do the work now and become as a great a person as you can be now. Examine your life with a fine tooth comb. Give yourself the critique you find yourself giving to others. Catch yourself when you are destroying someone else's life in the many harmful measure of ways that exist. Be aware of everything that is happening outside of your physical body and your material needs. Be mindful when you are walking out on someone in a soul mate connection who is good to you.

Karmic debt is not resorted to the criminals of society. Even good souls build up karmic debt. It's almost impossible not to build up karmic debt because you're having relationships with other souls that have complicated emotions tied to it. This is where soul mates come in. You might have a tempestuous love relationship with someone where it ends badly. Years have flown by and you still have not forgiven this person. This is displayed in how you continue to speak ill of them or scoff when their name is brought up. In this case, you have built up karma. The karmic debt is not that you reincarnate in a horrible circumstance necessarily, but you typically reincarnate with that person repeatedly, one lifetime after another, until you are on even keel with their soul. Reincarnating on Earth is the choice of both souls.

Reincarnation is the belief that when your soul exits your body it immediately reincarnates into another lifetime. There is a time period that goes by before you reincarnate. You have the choice to do so or not. The newer Earth souls do reincarnate more than once. One Earth class isn't enough especially if that soul did not evolve or gain crucial knowledge in the first lifetime. There is a difference between reincarnation and incarnation. Reincarnation is the soul re-surfacing in a new Earthly life to balance out previous karmic debt. They will learn additional lessons that were not gained on the previous round. Whereas incarnation are the souls *choosing* to incarnate in order to contribute something positive towards humanity and the planet.

There is much talk and fascination about reincarnation and past lives in many circles. My Spirit team has said that knowing ones past life is not important. It's fun to know for entertainment purposes and out of curiosity, but most of the time it's withheld from your memory bank because it's considered unimportant. What matters is your current life. You have worries, stresses, and concerns throughout your life. Can you imagine if you had these same worries about circumstances that happened to you in another life? This is why it's withheld from your memory bank.

What would it be like if you recalled all of your past lives? You're upset and someone asks what you're upset about. You say, "Oh something I did in the 14th century still plagues my thoughts."

The only importance knowing your past life has is that it helps you heal major ongoing issues you're carrying and battling with in this lifetime. If you're someone who has spent their entire life focused on lack, then there can be a connection between that and a past life of yours. If you're always having love issues or you have trouble forgiving others, then there can be a connection that exists in one of your past lives pertained to that. This isn't to be confused with one's current upbringing where fear may have been instilled in you in this lifetime at the hands of someone else. It may have nothing to do with a past life. As it stands human souls love to

40

conjure up fear energy. Just log onto the internet and read the headlines of the latest news and gossip stories. The darkness of the ego is prevalent on every street corner.

Chapter Six

HEAVEN'S GATE

On the ancient book it talks about how people lived for hundreds of years during the beginning of Earth's conception. To get into a book that is popular and controversial in a measure of ways would prove exhausting. I can only relay messages that my own Spirit team passes through me and not what human society says or follows. There are some altered truths and some fictionalized accounts within the book due to the perception of society during that time in history. If it is clear at how easily led humankind is today, then it is understandable how even less evolved they were hundreds of years ago. Look at how the masses follow one another like cattle today. Notice how they rally together in lynch mobs to crucify others they disapprove of. This is evident in the media and in the comment boards online alone. Behavioral instincts are predictable in the way others follow one another. This is apparent in how human souls treat each other, which is often in every way, but kindness. Look at how they are on the playground growing up as children in grade school. See how some of them are within the confines of their own households. If this is the case today, then you can imagine what humankind was like centuries ago when a book like the Bible was being put together.

Back in historical times, human souls were more in tune to all things beyond. They spent a great amount of time outdoors in nature and amidst the fresh air. They did not have phones, cars, computers, and all of the other electromagnet technological gadgets that prevent others from truly spending time with one another today. Being able to connect to someone today so quickly has its grand advantages, but what about the disadvantages? The radiation that exists in all of these devices and appliances is contributing to rapid health declines. Technological communication gadgets have caused decay in face to face connections that used to be long lasting. When you grow up in a world that trains you to receive gratification instantly, then you're going to experience some issues.

Anything having to do with fear, guilt, or low self-esteem in the great book is mythology. Only a human ego would write something like that, especially during a superstitious patriarchal society. Women were not considered equal until far into the 20th Century.

Some of the truths are that people did live longer than they do today. How the Bible or historians have come to the rough estimated numbers on how long people were living would deem unfeasible considering that the Calendar had yet to be invented or perfected back then. Despite this, I have been shown that humankind did live longer than we are now. This is easy to grasp considering that humankind had not yet turned the planet into the ticking time bomb that it is today. The stresses that are placed upon humankind now have become largely unreal and too complicated to understand. These are stresses that did not exist at the beginning of time. They did not have mortgages and rents. Humankind has turned their needs into complications. They have created this mess and others are here to attempt to reverse and correct it.

When life was simpler centuries ago, humankind was outdoors in the fresh air and that air was breathable. They'd wake up as the sun rose every morning and head out into nature for the day. They were not confined to boxes all day long. This is the way they do now in cold lifeless offices with poor unhealthy lighting. Imagine the toll that will take on you. Envision the repercussions on your health and physical body after a couple of decades. When human souls leave their office at the end of the day, they race home in a box that is their car only to walk into another box, which is their home! The amount of time that humankind actually spends outdoors is limited compared to how it was centuries ago. You might race outside for a quick walk only to retreat back inside immediately. The diets and foods were not yet contaminated, processed, and pumped with every toxic chemical you can imagine. In the beginning of Earth's time, human souls were not consuming hot dogs, chips, and ice cream on a daily basis. It's likely not surprising that in the beginning of time humankind lived a lot longer.

Some human souls are placed in the back seat when they pass onto the next world. They are on hold in Heaven above. They do not go through the front gate where you are greeted by angels, but through the "back gate". These are the souls who were careless or inhumane. It's the place you move to in order to learn about forgiving yourself for harm you have caused others. It is where you make amends and choose to work on your soul to be a better person in the next life. This can take some time to come to fruition. Others who lived in the Light on Earth and contributed positively towards humanity grow small light wings.

The back gate is another tunnel of light that is more or less taking the long way around into Heaven. This route is typically reserved for those who caused a good chunk of damage to other people while on Earth. They have quite a bit to amend, review, and come to terms with. The length of this path depends on how much needs to be reviewed with that soul. This is to also prep them for the work that lies ahead in the spirit world. This process also includes restoring their soul beyond the human part of their ego which is still with them.

You are having an Earthly life to elevate your consciousness by opening up all of your senses which enables you to be a conduit of the light. Be aware of what's going on around you, but remain detached from any drama. Do your best to be in tune to your soul's higher self. Focus on the source of love that resides inside you. This light of fire and spark dims due to the influences that human souls are assaulted with regularly. This light never truly dies and is always accessible at the hands of your higher self. Avoid becoming lost in the fog that finding the light within you is difficult to locate. It exists and resides permanently within you. Crank up the volume of this light and allow it to wash over you in a baptism.

Your personal team of Guides and Angels know more about what's coming for you, than you do. They don't always share or reveal this because there are experiences you need to be enlightened about on your own. This is why they insist that you learn to trust them and know that all will be well in the end. They know that what might be currently going on in your life is for good reason. Nothing lasts forever, so patience must be practiced. Have fortitude and understanding that there is a plan. On the flip side, some effort on your part must be put in as well depending on what the circumstance is. For example, if someone is complaining they do not have any money and yet they're sitting around at home surfing the internet instead of being diligent about looking for work, well what do you think will transpire out of that? Your Guides and Angels meet you half way when you show that you are doing what you can to assist as well.

Human souls have destroyed and wreaked unforgivable havoc on Earth for centuries. They continue to function in chaos at an accelerated rate. Throwing Children into a room full of toys will inevitably bring on tantrums and power struggles. This ensues as the child's ego attempts to dominate and nab the toy of their choice before anybody else does. This is animalistic and often seen as innocent by the parent or guardian's ego of that child. Heaven knew this would be the case at the conception of Earth. A place was needed where new souls would go. It was known that it would be much like throwing Children into a school playground in hopes they all get along.

There is great optimism in giving human souls the benefit of the doubt that they will carry this love they are born out of through the duration of their life. It is intended that the human ego will not drift too far astray. It is understood that catastrophe would be and is possible. Angel soldiers and souls on the other side stand in line to be born into a human body. They are the human souls contributing goodness for the betterment of humanity.

Earth is a place God created where souls are sent for the

purposes of learning, teaching, growth or to have a first life run as a human soul. The ones on Earth for the first time tend to have the most amount of ego. They are naïve and innocent in their actions through the eyes of the angels, but they will not get away with harming others for free. A debt must be paid back from their actions. This will be collected at some point for that particular soul. They are the ones that harm, hurt, and hate with no care in the world.

Chapter Seven

RECEIVING MESSAGES FROM HEAVEN

When you grow spiritually and transform into a warrior of light, you will find the messages from Heaven cracked wide open. At times I use the information I receive from Spirit and incorporate them into whatever I'm working on. I have always received messages from my Spirit team asking me to step in and assist particular people. I tend to volunteer the information without always telling that person where I'm getting my answers. Some might get uncomfortable when they know the source. Only when I know they are open to it do I reveal where it came from or how I know something that has helped them. To connect to your Guides and Angels it's important to breathe. Take a deep breath in, hold it for a few seconds, and exhale out any negativity. Continue to do so until you are deeply relaxed. This can take anywhere from five to fifteen minutes or longer if needed. There is no set time frame as every individual has their own process. The point is that you are completely relaxed and stress free. You might be under stress and not realize that you are.

The messages from Spirit reside throughout the elements of

your breathing. This is one of the reasons it is important to exercise regularly because that increases oxygen that is fed into all of the cells in your body. Those cells are all telecommunication receptors with your Spirit team. Those same cells close up when you are causing damage to them through things like poor lifestyle choices, diet, addictions, and negative emotional states such as anger, stress, or depression. Head into nature whenever you can to soothe and center your mind and mood. I have found the communication with my Spirit team to be clearer in those instances. I am always active and on the go. I do not sit still or relax easily unless I'm writing. For me to be able to reach an immediate calming state to connect even deeper means that anyone can if they put in a little bit of effort. You do not have to sit Indian style in the grass by a tree. You can stroll through a park or hike into the mountains breathing all of that wonderful nature in.

Do not allow your nasty ego to pull you under and obsess over triviality. When it takes over, you fixate over what you don't have, or what you feel is lacking in your life. You panic with impatience over circumstances that are not taking off quick enough. You grow upset that no one understands you and you feel disconnected from others. God and your Spirit team understand you and that is all that matters. Take a step back and be of service and gratitude instead. The angels and your guides are perfectly content and blissful. Many of them including those that have crossed over become of service in some way and that brings in good vibes to everybody involved. To get to that space, close your eyes, take a few deep breaths until you are super relaxed, and mentally or out loud ask, *"How may I serve?"* Allow whatever positive impressions you receive to be the answer. This can come to you through any of your clair communication senses such as seeing, hearing, knowing, or feeling.

TRUST IN DIVINE COMMUNICATION

It took me a long time to trust anything. There were times I did not trust my own abilities. My Guides and Angels point blank said something terrifically beneficial that applies to all of us: *"We want you to know that the messages you're receiving are not your imagination. You are discounting your own abilities by continuing to question your reception of input given specifically to you by us, often to help others. We ask you to stop doubting and trust more so that you can make better use of the input you get and not question it so much."*

A solid way for you to track your own interactions with your Guides and Angels is to keep a journal of the information you are receiving. Even if you think it might be your imagination write it down anyway. Keep this journal for one month. Record each message you believe you have received, whether you believe it's from your Spirit team or your own intuition. After a month, go back to it and jot down the outcome of that message. You will be able to tell the difference between the self-generated messages and the messages received from your guides. Trust the messages you receive and do not doubt it. If you make a mistake or you end up being wrong about something, big deal, keep on going. Your ego gets in the way and creates unnecessary negative self-talk that is not based in truth. Sometimes you make a mistake, but with practice you improve at focusing on what is your higher self and what is not. Anyone can connect to the other side who works at it. You have to take care of yourself on all levels, such as physically, spiritually, mentally, and emotionally. When you have raised your vibration on those key well-being traits, then the closer you are to receiving accurate, mind-blowing, heavenly communication.

Everyone connects to the other side in various ways. For me as a clairaudient it can sometimes be like tuning into a station on the radio. I can hear the static in my left ear as I'm tuning in and moving the dial until I hear my Spirit team clearly. This is how I heard about the 2012 United States Election trajectory and outcome over a year prior. With all of the noise in the world, I tuned that out and heard the real voices of Heaven break it down for me. They listed each of the running candidates that were dropping out of the race in order. They told me who would be the United States President in 2012, which later proved to be accurate. My mind then drifted off wondering what an incredible place this would be if politicians and its people were all in tune to their own Guides and Angels.

People get so caught up and obsess in the meaningless drama

in and around their lives that it bewilders Heaven. You just want to slap them away from that place. Some of the tougher spirits on the other side absolutely do that for you. It's a waste of time engaging in pettiness instead of focusing on high vibration activities. Gossip, arguing, and negativity are the biggest time wasting culprits of all. There are people who live in that state around the clock. It contributes absolutely nothing beneficial to anyone especially yourself. The energy is toxic. Clairvoyantly it appears like a dark, old attic filled with mud. There are stringy webs, cords, and insects crawling all over this attic. This energy within that person festers and grows like mold. It is a big contributor to common diseases such as Cancer, Hypertension, Diabetes, and much more. This is why you must take care of yourself in all ways and take the body you have with great earnest.

EXAMPLE OF SPIRIT INTERVENTION

One night I felt extreme thirst, which was odd considering I had just finished drinking a huge tank of water. I eyed my bottle of water, but then something prompted me to crave juice, which rarely ever happens. I buy juice and it sits there. I went into the kitchen and opened the fridge door eyeing the juice selection I had. I heard a hissing noise as I was pulling the juice out and poured it into a cup. I put the juice container back in the fridge and heard the hissing noise again. I opened the fridge and peered in confused looking at the light bulb. "Is that where it's coming from?" I closed the refrigerator door and was startled at the stove on my left. The stove burner was still on! I quickly turned it off, "Oh my god, I'm gassing the place up full of carbon monoxide!"

Had I not received a sudden craving for juice, I would not have gone back into the kitchen until the next morning. It would have been another twelve hours later to find the stove still on or an explosion. Who knows what would've happened. The thirst *(also known as clairgustance)* and sudden crave for juice was prompted by my Spirit team. I was nudged to head into the kitchen in order to catch this. This may appear so insignificant and slight that someone's ego may discredit it calling it pure luck. When you are fully aware and in tune you start noticing all of the little synchronicities and signs that are put in your path at the right time to help you. You do not notice these signs when you are oblivious or absorbed in your ego. The way your Spirit team guides you is also through these seemingly insignificant situations.

Receiving Messages Through Multiple Clairs

I was on the phone reading for an inquiry. I breathed in and out mentally asking to receive messages on him. Purple forms and shapes came at me. Seeing purple is common when your Third Eye Chakra is open.

I said, "I am shown a red car and a guy with brown hair driving it."

He said, "What kind of car?"

Hearing the word through my clairaudience channel I said, "Ford."

I continued on describing the clairvoyant pictures I was seeing. "The weather is sunny out, but it's cold. People are rushing around in heavy coats. There are tall buildings around and it looks like a big city. There is a subway or trolley rushing by above ground."

He said, "I think you're talking about my brother. He has brown hair. He just bought a red Ford Focus and he's in Chicago right now. They have a train that is above ground."

Hearing the word through my clairaudience again I said, "Who is Michael?"

He said, "That's my brother. He's the one you saw with the car."

I said, "I don't know why they showed me him when I mentally asked about you."

Then through my claircognizance and sense of knowing channel I said, "Okay, he's moving or wants to move."

My friend said, "Yeah, he's in Chicago, but has mentioned

moving to San Diego. I don't know how serious he is about that."

There are times when just enough information is revealed, but you are not always shown the entire picture. One of the reasons is that your Guides and Angels will not live your life for you. They may offer suggestions, but then it is up to you to figure out what is the best course of action. If you make a mistake, then they will help you out of it if you ask them to intervene. Your life will brighten in beautiful ways when you invite your Spirit team into your house.

It is not necessarily fun when you know the person you're in a relationship with is straying. When I was twenty-nine years old, I was in a relationship with someone who was not faithful. My guides showed me the one I was with in a moving vision along with a dark figure in the background. They told me there was someone else in the picture with us. Two weeks later I discovered it was true and I left the relationship.

A friend of mine called me to talk about someone he just started dating. He gloated at how this guy made him feel. His voice trailed off as he spoke. I took a deep breath and closed my eyes. I mentally said to my Spirit team, "Show me this guy he's talking about." I saw a guy with dark hair flash in front of me. I interrupted my friend and said, "This guy you're talking to has dark hair."

He says, "Yeah, it's black, so Kevin, then he…" He continues on not realizing I'm in a different space.

I saw the flash of a tattoo on this guy. "He has a tattoo on his arm and looks like on his back too."

My friend is quiet and low. "Yeah. He has one on his arm and it wraps down his side and onto his back. Wait a minute. How do you know this? Never mind. I know how."

You have access to Divine information about others when you are in tune to the vibrations within and around you. Breathe, relax, and connect with the other side. You'll be amazed at the messages you receive.

HEARING THE RIGHT VOICES

There are times where you might not know if it is your

imagination or your Spirit team. When I was a child I would sometimes wonder who was talking to me. I grew to understand that I'm super hard on myself, so that's how I am able to tell the difference between what's me and what is a higher being communicating with me. Your Guides and Angels do not give you a hard time. You give yourself the hard time. This is your ego and how you differentiate. Your ego wants to make you uncomfortable and insists that you are incapable of doing anything.

Spirit starts sentences with, *you* or *we*, while you or your lower self and ego start sentences with, *I*.

For example: "**I'm** not going to take that art class because they will all discover **I** am not creative." Whereas the angels will say, "**You** will take this art class as **you** are going to be a successful painter. Pay attention when we communicate with you as we have important guidance on the next step once you complete this action."

Knowing that you are not alone and there are Spiritual Helpers on the other side assisting you to have a peaceful life full of abundance takes practice, faith and trust. I have off days as we all do, but I'm fully aware of those days. I pray to release the burdens that I accumulate as it comes. I have battled trying to connect with so much going on in my mind that it's impossible to shut it off. There was a time in my earlier life where I worried whether or not I was on the right path just like anybody else. I would be working on writing pieces where I'm blocked and experiencing a blank slate, then when I'm knee deep in it I would wonder if I was making a mistake. You can see how the lower self wants to argue with your true higher self and delay you from doing anything.

Chapter Eight

Ignoring Heavenly Messages

Sometimes reading for others or intervening to help someone does not always go beautifully. There are times where I've read for others in the past, or relayed messages randomly to someone, yet they refused or denied the guidance and messages. This ultimately ended up creating a downward spiral effect as explained in the next story with Lisa.

My Guides and Angels asked me to let Lisa know that she needs to get outside more. This could be a calming locale such as a park surrounded with trees and flowers to awaken her state of mind pulling her out of isolation. They said she needed to open her windows and let fresh air into her place daily. She also needed to exercise more than she currently was. This much needed advice was blocking her and preventing her from reaching a higher happiness with work and love.

Her response was she "can't" leave her house and doesn't have time to add in an extra day of exercise. She informed me that she is unable to open up her windows as they are purposely boarded up. She was upset with the messages I relayed. I was shown that she would remain stagnant indefinitely unless these simple steps of progress were made. I did my part, which was to deliver the messages. How someone chooses to respond to them is not my business. I deliver the messages or guidance and then I walk away. In the end, it was discovered that four years after this read, she was in the exact same place she was when the messages were originally given. No movement in career or love had been made. When you shun Heaven's guidance, then you're not shown the next step. This can take years if you choose to ignore the original message.

Your Guides and Angels relay messages that will take you from Point A to Point B. Sometimes these messages are not what you want to hear. They may advise you to stop drinking alcohol as it prevents you from pursuing a successful career. Your ego will not see the two going hand in hand. Heaven knows exactly what you need to do to get to the place you are dreaming of. Paying attention to the guidance of your Spirit team will help you reach greater heights. If they are asking you to get outdoors or clean up your diet, trust it is for good reason.

When you refuse or opt out of following the messages and guidance of your Guides and Angels, then you essentially choose a path of continued misery with no hope for a breakthrough. The wisdom from Heaven may at times seem outlandish or impossible to follow at the time it is given, but it is important not to discredit it. They are doing this for your benefit by assisting you with making major life changes so that you can achieve a higher happiness and be at peace. Ask them for help if you are feeling fear and afraid to leave your home. Archangel Michael is the Archangel who helps with fear. Ask your Spirit team for help in finding a better doctor if needed. Archangel Raphael can assist with this too. They will not throw you to the wolves unarmed. They know the direction your life will take once you start taking active steps to improve your situation. Life is not always easy and there are and will be turmoil and troubles that enter your vicinity from time to time. There are other times where your decisions or lack of making a decision brings you unwanted chaos. When you have your Spirit team working with you, then the roadblocks that pop up will be more manageable, than they would be if you hadn't invited them into your life.

You remain in relationships longer than you should have only to discover you were with someone who was using you for superficial reasons. You spend fifteen years living with someone only to run into one argument after another. Neither of you seek the assistance to stop the cycle or end it, so it endures causing strife and heartache.

You have two people in love, who are drawn to one another and should be together, but both live in fear that if they take that leap in joining together that it might end badly or they'll get hurt. Avoid self-fulfilling prophecies and know that you have the power to manifest whatever it is you want. There are countless books written about this. They all talk about the same thing. The reason they all talk about it and write books about it is because it is true. It does not matter if it is a holy, spiritual, or philosophical book because the content is all similar. It has been proven that someone with a positive mindset ends up achieving and fulfilling all of their dreams. Those same people that received miracles due to constant optimism can all attest to this.

Someone who is buried in negativity will struggle against the choppy current growing weaker by the day. In order to evolve and grow your light spiritually, you must seek to improve yourself and become a healthier person by making sound choices. Those who refuse heavenly guidance end up stuck in the mud. If someone's ego is too big, then they don't want to hear how they can improve themselves. They are under the delusion that there is never any need for improvement. There is always room to progress, as that is what growth is. As a Wise One from the other side, I have a larger ego than more sensitive earth angel souls. However, my ego is not the kind of ego that deludes me into believing I do not need to grow and change. I'm an ever evolving work in progress.

When you go through a rough time, retrace your steps and examine how you arrived at that place. You create and manifest your future with the decisions that you make today. If you acted naively or blindly in a previous love relationship, then you welcome in the potential hidden deceit that hits you later. This is what some call Karmic retribution. If you do not notice the red flags, then you will bear witness to the outcome that leads you to a negative place at a later date. When you are in this state it could feel as if you will never get out of it. You are in a place with immense possibility and freedom to carve out a life on your own terms. You do not want to allow yourself to be hindered deeply in the past. Marinating in anger, stress, or any other negative emotion blocks you from moving forward. You have likely known or heard of someone who is in that state around the clock. This person may be in that circumstance for decades over one incident where they felt crimes were done on their psyches. Do not allow that to stop you from finding peace and love within and around yourself. I had a rough tumultuous life growing up. I did not allow that to prevent me from seeking happiness and going after the things I wanted and getting them.

TAKING RESPONSIBILITY

Life on Earth moves super-fast in this modern day world. It is overcrowded and spilling out over the edges. Everyone needs to pull their own weight and contribute something towards humanity in a positive way. For many, seeking out a partner in life whom you love is beneficial. This is so that you can share the journey with an immediate companion and share the expenses. You have the soul fulfilling through the means of a soul mate companionship, and you have the practical self taken care of all at the same time.

Back in the late 1940's and 1950's, America in particular had crafted out a neatly organized plan where a man married a woman and went off to work to provide for her, their family, and their home. The women stayed home to keep house, clean, cook, and raise the kids. It wasn't long before women noticed this imbalance. They had a burning desire to contribute something beyond keeping house as well. America had a real taste of it when World War II happened. The men went to war while some of the women took on the jobs that men would typically do. It's now essential that couples share the responsibilities, regardless of the genders involved within the love relationship. Living expenses and survival modes continue to rise, while work pay stays relatively the same. We're all somehow supposed to accept this greed mentality of taking from others while making them pay a higher price to receive the basic necessities of life.

Stephanie stopped working after she married her second husband, Matthew. There was no reason for her to stop working and I only saw danger up ahead when she did. The job market and the economy were going to weaken in the early 2000's as I was shown. If one of you within the duo loses their job and is unable to find another one, you're going to have more problems than you are prepared for. You can see how making unwise decisions in the past can lead you to where you are today. There is a cause and effect to the decisions that you make on a daily basis. Everything can always be corrected once you are aware of how you played a part in it. See the steps you need to take to improve and do it.

The immediate reaction of anything negative that's happened to you comes from the ego. This is where it quickly goes into blaming someone else for leading you to where you are. There is a profound saying that says being a victim is not your fault, but staying one is. Pull yourself up by your bootstraps and get to work at empowering you.

Stephanie's reasons for not looking for a job would be things like: *I'm too old. No one is going to hire anyone who is fat. I don't have a degree.* The ego makes one excuse after another to stop you from doing anything. People of all ages, looks, and those who do not have a High School Diploma go out there and find fulfilling jobs because they have something else: Drive, persistence, and passion. They are self-taught and believe in themselves. Let your true-self shine through every interview and endeavor you undertake. The majority of the jobs I obtained had nothing to do with anything except my personality, passion, and drive. I walked in unqualified and untrained for each position. I would become friends with the employer during the interview. They would be connected to someone with a personality rather than just another face answering the same job preliminary questions. I'd take over the meeting and would wind up obtaining the position over someone who had more experience or a college degree. In fact, I recall one employer who said he was meeting other candidates who had the fancy experience and degree after our meeting. Yet he added, "…but between you and me, I'm going to be hiring you. I still have to meet them out of courtesy." He did hire me as they all did. Communicate with your Spirit team and ask for their assistance with you when job hunting. I've mentioned this to some who discredit it. They do not ask for help and therefore do not get it. The world is changing rapidly and many are paralyzed with fear and anxiety about the future. The angels can guide you through these changes and give you solid guidance that you can trust. They help you stay calm during crises and heal away negative situations, while extracting the lessons contained therein as well.

SPIRIT IN THE SKY

One morning I awoke and immediately went into a channel with my Guides and Angels. This is common for me as I always find it to be a great way to start the day. You are super relaxed and open to communicate. I have heard from some that the second they open their eyes they have worry on their mind. This is no way to set the tone for your day and I've been guilty of it too in the past. Give your worries to Heaven in a mental prayer or affirmation in the morning. Start your day right. Whenever you are stressed or tired, then that is your body trying to tell you something. The angels urge you to pause and retreat as much as possible so that you can see the answer. They know when your soul is over stimulated and when you cannot afford to absorb any more input from the outer world. The energy of the outer world is intense everyday now, which is why it's crucial to take several time outs. On days that you are unable to, please do your best to sense, feel, hear, or know the voice of your higher-self coming through the noise. Even if you're unsure if you're making contact, know that you are. They are always responding even if you're temporarily blocked and not in the mind space to receive.

This one particular morning when I awoke, they asked me to turn the radio on. I reached over and hit the "on" switch near my bed.

The first few chords of the next classic rock song began called, "Spirit in the Sky". I thought that was incredibly fitting and pretty humorous. Those in Heaven have great laughter and senses of humor. This is why they urge you to have the same. They prepared me for the day and to remember that we're never alone. They prompted me to get a move on. Your Guides and Angels around you communicate to you in various ways and sometimes through music! This was their way of telling me they enjoyed connecting if only briefly after I woke up.

Have faith, trust, and open your heart to Heaven and your Spirit team. Pay attention to the repetitive signs and symbols around you, as they can be the answer you've been looking for. Remain detached and connected to your inner voice as much as possible on a daily basis. It doesn't matter if you're mentally checking out at times when you have practical priorities to attend to. You will still get those done by keeping one foot on the ground and the other in the spirit world. You're advised to take pause, relax, and contemplate often. In this process, you're clearing out all the old energy accumulated in and around you, which can be draining on your overall being. Your soul needs constant rest amongst the demands of Earthly life, therefore it is always okay to take regular time outs and not feel guilty about it.

Chapter Nine

REACHING FOR THE WARRIOR WITHIN

I have lived several lifetimes in one having grown up open to a wider variety of experiences than most people can handle. And many cannot handle some of the things I have partaken in. I discuss my rise from the ashes to becoming a Warrior of Light in my book, *Reaching for the Warrior Within*. I grew up in an abusive household. This led my personality to fragment and split off into many different "selves". I was smoking cigarettes from age fifteen to twenty-five. I started drinking alcohol heavily before I was seventeen. By the time I was the legal drinking age of twenty-one, I was already a full-blown partying alcoholic. This then led me to heavy drug use from getting stoned daily with marijuana to cocaine and Methamphetamine use. I was involved with drug dealers and those in escort services in relationships when I was in my late teens and early twenties. I was in one dysfunctional relationship after another where they all strayed at some point in the end. They were searching and dating around or were bathed in their own nasty addictions. They were committed one week, then non-committal and confused the next.

Sometimes you have to get beat up a bit to get a little street smart. Once you've been in the darkness, then you can easily help others navigate out of it. I dissolved or reduced my addictions with the help of my Guides and Angels. A complete turnaround was made when I was twenty-six years old. Before that, I was putting in energy to obtain toxic vices. I was soon putting that energy into more healthful ways of living. My connections to the other side opened up again in miraculous ways when I went clean. Since I was a teenager, I was guided by my Spirit team to study nutrition and health conscious ways of living. This was regardless that I was abusing drugs and alcohol. I've been exercising regularly since I was a teenager, but in my early 20's my darker side and the lower self was running the bigger part of the show. The situation would entail me doing a line of cocaine and then chasing it with a glass of carrot juice. I lived in immeasurable degrees of good and bad, light and dark, walking that fine line into both elements equally.

My earlier life was about survival and living in fear. I ran for shelter in a plethora of toxic poisonous addictions instead. They were harmful to my body, my psyche and well-being. There was always one bad circumstance after another going wrong. I gradually and quickly began to discover early on in my life that I was happier and more successful not partaking in those previous poor ways of living, but it took some time to get there. My Spirit team was always with me backing me up. They helped me obtain all of the jobs I ever wanted, including getting into the entertainment business and getting in front of the right people. It was like hitting many forks in the road that included a different choice.

I was clearly shown each choice down each road. One road was full of rocks and thorns surrounded by drugs, alcohol and other toxic addictions including people. The other road was lit up with a bright light and a timeline of positive events headed out into the distance for me to see. It was clear to me which road I should head down on. I was an intelligent young man, but breathing in constant pain. Despite hopping from the light road to the dark road sporadically, I knew I did not want to blow it. I knew what they were handing me and I needed to receive it in the right spirit. This would be by responding positively to these Heavenly gifts. Doing so would ensure I am taken care of in all ways. This ended up proving true. I have always been communicating with a team of

Guides and Angels on the other side. We all have this ability, but for me it was as natural and fluid as you call a friend up on the phone. The communication with them was dimmed to a good degree as a teenager when I rebelled against authority and swam in a sea of addictions. With the constant assistance and guidance of my Spirit team, I cleaned up my act and made a commitment to Heaven.

Although the demons live buried in me, I have quieted and tamed them for some time. Today I live comfortably and happily in the Light. I love me more now than I did growing up and into my twenties. My whole life has been a series of phases that has led to the joy that I experience now. I haven't wasted one-minute in my life always changing, forever evolving, gaining knowledge and life experience beyond someone who has lived 100 Earth years.

The biggest phase was when I made this official spiritual transformation as described in my book, *Reaching for the Warrior Within*. It was a pivotal transition, almost like a graduation in a sense. My world became brighter, but there were significant life choices I had to make to get to that place. This was not done alone as my Guides and Angels have always been communicating with me and guiding me down the path I needed to be on. I left one juncture of my life that was full of intolerable circumstances and entered blissfully into the next one with immense excitement.

I can listen to other people's stories, trials and tribulations without judgment and follow it with my input, which includes the wisdom, inspiration, or healing words that Heaven has taught me over the years. Even while buried in my own addictions, my Spirit team filtered the answers and guidance through me. I had blocked much of their instructions out from being high, drunk, full of anxiety, or depressed. Addictions and negative feelings of any kind cause a block between yourself and your Spirit team. They are always communicating with you and nudging you along your path of course, but you are not in a state to receive their communication. You are ignoring them without realizing it. This is until you get a smack in the back of the head to take notice of the danger you have been putting yourself in.

My work and communications with my Spirit team of Guides

and Angels grew to be daily during my official spiritual transformation. Before that, it was randomly and whenever without effort. Then I made a commitment to invite God and my Spirit team into my life permanently. They were instrumental in working with me to remove anything that was holding me back. They assisted me in adopting a new improved lifestyle and way of doing things.

Because the changing that was taking place was on the extreme side to something better, this would mean that I could no longer be around certain people. This was similar to when I quit drugs in my early twenties. Even though I had stopped doing drugs, I still hung out at the homes of these drug dealers, hustlers, ex-cons, and users. It was about two months after I stopped the drugs that I cut them all out as well. Not only could I no longer relate to them sober, but their energy was lost in the darkness and self-destruction. I was quickly moving onto a brighter path and had to eliminate it and them, or my foot would always be on the wrong side of the road. I never questioned it. It was as if I was standing in front of an open golden door feeling excitement and anticipation. I turned around to see the drug users one last time in their disintegrating dark hell environment. I smiled and waved goodbye. There were truly greener pastures, a rainbow, and a pot of gold shining at the end of that yellow brick road I headed down instead. That was more attractive than the previous life I was living. There would be no way I could deny it.

Chapter Ten

RANDOM MESSAGES FROM SPIRIT

Guides and Angels do not always divulge ALL information on what's to come for each individual. Some of the reasons are that you need to have certain life lessons and experiences on your own before you are shown the next great step. You need to be content with where you are at before the good stuff comes in. Some souls can take years before they get comfortable with that if at all. Come to the realization that it is best to be grateful for what you have now. Complaining or being upset about it doesn't do you, your body, or soul any good. I've witnessed others live in that perpetual state of unhappiness indefinitely wondering why no miracle has come about. The odds are that these mini-miracles have been brought to them, but they were too over-involved in despondence to notice. I've certainly been there myself, but I've noticed that the moments where I am completely content and not fixated on the future, then the great career position comes about or the next love relationship enters my life.

HALLOWEEN

Halloween is one of the more popular holidays celebrated on October 31st. Nowadays it is mostly a time where people have fun with it by dressing up in costume, watching scary movies, or visiting haunted houses and theme parks. There are myths and legends associated with the holiday, but most of it is not true according to my Spirit team. It is a day to remember the deceased. It ended up taking on an entirely new meaning over time. People started to associate the dead with ghosts and goblins. You can see how the holiday can easily take on a life of its own.

When I asked my Spirit team if the veil is thin between our world and their world, I received a surprising, 'yes'. The reason is mostly due to there being so much energy focused on the dead by human souls around Halloween time. Because this energy is so potent on the day of Halloween itself, this invites and attracts more of that energy in from the other side. Even though people are doing it just for play, it is having an effect. The effects are harmless to an extent, although you should shield your soul on Halloween or October 31st. Take precautions that you do not invite unwanted negative spirits into your vicinity who drain your energy. Those on the other side are pure, but there are spirits who are what some might describe as being in limbo. These souls refused to enter the light sometimes due to fear of what might exist such as judgment, etc. Instead, they attach themselves to human souls. They are usually attracted to darker lights and people bathed in addictions or in negativity in some manner. They coax that soul to continue on with the addiction or negativity.

The period around Halloween is actually a time of "transition" and "abundance". This is right on par with being about mid-way through the Fall or Autumn harvest in the Northern Hemisphere. My Spirit team did not get into the whole Halloween thing, but focused on using the Halloween energy to manifest abundance. Sow the seeds of what you want in your mind. It is a very powerful time including on All Saints' Day which falls right after Halloween on November 1st, as well as the Day of the Dead, which runs from October 31st through November 2nd typically.

THE EGO'S WRATH

The ego is what convinces you that you are not qualified. It delays you from moving forward with your life purpose. It prompts you to experience any negative emotions such as jealousy, stress, sadness, or hatred. The ego is your lower self, which is not of God. It is the part of you, which acts childish and immature or causes drama. Frustrated and fearful human souls might join in a gang or cult. It covers up what they feel is lacking with a false confidence. It is also a learned trait. A human soul does not enter this life desiring to enter into a cult or gang. When you think for yourself, you do not have any interest in latching onto others to form a gang or group. Do not allow your ego or anyone else's for that matter to convince you that you are not qualified or not ready for something. You were born ready and qualified. Ignore the negative voices that attempt to sabotage you. Go after what you want and do not allow doubt or reservation to enter the equation

Human souls must live with one another and learn how to love. You learn how to love when you accept that others are not like you. They do not live the way you do. Outsiders who have different interests and lifestyle choices than you will enter your vicinity. Your vicinity is your community, city, workplace, or on any level. Do you welcome them with open arms or are you immediately suspicious? Accepting someone with love is having an understanding that different people live in this world with varying belief systems and this is okay. This does not mean you must accept and love someone who is harmful, gossipy, and violent towards others. Accept and love those who have a different way of living than you without judgment. This includes those who have varying religious or political beliefs. This also includes those who are of a different nationality or sexual orientation than yours. If someone is acting out from their ego with these types of circumstances, then pray for them and walk away. I realize this can be easier said than done, but I'm sure you've noticed when you have been equally judgmental towards them that you've experienced an uncomfortable feeling inside.

A greed mentality exists in every part of the globe. One

example would be the kind that plagues America. One of the biggest shopping days of the year in the United States is called "Black Friday". This takes place the day after the Thanksgiving holiday every November. It is a day when material items are marked down to a great degree. It is only a handful of products which are marked down for a specific time limit. They are mostly products you do not really need. This leaves many fighting over material items. If you do an internet search on the crimes and violence broken out on Black Friday, you would be amazed. Thanksgiving is a holiday that has more or less forced most of America to head to their family's house to break bread and cook a turkey. The meaning of the long weekend has lost its flavor. It's now all about shopping. It's about Black Friday and now Black Thursday. More retail stores are opening in the late evening on Thanksgiving Day. This is of course a backwards step for humanity, where human priorities are dominated by greed. Close up shop. Take a break. Chill out and relax!

This is anyone and everyone that is participating in Black Friday on Thanksgiving. The exception is the employees who are expected to work.

I've always found Thanksgiving to be an odd holiday. This is especially when you dive into the history of how the holiday started to begin with. Human ego started a war on another culture of people in order to take over the land. On the flipside, I'll accept a holiday that does its best to bring people together. This is the point of Thanksgiving in current modern times. There will never be enough of bringing people together going on. What is unfortunate is that a holiday needs to happen in order for this to be accomplished. This should be all year round.

When I connected to my Spirit team for messages for Thanksgiving and Black Friday weekend, surprisingly the first thing that came up was LOVE. Love is the biggest feeling experienced when you cross over. It is Heaven and the spirit world's mantra. Love. Joy is right up there with love. Remember what is ultimately important to your soul and why you are here. It is to love. It is to give and to spread love. This mantra should be adopted everyday and every minute of your life. When all else fails, remember: LOVE.

Think and breathe the word always. Be grateful. Be thankful and above all....love. When that fails, love again, and repeat.

One of the strengths that everyone has in common is the capacity to operate purely from a place of love. Everyone was born with this gift. Negativity, stress, emotional instabilities are all learned traits. Love is what you are made of and what you were born with. It is the only place you can find true power and strength.

Anyone can connect to Spirit who works at it. You have to take care of yourself on all levels, such as physically, spiritually, mentally, and emotionally. When you have raised your vibration on those key well-being traits, then the closer you are to receiving accurate, mind-blowing, heavenly communication.

We are all on the precipice of a new energy. Heaven has sent millions of souls to enter this world to usher in this change and set the example in a myriad of ways. The spirit world has been sending souls to enter into human form throughout history to enact particular changes that progress God's Earth. These same human souls were crucified. They were people from Jesus Christ to those who were accused of witchcraft. They are and were those who had views that were out of this world. The new group of what some refer to as Light workers, Indigos, Crystals, Rainbows and many others has increased with great magnitude after the 1960's. More of them were rushed in through the 1970's and even more into the 1980's, 1990's and beyond.

RAINBOWS

The Rainbow colors are a mixture of colors that different hierarchy spirits exude and radiate. They are high vibrational colors and lights. Archangel Raziel shows up wherever rainbows or rainbow colors are. There is nothing negative or cryptic about a rainbow connection. They are reflections of light created as a message from Heaven. They are one way that someone on the other side is sending you a message if you are seeing the same symbol repeatedly. Heaven will communicate through repeated symbols and signs that have the same pattern. It would depend on what type of help you are asking for if any to decode those symbols.

If your question or request for Heavenly assistance were in regards to a work promotion or something having to do with material success, the rainbow would be a sign that the pot of gold is coming up or good news. The rainbow can also be a bridge or a passage that things are looking up. It also means hope and assurance that God is indeed present. Of course whenever God is present it is always a reminder that you need to be exuding love more often. He is always present, but when He is showing signs of His bigger presence, then it would show up in many forms including rainbows. He does not reveal his presence through violent acts despite what some might believe. Those are the acts of human ego. God is all love.

Chapter Eleven

PSYCHIC INSIGHTS

Heaven and the Spirit World have an aerial of view of the trajectory of your life. They tell me that if human souls could see what they could see up ahead for them, they wouldn't be complaining and whining so much. Every human soul can see what's up ahead for themselves. Someone had mentioned they did not believe in psychic abilities, but they believed that people were intuitive. Psychic or intuitive is the same thing. It does not matter what you call it. You're tuning into your core senses, which are communication receptors with worlds beyond this one. All souls have this ability to read better for themselves than anyone else can. Accurately reading for yourself or anyone is impossible when your ego is ruling the show that is your life.

How often have you received an internal jolt that something in particular was about to happen, and then it did? Even the non-believers can take a step away and recall those incidents where the psychic phenomena did indeed occur for them. You can do this by raising your vibration and tuning into what's outside of physical distractions. Trust the repeated messages you receive. No one can do that for you better than you can. Have patience and faith that what you desire will work out in your favor in the end. Sometimes it's not what you predicted or what you hoped, but you learn to realize that in the end, how it turns out is much better than you had envisioned. There is a reason you're living the particular life you are at this time.

Heavenly guidance sifts into your consciousness almost effortlessly while in a dreamlike meditative state. When you wake up from sleeping at night, it's almost immediately that you have forgotten your dream, even though you awoke from it minutes ago. This is what it's like before you enter an Earthly human life. Before you enter this life, your memory slate is wiped clean except for hints that include your life purpose. This is similar to your memory being wiped clean when you awaken from a profound dream. Only hints of this dream you had while sleeping are left if at all.

You made a contract with your Spirit team before you entered a human life. In this contract are things like the soul mates you would encounter, the things you would endure, your life purpose, when you will pass on and head back home. This is similar to the dream state when you're sleeping. Your memory is fully restored when you cross back over and head home into the next plane.

Some live an entire Earthly life and do not fulfill their contract completely. They may not come to this realization until the final days on their death bed as a human soul. They realize they are indeed going to leave their physical body. The reality and the fear might hit them at that point. They might say, "Why didn't I forgive him or her?" or "Why didn't I allow love in from this person?" These words filter through your consciousness as you transition home to where you came from in the spirit world. Your Spirit team on the other side greets you along with Archangel Jeremiel. They go over your entire Earthly life. This consists of things such as what you did and what you didn't do. What you did to others and what others did to you. What you accomplished or neglected and so forth.

I receive some pretty common psychic related questions. The first common question is about love. Readers write me frustrated about not being in a love relationship. My Spirit team says that the desperate need to have a lover is what blocks one from obtaining a lover. It's the negative feelings associated with that need which includes a fear that it won't happen. This goes back to the saying:

"Let go, let God." When you let go of the negative desire and panic to obtain a lover, then the lover shows up. I can attest for me personally that this is true. Every serious love relationship I have been involved in throughout my entire life to date came to me and developed when I wasn't looking for anything. I was in a state of perfect contentment before it happened, and then it happened naturally.

The second common question is surrounding one's career. Others are trying to figure out what type of career they want, or what job they should go after, and in what industry. The response my Spirit team gives me on that is to think about what your passion is beyond making money and then you have your answer. The desire to chase money as one's sole purpose will leave you dejected. I can also attest that the response to this question was accurate for me. I have never gone after a job or career position for the purpose of monetary gain. I went after it because I had a passion and desire for that type of work or position. The money wasn't on my radar. It ended up flowing in naturally and in great abundance more than expected. The increased financial flow for each work position I accepted in my life was the icing on the cake.

Pay attention to your senses when deciphering the incoming Heavenly guidance while on your life's journey. The guidance could even come in the guises of déjà vu moments. Déjà vu moments can be psychic hits of the future or of the past. The past can be a previous life or someone else's past. This can be the case even though the déjà vu moment is playing out as if you're the main character.

The future is what's to come. This also means not necessarily a vision of what's coming for you personally, but it can be someone around you. The way dreams and clairvoyant images come to you are not always direct. It may show you a particular vision, but one that is not necessarily going to play out exactly in the manner it's being displayed. Clairvoyant hits sometimes need to be decoded and interpreted.

The ego desires things now. I'm impatient myself regardless of knowing what's coming up ahead at times. Part of working on spiritual evolvement is learning the nature of patience and tempering the ego. Sometimes another person's guides will communicate with mine. My guides will then interpret what the other person's guides are relaying. They communicate at a fast pace that it overlaps with one another. It's much different in communicating than the way we do here on Earth in the physical body.

Since all souls are born with measuring psychic gifts, this means you can also all train yourself to pay attention to the input you receive. You can train to give tarot or angel card readings for yourself or for others. It takes work to strip away the materialistic life that you have built up within your DNA in this lifetime. With practice and work, you can be just as capable of giving reads for yourself as a professional psychic reader can.

Those who are professional psychic readers or mediums find it difficult to read for themselves, since their judgment is clouded and not objective. This is why many will read with another reader to receive a read from someone who is not emotionally invested in their life. This is also why many psychics do not read for friends as it becomes a conflict of interest. They have emotion invested in their friend and may bend the read to favor the friend. In the end a false read is given and the friend is not helped. Sometimes it causes the ending of a friendship where the friend feels uncomfortable by what their psychic reader friend has relayed to them.

Searching for the right psychic reader can be challenging and much like searching for the right Doctor. Readers read in a variety of ways. Some are angel readers, some are fortune tellers, others channel messages from the other side, and some use objects, while others use nothing, but their own body. There will be a synastry between you and the reader that feels comfortable for you both. No reader should ever tell you what to do.

For example, they should never instruct you to leave a lover unless of course the lover is abusive. The role of an ethical reader is to simply guide you or inform you of what they are seeing about a particular person or situation in question. They should remain completely objective and neutral in your situation. An ethical reader would say something like, "If you stay with this person, the philandering will continue. It is up to you to decide on your next course of action." You have free will choice to decide what's best for you knowing this information.

I've had angel reads, psychic reads, tarot reads, channel reads, and intuitive reads. I've watched others use no divination tool, those who use boards, rocks, or other devices. I love the craft and all points of view. I love the differing ways that others read. You gain different insights and perspectives with a different reader. It's a personal decision when choosing a reader to go with, just as you would in choosing a relationship. One person may love a reader that someone else did not gravitate towards. There is a synastry between reader and readee.

Sometimes others who enjoy the craft love to know what methods other readers use when reading cards. When using a card deck, I do not always use the three card spread. I've rarely if ever used the past-present-future spread or Celtic Cross spread. I don't have a pattern that I stick with when reading. I follow what my Spirit team is telling me through my Clairaudience channel. I pick the deck up as I'm saying, "I want to know about love for this person." I'm already shuffling before I've finished my sentence. For example, I will hear them say the number six. I nod, "Six. Okay, show me love". Some readers take the top 6 cards off when they're done shuffling. I shuffle for each 6 times until they have me stop on the card. This doesn't mean anyone should do it this way. You adopt the method that works accurately and best for you.

Ask your guides and angels for clarity when you're puzzled by their information. Request they show you signs and symbols to confirm what you're receiving from them. This is one way to determine if you're receiving accurate information or if it's your ego dominating the read. Every soul is born in tune to the other side and connected to God. The more a human soul allows their physical surroundings to influence them, the further away from God and heavenly communication you go.

Do I Volunteer
Information To Others?

It is best to avoid volunteering psychic related information to others unless they've asked you for it. It's not particularly enjoyable watching others head for a cliff and not being able to say anything. You cannot interfere with others free will choice. They have to learn lessons on their own. I just keep it to myself unless I'm specifically asked if I'm seeing anything. There is the asking me what is the best course of action to take with a decision. I let them know what I'm getting. It goes through one ear out the other. They do the opposite, then come back to me to say, "Okay you were right, now what do I do? How do I get out of this?" It's uncomfortable to not come off as if you're shattering someone's dreams. I'm all for one going after what they want. They're very excited about something and you do not want to crush that for them. You see it being a dead end or not ending well, and they ask you about it. You have to be delicate in the delivery of what you're getting, while still allowing them their free will choice to make the ultimate decision while also being supportive too.

I'm Hearing Voices Telling Me
They're Going To Kill Me!

Another common inquiry I receive is someone hearing voices that they are going to kill them. The inquiry comes to me wondering if it's a spirit on the other side. When one is hearing harmful voices, then this is typically the voice of ego. Spirits in Heaven only communicate with love, while the ego communicates in hate and negativity. If it's a demon possession, they would take over your entire soul and body, but those cases are extremely rare despite how common it seems in Hollywood horror films.

The harmful spirits in limbo mode that feed off a human soul's addictions merely prompt that human soul to dive harder into a particular addiction. They don't have the kind of power to whisper they're going to kill that soul. It would defeat their purpose as well, since their goal is simple. It is to get high through the human soul's addiction or vice.

If you're hearing negative voices speaking to you, it's important to first rule out if you've had a traumatic experience in your life. Sometimes traumatic events in one's life trigger negative self talk where it feels as if an entity or spirit is saying harmful negative things to you. Some post-traumatic stress side effects cause one's mind to splinter into different selves where it feels as if it's not you saying particular harmful things, but an entity or spirit. It can happen months or even years after the traumatic event. Most people have had at least one traumatic event or circumstance they can recall through the duration of their life that stands out. It can be something seemingly insignificant to someone else, but which is not to you. Circumstances such as a love relationship breakup that left you wounded and depressed.

If the harmful voices are something that continues indefinitely, then it's best to seek out a mental health practitioner to adequately treat and/or diagnose the underlying cause. This can also rule out any deeper issues that might reside within you that need addressing and healing. The next step recommended is to go to a highly evolved healer, counselor, or therapist as you continue down your individual spiritual path.

Questions such as this one can be uncomfortable to answer, but the response is always the same. This type of question is best suited for a mental health professional. It's not mine or anyone else's jurisdiction to diagnose a mental health issue, but left for someone medically qualified. It would be poor etiquette and bad practice on my part. I can only offer what my Spirit team relays to me, which is the same response for most common questions. There is nothing wrong with seeking a professional who specializes with mental disorders. One's mental health is extremely vital, and being someone who has fragmented and split off into various selves as a child, I understand the importance of addressing it. This is in order to take care of it and examine the underlying cause, so that you can be clear minded. With practice, you will be able to decipher what are your guides and angels, and when your ego mind is playing tricks on you.

THE "OVER SOUL" AND "WALK-IN"

There is what some call an *Over Soul*. Your soul has a higher self and a lower self, and both are distinctively different selves. To some it would appear to be that all human souls have a split personality to an extent. This is depending on how often they vacillate from their higher to their lower self on any given day. Yet it's only one soul, not two. Everyone has a dark side and a light side. There are cases where a soul will take over another soul's body at some point in their life. It is noticeable to others around them after this happens. The rare soul switching happens during a traumatic event such as a car accident or near death experience. This is where the soul switching takes place. Both souls agreed to have the switching prior to their Earthly life.

Once the soul switching takes place, others begin to notice the individual is not quite the same person they once knew. A pivotal event prompts the person to do a turnaround. They have suddenly changed their views; career, lovers, lifestyle choices and you name it! They almost seem like a stranger to those they are close to. There are elements that are the same since the memory banks of the previous soul have been transferred to the new soul. It's not like the new soul has amnesia. They're able to subconsciously reach into the memory banks of the previous soul's upbringing, but will not recall much. They will feel a detachment to it as if they weren't personally around for it. Some also call this a *Walk-In*.

Chapter Twelve

PSYCHIC TIMING

$\mathcal{O}$ne of the questions most often asked in a psychic read is, "When?" When will a particular circumstance happen? They want an exact date as to when they will meet that lover, start that new career, or buy that house. This is understandable since you are in a human body and crave immediate material security. This physical comfort could come in the form of the great job, money, or awesome love for example. When these things do not seem to be forthcoming for a prolonged period of time, you might begin to grow permanently solemn, frustrated, or disappointed. This state lowers your vibration, which could block or delay the event from taking place. This energy certainly does not bring the event to you any more quickly. It is always best to remain optimistic and cheerful, since that energy is what attracts in positive circumstances.

No psychic reader can necessarily predict when something is going to happen for someone. Those in Heaven who are relaying information to the psychic conduit live in a world without devices such as calendars and clocks. Those are manmade designs to give Earth life some resemblance of structure and order. There is no time that exists for Heaven in the way that human souls have made it on Earth. Therefore, it's near impossible for spirit guides and angels to give a particular psychic conduit an accurate time to give to their client as to when an event will take place. Time is fluid to those in the spirit world, so when they see a human soul wanting to know when something will take place, they do their best to give an estimated time frame. This time frame should be taken with a grain of salt. There are a great many factors that can and will often delay something from happening with any time frame predicted.

There are psychics who nail timing more times than not, but for the most part it's challenging to nail timing. You are gambling with someone's free will choice, which is unpredictable. I've nailed timing in the past and witnessed it happen later. I have had the person I've relayed the information to come back to me a year later. This was in order to say that something I stated a year ago has come true for them. The majority of the time where I've read for others, I avoid giving timing answers, since that is a dangerous risk. It's rare to predict it on the mark because free will enters the equation. When someone asks for timing on something, I will rarely relay it unless I hear a month or date slam into my aura during a read. The circumstances where I offered accurate timing were voluntarily on my part because my Spirit team happened to be highlighting a month, day, or season through my clairaudience channel. I just included it as part of the read. If they say nothing as to when something will happen, then I will say "I don't know. Soon." There are reasons they're not telling the human soul. Sometimes information is on a need to know basis. Your ego wants to know when something is going take place. Your higher self is not interested in the when or how. It knows all is well and what is intended will be.

The timing that is given by a reader is the *probable timing* pending that you or other circumstances connected to your desire are not hindered by any of the party's free will. Free will is not taken seriously enough when it comes to a psychic read. Most human souls operate using free will choice. They rarely listen to their guides and angels. It is more about obtaining their desire immediately. For example, in a love read no one can predict the impulsive choices you or this potential lover might make on any given day. This alters what was originally predicted to happen.

There is a danger when a psychic gives someone a time frame

as to when an event will happen. If the time frame the psychic gave comes and goes, then the one who was read for will debunk the psychic as being inaccurate or that it just isn't in the cards for them. Yet, months or even years down the line, it turns out that the event does eventually take place, but it is so far into the future that they've forgot all about the read to begin with.

When I was sixteen years old, my Spirit team had told me that I would be working in the entertainment business in the "near future". I didn't know what the near future was and I didn't ask them when exactly. I just knew without a doubt that it would happen. Of course, I didn't sit around waiting for it to land on my door step. I actively began researching the business at the library and investigating potential companies I could possibly work at.

To make a long story short, years passed and I was still researching and trying to get in. I grew frustrated and disheartened at times, but the desire to get in did not stop me. Weeks after my 23rd birthday, I was offered a position working for a major Hollywood actress at the time. This is to illustrate that I was shown this would happen at sixteen years old and in the near future. The event happened when I turned twenty-three. This dream came to fruition at full throttle about seven years *after* I clairvoyantly saw it coming initially. The point is that it did happen eventually. Can you imagine if I went to a psychic reader who told me, "You'll get into the entertainment business within the coming year?" I might have given up and said, "Oh they were wrong, that never happened." This is why psychic timing cannot always be accurately predicted on the mark. If it is, then keep an open mind that the reader is merely estimating the probable future. Just because the event doesn't take place when they said it would, does not necessarily mean that it won't ever happen.

One way to look at it is that a reader or your own guides and angels are informing you that something is indeed intended to happen. Don't worry yourself over the when and how it will happen. Otherwise you'll drive yourself into a mental obsession. This obsession is what lowers your vibration. When you are in a state of joy and contentment, in the here and now, then this raises your vibration. This then allows positive events to unfold, and even greater opportunities to reach you sooner than later.

I'm one of the most impatient people I know, so this is something I can relate to. I know what it's like to want to know when something is going to take place and how frustrating it can be when time has gone by and nothing has come to pass. Heaven says to trust, have patience, and keep the faith. Know that the path you're on is the way it is for a reason. The choices you've previously made have led you to the place you're currently in. What you desire will reveal itself to you at just the right time. Speaking from personal experience, I can attest that this is true.

Additionally, it's important to remember to follow the nudges, signs, and guidance that your Spirit team is putting in front of you. If they are constantly dropping the same signs in front of you to go to a different part of town you normally go to, or another store that is off your typical route, then trust that. It could be they are trying to orchestrate something beneficial for you. A psychic reader can rarely assist you with something like this. They might tell you that you're going to meet your next lover in October. October comes and goes and you wonder why it never happened. Were you sitting around at home hiding out between the day of your psychic read and October? This makes it impossible for any lover to find you unless that soul mate rings your doorbell like the postman or delivery person.

When a psychic informs you about a probable situation coming up, then keep an open mind. Take steps that can help it come along to you more readily. If this is a love partner entering the picture, then this means get outside and mix with other souls. Go out more often so that this wonderful lover can bump into you. Pay attention to your Spirit teams nudges on where to go if you're confused.

While out and about, if this potential lover approaches you and strikes up a friendly conversation, then let your guard down and throw on the charm with them. Smile, be engaging, warm, and open. You might not be immediately aware that this person is the potential right away when they approach you. They might not be what you were originally envisioning or thought of, so you end up closing yourself off to someone who desires to engage with you in conversation.

Another important action step can be that it is you who will approach this lover, instead of waiting for them to approach you. This is an easy step for an extroverted soul. If you're an introvert, then practice using your gifts of non-verbal telepathic communication on this potential. You can do this with a smile or by giving them a simple, "Hello." Pay attention to their body language and how responsive or unresponsive they are. This also means pay attention to your own body language. Do you stiffen up to a block of ice with an expressionless face when this person enters your vicinity and notices you?

This is a cold closed off world and some souls may have an automatic fight or flight response. They could be stunned that someone said hello to them let alone an attractive stranger. They might button up and turn away from you or give you a grunt of a response. Does that mean they're not interested? Not necessarily. When you're in tune to your surroundings, you can gauge whether someone is interested or not. Watch for the subtle cues in their body movement. Do they pull away from you feeling uninterested, angry or threatened? And do they suddenly soften and move back towards you with acknowledgment? Their movements may be subtle that you might not notice it right away. You assume they're not interested, when they may either be shy or thrown off that someone good looking is engaging with them.

Unless someone has been drinking in a bar to loosen up, most people are not used to others being nice to them, especially if you live in an overpopulated big city. Going to a bar or club with the goal of hoping to meet your long term relationship soul mate is a mistake and you'll wind up disappointed. Unless you're someone who loves hanging in a bar and looking for that likeminded soul who enjoys the same drinking habits.

If you're a woman, you might have a traditional way of believing how relationships should form. This is where you prefer the guy approaches you and strikes up a conversation. That was the way things once were, but times are significantly different. Now both men and women have to do the work if they want to find a long term loving relationship. If you're a woman, then you approach him with a hello.

If you're interested in a same sex love relationship, then you have additional factors that come into play or ones that might cross your mind. They might be things such as, "What if I approach this person and they don't go my way?" Or what if they have a negative reaction to my sexuality? Of course, you would use precautions regardless of what your sexuality is when approaching a stranger. You're not going to blurt out: "Hey, I'm interested in you!" This method could work, but being subtle and polite in your approach can go a long way. This is where you are striking up a conversation as if it were a potential friend. You'll eventually pick up on enough energy vibrations off the other person to determine what their interest level is. There are human souls who are super sociable and friendly. It doesn't mean they're necessarily seeing you as a potential lover.

Your Spirit team is not going to drop the great lover at your doorstep if you're hiding out at home and you never go out to mingle. They're not going to drop an awesome career opportunity in your life if you've never sent your resume or credentials out to potential employers. Heaven helps those who help themselves. They help those they see are taking action steps to make it happen. When you're passionate and positively driven to achieve this desire, then it's that much quicker to arrive.

Chapter Thirteen

A Look at Some of My Guides and Angels

There are seven main Spirit Guides and Angels that are part of my Spirit team. This includes my one main spirit guide and one guardian angel. They have both been with me since birth as everyone has this same deal. The other guides and angels around me came in one by one as I was growing up. They've remained permanently by my side in my current lifetime. There is also Saint Nathaniel who has been with me since around 2009. I was about to embark on a major transition once the healing from a relationship was complete from that particular connection. Saint Nathaniel is the tough love messages I feature in some of my works on humanity as a whole. He is the *warrior of light*, Wise One and task master who instructs most of the harsh stuff on humanity I sometimes bring up.

There is no set pattern that is consistent in how Guides and Angels communicate, because other factors play a part in that. It's a frequency that is shifting up and down all throughout the day and everyday depending on what's going on in your world. What your guides say is on a need to know basis. I've had letters sent to me by others who say their Guides are expressing frustration with them because they're not listening. This is not a Guide, but the ego taking over. An angel or heavenly guide is not going to tell someone that they're not listening and that they're tired of telling someone what to do. If you believe that they're telling you this, then you would hear the rest of the information and not just the frustration language. Scolding is a lower energy or the ego taking over. Angels use high vibrational words and energy when they communicate. They heal, comfort, inspire, and guide delicately and positively. They have an endless reserve of patience so it's not likely an angel who is getting frustrated, but the ego.

It is also possible it can be a departed loved one, since they have a good measure of their human ego intact as they work to strip it away on the other side. If that's the case, then you'll want to request a higher vibrational guide and ask that the departed loved one be removed from the duties of assisting and guiding you.

There are other guides and angels that come in and out of my vicinity for different reasons, but the main seven, plus Saint Nathaniel, are the permanent team that never leave or are close by. There are occasions where I'm communicating specifically with one who I've addressed directly. Depending on what's going on or what the situation calls for, the right guide or angel steps forward. They take turns orchestrating certain events that are in my favor. One guide may be working on bringing the next love mate to me, while another is working on the career or work stuff. Their goal is to ensure that I stay on path teaching, writing, inspiring and entertaining. I have long lists of things that need to be said and done. One guide is not enough for all of it. There are times where they do speak in concert, except for Saint Nathaniel who works separately with me.

The names of my Spirit Guides and Angels around me are Luke, Enoch, Veronica, Matthew, Jeremiah, Samuel and Jacob. Saint Nathaniel sometimes known as Bartholomew leads the pack.

Luke is my main Spirit Guide and has been since my human birth in this lifetime. His main role with me was and has been my entire work and career life to date. Every job and work position I ever received since I was seventeen were all part of the plan to gain additional tools and knowledge that would lead to the role I am in now. Luke has been instrumental in this process and continues to be so. He works closely with Archangel Gabriel and Archangel Uriel who comes in when it comes to my writing and promoting my work.

Veronica is my main Guardian Angel and has been since birth. She has been the front and center angel that has kept me on a healthy path. I knew from the early age of eight the importance of exercise and health. This was instilled in me primarily from Veronica. There were times where I indulged in addictions that would lead to one poor situation after another. Both Luke and Veronica would scream through the thud to get me back on path as soon as possible. Luckily, I listened to my Guides and Angels, otherwise I may have checked out early.

As I grew to know my guides and angels, I discovered some interesting historical facts about them that they did not reveal immediately. The reason they often withhold information from you is for a variety of reasons. One of them is that sometimes it's a 'need to know' basis. Other times it can be that you may not be in a position to accept the answer.

Saint Nathaniel

Saint Nathaniel is one of the many Ascended Masters on the other side. Ascended Masters are also Saints who often act as spiritual teachers and guides to advancing or evolving student souls on Earth for specific purposes. This is when you are ready to take on a more serious role in this lifetime that entails helping others through communication, leading, teaching and inspiring. It is not uncommon for Wise Ones to have guides who are ascended masters. Nathaniel started popping in for me in a regular appearance in 2009-a catastrophic year for me personally. It was crucial in that it was the ending of another chapter part of my life. It was the final chapter of all my years up to that point. Nathaniel knew where I would be embarking to next, which was an entirely different book, rather than the next chapter. The life lessons, class and karmic debt were wrapping themselves up. My soul vibration was rising to a higher degree. I was climbing out of the confinement of my material body.

Nathaniel instructed that I move into the role of the empowering teacher that all of my guides had been showing me for the ten years prior, but my ego denied this. My work life would be shifting and I would go through a powerful spiritual transformation. This is described in my book, *Reaching for the Warrior Within*. My Spirit Guide Luke had informed me that in November 2010 I experienced what someone might consider to be a near death experience while enduring a physical work out injury. This lasted for a millisecond in Earth time. Something shifted and turned in me where I would never be the same again after that month. This was simultaneous with the death of my father within that same month. This marked where my soul was freed and my former karmic debt officially paid off. I merged effortlessly and immediately into the role of a Warrior of Light full time. The change happened so gradually and fluidly by sheer magic. It was as if some strong force did something to my soul that profoundly shifted something within me at that point. I was awakened! My state of mind has been awesome ever since.

Saint Nathaniel appeared in 2009 just as the transition was about to happen in order to start aiming me in that direction. He knew what was coming. When I was on the other side, he and I, along with my other guides all discussed the agreement that included when they would reveal themselves to me during my Earthly run.

In the summer of 2011, I asked who was guiding me with all of this new stuff that I seemed to know involuntarily. He said his name was, Nathaniel. He didn't seem like the usual suspects around me, but instead came off quite stern and authoritative. His language had a biblical tone and was decoded into English in order for me to understand. It's like talking to someone with an accent. I asked why he sounds as if he is ancient. He informed me that he is not one of my guardian angels, but a hierarchy Saint and Ascended Master. He has been a crucial force in any and all words I utter that are aligned with humanity. Humanity is in desperate need of a real awakening. That is obviously coming from Nathaniel since before that point I could care less.

There was another spirit with the same energy as Nathaniel who started communicating with me around the same time. He said his name was, Bartholomew. Months later, I realized that Nathaniel was and is Bartholomew. I didn't understand the point of the interchangeable name.

Nathaniel/Bartholomew has ushered in the important messages in many of my spiritual books. When those works were complete, he informed me in greater detail who he was in a human life. This was in order to not distract me from the work of those particular books.

Saint Nathaniel is from the tribe of the Wise Ones. He is known to some on Earth as one of the three Wise men who brought gifts for the celebration of the birth of Jesus Christ. To some he is known as one of the Twelve Apostles. It was suddenly all being pieced together for me. Some on Earth also knew Saint Nathaniel as Bartholomew in those ancient days. Saint Nathaniel is from the Realm of the Wise One and was a Wise Man on Earth. He's worked with Christ and was a well-known astrologer in those days. All of these mark the traits of someone who is a Wise One. His authoritative teaching tone when he speaks, display a highly evolved Ascended Master.

When further discovering this information, my Guides and Angels pointed out who they were. They are prophets, angels and teachers from what some consider the biblical years. They have been referenced often in various philosophical texts.

Many prophets come from the Realm of the Wise One, so I did not find this surprising that they were my guides. Wise Ones in human form travelling with the big guns is not uncommon. Incidentally, Saint Nathaniel was known to have carried the Book of Matthew when he was a human soul. Matthew and Nathaniel are the guides that work with me. My main spirit guide, Luke, was considered to be an intelligent writer and scholar during biblical days in human form. He has a section featured in the Bible called the Book of Luke. One of my Guardian Angels, Veronica, wiped the face of Jesus before the crucifixion according to some texts. She allegedly appeared as human to the physical eyes which is not uncommon of an angel.

My Spirit Guide, Enoch, is a Wise One who incarnated on

Earth to teach about humanity. He wrote books about the sacred knowledge of creation. Enoch was a profit who walked with God in Genesis and never wavered even though some ridiculed him. He resurrected when he crossed over. His great grandson was Noah of the famous, "Noah's Ark" story. He is a descendant from Adam of the "Adam and Eve" story. I went to Bible school as a young child, but it did not have a lasting or profound effect on me. As someone with ADD and ADHD in a human body, it is challenging for me to retain information, especially memories from Childhood. Remembering the names of those listed in the Bible from that period are impossible. This is why I rely on my Spirit team to filter in the information naturally. My eyes narrowed with skepticism and soon evaporated as they pointed out that they are indeed mentioned in the book. It was only after I discovered who was around me that I noticed the irony. Leave it to me to bring in the big guns from the spirit world.

SOUL MATES AND TWIN FLAMES

Attracting in Love, Friendships and the Human Heart.

Chapter One

SOUL MATES

℮veryone is interested in love and relationships whether they like to admit it or not. Even the most hardened human soul has fantasized about having a love interest, companion, or a partner in crime. One of the main reasons all human souls are here is for the sake of love. This can be to learn to love or to exude love. All roads must lead to love in the end. This is not only in intimate relationships, but with everyone you come into contact with. You must accept someone else's differences in the way they choose to set up their life, as long as it is not harming someone else or themselves. It is in the core makeup of all human souls to want to help others out of love even if it is in the form of tough love. This love message was demolished somewhere along the way within in the human soul's upbringing. It is one of the major damages that the human ego has caused on the planet.

Relationships have grown complicated over the years. Society has imposed particularly rigid values and rules when it comes to how relationships should be. There was a time when interracial marriage was banned. Now there are laws on the books allowing same sex couples to marry, or the law is attempting to ban them from marrying. There was a time when divorce was seen as sinful and you would be permanently ostracized by society. If you committed adultery, you would have to wear the scarlet letter "A" for adultery as you made your way into town, so everyone could see that you committed a big no-no. You were forced to walk in shame upon judgmental and critical eyes. Divorce and adultery still go on today, but you're not forced to wear a button that says, "I'm a cheater."

Cheating is still frowned upon, as it brands someone's character as untrustworthy. Most human souls hope that someone they're intimately involved with can control themselves and be trusted not to stray. You cannot be with someone around the clock even if you live with them. The angels are egoless, and therefore do not judge someone who has cheated and nor do they brand them with a label. They see the underlying cause within that individual that prompts them to stray. They want to assist them in healing the source or fundamental origin that leads that person to seek out false fulfillment in toxic or harmful ways. They can only do so when that person has acknowledged that they desire help. If the human soul feels they are doing nothing wrong, then there is little your Spirit team or anyone else can do to help them. Make an outpouring request to the universe that you need some assistance and intervention. An angel or guide will enter the picture and work with you in ridding yourself of addictive temptations. Uncontrollable desires can cause hurt and pain in your relationships and ultimately to yourself.

Divorce is something that most cultures have come to understand and accept over the centuries. Your Guides and Angels will never urge you to leave your partner unless that person is emotionally, verbally, or physically abusive. They are about working on your union since there is no such thing as a perfect relationship. There will be times when you feel misunderstood, or are not being heard by your partner. This is your ego stomping its feet demanding attention.

When a couple hits a roadblock in their relationship, the answer is usually simpler than the human ego can see. The angels understand that some couples grow apart or stop seeing eye-to-eye. This is why they have performed miraculous interventions with couples that have reached a place where they are no longer speaking to one another. After the angels have intervened, that couple begins to see each other in a new light and are able to rekindle what they once had.

There are cases where there is no other solution within the relationship except to dissolve it amicably and peacefully. Every union's issues vary from one couple to the next. The bottom line is that relationships and love are a big deal to many people. You want to connect to others in a positive way and it disheartens you when it fails, or does not go according to expectations or plan. The angels watch you and your partner wrestle with hurt. They see the many miscommunications going on between you. The angels see the answer that can correct any misunderstandings and they want to help you see it too. Once you reach this place of understanding, then you achieve bliss within the partnership again.

There are those who prefer to be a lone wolf, but even they have moments where they wish there was someone in their life to do things with or communicate to on occasion. There are committed relationships that work where both partners do not live with one another, or they see each other irregularly. There are also many who prefer to live together almost immediately and often prematurely. Your Guides and Angels understand that it is a human need to want someone to share your life's journey with. This is why they work with those who request their help to bring in a loving, committed partner.

We all have certain requirements in a relationship with someone else that isn't always fulfilled. For instance, you may crave a passionate sex life with your partner, while they look at you as someone to hang out and go places with on occasion. They may not be romantic or passionate, and nor have a desire for the kind of hearts and flowers love that you crave. This can ultimately end a relationship if this issue is not accepted or addressed. The way to avoid an ending is to accept that this is where you are both different and then put in an effort to meet the other one half way. If you crave that passion around the clock, then ease up on that need, while the partner that does not have a desire for it should put in some time to be passionate with their partner that wants it. If one or neither party puts in an effort over a prolonged period of time, then the relationship will become frustrated and end.

Bigger issues that cause relationship break ups are where one person wants children and the other does not. Issues can be worked around to an extent, but these types of major issues should be resolved during the dating process, rather than when you are knee-deep years into the relationship. Many jump immediately into a relationship without truly knowing who they are joining in with. Before I ventured into other territory in my work such as spirituality, I was writing about love, dating, relationships, and sex. This is an area that I was born knowing about. With a heavy grasp of the human condition through claircognizance, I gained additional guidance and messages from my Guides and Angels. Because of this and through life experiences, I have successfully assisted and navigated many through the challenges and questions revolving around their love and relationship lives.

SOUL MATES

Everything you do, and every choice and decision you make every second has an effect. This effect is what attracts particular circumstances and people to you. Look back on the course of your life and the decisions you made and take note at what the results were. See yourself in an objective light. This will enable you to discover what part you played in a specific outcome in your life, and whether that invited in something good or bad. Your ego blames everyone else when there is no one to look at for your unhappiness, but yourself, your thoughts, choices, and moods. Sometimes you are in situations that you have no control over and are powerless, but in truth you are never powerless. You own your life and have complete control in the decisions you make daily. You may not even be aware of every tiny shred of decision making you do every day, but you are making them regardless of your awareness of it or not. The exception is a child who is under the care of an abusive parent. When you are in the grips of someone else, stop and be still, and connect to your Spirit team for the answers that will get you out of that situation. Ask them for help and intervention, then step out of the way and let them get to work on it. It's important to not just ask for assistance, but listen and tune in for the answers that are being delivered to you. The answers are not always immediately forthcoming, but you will eventually receive that heightened moment of clarity where you know it is divine guidance.

Heaven never ignores you as they are always communicating with you. If you are not picking up on their messages, then you might either be blocked or not aware that you have heard them. Sometimes you come to find that you already knew the answer. This is confirmation that you are receiving the messages accurately. You were unaware that was Heaven communicating those messages you knew all along. Ask your Guides and Angels to continue to show you signs until you know for sure what it is they are relaying to you, then always say thank you. Being grateful is an important part of manifesting.

You have more than one soul mate. You may want to meet your soul mate, but you may not be aware that you have already met several of your soul mates. Your soul mate can be a family member, an acquaintance, a business colleague, a friend or a relationship lover. Soul mates are put in your path for the purpose of your growth. You both have something to learn from the other one that will benefit the progress of your soul. You will also know if someone is your soul mate if they challenge you in a way that prompts you to make positive life changes. They may get you to take a good hard look at what you need to change in your life in order to be happier. They might push you to accomplish your dreams or positively improve your soul. One example can be if you are lacking in self-confidence, but then an employer pushes you out onto a stage in front of an audience to give regular speeches. Those speeches change the course of your life where you gain confidence and a new career in public speaking. The union was successful in that it pushes you out of your comfort zone to conquer your fears. This colleague is your soul mate who you were meant to cross paths with at that point.

The people you meet online for a shallow rendezvous, or who you pick up in a bar, are not to be confused with being your soul mate as they are a distraction delaying you from your purpose by negatively feeding a part of you that feels empty. This isn't always the case, but if you do meet someone in this way and something happens with that meeting that triggers a drastic life change in you such as permanently giving up alcohol, drugs, or any other negative block or vice, then that person was sent to you for that reason. Soul mates can be the people you come into contact with for any kind of important positive connection that changes or improves you. They are especially evident in the form of a friend or lover as those types of soul mates may be in your life longer than others.

You may have witnessed certain friendships that were once tight drift apart. This is because the connection was made to get you to a certain place in your life, but then it fulfilled its mission. One of the two parties might have grown and evolved spiritually in some way, and the soul mate friendship achieved its purpose. That soul mate may have been brought to you to help you start a successful business and then you find that the relationship deteriorates after that. This can also be a sign that this person was a soul mate to improve you in a certain area of your life. This purpose benefits everyone involved in a positive way and then it is time to disband the partnership. You take away only the lessons and love while being grateful for that connection.

A soul mate can be a friend who had appeared for you during a rough time when you needed it most. They offered the compassionate ear coupled with profound wisdom that helped you heal and get through a negative circumstance more quickly than if you had to go through a rough patch alone. If that person was not around at that time when you needed it, then you know that you would have had it much harder. This other person had the benefit of being a teacher, counselor, or healer to you in some form for that particular circumstance.

Soul mate relationships can be challenging in that they force you to examine yourself by holding a mirror up to your negative flaws. With soul mates, you often bring things to the relationship what the other one is lacking or missing. Every relationship you had whether good or bad was not only delivered to you for the purposes of your soul's growth, but you attracted them in through the Laws of Attraction. If you are covered in addictions, you will attract someone similar or on your level. You will not attract in someone who is well to do and who owns their life. Why would a spiritually minded health conscious person be with someone who falls prone to a plague of addictions on a weekly basis? If you want someone who appears as if they are on a higher caliber than you, then use that opportunity to start making long-term improvements and life changes for yourself so that your vibration will rise. You will have a bigger shot at attracting that person you are interested in for good.

My guides have shared with me that: *"50% of the people in the world cannot be in a relationship even though they ask us for one. They soon realize they don't want to be chained or tied down. They don't want to have to keep answering to them texting, calling, letting them know what they are doing and why or where. You don't do those things because you have to, you do them because you love them and you want to. You don't want them to worry up all night wondering where you are. We laugh here because many of you do not understand this today. You want it, but then when you have it, you can't do it and want out."*

Everyone wants companionship, but I often hear many complain that it is difficult to find a suitable love partner. There are various reasons for this and some of them are:

➤ You are expecting unrealistic perfection.

➤ Sometimes the soul mate love relationship the angels are bringing to you is being prepped and not ready for you yet.

➤ Your soul mate could be going through a transition in their life that ultimately prepares them for you and then the meeting will take place.

➤ Your vibration has risen to a higher level of spiritual growth and you are repelling those you were once attracted to. Your Guides and Angels are prepping a new soul mate for you who will match that vibration.

➢ Your next soul mate might currently be in another relationship with someone else that your Spirit team knows will be ending eventually. They are waiting for that relationship to run its course before they orchestrate a meeting with you and that person.

➢ Often times a suitable companion was sent to you, but you or the other person denied it or did not act on it. Your decisions to deny it are due to Free Will. It's more or less back to the drawing board for your Guides and Angels to find another potential soul mate.

➢ You might not be in a place where you are ready for the kind of soul mate relationship your guides want to bring you. You have your own transition and growth to take place before you are ready for a real lifelong love partnership.

Times have changed and half the world does not value relationships the way they once did. Many may not work at these relationships when they are in them. They are out seeking impossible perfection. They are under stress or bathed in addictions unable to attract a proper soul mate or even keep that person in their life. You have some work to do on yourself so that you are more ready for this right person.

Ask yourself what you have to offer in a relationship. Often many wonder, "What will this person do for me?", but this attitude is incorrect. There needs to be giving and receiving energy being reciprocated in all relationships in order for them to remain balanced and successful.

It's taken me a long time to get into the cycle of giving and receiving. I am a natural giver and have been uncomfortable receiving. This created issues in my past relationships. When you give and overcompensate, then that creates an uneven connection. You need to give and receive which creates an ebb and flow of energy. The same goes for those that are always receptive or receiving gifts, but not giving back in any way, then that creates imbalance and blocks in the relationship. This does not only apply to relationships, but it applies to your life in general. Giving can be as simple as smiling or saying hello to a stranger in passing. It is essential that all relationships have a give and take. All relationships need to have a healthy steadiness of giving and receiving otherwise there will be imbalance. The energy needs to flow freely back and forth to have a successful relationship of any kind.

You can only attract in someone good as soon as you become good. Do a thorough self-examination of yourself and be completely objective so that you can find out what you are doing that is harmful to your personal growth. Do you fall into a daily negative pessimistic cycle of constantly talking yourself down that you are not good enough? Where are you going to meet these potential soul mates? Are you hoping they will show up at your front door? Are you hanging out in bars, clubs, or even on those nifty little phone apps disguised as a way to meet friends, but are sexually charged for fleeting moments with no-name suspects? You will not typically find a put together, well rounded, secure, stable, busy professional hanging out there. This is ultimately what you need to embody for a successful long term relationship. In those settings you will usually only meet one type of person and they are after one thing in the end. They are lonely and bored souls who are looking for addictive ways to fill up their emptiness and insecurities. They are not ready to be in a healthy, committed relationship. Even if you do find that something is developing out of that, it is rare that it will be long lasting. Soon they will be logging back online to "chat" with other potentials. It is not the place you would likely meet the one to spend the rest of your life with.

Do not go diligently searching for your soul mate. You will cross paths with them naturally at just the right time. All of the soul mates I have come into contact with whether they are friends or love relationships came to me when I was not looking.

Take your time getting to know this person when they enter your life. Closeness and trust must be earned with new people instead of blindly and naively latching onto them.

When you merge in a relationship with someone new, then the real challenge begins. Everyone tends to present their best self in the beginning, but you can only keep that up for so long before your true colors begin to show. This can take about six months before you start to discover things about your date that you're not thrilled about. Everyone is flawed and those imperfections are magnified in a relationship. The real test when you're a couple is how you dance together and work peacefully through any challenges that arise. It's around eighteen months when you really know if the relationship is working. I would not recommend moving in with one another until you have been together for at least a year and a half. This is when the honeymoon blush wears off and you know that what you have is working or not. At that point make the gradual transition into merging your souls physically under the same roof if you both choose.

When the initial attraction to your partner declines you get lazy and the ego kicks in and wants control over the relationship. It is not the real you. The real you is when you experienced happiness as you were getting to know this new person. They reminded you of the love and joy you were initially born with. A relationship is not about having all of your needs fulfilled. It is about giving and sharing with someone else. It is about companionship and learning to love. It is about lessons and personal growth.

You cannot enter a relationship and expect it to be successful until you are experiencing contentment and peace in your life first. If you are blinded into believing that some perfect person is going to sweep you off your feet and then you will experience happiness, you will be sorely disappointed. The all-encompassing love you crave is your detachment from Spirit and God's love. Another person cannot fill that void or emptiness. They do not have that kind of power to give you an impossible love. They may fill it for a brief moment, but then you will be right back where you started as your previous feelings of unhappiness begin to rise again. This is why it is important to make your peace with yourself and your life first before you enter a love relationship. Be content with you and the direction you are headed and then will you begin attracting in soul mates at higher levels. You will be more apt to having a successful long-term relationship that goes the distance.

Chapter Two

TWIN FLAMES

$\mathcal{Y}$our Twin Flame is the other half of your soul. Most people do not meet their twin flame in this lifetime. Twin flames are a higher form of a soul mate. For some, your twin flame is waiting for you on the other side. They are not sitting around idly waiting, but are assisting you to manifest soul mates for you in this lifetime. If your twin flame is in the Spirit world, then they do not want you going through life alone. They want you to have someone to share your journey with while you're here. If your twin flame has reached a high level of spiritual growth that has surpassed yours, then they will already have moved onto the other dimension. You will meet them again when you cross over. You will not meet your twin flame in this Earth life if you have not reached a high degree of spiritual and personal growth. If you do happen to be in the rare category where you have grown spiritually and therefore come into contact with your twin flame in this lifetime, then you may find that it won't be easy for you both. The intensity you have for one another are extremely deep. It's that true saying: '*I can't live with you – I can't live without you*'.

There is often an age difference between yourself and your twin flame of about ten years or more. They may be from a different state or even country entirely having varying cultural beliefs and backgrounds than yours.

The connection between yourself and your twin flame is so powerful that often one of the two of you finds it difficult to pursue a relationship with the other. The passion for that person is so great that it can make one or the both of you uncomfortable. Instead they choose to date and get involved with other people that are ultimately meaningless to them. It feels easier to them to do this than pursuing the relationship with their one true twin flame for fear of getting hurt. They are unable to control the intense feelings they have for them. They cannot get hurt as they are meant to be with one another. They will continue to cross paths until they accept that it truly is destined.

While one of you is in these mini-relationships with these other people you cannot stop thinking about the one that is your twin flame. You are not aware that this other person is your twin flame, but your thoughts always lead right back to the person you are consistently drawn to over the years. It does not matter how much you hide it or convince yourself that you are happy with this other random partner you're not serious about. Your thoughts always wander back to your twin flame, but fear stops you from making a move. When you finally do come around, you find that your twin flame has put up a wall and is inaccessible for the same reasons. You are both seldom on the same wavelength of '*let's do this*'. When you both do decide to merge, you experience the kind of fireworks that last lifetime after lifetime. It may take several tries over the course of many years before you ultimately surrender to the connection. You accept it and become fearless.

Because your souls were split at conception, the pull to one another is unshakeable. This is not conception of your human birth, but your soul's birth. You will continuously be drawn to one another in this and other lifetimes no matter how much you resist it. If you keep on running into or crossing paths with this person over the years and you are both experiencing a heightened intensity that never wavers, then you may have met your twin flame. You will often find that you have strong feelings for this person over the years without it ever faltering. There can also be a love/hate relationship. This is not to be confused with tempestuous relationships, which are more Karmic.

You could end up getting married to someone else and yet you find yourself unable to stop thinking about your twin flame. Years pass and you are in another relationship that ends up in divorce or a commitment break up. During this time, you continue to run into this twin flame denying that it's the one. If you have a reciprocated and deep attraction for someone that continues on for years, then this could likely be your twin flame.

You do not reunite with your twin flame until you have improved yourself and your lifestyle. However, if your twin flame has improved themselves and their lifestyle, but you have not, then it could still be your twin flame. You were brought to them at the right moment where Spirit knew you were close enough to grasp these changes. This would prompt you to begin improving yourself in the process to match their vibration.

You must connect with a higher power such as God and make yourself truly whole before you are united with your twin flame in this life, the next, or in the spiritual plane. This is why it is rare to meet them in this lifetime, as you are here for the purpose of spiritual and personal growth and to learn to love. If you reach that level rather quickly in this lifetime, then it is likely you will connect with your twin flame. You do not need to take a retreat in an Ashram to be spiritually enlightened. It is remembering who you as a soul are. It is being aware of everything around you, being a good person, and having integrity. The message and theme is in every spiritual, religious, or philosophical book written: Love thy neighbor as thy self.

You can find someone you enjoy being with, have a connection and live with them your entire lifetime in a marriage union, and yet they are your soul mate and not necessarily your twin flame. It can be confusing when you first fall for someone and wonder if they are your twin flame. This is because you might experience an immediate deep attraction for someone you have just met. This does not mean it is your twin flame. You will know they are your twin flame if you have the same immediate deep attraction for them in five years as if you are meeting them for the first time. There is also an ever-evolving spiritual growth with the twin flame relationship in one lifetime.

The intensity never leaves with a twin flame. Going days without hearing from your twin flame starts to take its toll on the both of you. All you think about are being in the same room with them, seeing them, or even just falling into a hug, all of which are oxygen to you both. This is years after knowing them rather than weeks, which is everyone's expected behavior in the beginning of dating someone you first meet. You are not typically this intense with others or in any other relationship. This is a rare case where you find it to be unusually powerful and it continues to be so with that person.

Where a Karmic relationship may be negatively volatile, a Twin Flame connection is beautiful and compassionate. It is reciprocated between both partners. It is not negatively unbalanced the way a Karmic relationship might be.

When twin flames connect in the beginning it is not easy. The energy is generally too strong for one of the partners who may continuously sabotage it. They have not reached the level of spiritual growth that you have. You are close in understanding the nature of personal growth since you've both incarnated relatively at the same time, but generally there is a large learning gap, which contributes to one of you not being mature enough to both evolve together just yet.

When you are together it feels like home, but when you are away from one another, eventually your heart aches and you want to be near them again. You can certainly function and you're not bed ridden, but your thoughts keep wandering back to them. These thoughts reside in the both of you.

Twin flames are not an unrequited or one sided love. It will be as if you have been waiting for this person your entire life and suddenly everything around you makes sense. In the rare case that you meet each other in this lifetime it will be kismet and magic. You will both know this is it instantly without second guessing it. You will be drawn to one another like magnets. You will both gaze at each other as if you have known one another your entire current and past lives. You will immediately be attracted to one another decade after decade. Your energy and aura pulls you both together indefinitely throughout the course of your lifetime.

THE DEEPER LOVE OF THE TWIN FLAME

The Twin Flame is the highest and deepest form of a soul connection. Twin flames rarely incarnate at the same time, even though there appears to be a trend that many are searching for their other half twin flame soul. It is not the goal to find one's twin flame since they cannot be found. When it is time for a soul to connect with their twin flame while on its soul's journey, then it will happen naturally with no effort. This is similar to the image of magnet attracting in steel. Most human soul's twin flames are on the other side. Searching for someone who is not living on the Earth plane may result in prolonged disappointment.

Every single soul knows their twin flame personally, even if they do not remember them while living an Earthly life. Your soul is part of their soul. Your souls split apart breaking into two when your soul was formed and sparked out of God. This is like human twins who have formed out of the same egg. With that come the many similarities and natures between them. Those who have a twin sibling mostly do not always look identical or have exactly the same interests. Your twin flame does not look like you, but there will be a great deal of similarities and a huge bond and attraction that never ceases throughout the course of your Earthly life. Remember it is not one sided as both of the twin flames feel this attraction and intensity for each other indefinitely. This is the case even if they temporarily separate or one of the partners flees out of a need for independence. Fleeing is common among a twin flame. Their ego will want to focus on more practical matters rather than succumbing to the depths of an intense love connection with someone.

On Earth, usually one or both of the twin flames are involved in positive spiritual or faith based pursuits. If one is more involved in it than the other, then the other soul will display growing signs that they're heading in that direction. They are likely the younger partner of the duo, but not always. This is a human soul who has evolved to the level greater than the superficiality of the physical world. This isn't to be mistaken with two people who are involved in religious pursuits which harm others through words or violence.

The twin flame soul is highly evolved beyond hate filled dogma.

It is near impossible for twin flames not to merge together in a love relationship. It's too heartbreaking on both ends for them to be apart for too long after they've first connected. The twin flame connection can be a tough connection to bring together at times. Sadly, some twin flames connections come together, break apart, come together and break apart and repeat. This is due to one or the both of their egos denying they're meant to be. One or the both of them may sabotage or pull away from the connection due to its intensity. Yet they manage to end up right back together months or even years later again. There's a cycle where they are two peas in a pod, then a period where they have little to no contact with another, only to be back in one another's arms years later. They wouldn't be able to function or continue on through life indefinitely without the other one. This is on both ends and not just with one of them. If it's just with one of them, then that's an unrequited love, karmic connection, or soul mate relationship.

There's nothing wrong with someone being a soul mate relationship over a twin flame. In fact, the soul mate connections are at times easier than a twin flame union. Soul mates experience friction as well, but twin flames are more intense and feeling oriented. This contributes to the additional difficulties. The friction with twin flames is in coming together. They have trouble connecting and sealing the deal. This friction is due to ego. Human souls grow uncomfortable or over emotional when feeling a heightened love attraction for someone who feels the same way about them. This goes beyond a physical attraction and into an unwavering deep soul attraction. The more insecure partner of the twin flame connection may end the relationship more than once. Sometimes this is to pursue selfish ego gratifying needs, yet their twin flame partner will always be on their mind, or will continue to surface in their mind indefinitely throughout their life.

Everyone is with their twin flame at some point on the other side before they incarnate on earth. Many souls come to Earth either as student or teacher. Earth is school and all human souls are in class. When you graduate, then you go back home where your twin flame is waiting. This is why it's rare for the twin flame to be on Earth when you are, because one of them is usually more evolved spiritually. If that's the case, there is no reason for them to incarnate into a human body, unless they agree to an Earthly life in the role of Teacher or Leader.

This would mean that if your twin flame has also incarnated into a human body, they have done so as student. The Twin Flame mix on Earth is either Teacher-Student or Teacher-Teacher. This is also why there is often an age difference between both Twin Flames who are in a human body, since a student might likely be younger, but not always. This is additional friction compounded onto the two souls. In Earth years they are in varying levels of human development that rub against each other uncomfortably, and sometimes even human generational gaps. The exceptions are if the younger soul is evolving rather quickly and maturely, while the older soul is tolerant and patient with the level the younger human soul is at.

Twin Flames might also be from different states in North America or they might be from different countries. They could incarnate relatively at the same time in order to assist one another with their individual life purposes. This is regardless if they choose to remain together as a romantic couple or split apart due to ego practical concerns. Not all Twin Flame connections are romantic and nor do they necessarily sustain the distance.

A quick Twin Flame recap:

You have many soul mates and only one twin flame. Most people do not connect with their twin flame in this lifetime. Twin flames are highly evolved souls. Since you are here for the sake of growing your soul, it is rare that you incarnate at the same time as your twin flame. Your twin flame is the other half of your soul. If your twin flame passes onto the other side long before you do, they will wait for you on the other side. They may choose to be one of your guides in order to work with your Spirit team to place potential soul mates in your path. They help you cope and strengthen your soul so that you can continue on the rest of your current Earth life.

They do not want you to suffer or grieve over your temporary detachment from them, especially since they are alive and well. You have other important matters to attend to while you are here. Your twin flame does not want you distracted from that because they are in a different spiritual plane. You connect with your twin flame in this lifetime if you are on a higher spiritual path or you have evolved. Your twin flame would need to be in this same space as well or at least close to it.

It's sometimes difficult for a human soul to comprehend or connect with their twin flame on the other side, even though they are without realizing it. To your twin flame from the spirit world, they're very connected to you more than you know. You will be with your twin flame soon enough. To them, your life is a blip that lasts one minute in the spirit world. You may feel the presence of your twin flame at times as they send love to your heart. Even if you are feeling love for a new soul mate in your life, your twin flame is playing a part in opening your heart up to that soul mate. Your twin flame can also be of the same gender as you. Twin flames are the deepest love relationships that last lifetime after lifetime.

Your soul does not always re-incarnate immediately if at all. The ones that typically incarnate are new souls and teacher souls. You and your twin flame choose the when or how you will incarnate on Earth together if it is intended to happen. You agreed to this particular design. You likely won't remember that now, but your memory is restored when you cross over. You will re-connect with your twin flame when you cross over if they are currently in the spirit world. They are one of the many souls that greet you as long as they're not already living an Earthly life at the time of your human death.

The souls that re-incarnate immediately are the ones that had an Earthly run just to have an Earthly life with no other purpose than that. Human souls that commit suicide will generally re-incarnate sooner than later. This is because they cut their life short before they could fulfill their purpose. They need to go back and finish what they started. They move through an incubation process where their soul is restored before that happens. No soul is forced to live an Earth life. They make that choice with their Spirit team.

They usually want to have an Earth life as they have more perspective while on the other side than they would on Earth. There is an importance in terms of their soul's growth on Earth that is understood. Other souls agree to incarnate in order to be a spiritual teacher on some level. The spirit world understands the significance of improving one's soul, other souls, and God's planet.

Chapter Three

KARMIC RELATIONSHIPS

Karmic relationships are usually ones where you are incompatible in every way with this relationship partner, yet you both cannot stop from making a beeline to one another. It's like an unhealthy addiction. The relationship connection is more negative than positive. The negatives are obvious because it is deliberately antagonistic. One or the both of you might be abusive in some way such as physically, verbally, or emotionally.

There will be other addictions involved between you two such as you both drink heavily or do drugs together. Basically anything that clearly does not benefit your higher self. The problem is that many people are unaware that the relationship cannot be saved and it is best to get out while you can. They might know that something isn't right in their relationship, but they do not know that they need to get out of the connection. One of the partners may continuously want to save the other person. They protest how much they love their mate with their friends. Yet, their friends may narrow their eyes in suspicion wondering what their friend sees in this partner. All they hear from their friend is one drama story after another.

These stories are the kind where one partner is constantly cruel to them. Perhaps your partner is always belittling you or making snide remarks. Maybe your partner is cheating on you, or you are having obsessive thoughts that they are cheating, and therefore always confronting them and making empty accusations. Perhaps one of the partners is jealous to the point where they act out physically by starting violent fights. It's normal to display signs of jealousy from time to time, but displaying that emotion in a heated way on a regular basis can be draining and will kill the relationship.

This may sound like a soul mate relationship, but soul mate relationships are not violent, negative, or antagonistic. There might be disagreements or minor bickering among a soul mate partnership, but a Karmic connection is more antagonistic than not. Soul mate connections offer assistance in your personal growth of a positive nature. This is where they make you an improved soul. Karmic relationships are destructive. Those in them tend to either stay in these types of relationships or are always attracting them in. The way to break this type of relationship is by learning from it and stopping the cycle. Be aware of the lessons involved in this kind of hurtful relationship. Gather enough strength to end the connection. When you learn from it, you are in complete awareness of how being with someone like that is not good for your higher self. You also forgive this person when letting go of it. Change your way of thinking and living in order to attract a more loving human soul mate.

DYSFUNCTIONAL RELATIONSHIPS

You attract in people that are similar to you. You will also attract in those who you must learn something from or teach to. I am not going to be attracting the bad drug-dealing user I was at age twenty-two. I always wanted to be in a committed, love relationship where I would grow and evolve with one person. By the time I was sixteen, I was ready to settle down. Of course it didn't happen quite so simply. I did not have a positive view of successful relationships as I grew up amidst adultery, violent, and negative unions. Some human souls are flawed and operate with a dominating ego. Be fully aware of how you treat others as it should be with respect and love. Spirit embedded the true long-term view of love relationships in me at birth. Having grown up disappointed, I stopped trusting other human souls. All I desired seemed simple enough, and yet I could not figure out why that was incredibly difficult for most others to do. The basic necessities of life are love and security. The irony is that you seek those two things out from other people when they can be perfectly supplied by the one true source.

As a result of my upbringing, I grew to be suspicious of anyone who attempted to get close to me. I would create self-fulfilling prophecies while in a relationship such as saying, "How long is this one going to last? How long before this person takes off in search of something else? I wonder what they want from me or if they have an ulterior motive." I came to the conclusion that was the norm. I soon realized I was attracting the same type of person into me repeatedly, and not everyone is the same. There are good people out there who would make a loyal, loving companion.

As a super, passionate, hot-blooded guy I would choose to get serious with those who were uncomfortable with being touched. When I finally did attract in a relationship with someone who was equally super passionate, then that person eventually strayed. My lack of trust in relationships did not help. The days where I was not with any of them, I would assume they were up to no good since they all ended up doing that anyway. I had to drop my guard and have faith that not everyone makes those particular choices. I had to find a way to stop attracting in the same types of characters. Anything less than compromise is unacceptable in a relationship.

My vibration had risen to a great degree in my mid to late thirties. I made a pact to never get involved with anyone who I considered less than my equal. The only exception would be if I was meant to teach them how to be in a relationship per my Spirit team's instructions. If this happens to you, then you will have to know the difference between someone willing to learn and someone who is uninterested in gaining knowledge, but instead antagonizes you. If they are not in it to learn, but criticize you, then it's time to end the relationship. You are in soul mate relationships to teach and to learn from one another. I reached a point where I decided to sacrifice myself by waiting for the right one, rather than being with someone purely out of loneliness or the desperate need for companionship. You can have companionships in friendships. You do not need to have it in dysfunctional love relationships. Some human souls are commitment phobic for fear of being in the wrong relationship when the right one shows up. Relationships are not perfection. You are meant to work at something together and learn the nature of compromise, support, and compassion. There are no relationships that are 100% perfect.

I have been around the block more times than I can count. I have had more experiences than I would care to divulge in. This does not mean that there are not those who have done far more, but I am hammering home that it was quite a bit of experience. I have been out on so many dates and physical connections in my lifetime that I would never be able to tell you how many as it was off the charts. I was the serial dating King and I never asked anyone out. I figured if they wanted me bad enough, they would court and pursue me. I am not that unobtainable or difficult, because I would always meet the other person more than half way. If they made the move, I graciously reached out my hand and pulled them in with me. In the end, I gained a degree from the dating school of hard knocks. Without intending to, I had mastered the art of relationships, dating, and sex. This happened through my own experiences coupled with my instant knowledge on relationships delivered to me by my Spirit team.

When someone is having love troubles or questions, I am the one they contact in my circle of friends. I soon took those lessons and began teaching it professionally through writing and books. I always found it ironic considering that my own romantic relationships in the past were typically unsuccessful due to infidelity or instability with the other partner causing a drastic imbalance. I had to examine how and why the romantic relationships I was in were with someone who was up to no good. Add to that, they were swimming in addictions such as heavy alcohol or drugs. They were experiences at that time that I do not regret, because they served a major function in my growth and purpose. Despite the relationships ending early, I knew that it would be good practice for me to drop my walls. It was important to open myself up more to fresh possibilities and ways of interacting in new stronger relationships with more evolved people. Each of my love relationships improved over the previous one for that matter. It can take years of effort to stop the cycle of attracting in dysfunctional relationships. You can get to that place when you put in the effort. Do the work and make positive changes within and around yourself. You'll become a radiant magnet attracting in a healthier relationship with a stable partner.

RECONNECTING WITH A PAST EX

Sometimes you cannot meet another potential partner if you are still hung up on a past love or an ex who hurt you. Ask your Guides and Angels to either help you release your ex, or mend the relationship if it is meant to continue in an improved way. Your Spirit team needs to know that you are absolutely ready before they can get to work on it. If you have a huge pull towards your ex that is not negative, but a lingering attraction, then there could be a couple of possible factors. You both merged together the first time prematurely and this is why it ended. One or the both of you were not quite ready to receive the relationship in the right spirit. Or one of you was rushing it before it was time while the other was moving too slowly.

It is not uncommon for people to re-connect with their ex only to discover that the relationship is better than it was before. They had time to live, learn, grow, and mature. Another reason ex's get back together at a later date is if there were no threatening reasons for you two to split to begin with such as addictions, cheating, or abuse. State clearly with your Guides and Angels to either release your ex, or if you are meant to reconnect, to allow that to happen that benefits all involved. This is in keeping that you are both healed enough to forge ahead with a new relationship with one another, or dissolve your love peacefully so that you can be open to the right soul mate relationship.

I had some residual emotional damage from all of my past love relationships and this had built a wall around my heart that required a monumental effort to scale. I guard my heart carefully and with good reason. If one wants to finally have the type of relationship that you crave, you will have to let your defenses down. You will have to know the person well to be comfortable enough to do that. The person you get involved with should have an openness about him or her that will allow you to open up to them on many levels. This knowledge will help you feel safe and secure enough to trust someone new.

When I went through my own major spiritual transformation, I had added, *"Please assist me in eliminating all of these toxic, dramatic, unnecessary relationships that are only hurting me, so that I will be completely free and clear to receive this great soul."* You do not want to be prevented from connecting to your soul mate because you are drowning in pain over your last one that hurt you.

I am a love addict and with that I have ended up in some serious jams in my dating life. I have found many to latch on to me like a snake to a vine as if I have opened them up in ways where no one has. I would often hear them say at some point, "I have never been able to open up to anyone the way I can with you." Naturally they would be falling in love, but I would not be in the same way. I adored them as I do all souls, but I did not experience that kinetic spark you have when you know this is a potential partner for you. I was aware of this pattern throughout my dating life. One of the main roles my guides have shared with me is that I am a love teacher. These prospects and suitors were meant to cross paths with me in order to learn how to open up their heart center Chakras. The gain I had with each of them was mainly to teach them about love while learning to accept that this is the position I am to exude. They were essentially a student and whether they were older than me or younger is irrelevant as it was the same class lesson for all. Age has no relevance when it comes to Spirit and Heaven. Those restrictions and fads are what human ego has imposed as socially acceptable or not.

Chapter Four

THE HUMAN HEART

Express love with those you come into contact with. Be aware of how you behave towards someone else. Many complain about what someone is doing to them. They do not take any accountability for the part they played. Be mindful of your own faults so that you can improve yourself and your life in the process. This is not to say that if someone is cruel to you out of nowhere that you are responsible. It is that you do not need to be a victim of someone else's cruelty. It is walking away from it and not allowing it to continue. You are not here to live carelessly and recklessly with abandon. Do not assume it is okay to treat people badly. Wake up and give yourself the occasional scrutinizing self-examination on how or where you are acting out inappropriately. Include how you are with strangers and especially those close to you. This waking up realization is in the same vain as someone who drinks heavily and one day comes to the conclusion that they want to stop. "Admitting" is the first step to recovery, because then your focus is on cleaning up your act. You hit that awareness point when you are accurately receptive in receiving clear messages from your own Guides and Angels urging you to eliminate certain people or negative behavior patterns in your life. It is your Spirit team who has been nudging you all along, but your ego denied it wanting self-gratification to feed the emptiness within you. This is the point of higher consciousness where you are totally clear about your behavior patterns and your lifestyle choices. Growth takes time and does not happen overnight. If you are doing the work, then people who haven't seen you in years will notice the positive changes in you. They will know that you are not quite the same person you once were, but you are better!

Everyone has their lists of wants and needs in someone they want as a partner and yet some of them are unrealistic. The one thing rarely seen on these lists is the word 'love'. How about, "He/She has to be able to love and give love." They might say they have much to offer and go down the list, but few fail to say, "I have a lot of love to give." Why do you want to be in a relationship if you do not feel you have much love to give?

I have been out there in the trenches coming face to face with the ego in others on a regular basis. Many do unless you are living in a quiet, rural, or country setting where Spirits power is heavy and easily accessible. This is the term when you hear the phrase "power place" in areas such as the mountains or the desert. Wherever there are vast regions of nature and quiet will give you a good idea where to go to re-center and connect to your Spirit team. You can connect with them anywhere, but it is doubly effective when you are in calm surroundings.

You were born out of love and with the greatest capacity to love. Unfortunately, negativity and ego-based thoughts like judgment, hate, and anger take over. All of those negative thoughts and feelings stem from deep-rooted fear or addictions you're consuming. You need to have great strength to not allow yourself to be swayed by others or your own ego. The ego is strong and can overpower the more sensitive. Ultimately the sensitive are more powerful than the ego in the end. This is why you hear that love conquers all. People are afraid of being alone so they conform to their peers, their community, and family so as not to be an outcast. They go along with false friendships, relationships, and acquaintances to keep from being lonely. They mistakenly believe that if they sell out and conform, then they won't have to be worried about being lonely. Nobody knows who you truly are in that state.

You have been inauthentic and are putting on a forged face. Go it alone even if it means you will be alone. Do not compromise your integrity for fear of loneliness or being misunderstood.

ASKING FOR HELP IN FINDING A SOUL MATE

Ask your Spirit team to work on bringing a soul mate partner to you. You can call upon a *band of angels* that is at times referred to as the Romance Angels. They are similar to the cherub angels one might find depicted in Valentine's Day greeting cards and memorabilia. Yes, they really do exist! They often work as a team of three's. It does not matter who you choose to ask for assistance as your request is heard and the right spirit guide or angel to assist you in your goal will come in to help. Asking God for help with anything is the ultimate go to power for your Earthly needs, including manifesting soul mate relationships. If you are calling out to your guide or angel you are simultaneously bringing in God. You can do this the same way you ask for their intervention for anything else such as mentally, out loud, or in writing. I have found in the past that I would write them a letter describing the kind of soul mate I wanted, but I would neglect to be specific.

Every soul mate I was in a serious love relationship with in the past seemed to regularly hang out in the bars, the clubs, or other sketchy places that the average person might question. They would meet people there and some would even go home with them, or bring them home to their place, and even forge a short lived relationship! They would stray or date around and chat with other potentials while continuing to "hang out" with me. All of the people I romantically attached myself to in the past had exhibited this behavior at some point. This is what I was attracting into me. No doubt they were Karmic connections. I had to take a good hard look at who I was allowing in my vicinity and to put my foot down. The irony is I didn't meet any of them that way so I naturally assumed they had the same values I did. Since we are not as objective about our own lives the way someone else might be, a block is formed and you do not pay attention to the red flags until it is too late. By the time I was deep into these relationship scenarios, that's when it was revealed to me on how they spent their free time. It was always along the lines of what many consider to be up to no good.

I reverted back to my letter to my Guides and Angels and revised it by adding something like: *"This potential partner is not someone who hangs out regularly in the bars or the clubs, and nor do they go home with these people they meet through these avenues. This is someone who is not dating around, and in fact, is also like me in that they are waiting for the right one before uniting with just anyone, even if it takes years."*

It is important to be clear in your request, because your team may bring you the perfect soul mate, but then you discover things about them such as they are not passionate or romantic and that's a big deal to you. Or as I stated in my case, they are not out there searching and meeting other people. The right person for you is going to be sure that you are the one. There will be no confusion about that.

You need to compromise and accept certain issues about your partner. There are also some things that you know you absolutely will not tolerate in a partner, such as they smoke cigarettes. The things I suggested for myself are what many people want when it comes to a soul mate. We all want a solid, healthy partnership. I would have no problem sitting in a lounge with the one I am with for a glass of wine or a beer. It is another thing if that person I am with is at the bar alone regularly or meeting new people that way. There is a fine line between both and yet it is important that you do not jump to conclusions even though what appears on the surface might be questionable. Sometimes having a conversation can clear things up before it turns into unnecessary drama.

When looking to get into a serious relationship with someone, you do not want to end up with someone who is not ready for a real relationship where there is no out. You cannot be with someone who needs to have an escape route or who is commitment phobic. Many souls have experienced this with others they cared deeply for, or they may have been that way themselves. I can attest that I have and so have my suitors. Even though that person might tell you differently and that they just haven't met the right one. The truth is they are not ready and will find excuses to avoid settling down. They equate settling down to losing their edge. On the contrary, the right loving, committed relationship is exciting and beautiful. It is true that not everyone is meant for a committed love relationship, but those that are not meant for it have trouble experiencing deep connections with other souls in this lifetime. It's generally fears that they will be tied down. They want to continue having fun in the form of feeding their toxic appetite. This is where their soul's growth is, which might be inferior to where yours is on the scale of personal growth. You cannot force, bully or trick someone in that space to be your marriage partner.

Write a letter to God and your own Spirit team of Guides and Angels pouring your heart out about what traits you are looking for in a romantic partner or friendship. Let them know what you will not be okay with. Ask them to bring you together and to give you the courage to speak to each other when you cross paths. This is important because how often do you find that you are attracted to someone who feels the same way you do and yet you are both silent and afraid to say hello? You end up passing each other like two ships at sea. Some do not realize that the one for them has been in front of them all along. This is because they might be addicted to the adrenalin rush that comes with pining over the wrong one. They may be disillusioned to believing that there is something better out there. They may still have some things to work on within themselves first before they can attract in the right person.

The stable love interest that comes into your life is actually the one that is more likely to be the one for you. They may seem nothing like you would typically be attracted to. Perhaps they might appear on the boring side or too domesticated at first. The truth is that the excitement of chasing someone who appears to be immediately electrifying is actually wrong for you. You are chasing after a mirage and therefore ultimately get burned or disappointed in the end due to their instability and ability to not commit. The often less glamorous choice is generally the one that turns into a real and lasting love relationship. This isn't to say that you are settling for a life of boredom. In fact, it's the opposite with the right one! Your Spirit team knows that you might crave a certain type of relationship with one person. This person is loyal and disciplined, and yet is also powerfully passionate in the bedroom. Ask and you shall receive!

I would go back to my relationship request letter to my Guides and Angels and continuously revise it. Naturally the letter grew to be a couple of pages long. After being disheartened by another suitor's behavior choices, I would add additional things like: *'It is mandatory that this person be loyal, loving, and compassionate. They must know the value and rewards of building a slow and steady long-term relationship that has security and friendly companionship.'*

You would think that those would be obvious traits in a partnership, but you would be surprised how often it is not. You might want to end your letter and request with, "This – or something better God." You do not want to limit yourself from being with someone that your Spirit team knows you will enjoy more. I still ask that we be attracted to each other knowing that this is a given anyway. You are not going to run off with someone you are not attracted to. There is a difference between lusting over a good-looking six packed Barbie doll model and someone that you have true feelings for their soul.

You might also be delivered someone who is attractive to others, but you find that you are not attracted to them until you get to know them over time. There are endless cases where couples admit that they were not initially interested or attracted to the person they are currently in a long-term relationship with. This is real love which grows over time, whereas fleeting love is one where you are immediately into someone for a couple of weeks only to have the feelings die off leaving you feeling dejected. The younger you are, the more likely you are attracted to something immediate that has no substance in the end. This is because you are lacking in life experience, maturity, and knowledge to appreciate someone's true soul and character.

Since being passionate, romantic, giving, and intimately sexy are a big deal to me, I would add that into my letter as well. I even added that I want a highly charged sex life with this one person. For me being physically touched and kissed repeatedly is oxygen to me. I have been this way my entire life and it's not going to change. I am a walking love bug, which can be a handful or detrimental to my well-being state if I put it in the hands of the wrong suitor who is passion-less, unromantic, or non-committal. This is the same endorphin releasing I get through exercise.

Touch has therapeutic benefits that promote a healthy body. If you are someone who is not particularly passionate and are interested in being with someone who is romantic and always touchy feely with you, then this is an important detail for you to put into that request. You do not want to have a suitor delivered to you who is always showering you with kisses only to find that it continuously gets under your skin prompting you to pull away. You both end up suffering and the relationship crumbles. It may lead one of the partners to seek out what's missing in their relationship with someone else. This is never advised, as you should always mend the relationship and work on it first. If all possible angles have been established and you have both come to the realization that neither of you have been happy after a long period of time, then dissolve the union peacefully.

When I had previously made my dramatic spiritual change and growth I had to add an extra detail to my letter that was not there before. It had to be revised so that I could request that this person be spiritual in nature or spiritually minded. This person does not have to practice it or even understand it, but this is a big part of my life. If I can't talk about it for fear of being judged, then it is not going to work with that person. If I'm with someone who attempts to continuously debate it, then I'm with the wrong person. It's safe to say or request that this person be spiritual themselves or at least be open minded, accepting, and supportive of it. I am walking the talk and living as healthy of a life as I can. If I find myself involved with someone who is out partying all night, then I've made a mistake in what I have attracted in. That was my former life that attracted in those types of characters and I am no longer attracted to that. I cannot fake interest because we are two different types of people with different values and lifestyles. I have had enough experience to know to pull out of the connection immediately if I suspect something that no longer jives with my values.

My letter and request would eventually grow into several pages long wrapped with layers of detail. I am using what I have done as an example of how trivial it might seem to someone else, but to you it is not. These are things you enjoy doing. You want to be able to do them with this one person in a relationship. You are also manifesting this and attracting it to you by writing it out in a letter similar to a vision board.

I would add extra colorful things to this letter such as this person must be nice, caring, and stable. They are someone to relax or have fun with. Sometimes we go out for date night once a week, while other times we are perfectly content to stay at home and watch movies entangled on the couch or on the bed together. We are developing something meaningful over time. It is someone who does not date much, but has mainly been involved in long-term relationships.

This person has not had many romantic relationships or dated around. The reason for this is those who tend to date around quite a bit, or who are having several mini-relationships that only last an average of a couple of months, are more likely to be unstable and non-committal. If they had done this in an earlier part of their life as I had, then that was who they were then, but not who they are now. Those who are not dating around are careful in choosing a mate, because they take the process and that person seriously. They are investing themselves and their life with this person and expect the same in return. They are completely ready for something real and tangible with someone else.

When I had my major spiritual transformation, I was no longer going out with anyone and everyone who showed the slightest interest. This would deem impossible anyway considering that I receive messages in abundance regularly. I made a pact to move towards those who practiced a healthy lifestyle as well as positive thinking. This eliminated about 99% of them! You can get a good grasp of the circles I was travelling in. Besides the typical wear and tear, peaks and valleys of relationships in general, I know that there will be issues every now and then in any relationship. The problems that arise with myself and the one I'm with will be tepid. We will work through them swiftly and always make up immediately if there is a minor rift that pops up.

Write a letter to your spirit team of guides and angels that includes what you're looking for in a partner. You may choose to include in this letter that the potential mate be physically attractive to you, but remain open minded to how this soul mate will appear. This can also work for career, health, or anything else you desire. You're merely having a one on one dialogue with your spirit team. It doesn't matter if you handwrite it or type it into an email and send it to yourself. What matters is the feeling and intention behind the letter.

Reading the letter to your Spirit team every day is not necessary. If reading the letter everyday to them gives you added optimism by partaking in that additional step, then that's fine too. It would be a personal preference, but not mandatory. Write the letter and then release it to Heaven. Those who enjoy cooking might pick up a cooking recipe, but then will start making slight changes to that recipe so that it works for them. This is the same concept as when you take on a suggested formula such as writing a letter to your Spirit team. Follow your gut on what feels right for you and trust that. Remember to step out of Heaven's way once you've released the request to them. There is no time limit on when a soul mate will be delivered. It can be weeks, months, and even years, but the point is to not lose hope. In the meantime, get into the fun and joy of your life with positive activities. This will help you shine with radiance, which attracts in potential soul mate interests shifting in and out of your vicinity.

What I have described is an example of what you can put into this letter to your romance angels or guides. You do not want to forget the details because you would be surprised that the angels fulfill your request as you have asked. You finally meet and connect with this wonderful person who exudes the qualities you asked for, but then they display a negative trait you forgot to mention. Start bringing more love into your life today by exuding and displaying those traits yourself too.

Chapter Five

The Power Of Love and Relationships

The only thing that matters in the end is love. It is the #1 reason you are here. All souls have this love gene within them. Everyone has the gift and ability to love and express love, yet so many stop living in this space full time. They give or expect love with peculiar conditions behind it. If you do not feel love or do not have any love to give, then take steps to elevating your consciousness. Do not allow the wrath of your ego to dominate your behavior. The ego has no love. Any love that it does show has an ulterior motive behind it. This motive aligns with qualities such as greed or betrayal. It will crush your spirit and turn you into something cold - which is also a front. I have witnessed this happen in others where past circumstances have caused them to shut down from giving and receiving love. They are unable to be intimate in their relationships or in friendships. This is unfathomable to me. Love and joy are the highest vibrations that exist. Love is the nourishment that keeps your soul riding on cloud nine. It keeps you healthy and lucky in attracting in positive circumstances to you. Make a pact to live in the space of love full time.

A potential love partner comes to you when you least expect it.

All of the serious relationships I have had in my past happened when I was not looking for it. Each one of them came about in the same manner. It did not happen when I was purging, in the middle of a change, or other major internal transformation. These soul mates showed up after I had gone through a mini-shift, which allowed me to experience peace. I was in a place of total contentment when every one of my romantic soul mates entered my life. As a love addict, I've always been consumed with an overflowing feeling of love. Growing up, I would use my pillow as if it were the one I was with. I would daydream of falling asleep with someone and having a profound connection with them in a loving, committed relationship. By the time I was sixteen, I was ready to unite with a soul mate in a marriage for life. I am a love bug and place the bar high when it comes to all things love.

Before the days of technology, relationships lasted throughout the duration of the couples Earthly lives. People stayed together and worked at it. There was less materialistic ego getting in the way that has a habit of crumbling the connections today. There is no perfect partner and yet through my research and interviews with single people, I've discovered that many of them are seeking perfection. This is a time in the world that is dangerously fixated on the media, fads and sexually charged images. Newer generations learn about this instant gratification desire. Fed to them since birth, they absorb this illusion and ultimately meet disappointment head on. There is perfection created in the media and in these images. They display false interpretations of reality. This is with the use of great lighting, camera angles, make-up and hair people toying with the one in front of the camera to make them look out of this world. Having worked in the entertainment industry for a good chunk of my life, and raised in the business, I have seen how they orchestrate everything to create the perfect shot. Most people have admitted to touching up their own "selfies" before posting those photos on social media. This is connected to self-esteem issues that have risen in astronomical numbers in others due to the internet's perception that everyone must be picture perfect. What happens when you meet these picture perfect photo people in person for the first time? Both of you are not exactly what you expected each other to look like and therefore you've wasted one another's time. The sole reason you met them to begin with was you expected a flawless appearing human being who looks as if they jumped right out of a fashion magazine.

All souls are shifting in and out of each other's lives for numerous purposes. Soul connections made have no set period in how long they last. They might last a week, months, years or even a lifetime and beyond. Some come into your life so that you can learn important life lessons that prompt you to change and grow. This is where the connection might be a challenging one, but in the end it enhances your soul pending you learn valuable lessons from the connection. It must happen or you would not be ready for the next big step. You connect with that person in order to join forces with them on a particular quest or to gain specific knowledge. They may be your soul brother or sister. You connect through several lifetimes sometimes just to say hello.

MESSAGES ON LOVE

Sometimes you overlook the potential suitors sent your way. They may not be the kind of person you were expecting so you do not bother with getting to know them. You do not feel like you have a shot. When you run into this person, you instead avoid them. Your own Spirit team sets up these chance encounters. They work together with the other person's guardian angel and spirit guide in order to orchestrate a meeting or a place where you will both cross paths. They will not bring a romantic soul mate into your life to replace your current one. If you meet someone while with your current mate, this does not necessarily mean your Spirit team sent this person. Heaven is about working it out with your current mate before considering bringing another into your life. Your current relationship would have to end. Time would need to be spent working on yourself afterwards before a new soul mate is delivered to you.

There is one exception. For some, they have a lifelong soul

mate or twin flame relationship that will come to them regardless if they are already in a relationship. This is because you and this other soul chose to meet at such and such time no matter what. It was set up and designed long before you were born into an Earthly life. You will know this is the soul mate if you end up with this person for the duration of both of your Earthly lives.

It can be challenging, because many people do not follow the guidance of their Guides and Angels and may be more prone to act on free will. There will be times where you or this other potential does not happen, because one or the both of your egos refuse it. Your Spirit team will continue with the search of putting other potential possibilities in your path hoping you both notice each other and strike up a conversation. They will at times continue to put the same person in your path for months and maybe even years trying to get you two to notice one another if it is indeed meant to happen this lifetime. This is why some couples have later recounted that after they became acquainted with one another they indeed had some near misses. They discover they had many missed encounters where they would have been together much sooner if it were not for their ego denying it or the fault of poor timing. Perhaps they were at the same store location, but missed each other by a couple of minutes. They can be the two people who work in the same building together, but continue to miss one another in the lobby and elevator by mere minutes. These unforeseen circumstances cause long delays between soul mates meeting and uniting. You and your potential soul mates Guides and Angels can only maneuver and control so much in order to get you two to connect. It's challenging for them to work on delaying or speeding up morning traffic in such a way that you both manage to arrive at the work building at the same time. They do indeed perform these brilliant miracles, but this is to illustrate the amount of challenging circumstances they have to move around to get you both in the same elevator together.

I receive questions from others regarding personal psychic or angel reading sessions they had with a reader. Sometimes the question might be regarding messages they received from their own Guides and Angels. One of the questions is they are told that they are meant for a specific person in a relationship, but that the person in question is already involved with someone else. The answer is an easy one. He/she may not last with this other person. When it is complete, then you will both cross paths and merge, pending that no other circumstances have taken place with either party. Two human souls who are meant to have a soul mate connection with each other will cross paths with one another repeatedly over a lengthy period of time until they finally notice one another and take action. If they do not take action, there are several reasons for this below.

There are people who are supposed to meet each other and yet they never manage to connect in this lifetime. This is mostly due to free will. Most human souls have saturated themselves into the material world. The media, their peers, and society heavily influence their nature. This blocks the important messages and guidance coming in from the spirit world. This makes that person more susceptible to ruling from their ego. For that matter, they tend to act upon free will. When you act upon free will, then you miss the gifts and wonders that God is placing in your higher path including a beautiful all-encompassing love relationship.

When it comes to two people connecting in a soul mate relationship, one or the both of you acts on free will and denies that the person they have crossed paths with is the one. Their ego convinces them that the soul mate potential is not what they are attracted to. They write off behavior patterns or habits this person does without giving them a fair chance. There are habits in others that are an understandable definite no such as they drink heavily, do drugs, stray, sleep around, and hang out in bars regularly as a fixture. The habits I am talking about are much smaller and forgivable such as they did not return your text immediately that day. Or they are not tall, blonde, and built to the nines. Your ego quickly writes them off, not realizing that this person is the one you are to connect with in this lifetime.

Before the media took over and dominated its influence on humanity, there was a courting process between two people. The couple in question was much more accepting of the other's idiosyncrasies and foibles. They also took their time getting to know one another before anything physical happened. This not only made the physical emerging sexier and hotter, but it also contributed to the longevity of their connection. The connections today are immediate and fleeting. This prompts many couples to split long before they truly know each other.

You cannot call one a couple or say that they are in a long-term relationship until they have been together for at least a year. Half of the couples that connect today do not make it that long. This creates a combination of loneliness and aloofness among souls whose basic nature is supposed to be love. This makes you grow cold and detached while continuing with your search for something instant to give you immediate pleasure and satisfaction. All the while wondering what it would be like to be with someone in a long-term marriage like relationship. Years pass and this pattern in your life increases to an astronomical and unmanageable degree. The image of this soul mate connection starts to take on a picture perfect vision that makes it even harder to believe it will come true. The person you seek and which you have conjured up in your mind has perfect qualities that no one in the world could fulfill. This perpetuates and delays any connection to any potential soul mate partner.

When you are in a relationship, then be unlimited in love. I used to say that I was difficult in love. Due to my past relationship experiences, I assumed the love I demanded was over the top or outlandish to a degree because I discovered no one knew how to do it. The intensity is beyond what an ordinary human being can give, but those who are no ordinary human souls understand this. Sent here with our individual purposes that have the capacity to be far reaching, one can find disappointment in ordinary human soul love. Our hearts are just too big for our body to contain. The truth is the right one has the same equal belief systems, values, and desires as you do. It is the same give and take. You cannot allow the quality and size of your Spirit to squeeze itself into a limited system of values. You are whole, perfect, and full of immense love. Allow this to shine so bright that it attracts in the right mate for you. Be completely together much more than you realize! Get out there and continue to live life. Go to the places you want to go and do not allow anyone to stop you from living and loving. Let go of the need to control the need to know when the soul mate connection will happen. Trust it is evolving on divine timing.

Know that some soul mates are an awakener for you. This is by allowing you to experience the emotions and thoughts that you had unknowingly closed off. The soul mates purpose is to bring your true soul out of the human body to get some air!

CHEMISTRY

Having chemistry with another human soul is only the beginning of where it could potentially lead if anywhere. This is a comfortably, strong, and deep attraction that is experienced by both people when they are together. Chemistry is a positive, mutual, reciprocated feeling with another person. You cannot act on chemistry alone though. Having chemistry on a first meeting with someone is natural for any human soul who is connecting to the newness of someone you have crossed paths with. This does not mean it is meant to move forward beyond that. Chemistry can be a dangerous thing depending on the scenario. Human souls are always experiencing chemistry with other souls, but that does not mean it is a love relationship waiting to happen. You can have chemistry with your closest friends and that is all it is - a friendship.

There are many different levels of chemistry. There is the, "I just want to have sex with this person", chemistry. There is the, "This person really gets me on a friend level", kind of chemistry. A successful relationship experiences chemistry on many levels. You are physically attracted to each other. This person is also your friend. Drawn to one another you find yourself heading back to that person and they are drawn to you. Being with someone who is exactly like you in every way can lead the relationship to grow stale. This works for friendships that you communicate with on a regular basis, but not so much love relationships, which require some shades that are slightly different from your partner. The hues are not vastly different where it causes constant friction of course, but different enough that it continues to attract you to this other person.

They are not quite like you, but there are elements about them that pull you in. Although it is important to have similar interests and values to an extent, it is even more so important that both parties involved in the relationship have some differences. This is somewhat close to the saying that claims opposites attract. The fine print version of the opposites attract syndrome is that they should not be too much of an opposite because then you will not connect completely. An extrovert can indeed be in a healthy long-term relationship with someone who is an introvert as long as they are facing the same direction. This is a case of opposites attract working.

One of the many reasons love relationships happen is for the sake of your soul's growth. For this reason, being involved in a healthy long-term relationship is beneficial when you are with someone who has some elemental differences than you. You will gain knowledge and lessons from this soul. It will also teach you to love someone who is not exactly like you. The relationship in general will teach you to work with others through compromise and communication. These are life lessons that build character and thus enhance your soul's growth. There does come a point where the differences might be too vast for a relationship to thrive. These are what might seem obvious in the realms of common sense. If someone is incredibly different from you on every level, then coming together might be impossible. This is not the case if it is a sexual connection. Human souls do experience the kind of chemistry that takes place with someone you are simply lusting after in a sexual way. Anyone that has partaken in such chemistry knows that it is short-lived and not long lasting. This is not to say you should stay away from that kind of connection. If you are one hundred percent single and alone, then there is nothing wrong with connecting in a physical way with someone you are having strong intense feelings for sexually. Ensure you are being responsible and using safety precautions, but know that it will not assist you in finding the love you crave.

When strong feelings are involved, your dopamine levels rise. Dopamine is the naturally producing chemical in the brain that prompts you to display loving feelings. Being a Don Juan Casanova type myself, I have met no other who knows about breathing in this dangerous chemical full time. What is hazardous about it is if you target this love towards someone who is wrong for you. Having this feeling for someone you meet while currently with someone in a relationship is not for the right reasons. The Romance Angels say that taking off in search of greener pastures is like chasing rainbows that eventually fade. The love chemical in your brain can cause you to see things with rose-colored glasses. It is unsafe to your heart when you direct this towards someone who does not share this same love with you. While there is nothing wrong with loving love, keep some measure of a reality in check so that you do not get hurt.

When you have chemistry with someone at the beginning of getting to know them, you likely do not pay much attention to the red flags. Later when your union hits a wall of unhealthy issues, you look back in hindsight remembering how you did see the red flags. You failed to think much of it until you dove too deep into the connection. You might use the excuse of, "Well had I known this I never would've moved forward with the relationship. By the time I discovered all this, I was too emotionally attached." In truth, if you take a step back you might be able to hone in on where the red flags were apparent. It might've felt so subtle at the time that you failed to think much of it. Most human souls tend to have the rose colored glasses on when they experience immediate soul attraction to someone who is feeling the same thing. Rose colored glasses give you the great love high, but the mirrors of the glasses are fogged up to the point where the real reality is distorted.

If you are in a loving, committed relationship and a red flag pops up, that does not necessarily mean to leave the relationship. At that point, it is more about addressing an issue that is extreme enough to rock the foundation of your connection. Your partner is in the relationship with you at that point and should be open to working out whatever the issue is. If you notice they're flirtatious with others when you're out together, the chances are they were always flirtatious by nature. They don't suddenly become flirtatious way into your relationship.

Sometimes long-term relationships lose their chemistry, but if the couple was able to come together repeatedly over the course of time, then the chances are they can restore the chemistry and balance in the relationship. A long lasting relationship goes through highs and lows while they are together. They are fully aware they fall in and out of love with each other over the course of their life. Falling out of love does not mean hatred or leaving the relationship. It is having an understanding of the basic nature of the human ego, because your higher soul is all love and never falls out of love with anything or anyone. There will be periods of detachment between one another while in a committed relationship. Allow your partner the space they need and be willing to communicate about anything important. Knowing when the other person needs space is vital. The partner having a temporary moment of detachment could be going through a personal transition or transformation. The other partner senses this and grants them the required space, while remaining nearby should their mate need them. Any couple that takes their partnership seriously realizes that they may hit a wall where it feels as if the chemistry has evaporated. The partnership is strong and rock solid enough that one or both of them soon rise to the task to rekindle the fire that never truly extinguishes for good.

INVITE LOVE INTO YOUR LIFE

Over the course of entertainment history, there have been love songs recorded, romantic movies filmed, and books written about having a secure, loving, and passionate relationship. Someone felt those things, craved it, experienced it firsthand, or witnessed it in others. Love is a universal need. It is your soul's innate nature even if you lost the ability to operate from that space. You can find that space again because the love you were born with never leaves. You just bury it beneath layers of cement.

Many singles feel discouraged about love. They crave and desire it, but when pining for a wonderful soul mate has turned to years of rejection or no success, then it can cause one to become everlastingly disappointed. The Romance Angels say that remaining optimistic about love is what is going to bring you this love. I can attest personally that I understand how difficult that can be, but through work you can get there. Doing the work means catching yourself when you find that you are negative whenever it comes to the word love. Be aware when this happens and then shift your state of mind into something positive.

Think something like, "I am blessed with a loving, soul mate relationship." Say it as if it is already here. It's about believing that it is happening now, rather than it's going to happen. Nothing is going to stop you from obtaining it. Get into the joy of your life. Feel the feelings of optimism when it comes to all aspects of your life. This opens up your heart chakra to receive love. When you are playful, lighthearted, joyful, and allow your inner child to shine, then you will attract in wonderful soul mates to you.

One way to focus on love is when you head to sleep at night. You are lying down in bed as your thoughts drift. Allow your thoughts to move into a visualization of you in a relationship with the kind of person you envision yourself to be happy with. Picture yourself in the house together with the picket fence and the animals. Go all out and do not withhold for fear of it not happening, or that you are being what someone's ego might call cliché. This is about you. What do you desire? Allow your mind to play you this mini-movie of this relationship you seek. It may come to you quickly or it may take some time, but never give up on love. Love yourself and those around you more. Become more appreciative of having these loving thoughts.

You can purchase some Rose Quartz crystals and leave it next to your bed. You can also put it under your pillow when you sleep. Carry it in your pocket, car, or purse. Lie down on your back somewhere comfortable in meditation and place this crystal on your heart. Take a deep breath in and exhale, then repeat this step as you relax. Visualize the crystal opening up your heart and allowing love to pour into your heart. Envision this love pouring back out of your heart and into your love's soul light across from you. Allow the light to envelope the both of you. It is not necessary to have a specific vision of what this person looks like and in fact it will be equally powerful allowing them to be faceless. This means you're leaving the door open for the angels to bring you a soul mate who might be more amazing than you initially imagined.

Purchase some *rose essential oil* and dab it on your heart. This is beneficial when you have been feeling closed off from others. Breathe in deeply and see a magical pink light shooting into your heart from Heaven. Send this light out tenfold back upwards and out of your body like a geyser. It is not necessary to go all out and purchase Rose Quartz crystals or rose essential oil, but it most certainly will not hurt it. You can manifest what you want with the power of your own mind. Love will come. Love is here. Love is within you and always will be.

Love yourself more in order to open up the feelings of love within and around you. This can be in the form of self-love, which is admiring all that you are. Love how you physically appear. Strip down and look at yourself in the mirror and say, "I love my body." Buy yourself a gift as if you are buying it for someone you love. Watch a romantic movie, have a massage, some pampering at a spa, or take a mini-vacation somewhere. Dive into your hobbies that bring you joy. All of this is self-care, which not only opens up your heart chakra, but also assists you in bringing those love feelings to the surface. You glow in this state and other potential suitors or people on the street notice this. You are a magnet that attracts in love. If you are currently in a relationship, then this will add some extra love into your connection. Even more powerful is if your partner participates in this with you.

Keep in mind that sometimes the soul mate you envision or crave may appear in a different way. They might be right in front of you and yet you are not immediately noticing. This is because you have a specific vision of who you think they will be that you do not realize that this soul mate is already in your vicinity. They may not be what you were expecting and you might not even be completely attracted to them right away. There will be some measure of attraction, but it is so slight you write it off because you are not feeling all of the feelings you expect to happen with a potential soul mate. Those feelings grow even more as you get to know this soul mate. Keep an open heart and an open mind while on your search for a love companion. Release the need to know when or how this person will come to you. Find activities that make you smile and enjoy. This keeps your heart wide open. You will be so busy enjoying yourself only to discover your soul mate has arrived and you are having a conversation. Worrying about when or how it will happen darkens your aura, causes you grief, and prompts you to feel depressing thoughts. This does not make your light attractive to others and you certainly do not want to repel your soul mate from entering your vicinity.

If you have had a history of bad past relationships, use the time that you are single to make crystal clear intentions about what you will or will not accept in a loving, relationship. You will want to keep these needs somewhat flexible. If you are too rigid in your list, then you will repel the right soul mate for you. The kinds of things that are understandable of what you will not accept are things like cheating, abuse in any form, alcohol or drug addictions, etc. The list would not include things such as where you insist that your soul mate calls you back immediately whenever you send a text. Controlling demands do not invite a loving, compassionate, and loyal partner to you. It instead brings in a partner who exudes the negative traits you were hoping they would not have in them to begin with.

In this same respect, controlling your current relationship if you are in one creates a difficult situation. No one likes to be controlled or have harsh demands placed on their backs. If your current partner is behaving in ways that you disagree with or that do not jive with your values, then discussing it peacefully with them is the next step. If that does not work, then consider working with a couple's counselor. It also boils down to what you can live with. If your current partner is not abusive, or addicted to alcohol or drugs, and does not cheat, then put in some extra effort to work on the partnership before considering leaving. If you leave, you will find that you will be stuck with someone far worse than your current mate is.

When making a commitment to someone else, you are first making a commitment to you. This practice of commitment with your own self is what you will carry over into your loving companionship with your partner. If you are irresponsible in your own life, with your actions and decisions, then you are not quite ready to commit to another human soul. This shows if you have a tendency towards short-lived connections that have no staying power. Work on taking responsibility for your life, yourself, your soul, and all of your surroundings. Making a shift in that direction where it becomes second nature to you is what will make it that much more effortless when joining with another committed, loving soul.

While in a relationship, avoid divulging every little tidbit that goes wrong with those close to you such as your friends. They may persuade you to leave a divinely orchestrated relationship. The natural reaction from those close to you is that they will side with you and not your partner. This is unfair to the person you are with. It will cause you more confusion when you are influenced by the words of those close to you. You have no idea what action to take if any. If it has come to that, it is best to take a time out for yourself and disconnect temporarily from your circle until you have individual perspective.

Loving relationships that run into roadblocks or a stalemate can deepen their connection by spending time alone together. This means getting away for a weekend trip or hiding out in your house and creating a romantic environment for just the two of you. When you spend time alone with your partner, then your feelings grow. This is extra beneficial for a relationship that has reached a point where one or the both of you feel stuck. This is what it means when others say relationships take work. You have to put in the work. You have to care about it. When you care about your relationships, then you care about you.

I am a firm believer of date night at least once a week while in a relationship. Inject laughter and fun on your date nights. It should be a relaxed and playful time for the both of you to forget any cares, stresses, or worries around you. Love relationships have this benefit in that the right partnership is an escape from all negativity in the world. When you are with them, you remember what is truly important in this life. Love is all that matters. Loving relationships help you remember your divine heritage.

Chapter Six

THE SECRETS TO SUCCESSFUL RELATIONSHIPS

Most human souls desire companionship on some level. You crave someone to be by your side that understands and supports you. Someone you champion and who appreciates you in return. For some, it might be a platonic friendship, for others it might be a sexual relationship with the same person throughout this lifetime. Your soul split into two souls at its original conception. This other half of you is your twin flame who many long for. They are a part of you, although not everyone connects with their twin flame in this lifetime. You move through this life feeling like there is something missing. In essence, you are searching for your twin flame. For most human souls, their twin flame is usually on the other side guiding you to healthy soul mate relationships for you on your Earthly journey.

Jaded singles have protested a myth that they believe those who are in relationships are unhappy. This could not be further from the truth. Those in unhappy or volatile relationships usually contain one or both partners who are not ready for a real relationship. They have not done the inner work yet. They bring their worst selves, their ego, and negative habits into the relationship, and then place that burden onto their partner. The connection is full of toxic energy that never lets up. The couple might be the type that argues more than they express love. It is normal to have a disagreement with your partner, but it is harmful if you are butting heads on a regular basis. Those who are in successful committed relationships are happier, healthier, and more productive in their lives than those who are not in peaceful connections. The ingredients for a successful long-term relationship are vast.

One of the secrets to happy relationships is that both partners are open and communicative with one another. If you do not communicate openly, then how do you expect your partner to know what your needs are? How are you to work at it if your partner has no idea how you are feeling? Meanwhile, you are making plans that will affect your mate and they have no idea. It is not fair to leave the one you are involved with in the dark.

When you head to work or your job, you have to do more than show up. You actually have to do the work. Granted you are receiving money to do that work. Whereas in a relationship the payment you receive is the experience and lessons you gain with your partner that benefit your soul's growth. This is worth far more than any money earned. Money is temporary, while your soul lasts forever.

Another problem that can arise is that you or your partner feels uncomfortable or afraid to bring something serious up with the other one. This is not being assertive, but living in fear. You might fear that your partner will take it the wrong way or that they might attack you if you bring a concern up. If your partner always attacks you for opening up, then this is a red flag that you are with the wrong person. No one should have to endure any measure of abuse from anyone ever. If there is an issue at your job, most people have to bring it up unless they want it to blow up in their face down the line. If they do not bring it up, then disaster will hit. Someone will say, "This could have been prevented." Alternatively, they might say, "Why wasn't I notified?" In relationships, some couples are afraid to bring serious needs and issues up because they do not want to rock the boat. If you do not bring your concerns up or any potential issues, it is not going to go away. In fact, it will grow into a bigger problem resulting in more damage.

Your relationships are to be safe haven. You need to feel most at home when you are with your mate. You should be feeling safe enough to communicate openly and work through issues together by talking it out and taking action steps to mend what needs to be. Not being able to talk to your partner about anything is like walking on broken glass. This is no way to live a healthy and happy life.

You have been feeling suspicious that your partner is not being faithful. You do not want to mention this insecurity because you fear that you will be wrong. You worry that your partner will judge you, criticize you, get defensive, or attack you for the accusation. This is not a loving partner. A loving partner is understanding and compassionate. They reassure you that there is nothing going on with anyone else and that you have nothing to fear. If your partner does become angry and self-justifying, then this can potentially be an admission of guilt. They are uncomfortable with emotional vulnerability and therefore not completely equipped to being in a loving healthy relationship. On the other side of that equation, there is a difference between making a cruel accusation in anger and peacefully discussing insecure feelings. When you attack your partner, they will naturally become defensive and retaliate. All of this hostile energy flying back and forth, but no honest discussion with answers ever enters the equation. The ego of both partner's end up controlling the conversation leading you both nowhere, except more defeated and drained.

Those in successful relationships feel openly comfortable to discuss the touchy subjects such as vulnerabilities or insecurities in the relationship. They nip it in the bud immediately so that it does not grow like a dangerous toxic weed in their beautiful garden.

Successful couples have similar values and interests to a degree. For example, both partners have a desire to live in the same part of town. You will run into problems if one of you wants to live in the big city around people, while the other prefers a quiet nature setting somewhere in a rural area or countryside.

If one partner feels like they cannot keep their feet planted in one spot and the other is perfectly at home doing that, then you will run into problems. There is a limit to how far compromise can go on some of these bigger issues. This is where communication is key once again.

Relationships are work and it is like a job in the sense that you both have to show up for the task. There are many couples where one is always on the go for weeks on end, while the other is at the home base. Is the one at the home base okay with this scenario? What if the partner on the go decides to take off and never come back? Is this who you want to commit to? There are billions of people in the world and it is impossible not to connect with someone who shares your ideals to an extent. You will find another soul mate potential with similar values as you have. This would include offering you more stability or reassurance that they are in this with you.

A successful relationship is facing in the same direction. It is joining to fight for everything around you together whether that is a parking ticket or having your partner's back in support.

Having or adopting children is another area where compromise does not always work. One of you wants or has plans to have children one day, while the other partner vocally does not or is flip floppy about it. This is where they protest that they want children, but then on another occasion they reveal they never had any interest in wanting kids. You are stunned to discover this truth. You could have sworn they were interested in having kids one day, while your partner is wondering how you ever got that idea in your mind. This type of person is flip floppy around many issues surrounding one's values. Flip-floppiness is someone who is not fully committed. They do not know what they want. Unfortunately, they are more or less stringing you along. You stay with them thinking they will change or that they need more time. Years in you come to the realization that they are never going to change or settle down. They have fears that govern their relationship lives and connecting with other people. This prevents them from being a grown up and mature soul. Fear is a relationship killer.

Human souls grow and evolve, but not always. Many stay relatively the same. When you were sixteen dreaming of a long-term committed relationship, this will not change when you are thirty-five. You more or less will still want that if it hasn't arrived or if you are newly single again. The only change would be that you grow more realistic as you age.

Trust is another important factor in a successful relationship, but more importantly is communication. Successful relationships endure because both partners communicate with one another and think of each other as the other's soul mate. Their love and understanding grows over time instead of fizzling out the way a fickle connection might. They are supportive of one another. They accept each other for who they are - imperfections and all. They work together in assisting in one another's growth. They shower one another with love and compassion. They are a beautiful and magnificent team.

Heaven and the angels love seeing two human souls in loving, committed relationships regardless of the genders involved. They know that once you are in a relationship that the real work enters the picture. They are by the sides of couples that request their assistance in empowering and improving the relationship. When there is friction going on or a disagreement between the both of you, then call on your Spirit team to intervene and mend the relationship. You can pray to God to send an angel to help your relationship. Assigned to your case will be the right angel or spirit guide. You may also call on Archangel Raguel who restores balance in relationships that are suddenly off kilter. He can mend any arguments or rifts that have risen. He will bring peace to all parties involved. Archangel Raguel is happy to do this for any type of connection, whether it is a love mate, friendship, or colleague.

Chapter Seven

STAGES OF COUPLEDOM

*H*ave you been in a situation where you are dating someone new and yet you have no idea what you are? By what you are, I mean are you dating, are you friends, or are you in a relationship? What is the scenario? Many have professed uncertainty surrounding the appropriate title. They feel as if they are sitting in the dark not knowing what they are to the person whose company they enjoy. They might see the person they are dating as a good friendship, yet the connection feels like it is slightly more than a friendship. This will cause confusion and future pain if you are not talking about it.

You should never assume that you are together, but at the same time, your connection does need to be established. What if you are seeing someone who sees that you are both simply friends? You have wasted valuable time putting energy into a connection with someone who has no interest in a relationship. Another scenario would be that the other person feels you are in a relationship, and yet you do not. Therefore, you have been dating other people here and there while making a beeline to this other person who believes they are involved with you. This will also cause pain, heartache, and damage to your connection. This kind of harm exists if one of you has more of an interest in your partnership and yet you carry on with it knowing this information. Edward was seeing Lisa regularly

146

only to discover that there was never any clarity if they were together or not. They had been dating regularly for nearly a year at that point and had been intimate on top of that. Naturally, he assumed for that reason, that they were indeed an item. It turns out Lisa looked at the connection as if it were a friends with benefits union. She had been flirting with other people inappropriately outside of being with Edward.

The modern day world has come up with so many labels and tags to identify what people are that it feels like a buffet of noise. Labels are not important because two souls who operate on the same frequency know exactly what they are to one another. However, human souls feel more comfortable when they are able to identify what they are with this other person.

DATING

Dating is a word that has lost its meaning. The latest fad that seems to have taken a rise within the newer generations specifically is that they feel uncomfortable using the word, *'dating'*. Dating might mean that this is serious and I might have to commit. There is a ton of fear about merging with another soul. Merging with other souls is one of the main reasons you are here. It is an instinctive need to connect with someone else. Instead of using the word dating, there are great amounts of people who use the phrase, *'hanging out.'* Using the phrase, *'hanging out'*, can and will cause confusion in a partnership that has not established what they are to begin with.

Dating is the process of getting to know someone gradually to see if you are a relationship match. You are not getting married or entering a serious relationship with them. However, dating is what leads to the more serious titles. Some couples may date for a month and part their separate ways, while others may date for years. If you are 'hanging out' with this person, going to restaurants, doing things together and kissing and being intimate on any level, then you are dating. There is no way to run from that title. This is the definition of what dating is.

Those who use the phrase, 'hanging out', tend to bypass the essential dating stages. Instead, they rush into a relationship with someone else within a month of knowing them. This is not a relationship just because you change your social networking status to 'in a relationship'. You cannot define a real relationship as such in less than three months. Those that do so will find that the dating connection has ended sooner than when you began it. You should be dating for several months getting to know that person over time. This is where you discover their interests and what they are like. You are looking to see if this is someone that you could see yourself going the distance with in a real relationship for decades to come. Take it seriously and treat it with the utmost care. Having a blasé attitude about dating means you are not ready to merge into a serious connection with anyone. It is also giving you a clue that the outcome will be failure.

How far into your hanging out before you bring up the inevitable question about what you both are? What if you bring it up too soon and scare the other person away? One would hope that common sense would be evident that you are dating regardless. The rules that modern day society has made up in terms of what you are, has left most people living in a fog.

If you are hanging out with another human soul regularly, being intimate, or the attraction is present on both ends, then you should refrain from hanging out with other people beyond a friendship. Unfortunately, not everyone observes that rule. The media, peers, and society have decided to make up their own rules. This has contributed to chaotic confusion with love and relationships. Human souls have free will choice to do as they please. As creative as the numerous rules may be, unfortunately they do not ensure longevity for a long-term relationship. Nor do they teach a soul about unconditional love or working with another soul. Someone will feel left out or unsure. One or both parties will sabotage the connection at some point. Poor choices lead to a buildup of Karma on your life path. You need to have the talk and do it soon before it gets out of hand.

It was not this complicated before the 1970's and 1980's. This was before free love and the sexual revolution, which brought in its plusses and negatives in the process. Everyone grew to be free in a way that the courting process became too complex, dynamic and therefore much more chaotic. It was the end of long-term committed relationships as ego modernized souls would come to know it. Before that time, two souls would endure a lengthy courting process, which involved a form of hanging out. They felt and observed the sexual tension even if they had not kissed yet. You did not go out searching, chatting, and hanging out with other potentials while courting someone. Doing so is bad form and having no integrity. This is what shows you someone's character.

The Internet and phone apps that exist today connect everyone together, but they have also caused the relationship downfall. Technology did not shatter how relationships develop. It is the human ego, which has destroyed it. You give a child a new toy they are not ready to play with and you will have a problem. There are many who do not know how to properly court and date. Raised in a generation of texting, social networking, emailing, and phone apps have not helped with this. The ego wants more! It wants more friends, more people, more newness, more possibilities, more stimulation, more everything! The incessant search for immediate, self-gratifying, self-sabotaging sensations is a sign of detachment from your higher self, soul, and God.

CASUALLY DATING VS. EXCLUSIVELY DATING

Define what you are together and agree on it. If you do not agree on it and neither of you is compromising, then you will run into issues.

Are you both going to agree that you are *Casually Dating* or are you *Exclusively Dating*?

Casually Dating means that you enjoy each other, but you are not serious or looking for anything serious. This is more or less someone you enjoy hanging out with. If either of you decided to stop it tomorrow, neither of you would care all that much. You may also be dating each other while dating other people casually as well. Of course, it is important that you are both on the same page that this is the set up you agreed on. Casually dating someone can be similar to a serial dater. This is someone who is always dating someone for a brief stint and then abruptly moves onto the next new person that enters their life. They are in love with the newness of someone. There are no hassles, no commitments, and no responsibility needed. They are also chasing their tails. They may be dating several people at the same time or their dating scenarios with one person at a time are typically short-lived. They may also be the same people who add *'in a relationship'* to their social networking page status, even though they have just started dating that person. Within one to three months max they end up changing their social networking status back to *'single'!* They were never truly in a relationship to begin with. What they were doing was dating. They were never quite able to bring their dating situation to a REAL relationship efficiently. This is typically common with people younger than twenty-five who are inexperienced and tend to jump in immediately eliminating any essential courting process. It is not limited to someone under twenty-five as there are cases where people who are older do it as well. It is lacking in experience or having a deepened maturity level. This is a red flag, unless it is a scenario mutually agreed upon.

Exclusively Dating is where you are both loyal to one another through the dating process. You are incredibly interested in one another and you both want to see where it goes. You both imagined that you could be with this other person for life in a relationship. You are not dating around, seeing other people, or even chatting inappropriately with other people. You are investing time, energy, and love into this person.

Dating can be tricky, because you do not immediately slap on the exclusively dating label, but it does happen fairly soon after a

150

couple of months. You always start out with them as casually dating, but then as it continues to grow you are exclusively dating. You need to make sure that the other person is on the same page as you. This is the stage where you both may telepathically know you are an item, but you still have to clarify it. This should be easy for both as you are likely sharing much with one another to begin with. Exclusively dating one person is often termed also when the couple is not quite thinking of a serious relationship, even though they are seriously dating. The 'exclusive' terminology ensures that the couple knows they are devoted to one another only. The connection is a deep friendship, with some intimacy and the occasional date night. It might not be a full-fledged relationship, but to a degree, it is a relationship.

BOYFRIEND OR GIRLFRIEND

Some people are uncomfortable with the title of boyfriend or girlfriend. They are usually the same folks who do not use the dating word. Some acknowledgement of how you plan to refer to yourselves is helpful. Casually dating someone does not mean you are necessarily the boyfriend or girlfriend. If you are exclusively dating someone however, then you are a boyfriend or girlfriend. Clarify this title with one another to make sure there are no surprises. There are many who are unsure what their connection is. Therefore, they continue dating other people or chatting them up. When people are hitting on you or asking you out, your immediate response should be, *"Thank you, but I'm seeing someone. I have a (boyfriend), (girlfriend)."*

RELATIONSHIP

A relationship is where you are committed to the person you have been exclusively dating for some time. Exclusively dating someone is a commitment, but a relationship is taking it to a higher level. You might still be using the boyfriend or girlfriend title on occasion, but you are in a full-fledged relationship as well. This means you have both acknowledged that you are in a relationship with one another. You have gone through the dating process with them and have come to the realization that this is someone you trust, love, and want to share your life with at this point. This is not to say that you are not experiencing those feelings when you are exclusively dating someone, but a relationship is an entirely different ballgame. It is a beautiful moment and yet at the same time it will take work to keep it afloat. The Romance Angels know that the work has only just begun when a real relationship starts. They are present for those who request their assistance while in a relationship. In a sense, it is like buying a house to a degree. You have to take care of that house, work on it, and keep it up. The same goes for your relationship.

A couple who is mature and responsible about forging on in a relationship knows the value and benefit of coming together in an even more committed way. They understand that it is a perfected dance. You understand each other's quirks and know how they operate.

If you do not communicate, then your relationship will disintegrate. This means opening up and discussing everything including the serious matters. You are partners and a team who have made a pact to forge on in life fighting the same cause together. You work through difficulties the way you might work with someone at your job in finding a solution to issues that arise. It is to know that you will have to compromise especially when your ego wants to do what it wants YOU to do. This is not living in the Light, but in selfishness. When you are selfish, self-centered, and act out in your own interests, then you create bad Karma. This Karma grows when the particular choices you make negatively affect another human soul. This can include leaving a relationship to feed your ego. It is different when you leave an abusive relationship or that person has been engaging in intimate acts with other people. Even talking intimately with another person while you are involved with someone else is an emotional betrayal.

You might be riding sky high after you make a selfish move that affects the one you left, but the initial selfish act you participated in grows and suddenly things start going wrong in your life. Most human souls do not realize that it is their Karma. When you are selfish, how would you know you acted selfishly? You are too self-absorbed and narcissistic to care. Human souls have relationships throughout the course of their Earthly life in order to gain specific knowledge pertaining to their soul's agreement. No one is exempt from this regardless if one does not have at least one serious relationship in their life.

In a serious relationship, the couple usually tends to have their eye on living together at some point. There are many successful relationships where the couple has separate residences. In those cases, they are spending quite a bit of time practically living at each other's places. They might as well live together.

Relationships can also be anyone that your soul connects with for any length of time. This can be for a few minutes or a few decades. It can be your love relationship mate, your boss, colleague, a friend, or even neighbor. It can be someone you have met in an airport terminal holed up together for a two-hour delay. You share a conversation that enlightens or prompts you to make a positive change within you. They might have connected with you to deliver specific information that ends up assisting you with something more pressing in your life.

When you merge into an actual love relationship, you have likely experienced some ups and downs with that person during the dating stages. You know how to navigate effectively with each other when there is a disagreement. When you were exclusively dating, you might not have shared every moment or your whereabouts, however in a relationship, it is a mutual alliance. You will be receiving questions that you might not have had before. "I saw you talking to that girl. What was that about?" How about, "Can you accompany me to this work thing?"

In a relationship, you are already aware that your mate may need extra reassurance that you are with them from time to time. You know how your mate is and will not be exactly like you. Perhaps they need additional emotional support or physical affection. Maybe they crave heavy doses of romance or they prefer not to have the hearts and flowers kind of love. These are situations where the couple does these things for their partner, because they care about them. It might not be what they are typically into, but this is where compromise comes into play. You gain knowledge in the relationship such as opening up or revealing your heart more. You are here on this planet for love after all. Do you really think it's to work a 9-6 job for the duration of your Earth life? Sure, you need to make money to survive, but that's not why you are here. It is to learn to love and exude love.

It is awesome to be an enterprising person in business, and to strive for financial success that ensures the stability and security your human needs crave. However, you do not want it to take over your life to the point where you ignore your mate indefinitely. There will be times where you might have a busy period at work. It is another thing to allow it to consume and rule your entire Earthly life. The Romance Angels stress on the need for you to balance both your work and your home life. Doing this ensures that you are in a happier state of mind while attracting in the abundance your human soul desires.

By the time you are in a relationship with this person, you already know them pretty well. This means you know what some of their faults and moods are like. You know how they are, what makes them tick, or what upsets them. You need to be at a place of being open with that other person when you cross over into the 'in a relationship' territory. At that point, you may have already discussed if you will one day live together and what kind of places or cities you would like to live in. You discover if it is in harmony with the other person during the dating phase. You know if they want kids, or a family, or pets, etc.

How is your partner with children, animals or their own family? These are clues to what they might be like when you are living with them. When you are living with someone in a relationship, you are with this person day in and day out. Is this something your ego will be able to handle? It is certainly important that the partnership have their separate lives and hobbies to an extent. If you are with the same person every second, then you will be driven crazy. Human souls need space and independence every now and then. This helps

154

them realign and reassess their goals, visions, and thoughts. Successful couples are in constant communication with one another even if they are on a sabbatical alone while the other is teaching a class in another city. Many households have couples where both of them work all day. When they arrive at home at the end of the day, they may have personal activities to attend to. Maybe one of them enjoys swimming at the gym after work on Wednesday's while another meets his buddies on the field for a baseball sport. Healthy relationships welcome the separate, but equal lives they have together. This ensures the longevity while keeping it all balanced.

You are each other's friend and confidante. Having your own life is beneficial pending that you do not neglect your partner. Some long-term successful couples have protested that the passion or the sex has waned at times while together. Passion and sex in a relationship is a helpful component, but it is normal for happy committed couples to reach a place of no sex or a drought. When this happens, you must talk about it with one another. Take it seriously by finding ways to unleash the passions within you both. This should not be too difficult because all of the other positive components that keep you together already exist. This is why you are together to begin with. When you have the other positive qualities in the relationship such as a great friendship, companionship, communication, trust, and enjoyment together, then it is relatively easy to move it into a sexual way.

Growing subconscious fears contribute to lack of sex in a relationship. Some couples become too comfortable with each other where it feels like you are roommates or siblings. This does not mean your relationship is over. On the contrary, this is where you put those working on the relationship skills to good use. Find ways to re-ignite that exciting passion between you both. I have a strong sexual drive by nature, but I am also very patient with someone I love when it comes to that. You may need to put in some effort and not be afraid to talk sexually with your partner. Send them little sexual texts and emails or start complimenting them and their body. Your partner should be open and receptive to this. Drop your guard and those pointless walls built around you and let loose with each other. Come up with some sexual exercises that you can both work on together. Develop self-love for your own body and your lovers' body. If you do not love yourself, then how can you love someone else? Take romantic trips with one another and put together candle light dinners. Hold hands more. Cuddle. Hug. Get into it and put in some effort!

You should never jump to move in with someone in a relationship right away. Wait until the honeymoon blush has worn off. This is about the 18-month mark after you first met or started dating. If they have lasted that long with you, then you know there is a great shot at making the living together part work. There is no set time on when you have to move in, as there are couples that have been in relationships with each other for years, but choose not to live together nor have immediate plans to. Exceptions always exist such as an older couple who comes together and gets married within the same year. They have the maturity level to ensure it lasts. They don't have the excessive hang ups that come with someone who is younger.

There is no such thing as an open relationship despite the modern day world pushing for that title. Open relationships are essentially, *'friends with benefits'*. This is what it should be labeled. There are swinger couples that live with one person in a relationship, but might be unsatisfied sexually with that person. They prefer to invite another person into the bedroom on occasion. They are more into sex and agree on living together for companionship, while bringing in additional partners for sexual enjoyment. This is a mutually reciprocated agreement between them.

MARRIAGE, CIVIL UNION, COMMITMENT

Marriage, civil union, or a commitment ceremony is the next step after relationship. You have been in a relationship with the same person for years and you are both happy with it. You may both choose to make it even more official. This is where you are taking a big step in joining in a marriage under the eyes of human law. This includes all the tax benefits that it entails. This also includes the dangers if you decide to divorce. It can be taxing financially and emotionally if you are both not in sync when you decide to dissolve the marriage. Marriage is not always a romantic circumstance, although it can be. It is a business alliance as if you are starting your own business with a partner. This partner is your soul mate and they are on the same page with you. You both already know quite a bit about the other person and you function well as a team. You are each other's family through all good things and bad. Only marry when you have no problem knowing there is no out. You know there will be lows as well as great highs and you are still okay with that. You will work together to fix it as if it were your business. You would not walk away from your business immediately if there were problems would you? You would find ways to fix it.

Another label for marriage can be a civil union, or some choose to conduct an official ceremony even if the government does not recognize it. This might be the case with Same Sex couples in certain states or countries. The bottom line is that it does not matter what the law, government, or other people think about your relationship. It only matters what you and your partner choose to call it. You may choose to say you are married, even if you did not go to a government facility to have it documented under the eyes of the law. Some couples like to have a special spiritual ceremony whether it is personal between them, or an all-out wedding with all the trimmings and guests. This is in keeping with the fun and joy that a love relationship is. Love is a celebration!

Chapter Eight

THE EGO'S WAR ON LOVE

Human souls crave contact and love from others, even if the hardened ego denies it. Those who prefer to be loners, independent, or living in the middle of the woods with no one else around grew to be this way due to societal conditioning during their younger life's developmental years. Deep within the DNA of the soul's core, the soul desires a love companion. This is the case even if the love companion they crave is independent natured themselves. An independent minded loner would have a better chance of going the distance with someone who is similar in that respect. You do your thing, I'll do mine, and every now and then we do our thing together.

One might not call this a love companion, but a friend companion. It's still a love companion regardless of the title you give it. The nature of closeness you have with this person is irrelevant. Your one true long term soul mate this lifetime could be the same gender as you. You might be sexually attracted to someone of the opposite sex, and yet the love companion you choose to be around through the duration of your current Earthly life is of the same sex. This doesn't have anything to do with engaging in physical intimacy with this person. There are a great deal of love relationships between two people where they are with someone of the same gender, but do not engage in physical intimacy because sexually they're attracted to someone of the opposite sex. This is the same case with someone who might be attracted to the same sex, but their soul mate lifetime love is someone of the opposite sex. These cases are just as much a deeper higher love than any other physical relationship. This is someone you feel the most comfortable spending the rest of your current Earthly life with. Over time you come to the conclusion that the person you want to be with is this particular person.

Some might flinch confused believing that the one true soul mate intended for them is supposed to be someone they have a sexually, passionate, hot love relationship with. Yes, this soul mate can have those qualities with you, but this isn't always the case for many souls on Earth.

One of the bigger misconceptions about long term love relationships is that human souls have this misunderstood belief that if there is no sex with a love partner, then the relationship must be over or they're not with the right one. The angels say this myth couldn't be further from the truth in real reality. It is the ego demanding that relationships satisfy their insatiable needs. There is a great deal of soul mate love relationships where they experience a sexual drought. It feels as if they're stuck in a rut and have become more like roommates or siblings. There is a block that prevents them from being able to adequately move into a regular sexual physical relationship with one another. This can be shifted when both partners discuss this issue openly and with compassion. They both agree to take steps and make effort to be more physically intimate with one another. This is in order for the partnership to thrive and grow. Your higher self's soul is open in all ways conceivable. This goes for physical intimacy with a love partner too!

The other case is there is no physical sexual intimacy with the soul mate if it's a love connection with a friend who is of a gender you're not sexually attracted to in your lifetime. In this sexually charged world, this is a difficult concept for modern day human souls to comprehend, but Earthly life is slow to evolve to a higher space where complex circumstances unseen are understood.

The ability to love, give love, and receive love are part of every soul's make up when it enters into an Earthly life. Human souls were not born unfriendly, greedy, angry, and selfish. This is the human ego and lower self running the show. It is not one's higher self, which is pure love and compassion. When someone displays love, joy, and compassion traits all at once without wanting anything in return, then you can be sure that at that moment they're operating from their higher self's space. You've likely encountered this type of person in your life that exudes those traits. They are infectious and brighten your world just by being in your vicinity. Wouldn't you rather be in that space full time, rather than in upset and stress?

It is understood that you live in a world with tampering energies around you. If you live in a big, unfriendly city, then you likely know how difficult it can be to navigate through the tempestuous waters day after day with angry rushed souls around you. The love is nowhere to be found and you feel this, but often so does the angry soul. They've hardened becoming jaded and unlovable to themselves and other human souls. Yet, deep down at their soul's core resides the love they were born with. Their ego has rendered it inaccessible caging it and sealing in the goodness. This is why there are souls experiencing an Earthly life for the specific purposes of awakening and opening the hearts of these hardened souls. They might be someone the hardened soul crosses paths with and is showered with love and kindness from this other soul in passing. It allows a few cracks of light to burst out of the hardened soul's heart chakra.

It takes work to reach a state of serenity. Sometimes you will falter and lose your way. All souls are works in progress. This includes the teachers and leaders of the world. When you gain the tools necessary to pull yourself out of the ugliness, then it gets easier to do so in those moments when you waver.

Love relationships in modern day era have grown to become more than an effort to find and a struggle to keep. Since many human souls are governed ruthlessly by the external and the ego, this has played a huge part in the demise of loving relationships. In the United States alone, polls and stats are being revealed that slightly more than half of the population consider themselves to be single. This data isn't taken seriously by anyone, and neither is the tragic reality pointed out. This is a sad revelation that further demonstrates that humanity is not evolving as quickly as one would like to believe. It is ironic considering that love is the reason all souls are here, but obsessions center on needs, excess, and selfish satisfaction. This satiating need to sharpen in on external fixation was taught to others by the masses in the media, your peers, and society. This progression continues to be recycled generation after generation. It's a strange kind of zombie like transfixed eeriness that hones in on all things greed, material or external. Some human souls attempt to receive this need for love through external sources such as social media adoration. This is not love, but ego. It is done innocently at times since this is a soul who simply craves love.

It is easy to hypnotize a baby soul more than any other. Baby souls are on Earth for their first Earthly life run. The angels see them as naïve and innocent. Other spirits see them as dangerous, causing the most hate, destruction, issues, and drama around the world. The baby souls are all of those things combined. They are both naïve and destructive. They're easily influenced and succumb to the intoxication of the images being fed to them. This is done instead of diving deeper into pulling out their true higher self's soul. If this isn't the case, then the soul is terribly unhappy with some part of their life. They might be under stress and experiencing prolonged feelings of negativity.

Social media and phone apps have also contributed to the downfall of long term relationships. There are positive benefits to social media, but what are the benefits with phone apps? The lonely and bored typically log on to connect with preying predators looking for the next best thing, or to fill up the emptiness the ego created within. You are one in a long line of people that someone is sending the same messages to. The rise in phone apps to meet people is another avenue to come into contact with those in your vicinity. This has its benefits to a degree for those who are either temporarily single, living in a small town with little to no people, or for hooking up. This can be misconstrued as a broad generalization, but we're not speaking in specifics.

Through research, I've discovered most people ultimately use dating apps for the means of hooking up with you at some point. Phone apps are a way to meet people in your vicinity at the touch of your fingertips. This is an exciting and alluring way to hopefully meet additional people who you hope will become important in your life. The issue is that the ego is looking for instant gratification with many, instead of developing something meaningful and long lasting with one person. These avenues satisfy the ego, temporarily relieve boredom, and fulfill ravenous addictions.

Some of the common inquiries I receive from others are where they are dating someone new or already in a love relationship with them. It isn't long before they come to me with a discovery. They discover by "accident" that the person they're involved with is on a phone app. They express confusion and concern unsure whether or not to say something to their partner. They don't want to upset them or find out they're up to no good. Instead they hope they can trust their partner enough to assume they're just on the app for friends. Friends with a gender they are attracted to? Sure it's possible, but it would lead a rational soul to question it.

This further cements that most have already placed a negative stigma on the use of phone apps. There are good people wherever you go, including on a phone app. The flip side is that it can be a device for narcissism and addiction. You're logging on day after day hoping someone can fill the emptiness that resides within you. This soon lowers your vibration leaving you perpetually glum and dissatisfied. You're searching and searching for people to connect with on the app. What about the people you know in person? These are the ones who are already in your life. I've watched a great many throw that away only to log onto a phone dating app looking for new people to develop nothing with. It's a cycle that never ends.

Relationships are colder than they've ever been in this modern day, yet somewhat backwards civilization. The hyper-technological world has contributed heavily to the demise of real human connections. The irony is the issues going on in the world are stemming from disconnect with one's true soul and higher self.

Before the rise in social media and phone apps, human souls took the connections they had seriously. Now they disregard them on a whim for the next best thing that pops up on their phone.

162

Operating from ego, boredom, or loneliness ultimately lowers your vibration. One is craving instant stimulation from anyone around them. It doesn't matter who it is. Most on phone apps are ultimately looking for a one-night stand. Some will cut the foreplay and come right out and tell you, while others will work you a little bit before dropping the bomb that they're deeply and crazy attracted to you. You feel loved for a brief moment that someone finds your photo or photos attractive. Eventually your banter between one another dissolves as this person has moved onto someone else they're chatting with and saying the same remote things to. It's a cycle that repeats itself as you log back on and continue this drill with the next victim wondering if any of these people could be 'the one'. If they're not attracted to you, it's rare that they would attempt to get to know you at all. Everything is externally based. Do I like how you appear before I engage with more than a hello?

Your soul longs for the kind of eternal gratifying stimulation that cannot be fulfilled through immediate indulgence. It's an addiction within the ego that one feeds in hopes of finding the one awesome love, friend, or one-night stand. This tears down your soul thus lowering your vibration in the process. It's the search that crushes your soul.

I've reviewed many cases where love relationships fell apart. Both partners end up back on social media and the apps searching instead of working on the connection they had. One or both will say something like, "Well our relationship was great, but there was something missing." They'll make a variety of excuses that are fixable in the eyes of someone operating from their higher self. There is no perfect relationship and it will always seem as if something is missing no matter who you are with. This is how you learn important soul enhancing traits while with someone. You accept your partner's neurosis as they do with you.

The ego is strong in others and demands to have all of its needs met at once. This is a false reality that will leave the human soul perpetually dissatisfied. As you grow older and find yourself alone feeling even more abandoned, your mind sifts through the many options and choices of soul mates that entered your vicinity during the course of your life. There may be one soul mate in particular

163

that your mind drifts over to from time to time. You'll wish you could do things differently with them, such as make it work and not throw in the towel. Human souls are intended to partner up with one another in soul mate relationships and companionships. This strengthens your souls by merging both your lights. You have that loving, supportive companionship through all of your years on Earth. You are the anchor for each other when things get tough. It helps to have that other half to make decisions with while granting them and yourself the space your soul also requires for clarity. When you partner with the right soul mate relationship dynamic, then you add balance to your life that keeps you from diving too far off into the deep end.

When you ultimately merge into a love relationship, then remember to love each other up often. Touch, hug, and cuddle with one another. The physical body hugging another physical body adds positive health benefits. Clairvoyantly one might see the aura light around both people hugging. The light in both soul's merges and the colors of their aura shifts from a dark muddy color if they were stressed to brightening up. This is doubling the power and effects that the hug has. It releases Oxytocin in the brain and relaxes the soul. Tests have been conducted on hugging where they measure the blood pressure in someone who is stressed out. The blood pressure rises in the soul who is lacking of hugs. While the one receiving or giving a hug displays a drop in blood pressure preceding a stress event. Hug someone whenever you can and spread the love. You can hug a friend, a tree, and even animals. Although the hug of a love interest has a massive health benefit due to the high passion and love quotient between them.

Chapter Nine

BRING BACK MY LOVER

*L*ove issues are more frequent than ever before due to the heavy rule of ego in this materialistic externally based world. One of the biggest inquiries I receive surrounding love is that someone's lover abruptly leaves the relationship. This results in the one who was left to feel eternally dejected. The partner that was left desires heavenly intervention to bring them back together again. Heaven cannot force someone to act a certain way against their will. For some cases, they might plant the idea in that person's mind only if it will benefit both of the souls higher good. And if it is part of the agreement both soul's made prior to entering an Earthly life. There may be cases where you believe with all your heart that your relationship ended prematurely. This may be the case to your ego, but not to your ex-partner or your Guides and Angels.

Not all relationship connections are intended to last forever. It is not uncommon to have strong feelings for your partner after they've exited the relationship. Your mind goes through a whirlwind of feelings that include sadness, anger, and pride rejection. You miss the good times you had and love the security that the connection provided. You're left in a state of shock mulling it over in your mind repeatedly trying to understand how the breakup could happen. This causes confusion as you thought everything was fine in the relationship. You reach out to anyone who will listen to your troubles surrounding it. This is with the hope that this person you're reaching out to will offer you answers that will bring your lover back to you. This can be from friends, strangers, colleagues, therapists, to psychic readers. Inside you desire that they will all tell you that this is just a temporary break and you'll be back together before you know it. In some cases, this does happen of course, but not always.

I've been in those love connections in the past where it was bliss without any major issues or arguments and it ended only to be rekindled again years later. I've also witnessed the red flags in other people's relationship connections, which both partners were blind to seeing. The person who was left in a relationship is in a state of shock. They are unable to admit the red flags were indeed present if they examine the connection trajectory more closely. You ignore the red flags when you're in love. If you notice the red flags, you think the person will change only to later discover they've ultimately left you in turmoil and heartache.

If you were left in a relationship by someone you deeply loved, then request heavenly assistance from your Spirit team. Ask that they help re-kindle the spark lost between you and your ex mate. If your Spirit team sees that the relationship is indeed over and has run its course, then add that they help you heal and move on. If they intervene to assist your lover to come back to you, this doesn't mean that person will acknowledge the heavenly guidance and nudges. Many do not listen to their Guides and Angels due to the over consumption of the ego and material world around them. The exception is a spiritually minded partner, but a spiritually minded partner likely would not have left their mate in the first place unless they were abusive in some form or bathed in addictions. Another exception is that the partner is moving into a period of soul searching and discovering who they are. They require space for a major transition. However, a spiritually minded partner more than likely would've discussed the break up with you so that you are both at peace with the splitting up.

The soul mate you love has left you and chosen to pull away.

They distanced themselves from your connection for a myriad of reasons. You anxiously wonder and obsess if your lover will come back to you. You believe you received signs that they're interested in you regardless that they left. The angels know if a couple has what it takes to re-unite and make it work, but they cannot intervene with the other person's free will. If someone bailed out of the relationship, they do so out of free will and ego. This is powerful beyond any kind of heavenly intervention. It is important to note this since I have had others say they've asked Heaven or their Guides for help in re-uniting them with their ex in a love relationship, yet months have passed by and there has been no movement or sign of it happening.

Heaven does not have control over how someone chooses to respond or not respond to your affections. The person you desire will show how they feel about you through their actions. Believe them when they show this. They might be unresponsive to your affections after the break up. When someone is interested, they will let it be known. When you reach out to someone you have interest in to see if they have interest in you, then do it with the knowledge they might not give you the response you crave, if any response at all. Prepare yourself for this and accept any outcome. This person made a decision to extricate themselves from your connection. This doesn't necessarily mean you did anything to cause that, which is something else that may plague your thoughts. You're likely to go through deep self-analysis to see where you might have played a part in the crumbling of the union. Sometimes you'll see where you made mistakes. Other times the breakup doesn't have anything to do with what you or they did or did not do.

Friends may urge you to move on and immediately see other people. Feel whole and complete within before you venture out into the dating field. This is another side effect after someone has left you in a relationship. You understandably want to get over it and move on as quickly as possible. This isn't fair to someone new when you're not ready and still have deep thoughts lingering over your previous partner. Understand the lessons that have been learned in the connection that ended abruptly. If the connection was submerged in red flags, unhappiness, or abuse, then in the future make a pact to only accept soul mate relationships that are loving and supportive. These are ones that enrich and nourish you, while you give this same support in return. Refuse to be part of any drama with a soul mate that makes you feel less than others. Aim to be around people whose lives are working. Choose to be around those who are making positive contributions. Be around those who are growing, evolving, and making soul contact. Sometimes you need to release soul mates because they are harmful in toxic ways you might not have been noticing, either to themselves or towards you.

There will be times when your ego has a difficult time letting go of an ex. You have loving memories of the good times you had with them. The ego refuses to believe that the connection and lessons with them are over. You wait and hope for that small glimmer of hope that there will be some reuniting taking place one day. Meanwhile, years have passed and there's been no movement. What will it take to see that the connection is indeed over? Sure there are cases where there is a reuniting that takes place in order to complete unfinished business, but those are rare cases. Incidentally, I have personally had that happen where one of my soul mates and I re-united years later and moved into a love relationship. The relationship was stronger the second time around. Regardless, it is vital to move on and start living again. Get back into the joy of your life. If someone is meant to be with you including your ex, then the re-kindling will happen naturally on divine timing.

I never advise that someone wait for someone who left them, no matter how big the feelings are. An exception would be if you have both discussed that you're taking a break or one of you needs your space. If you wait around hopeful that your ex will return, then this can create a block from allowing someone new from coming in to an extent. It becomes difficult for a new person to enter the picture unless it is the lifelong marriage soul mate. A sensitive person or the kind of love mate you desire will sense an ex's energy around you even if they're not aware of it. It's in your aura. When you pine over someone no longer with you, then your body language may slump more than usual without knowing it. Your energy may be suppressed showing signs of a prolonged disappointment with something in your life. This energy you're giving off is not conducive to attracting in a new love partner. You have to move on with your life. If your ex comes back one day to mend your connection, then great! If not, at least you'll be living.

It saddens the angels to see so many struggling in love relationships today. You were involved with someone romantically, only to have them pull out of your connection unexpectedly. One day everything seems like it was going great and the next day you get a message out of the blue that they lost interest. You wonder how it was easy for them to pull out or how they sleep at night. It's almost as if a light switch was turned off and they were no longer interested in a relationship with you. You were kind, compassionate, and loyal to this person. You attempt to make sense of it and wonder what you did wrong. You grow angry feeling like they wasted your time. You might find it difficult to pull through each day. Meanwhile, you know they've gone on and they're busy with their life as if what they did had zero effect on you.

If someone pulled out in this manner, it's likely they were already entertaining the idea of leaving you for some time, but putting on the face that all is well beforehand. If they were merely looking to pull out a month before they did out of the blue, then this is a behavioral pattern with them where they pull out of everything with a snap of a finger. It's not someone you would want to engage in a long term relationship with anyway. It is a form of deception and having deceptive energy in a relationship is not healthy for a long term relationship. You may have bit the bullet with this connection. Treasure the great time and experiences you had with your ex. Make your peace with it and let it go. This will lift your vibration which will help attract in someone awesome!

Chapter Ten

GETTING OVER AN EX LOVER

*Y*ou've come to the realization that your ex who left you has indeed moved on. It's been months or even longer and there has been zero communication. They've either moved away or ended up in a love relationship with someone else. You now know that it is over. Coming to this reality might be painful, but it is also freeing on your soul as well. When someone leaves you, then you do not need to go through it alone. You will be tempted to email, text, and call this person with upset emotions. Some do the 'drunk dial'. The guidance is that you leave it alone. Nine times out of ten when you do reach out to them upset it has a tendency to back fire or blow up in your face. You come at your ex with heavy emotion and distress. Your ex is turned off and repelled by this energy. When you have no feelings for someone and they come at you with heavy emotions of anger and upset, the human instinct is to immediately display annoyance and anger. Although, if it's someone you truly love, then you want to talk it over with them. This is another clue that the person that left has lost interest at that time. Knowing this information is helpful as much as it feels like someone is killing you.

Write what you want to say to your ex-lover in an email or letter, but do not send it to them. Send it to yourself or a trusted friend who understands. Lashing out at the ex will not cause a dent except push them further away. They've already made the decision to walk away from you. They are not going to care much about how the split has upset you or what you have to say. They have absolved themselves of any responsibility with you.

I've received cases where someone wants to send their ex this letter. It should only be done when you know for sure that you are finished with them. Most of the time I've discovered that they're really only sending the letter in hopes of eliciting a positive response from their ex. Immediately the next day I will hear them say that there was no response to what they sent, or that it backfired with the ex telling them to leave them alone.

Why are you questioning that there is no response from your message to them? You sent the letter releasing the pain off your chest knowing that you're officially walking away. This letter does not contain anything positive, but is merely a recounting of all the times this ex hurt you. There is some colorful foul language sprinkled in it for good measure. Then they end the letter with, "If you still want to talk and work this out I'm available." This will not prompt the ex to grow a conscious.

You will need to work on getting through each day. Pre-occupy yourself with positive activities and healthy distractions as much as possible. Get to the space where you are feeling joy again. The depressing feelings surrounding your ex will be less hurtful as time progresses. It will be difficult at first as you push yourself to go to the gym when it's typically an easy occurrence for you. You just want to stay in bed or lie on the floor and not move. You grin and bear it. You pray and ask for heavenly assistance everyday and you keep going. Let go of the why's, how's, and I don't understands. Make your peace with the connection dissolving. There will be no way to wrap your mind around it no matter how you look at it and dissect it to death. You have to allow yourself to move through each of the stages of emotions such as sadness, depression, then anger and resentment. Eventually this is followed by a transformation where you reach a place of peace and forgiveness for yourself and for your ex love. This is where you accept that this is the path your ex chose and you respect that. You do not need to take any responsibility for their actions. Thank them for the time you had together. Forgive them for your soul's benefit and then let the energy surrounding them go. There is no timeline for these emotions to work themselves out, but reaching the place where you're completely content again is the goal. It is where you can think of them and it is no longer painful. You discover they're with someone new and that does not bother you. Any difficult emotions experienced do more damage to you than anyone else. No one is worth that kind of pain.

Avoid remaining in contact with your ex when possible. When you have heightened love feelings for your ex and you were the one who was left, then this can be taxing on your psyche. You never truly move through the various stages of emotions in order to start living again. You find you're getting used to moving on in life without them, then suddenly they surface with a text hello and you're right back where you started. The love feelings come up again. You grow hopeful that perhaps because they're remaining in touch there is a possibility of rekindling the love connection. Whenever your ex reaches out to you it prolongs the pain. You'll be afraid to let them go and avoid contact because you do love them. However, know that constantly engaging with them when you have deep feelings for them can confuse you into believing there is still hope with them. That is until you discover they have added the 'in a relationship' with someone else status on their social media account.

When experiencing heartache over a love interest leaving you, then call upon Archangel Raphael and Archangel Azrael. Ask to be infused with healing love energy daily until you discover you've indeed moved on. The thoughts of your ex no longer bring you any pain or emotional discomfort. This means that you are no longer affected by posts they put up on social media, or when you receive that random text hello from them. You'll know when it's safe to form a friendship with your ex if this is what you both choose. It'll be the moment where your ex is with a new love interest and that does not bother you on any negative level.

When praying and asking for help, understand that sometimes your Spirit team will not always bring you what you want if they feel it is not going to benefit your higher self in the long run. They know what's to come up ahead and what you must endure. You might profusely request help and ask that a particular soul mate contacts you, but it does not come to fruition. There are a couple of factors that would prevent that from happening. The ex's free will choice. Consider also that your Spirit team is blocking it from happening at that time for your own soul's benefit. The answers as to when it will happen cannot be understood until time has passed. This is when all will be revealed.

Ask yourself the serious questions as to how you wish to proceed from this point on. Soul mates come and go in your life. Not all soul mates are intended to stay no matter how much of a huge impact they've had on you. Ask yourself the tough questions such as: "Is the soul work with my ex indeed done? If so, how long will I allow this breakup prevent me from moving forward?"

It's not uncommon for some human souls to have that great love they will never forget. For some it can be their first love. It can be the one they had when they were younger before they grew older and became more jaded to love. Perhaps it happened later in life. Fear keeps people in relationships that are long over. They're too comfortable and afraid to make a drastic change by walking away from a connection they've been unhappy in for years. Change is disruptive to human souls. If you do not change toxic situations, then you'll remain miserable!

It can be difficult for some souls to emotionally detach from someone they were intimate with for a long period of time. Most human souls do not automatically switch to being friends after a serious love relationship ends. The brief connections they had which only lasted a month or two can merge into a friendship with no problem. This is because you're not emotionally attached to them. The long term relationships are another story where there was a stronger long term bond. If you have deep emotions over a love connection that only lasted one to three months, then take caution with future love potentials. Avoid wearing your heart on your sleeve so soon with someone you do not know.

Having to put on the face day after day is exhausting as you attempt to get over an ex. You still have to go to work or the grocery store. You're inevitably going to see and bump into people depending on where you live. It is okay to give yourself permission to not engage with anybody unless necessary. The hurt and pain will come and go. Sometimes you'll be fine and other times you won't be, but over time it will diminish. Just keep moving forward and take it day to day. It's normal to have confused emotional reactions to someone else's behavior following a breakup.

Those who pull out of a love connection with someone they love might be seen as being in a state of self-centeredness, or going through a selfish period. Sometimes this is the case, but other times it's not. It's easy for the ego to grow angry when a lover leaves them. It's important to also consider that this ex-lover discovered while in a relationship with you that it is not what they desire. They might long to be free and thought they could do the 'relationship thing', only to discover it's not for them. Or perhaps they have some soul searching to do that requires they leave the relationship. Everyone is on their own soul path. It's crucial to step away from the tantrums of your ego and respect that.

There are souls who indeed have a pattern of using others in a love relationship. They might be the ones who do not have a history of successful long term relationships. They have a history of being in short lived connections only to grow bored and leave most of them sooner than later. They are living in the moment and thinking of themselves. They are not in touch with how their actions might affect someone else. If they do know and do not care, then that would make them a sociopath. Sociopaths do not have deep emotions for others. Selfish would be a more appropriate word. Selfish people do not change overnight. Learning to be selfless takes quite a bit of time. The selfish individual needs to want to become more selfless, but it's difficult for their ego to convince them that this is what indeed needs to happen. The selfish person is not out to get you, but are thinking of themselves first. This becomes a bigger problem when it negatively affects those around the selfish person. The selfish person is too selfish to notice that their behavior is affecting others around them. Never wait for a selfish person to suddenly grow a conscious if it's never been part of their nature. In hindsight, if you examined the red flags in this

174

type of connection, then you might see the signs that your connection would not last to begin with. You likely brushed it off until this person really did something awful to your heart.

While in the dating process, pre-screen your potential soul mates entering the picture. This way you can get a feel for the kinds of relationships this person has been in and what they desire in a love relationship. Dates that are serious about you tend to ask: "How long was your longest relationship?" If the answer is three months, well, I think you have your probable answer as to how it's likely going to go. When your love relationship ends, remain strong and pre-occupy yourself with fun activities, even if you have moments where tears form. Do not put too much pressure on your soul. You deserve respect from those you have shown love to.

Nothing is ever final even if it feels that way. Your ego wants to convince you that the despair is real. It is real in the way that your human soul knows it to be real in the physical world, but it's not real in the grand long term sense. Allow your soul to breathe by moving swiftly through the traumatic experience. Moments of hurt will twinge your side from time to time. You might mask that with an addiction. While other times you'll push yourself to go to the gym. I've felt this kind of pain when it comes to a deep, loving relationship split. In my previous life, I found that I had a habit of attracting in soul mates that were living in the moment. They love you today, but tomorrow they likely will not. This is giving your power away to someone you put faith into. You realize they are flawed and have issues as we all do, but the issues they wrestle with have nothing to do with you. Unfortunately, sometimes it is at the expense of others. Everyone's lives are constantly changing and altering. Nothing stays the same even if one wanted it to. The ending of a deep love relationship feels like a death. Your views and life take on an entirely new turn. Someone loses their job they thought they would be at forever. Their life is altered by that one act. They have to make plans they otherwise would not have.

Perhaps months have passed and you're still battling cutting the cords with your ex. If you believe your connection with them is worth saving, then reach out for one last bit of hope. The odds of them coming around and initiating a move could be slim. At least if time has passed, the heated emotions might have subsided with you and your ex. You might be able to communicate peacefully. If you do reach out to them, do it knowing that you might not get the response you're hoping for or they might not have any romantic interest in you. However, you will have your definite answer depending on the way your ex has responded. This can give you peace of mind that it may be time to cut the cords from the attachment to this soul mate for good. This way you are not stalling your soul from experiencing prosperous new connections. If your energy is heavily invested in this ex soul mate, then this can deter a new suitor who is trying to enter the picture. Someone who is high vibrational can sense an ex energy in someone.

A relationship break up puts you at a cross road in attempting to forge on with or without them. You come to the realization that you need to make a choice. Will you hang on to your ex's essence in the hopes that there is still that possibility? Or will you open the door a crack for someone amazing and more aligned with you to enter the picture? This would be someone new who genuinely has an attraction and feelings for you. They're facing the same direction as you and value long term committed relationships. Even if you do move forward, it does not mean that this ex soul mate and you cannot become a romantic item at a later date, but until then at least you'll be out there living!

Chapter Eleven

SOUL CONNECTIONS

$\mathscr{I}$f the important love relationship soul mate is to enter the picture for someone, then nothing is going to stop that person from connecting with you. This includes free will choice. Free will choice can delay the connection from happening, but it will not delay it forever. Your guides and angels team up with your soul mate's guides and angels to orchestrate the connection. Once the connection is made, there is little that can stop it from moving forward. You both immediately take notice. Anything that does stop it from moving forward is temporary. Sometimes how it happens is that you continue to bump into this person until you both finally lock eyes. From that point, nothing stops you from communicating. You both know this is it. Note we said if it is the big soul mate that is intended to be the life partner mate. There is a synchronicity set up taking place in order to bring two souls together.

Everyone has numerous soul mates sifting in and out of their vicinity during the course of their lives. In this case, this is the love soul mate marriage that you connect with who sticks with you through the duration of your Earthly life in a love connection. These are not the soul mate relationships that come in the guises of friendships, colleagues or short lived love relationships. Those are soul mates as well who you made a previous agreement with. This is in order to connect to them briefly for a specific purpose. This can be such as balancing previous karma with that soul. They might be an awakener for you to prepare you for the REAL lifelong soul mate relationship.

If your soul is not ready for the real deal and you have additional tools to gain, then you will have a short lived soul mate enter the picture before the long term one comes in. You may even have many short lived soul mate relationships for a good chunk of your life before you are with the long term mate. If you are thrown to the wolves prematurely with the long term mate immediately, then it may end unhappily. You will both likely incarnate relatively at the same time repeatedly until the connection is balanced.

There is no stopping any soul mate connection from happening. If it's not happening with someone, then they are likely not the intended big relationship soul mate. You will know they are the lifelong mate, because you end up together for most or the rest of your current Earthly life.

LONG DISTANCE RELATIONSHIPS

There is a belief that one's soul mate might be living in another state or country. Your Spirit team would not place your lifelong soul mate somewhere else when you live thousands of miles away. If that were the case, it would be orchestrated or foreseen by your Spirit team that one or the both of you are going to eventually move to the same city, state, or country you live in relatively soon. This would be within one to five years after the meeting or initial connection contact takes place.

There are many cases where lifelong soul mates and especially twin flames have crossed paths with one another while not living in the same state or country. This is more common with the twin flame relationship. As discussed in this book, there would be key signs to look for if it is a twin flame. One of them is there would more than likely be an age difference of about ten years or more. The love intensity between the both of them continues on until the end of time. They have relatively similar natures and personality styles that are complimentary for the most part. They have the same values give or take. Of course there will be slight differences in all of these aspects, but when it comes to love relationships, they want the same thing. They both admit they're comfortable being around the other. It is rare to witness couples both desiring the exact same thing, so when you have it, then be sure to never take it for granted! The ego enjoys taking everything for granted especially in love relationships.

The soul mate or twin flame connection that is long distance ultimately brings both people to live in the same city. At least one of the partners makes it happen without hesitation by moving to the same city area as their soul mate or twin flame. This process happens naturally and without force. For example, one of the partners suddenly chimes up to say they're moving to the other one's city in three months.

There are exceptions where a long distance relationship soul mate connection works. To understand if you fall into this exception rule is that you would know without a doubt this person is your lifelong mate. You both know it and stop at nothing to make it happen. This would be where one or the both of you move to the same city after getting to know one another. You develop a healthy long distance friendship before it moves into love relationship territory. You're both smart about the way you're coming together, because there is a natural ease between you. This friendship could endure for a prolonged period of time at first before you become a love item.

A healthy long term long distance connection is one where there is no consistent drama, arguing, and issues throughout it. That would be a Karmic relationship, which would need to be dissolved as the lessons have been learned. The soul mate or twin flame partner who lives in another area is a blissful contact between you both where little to no trust issues arises. This would be rather difficult considering that trust is needed for a long distance connection. Most long distance relationships do not work unless both partners set up a system where they alternate visiting one another regularly. This can be at least once a month. Over time this puts strain on less stable connections with one or both of the partners. The trust factor in a long distance connection needs to be there naturally between the partners. Ultimately both parties in the duo have plans to live with one another or live in the same town fairly soon after connecting. Nothing stops them from making that happen. The pull between the two soul mates or twin flames is incredibly strong that it's near impossible for them to not make that happen. There is no second guessing when it comes to uniting in the same city for good. These are some of the signs on how to recognize what kind of connection one might have in a long distance relationship set up.

IS THIS PERSON MY SOUL MATE?

A common question asked is, "How do I know if the person I'm with is my soul mate?"

The instant answer is that if you have to ask, then it is probably not your soul mate. It may be one of your soul mates which sift in and out of your life, but not the lifelong love soul mate. You would not need to ask this question if it is.

The longer answer is that you will need patience to see how your connection with them plays out if you're questioning if they're the big soul mate. If the person you believe to be your soul mate has chosen to break away from your connection by ending it, then you're moving into iffy territory. The way your real life long soul mate connection will work is that nothing can stop you both from making a beeline to one another. The soul connection draw is too strong and magnetic to break. Even if there is a temporary break, it does not last long because the soul connection is too strong where both mates know without a doubt that this is it for them. It's not a one-sided unrequited love. A case by case examination would need to be made as to why both partners are no longer together and yet they both hold deep attracting feelings for one another.

ATTRACTING IN THE SAME TYPES OF MATES

The soul mate connections you make throughout the course of your life are vibrational matches to you. If you attracted in someone you are constantly unhappy with for a soul mate, then come to the realization that you attracted that person and their energy to you.

I often hear others protest, "Why do I keep on attracting the same type of lover to me!?"

In order to break from that cycle, you would need to take action steps in raising your vibration in order to attract in someone of a higher caliber. You can do this by shifting your perception and interests in life to something more positive. This takes work since human souls are innate and their basic nature stays relatively the same. The way an individual behaves is taught and learned through their upbringing and the society they live in.

Many find they go through several short term soul mate love connections that rarely have much lift off. This is to teach you important tools that prepare you for the right one. This also raises your vibration to the right one's vibration. If you do not learn from those short lived soul mate connections, then you will continue to attract in the same type of short lived soul mates to you. They are the class that preps you for the right one.

BEING TOO RIGID IN YOUR SOUL MATE SEARCH

Someone is single and looking to date, but they have the unbending list of what they're looking for in a partner. Many of the qualities on that list are of the superficial variety, such as what this potential soul mate should look like and how tall they should be, etc. This is someone allowing their ego to paint an unrealistic picture of a potential soul mate that has been airbrushed in a magazine. Falling for someone easy on the eyes does not mean it will be a lasting long term relationship. It takes more than good looks to be a stable loving partner. You will be on the hunt for a mate indefinitely until you release this inflexibility.

This is not the only way those who fall into this category see things with such severity. Most of their choices in life are learned. It's all they know because it was all they allowed themselves to know. Anything beyond their backyard is unseen. While all human souls have certain values of what they'd like in a mate such as the person be spiritually based or not be a cigarette smoker. Rigid egotistical qualities would be that this mate must look like an Adonis model or kiss the ground you walk on daily.

While having a physical attraction to a potential partner is helpful, it will not be what keeps that person around you indefinitely. Many are guilty of it to an extent as it's what the media has shoved into the minds of human souls during the developmental stage. If the person is not tall with a tight body and six pack abs, then you will not give that person a second look. You're searching for the image of a mate who has been airbrushed and photo shopped up in a magazine. You're looking for someone who resembles the Prince or Princess that exists in popular animated fable love stories. No one stays looking that way forever no matter how well you take care of yourself. The fit people in the world eventually witness a decline in muscle and body mass as they age. Bodies are not designed to last, even though it is vital you take care of your body, mind, and soul in all ways possible while you inhabit it. The truth is many human souls fall in love and end up in long term relationships with those they normally might've considered to not be their "type". They end up falling in love with that person and vice versa regardless. This is a true genuine soul attraction. It is the souls being drawn in and attracted to one another regardless that they're not what the media considers to be exceptionally perfect.

WILL A ROMANTIC FLING DELAY THE CONNECTION WITH MY LIFELONG SOUL MATE?

A brief romantic fling cannot create a hindrance in preventing your lifelong soul mate from entering the picture. Nothing can permanently stop the life partner that is intended to connect with you from doing so. If you're with someone in a mini-relationship or a fling, and then the one that you were intended to be with crosses paths with you, there is no way either of you will not notice. The pull between one another will be too strong.

Some have left marriages when they discovered they have met their one true soul mate. This is the case where they've left these relationship commitment connections for someone who ends up being their partner until they exit this lifetime. This is not the case where someone leaves their partner 'thinking' this new person is the one they're meant to be with and yet that falls apart too.

WHERE IS MY SOUL MATE?
I'VE BEEN WAITING FOREVER!

When you're content with you, your life, and where you're at, then the right love partner enters the picture. If you do not love yourself, how do you expect someone else to? I've witnessed others cry out in frustration that it's been years and no love relationship. It's the frustration energy that pushes the right person away. The right person isn't going to go after someone who has frustrated energy around them. This will turn off and repel the right one. Love yourself and be comfortable with being alone, while being open and receptive to what and who may come.

HAVING ENDLESS ISSUES
AND DRAMA IN YOUR CURRENT RELATIONSHIP

When you are in a healthy relationship, it will not feel like you're pushing against resistance. If you feel that you run into a roadblock with your current partner at every turn, then accept that this is how it is right now with your current partner, or choose to distance yourself from this connection. Being conflicted will not help in strengthening a love connection. In order for a relationship to thrive, you must let it go. You cannot wait for someone to come around because the odds of that happening are slim. This is not said to let you down, but the angels will not give someone false hope either. They are all about two souls working it out together. If both souls do not put in an effort to make healthy changes within the relationship, then it is likely to stay as it is.

Chapter Twelve

FRIENDSHIPS CHANGE AS YOU EVOLVE

When you walk down a higher spiritual path, your Guides and Angels will repel those you need to stay away from. In the process, you will attract in new people who aim for spiritual growth or who are already living in the light. Changes in your friendships are a normal process for those who frequently evolve. You find that you no longer have the same interests as those you had considered once close. When my vibration had risen to an astronomical degree from my previous way of life, I discovered that those I had once connected with were headed down a path I had no interest in. They were content to stay exactly where they are with no need for improvement. The interests they had were based purely on a superficial level. Many of them were prone to spending their days drinking, experimenting with drugs, or being a regular fixture in a bar. This used to be who I was in my twenties, but I evolved so rapidly I could no longer fake my interest in those activities. I'm not talking about the occasional get together with a buddy and a beer. This is about those who live a toxic life on a daily basis. There is no judgment of course if you revel in those activities, but when

185

you are doing your best to live as healthy as you can while pursuing your love of spiritual or religious interests, you want to surround yourself with likeminded souls as friends. I'm by no means perfect and I make mistakes just as much as anyone else. We're all works in progress.

How can you tell if your friends are true friends of integrity? When you're hanging out with your friends, are you always having an alcoholic drink or drug? If most of the time you are with them you have an alcoholic drink, then these are not real friends, but enablers. Do they prompt you to make poor life choices? They do not have to coerce you into making an unsound choice. If while in their presence you find that your negative addictions are fed, or you make repeated toxic choices, then you can be sure you're not surrounded by friends of integrity. True friends have your higher self's best interests at heart. This is not about the occasional drink you have with your friends, but rather the kinds of friends where you take on toxic vices every time you are with them, or the majority of the time you are with them. You feel temporarily fulfilled. Someone who is intoxicated pats you on your back in support when you're making an unsound choice, but their judgment is not clear. They are patting everybody on the back no matter what they're doing. This is not real love. You feed off each other's addictions and thus form a co-dependent connection. Some of this stems from fears of loneliness, a need for love, and desperation for friendships to the point where you will be friends with anybody, even if it is detrimental to your well-being. Months later, you discover that your life has been in the same place it's been in for some time. Call upon Archangel Raphael to remove any toxic addictions from your life and to help you get clear minded. Call upon Archangel Chamuel to assist you in finding friends of integrity and who are aligned with your higher self and greater good.

There was a point in my mid to late thirties where I chose to create a relationship with God and my Spirit team daily. This included working and communicating with them on a regular basis. I had finally come to the profound realization that my life before that was not as joyful as I believed it to be. I was unfulfilled by the mundane superficiality that so many were perpetuating around me.

186

I needed more! When I invited Heaven permanently into my life and let them know we were going to develop a serious relationship, only then did I notice the positive changes in my life take place. This enabled me to not only improve my life, but help others as well. Having an understanding of where we came from has assisted me in navigating through the often challenging roads were often faced with as human souls. I chose to be mindful and cautious of who I allowed around me. I was also careful about what I was ingesting into my body including foods, alcohol, and other addictions. My mantra became either keep it in moderation or dissolve it completely. My interest in it was dropping as I moved into that space naturally. Having those around you who operate solely on a lower vibration will contaminate your aura and own positive energy. This is a perfect example of why psychic readers or anyone who works with the general public should practice shielding themselves. This is by visualizing Archangel Michael surrounding you with white light.

I was hesitant to discussing my rising spiritual interests or in opening up about how I psychically knew certain things about someone for fear of ridicule with just anyone. I did not want to announce or say the words of where I was getting my accurate information about them from. I assumed that the majority of people around me were mostly atheists or who had no belief in God, a higher power, the light or whatever one associates God to be. The main reason I assumed this was they preferred living a toxic path. They had never uttered a spiritual word as long as I had known them. This does not bother me of course, because I do not discredit good friendships simply because of a different belief system. As long as both parties are open and accepting of the other person's way of life, then there is no reason to not be friends. You need a high level of maturity to be friends with those who have differing opinions and beliefs. You would limit, avoid, or keep your philosophical discussions to a minimum. However, there is a difference if they are partaking in certain deadly vices that are no longer conducive to your overall well-being. It should be common etiquette knowledge to never discuss religion or politics at a get together anyway, unless you know for sure they share your beliefs.

Human souls can rarely be swayed to your belief system after one conversation. This is a personal choice they develop on their own.

For others around me I noticed that if it was not about sex or something superficial, then they could not be more bored or uninterested. This started to limit my friendships as we live in a world that is hyper-media focused. They may not be all that interested in anything beyond superficiality. This is what they have allowed their communities and peers to raise them on. It keeps them distracted and disconnected from knowing who they are and why they are here to begin with. When there is no room for anything else, then as a spiritual person you lose interest.

If I posted something on my social networking page in the realms of spirituality, then there would be one or two bad apples that would comment something patronizing about it or make a joke. I was around those that were either spiritually open or sexually open. Since I fall into both sides, if I posted something in either category I feared mockery from one or the other. I felt that I could not truly be myself and there appeared to be no room for any of it. I moved into a place of wanting to remove all traces of me on social networking sites, but then my higher self grabbed hold of the reigns. *'Wait a minute. This is my life and I'll post what I want. If you don't like it, then remove yourself or I'll remove you.'*

I had to put my foot down and remove hundreds of people that I knew were going to have judgment towards the spiritual stuff or the sex stuff. These same people were around when I used to be slightly superficial myself. Although I had some measure of superficiality, the spiritual nature of who I was in truth, was present in there as well. When I shifted, I never reverted back. In fact, once the spiritual teachings blew up as part of my purpose, those friends who have been around me for years would comment that they were not surprised. They would say things like, "You always had your foot in Heaven's door for as long as I've known you. It was only a matter of time before it would blow up into this awesomeness that exists with you now." We are all unique individuals with varying concepts to share or teach. My Spirit team let me know that the right people who are more aligned with my new beliefs, and/or who are open and accepting to all of it would be attracted to me.

LONELINESS

Loneliness is a frequent protest among many human souls. They express feelings of loneliness and a lack of having any solid friendships or love relationships. This is due to a combination of several factors. The current way of life perpetuated by the media is one aspect. The rise in technology and the Internet has predominantly promoted superficiality and a lack of genuine relationship connections among humanity as a whole. It has created a larger gap and disconnect between the human soul and God. This gap has left the human soul feeling perpetually empty while craving anything that will fill the emptiness up. The soul will flip flop all over the place making poor judgment choices, such as getting involved with the wrong people to feeding their soul a toxic addiction in order to feel whole. None of this works as some have likely witnessed. The loneliness continues to be a common complaint from that soul over the years.

Loneliness is especially the case if you are going through a spiritual or major transition of some kind. The spiritual community is an open, accepting, and loving group of bright souls. It is still not easy for one to form friendships whenever there is any kind of transition in your life to begin with. If you are frequently evolving, then you are going through many shifts and transitions in your life. This process weeds out many of your current friendships. You must be comfortable being alone and with yourself before you can attract in new friendships. This is the same concept as searching for a soul mate. You cannot diligently search for soul mates and friendships. All REAL relationships and connections happen when you are not looking for it. They come to you naturally and effortlessly at the right time.

Loneliness is the human condition. You came into this world alone and you will leave this world alone. When you were born you were a perfect well rounded human soul experiencing joy, peace, love, in tune psychic abilities and contentment. It was society and those that raised you that inflicted all sorts of nonsense onto your soul causing you to experience negative feelings such as loneliness.

Loneliness is an emptiness that cannot be cured or filled up by another human soul or filled up with addictions. The emptiness is so vast it would be outlandish to place that responsibility on another person to fill. What you are craving is God's love. It is natural for a soul to attract in a healthy companion or other half while on their journey, regardless of the gender of that soul. Yet, the attraction of that companion should not be out of filling an inner void, because this taints the union causing it to be a false connection that will end. You're basically using the other person, not because you truly love and adore them, but because you have a lacking void within you that needs to be filled. When you gain solid relationship tools and knowledge in order to function in a healthy connection whether it's a friendship or love connection, only then will you be facing in the direction of happiness.

You will also not attract in the right kind of friendships in a state of loneliness or boredom. You will attract those that are similar or worse off than you. This will leave you to fall into a deeper despair. Get happy and productive first while allowing the right friendships to come in on their own time. You will be content with this new you that you will not have the time to notice when or if the right friendships have shown up yet. Find hobbies and interests to occupy your time off so that you are not sitting on the couch all day with a beer feeling deep loneliness. Ask your Guides and Angels to work with you on removing those feelings of loneliness and to help you experience profound inner joy.

You will need to look at where you are hoping to find new friendships. Are you going to the bars to find these new friendships? Many try this avenue and end up disappointed feeling more alone. When you meet someone at a bar, the friendships are typically short lived. You are meeting those that likely partake in the same escapism as you do. This is a broad generalization, but we're not speaking in specifics. What happens when you are friends with someone who is more or less a barfly? You fall into the bell jar together delaying yourself from achieving the life you dreamed of.

Bars are a place where many dark entities lurk. These are spirits that avoided the light when they passed away. They attach themselves to the drinking patrons permanently or for a prolonged period of time. They prompt the human soul to continuously drink or do hard drugs indefinitely. They prod them to make poor life choices. This is not in judgment as I will be the first to raise my hand to say that I used to love hanging in bars in my early twenties. It was where the drinks were! There is a difference between going to a bar with a friend once in a blue moon for a drink versus going to a bar weekly or even daily. Many of the friendships you make if any are with those who love you in the moment of high intoxication, but their feelings shift when they wake up the next morning feeling gross, moody, lethargic, and unfit. The only way to get rid of the feeling is to continue drinking. It's a cycle until you put your foot down that you need to keep it in moderation or give it up completely. It is no surprise that many who fit this description are starving for real friendships. You cannot attract quality friendships while in a state of addictions. You will bring in those like you, who are not the stable long term friendships you desire.

My friend's warn others not to use the word bored around me. This is because there is always something to do! To begin curbing your feelings of loneliness and boredom, discover what your true hobbies and interests are that bring you joy. Do you enjoy regular walks on the beach, certain sports, road trips or creative pursuits? The key is to choose an activity that is not negative or toxic, but rather productive and uplifting. This is where you are likely to find quality friendships. If you love painting in your spare time, then consider taking a course on painting at a trade school or college. If you love being physically active, then join softball leagues or rock climbing groups, etc. It does not matter if you already know how to do these activities, because it will get your energy out there in the right places. You will be spending several months or many weeks with the same people who have a likeminded interest. They are more apt to be quality people who are productive in their lives as well. You are spending your free time wisely by engaging in something you love doing. This raises your vibration to a more joyful level, which attracts more good things into your life including great friendships!

WE ARE ALL TEACHERS

When you shift into a more spiritually minded soul, then you appreciate the connections you make with those around you. You do not take them for granted. This can be a friendship, relationship, or an acquaintance. You learn something from someone that crosses paths with you because everyone is a teacher. This can be someone you met for as little as a minute. Take a look at the various people you have crossed paths with in the past. It can even be someone that cuts you off in traffic. What could that person possibly have had to teach you, you might ask. How about patience? Perhaps you are being taught to not allow the little things to affect you by remaining detached from any kind of traumatic crisis.

Examine the close relationships you formed which are long passed. It is easy to have disdain towards certain past relationships where one might have been hurt, but I don't regret any of my relationships, even the bad ones. There was knowledge I had to gain while in them as you are meant to pick up something of substance in relation to your growth. You attracted in that person at that particular time. It was designed with the goal to be of benefit for the both of you. There comes a time while in a friendship or love relationship with someone where one or both of you have served your purpose and the point becomes moot. This is when you know it is time to move on. With certain relationships, such as romantic, there can be two people who spend this entire lifetime together and act as partners in crime. They are evolving together and facing in the same direction. They gain knowledge while together as well as with those they come into contact with outside of the relationship.

DISSOLVING FRIENDSHIPS

Your true friends never ridicule or make fun of you, but instead support you. They do not place unnecessary demands on you or your time. They are flexible and know how you operate and accept this. If you have a friend that has been consistently upset over something you do or don't do, then this is a clue that it is time to consider distancing yourself from them temporarily. You may choose to dissolve the union altogether if it continues. You have different values and what you expect from the other. If you were once seeing eye-to-eye and facing the same direction, you have now hit a fork in the road embarking on separate paths with different views and interests. The purpose of your friendship has been fulfilled.

If you are negative and a gossip, then you will attract that same type of person to you. When you grow and walk a larger path, you will find that you can no longer relate to those people you initially attracted in. In fact, you find them to be energy zappers where you are drained after having a phone conversation with them. You become fully aware of your surroundings and how they have contributed to your negative state. You realize how miserable you are with them only to discover that you played a part in it too.

The only way to start attracting friendships with greater people is to begin the process of improving yourself first. There will be a transition period that could last anywhere from one to three years as you work on yourself in a big way. During this transition, some of your previous friendships will begin fading and newer improved friendships will gradually enter your life. There will be some friendships that might be difficult to dissolve. These friends may be the biggest energy zappers of them all. They feed on you like a vampire. They have their clutches in you and have no desire to let go. Pay no mind or attention to this. It's not your responsibility to be the source of happiness for someone else. Ask Archangel Raguel to assist you in peacefully dissolving the friendships and relationships that consistently cause you grief.

There were friendships I had in the past where I was not comfortable with in discussing my spiritual pursuits and the profound changes that were happening within me. You never share your dreams with those you have to convince. If people are critical, then it will shut down your Heavenly connections and block your communication with God. Their ridicule will affect your self-esteem and lower your vibration. I had friends who might not

193

understand my spiritual beliefs, but were delighted to hear about it. Most people find that they are curious or fascinated by it because there is something about it that reminds them of who they once were in the Spirit world. It triggers a past life or spirit world memory and offers them comfort. They could be at a point in their life where nothing around them matters anymore. They feel trapped in their body unable to connect to anything. There were others who never uttered a word of spirituality, but grew to be interested in that realm after hearing my teachings. They miraculously expanded into that world in an even bigger way.

My interests in certain friendships and people were changing as I walked down this higher path. Doors were opening and relationships were shifting by ending or improving. It was a period of adjustment and I would have previously approached that kicking and screaming, but instead it was a peaceful transition. I found those that were part of religious institutions had taken more of a liking towards me than atheists did. I was initially surprised by this, since I was formerly under the assumption or façade that those who had no spiritual belief system were more open minded than those who were religious. Even though religious and spiritual beliefs vary in certain areas, we found some common denominators when it came to circumstances like an afterlife, God, Heaven and angels. I sat with a religious couple over a dinner. They later commented to someone we mutually knew at how awestruck they were with me. They were blown away and moved by what I spoke about. There is familiar ground in varying spiritual belief systems if people remain open.

I've made enemies for being open about my beliefs. I've had people who volunteered to write me out of the blue through a social networking page and say, "Wow, I realize that I don't like you at all." They would then delete and block me. They were surprisingly atheists, who as stated, I thought would be more open than someone who was religious. I found the opposite to be the case in my personal experience. You ignore it and forge on with your purpose in merging with the Light. The Light will ensure all of your needs are met. It will ensure you are around good-hearted, compassionate, and understanding people who you feel comfortable around. The angels will deter those who are a danger for you to be around and extricate them out of your vicinity. A person such as this is consumed by toxic energy and rules their life predominately through their ego. You being a sensitive and in tune to your surroundings will soak that up like a dirty dish rag. Meanwhile, in the works are greater more important human souls operating from a higher place entering your vicinity. They are drawn to you as you make the shift onto a higher level of consciousness. This process takes quite a bit of time because you're growing and evolving at a rapid pace. There are people exiting your life much more slowly.

You will be hesitant to dissolving certain friendships because you do care about them and the good times you had, but at the same time they are not welcoming or responsive towards your new beliefs. They are living unhealthy lives that no longer jive with who you are becoming. You may choose to make yourself less available to them until they have moved into your acquaintance box. Before you know it, you will be communicating less and less. Some of these friendships and relationships might be with people who are heavily into negative substances and addictions. Long before you've made that spiritual shift, you were likely working on lifestyle changes gradually. This includes what you consume and shove into your body. You find the new friendships you make are with those open to what you believe in, even if they do not partake in it or fully understand it. Those unions are more beautiful, loving, and improved than you could have imagined with anybody else. They are pure and full of light. An uplifting energy is created when both of your soul lights are together. You surpassed a superficial mundane existence and expanded your consciousness.

My friendships changed to a great degree as my newfound interests moved onto a whole new level. Some shifted comfortably with my heightened interest. They effortlessly accepted this is the new me and not some whimsical fly by hobby. I have eternally changed and continue to do so. This is the same concept as those who claim to be born again Christians. They might have run into friendships that no longer shared their beliefs or talked it down. One of the differences may be is that my reason for letting people go is because they were not serving my higher purpose. They were not supportive or they ridiculed my rising interests of a healthier variety. Archangel Michael is by my side on a daily basis and he extracts those from my vicinity, often before I'm aware that they are close.

The spiritual transition I made in the past was empowering, but there was an immense amount of alone time because I was no longer interested in those I was previously connecting with. I was in an area where there were certain types of people I would experience a connection with. If I felt isolated before, then I felt inaccessible and disconnected from everyone during the transition. This is a normal and typical part of the process where your personal life might seem unfulfilling. You are removing your previous old way of life in order to bring in new people on your level.

I would continue to be approached and many would express great interest towards me, but I felt emptiness with them. I would wonder how long in before it was time for me to mention my spiritual interests, and then how quickly the judgment or skepticism would fall over their face. I knew that I would have to remain in the spiritual closet until it was safe to open up about it with the right people. It was generally not that long before I'd know whether or not someone would be in a place to hear it and understand. I had discussed it with certain friends who I assumed were spiritually inclined, but found that it would go through one ear and out the other. This would be the case whenever I would share the profound changes that were happening with me. It was as if they did not buy it or believe it, so they opted to ignore that it was said. I could tell by meeting someone who would be open to it after a few sentences spoken from their mouth.

I knew love and romance was going to be more of a challenge, as this person would have to completely understand. They would not have to partake in it or do the things I do, but that person would have to be open minded, supportive, and loving about it. What I do and what I experience with this is not up for a debate. I knew there would be no way I could be involved with a non-believer because this is something I do every day now. I would need to communicate openly with the one I'm with. How could I do that if

196

it would be subjected to ridicule? If you find yourself in that predicament, then ask your Guides and Angels to send you someone who is open and receptive to what you do without judgment. This is someone who is walking a spiritual path. I would first ask that they open up the mind of the person I'm with before making any sudden movements. This was not the only reason I chose to be alone. The portal was open into this new way of life and I was fascinated and immersed in study and research as I perfected the gifts I already had.

Never divulge your dreams or deepest interests to anyone you suspect to be untrustworthy or a negative naysayer. Guard your dreams and aspirations with delicacy. Don't blurt out your closest secrets to an unreliable soul. You can tell by the response you get from someone whether or not they support you, or if they are operating purely from ego. One who supports and coaxes you on with your dream is the real deal. Someone who always belittles you, or responds negatively to your dreams, should be dissolved out of your life. With all of the wonderful people in the world it's important not to waste one minute with someone who has issues about you, or who is jealous of you and the attention you receive.

I am impossible to control, which is another sign of spiritual progress. I act and function in complete independence. I do not follow the crowd and always had separate views that were not on par with the majority. No attention on my part is paid to how others feel about it. I've had friends in the past that were uncomfortable that I own my life. They would find some way to undercut something about me. They would say it as a backhanded compliment as if I wouldn't notice. Today, I no longer become friends with unsupportive people. Being in tune, you're able to asses that energy in the beginning rather than knee deep into the connection. I'm not this way with others because I live in a higher frequency than they do. Those types of personalities were disbanded out of my life. My detector is incredibly tuned in where I sense this energy immediately. There were those unaware of their lack of tact. I would continue to keep them around, but not hesitate to correct them on their naivety. Only allow those with the highest of integrity near you.

Friendships have to be earned and should never be immediate. This applies to romantic relationships as well. You attract friendships to you the way you attract anything, through the laws of attraction. If you are at a certain level of growth you will only attract those that mirror your intent. If you're consuming negative substances such as drugs and alcohol, what types of people do you think you're going to attract in? You're not going to attract in someone walking in the light. If you find that you have on that rare occasion, then there is a reason for it. The reason is that person who is a spiritual being was guided to you by Heaven. They see you are ready to grow out of your current phase. The wonderful spiritual being is your teacher and will not be around you forever if you abuse it. When they leave you prematurely, then you may continue down your path of self-sabotage and destruction. You are given an Earth Angel to cross your path to help you, and wake up and progress your soul. There are many out there threading through the world to get you to wake up and walk the path of love, joy, and peace. It is important to recognize who they are.

RAISING YOUR VIBRATION

Fine Tune Your Body & Soul
to Receive Messages from Heaven

Chapter One

FINE TUNING YOUR SOUL

How do I receive messages from my guides and angels? This is a complex question since every soul's methods vary. Souls connect with Heaven in a myriad of ways. Laying it all out in a step by step manner does not always work for some. The ways suggested could be too confusing or intermediate for those who do not consider to being in the advanced class. Those who are brand new at diving in at expanding their consciousness and raising their vibration have poured in requests that some basics be discussed. *Raising Your Vibration* is the beginner's class on picking up some of the immediate guidance to consider implementing in order to improve your soul and state of mind in this material driven physical world. One of the big inquiries others desire is to communicate with the other side in order to know what their future holds. Even if you are able to connect, this does not mean your future will be relayed to you. Your spirit team of guides and angels do not live your life for you. What is relayed to you is on a need to know basis that will enrich and grow your soul.

For example, you might become frustrated when years have gone by and yet the love relationship you desire has not been forthcoming. For certain circumstances, there are pieces to the puzzle that need to be maneuvered on your behalf before what you crave happens. There is an excess of possible reasons that could come forth as to why there is no love partner in someone's life. Each case would need to be studied individually.

Every soul is communicating with the other side whether they're aware of it or not. I could be walking from my car to the elevators in a corporate building and Spirit messages are sifting through me mostly via clairaudience *(clear hearing)* or claircognizance *(clear knowing)*. I'm not doing anything specific to make it happen. Nor am I attempting to conduct a psychic reading, or asking my Spirit team questions as I hurriedly walk to my appointment. The messages naturally fall into my vicinity without me wanting it or thinking about it. It's always been this way and it's all I've ever known. I was born with one foot in this world and the other in the spirit world. All souls who do not feel they have this ability can get back to that space by making healthy life changes. You were born connecting with the other side, but somewhere along the way blocks were formed.

One of the big ways of connecting with Spirit is by raising your vibration. Fortune telling psychic readings or someone with enhanced psychic abilities are unlike raising your vibration. Someone who is psychically gifted could have a low vibration or operate from ego, but they are still exceptional at connecting with spirit effortlessly. Raising your vibration is important for your soul's growth beyond becoming more psychic.

Your vibration is an invisible energy field that exists within the DNA of your soul, aura, and physical body. It is energy that would be seen by someone with heightened clairvoyance *(clear seeing)* or sensed through clairsentience *(clear feeling)*. If Archangels and Angels are God's arms and hands, then your "vibration" is your soul's arms and hands. Your vibration is made up of undetectable cells to the human eye. These cells fluctuate and change colors depending on your mood, your thought processes, who you surround yourself with, as well as what you ingest into your body among many other "negative" things.

Your soul and entire aura is an everlasting breathing energy field that has an effect on your state of mind. This is whether you desire to be happy in your Earthly life or miserable. A chief executive officer of a major corporation is an angry curmudgeon who is rude to the staff and only interested in making money in any way they can. This person might be financially successful, but they are still perpetually miserable and a spiritual failure. This angry state lowers their vibration which brings in an onslaught of negative circumstances and health issues at some point in their life. This is due to the angry stressed state they've endured throughout the course of their human existence. It builds up like mold in a damp basement, until the individual decides to eradicate it and make some healthy lifestyle changes. The changes put into practice would be with the objective of raising your vibration. When your vibration is high, you feel euphoric feelings of joy, love, peace, and contentment. You discover that what you desire moves into your vicinity much more fluidly. If something has not been forthcoming, in a high vibrational state, you are not bothered by that in the slightest. You operate from the space of being totally centered and together. The abundance that falls into your vicinity is your soul operating in its high vibrational state.

You are in a temporary physical body with an inflated ego that enjoys pushing you to experiencing negative feelings, such as anger or sadness, when a life circumstance throws you a curve ball. This can seem inevitable depending on the kind of life you live and who you surround yourself with. When you have felt and expressed negative feelings in the past, you may be able to point out that while in that state you were not thinking clearly. This might have prompted you to react harshly towards someone else, or you reacted impulsively by making a decision you later wish you could take back. The ego is your lower self which puts you in a state of removal from your higher self. It's almost like an out of body experience. You lose all logic while in that lower self state. This affects how you

203

communicate to others and the choices you make.

You could be a busy professional who works a job that drains your soul's life force; therefore working a job you despise will lower your vibration. You sit in traffic to get to this job you're unhappy at, only to leave at the end of the day and sit in traffic to get home. This stress in driving in those conditions lowers your vibration.

You are made up of energy since every living organism, plant, animal, element, and atom vibrates of energy. When you take a stroll through a garden or park alone, many sense a heavy weight being lifted off them. You suddenly feel a little elated and more relaxed. This is an example of what it might feel like as your vibration begins to rise, but then you get a phone call from a friend who is a gossip and begins to tell you about how someone did something they angrily disapprove of. Now your vibration begins to decline, and yet you didn't do anything except answer your phone to talk to this person. You were on the receiving end absorbing this negative energy your friend was outwardly darting at your soul. Now your vibration has dropped.

Some animals will dart away when they sense a hostile energy coming towards them. They're in tune with a high vibration that they guard their territory without second guessing it. However, some human souls will instead welcome the hostile energy and then become one with it. They will go along with whatever the person is complaining about to them. This drops their vibration. It's understood that you might have a complicated life and you live in ways that are not conducive to raising one's vibration. This could include living in a big city full of cold, heartless people rushing around. Know that this is all about being aware of what can and will lower your vibration, while doing your best to avoid the things you know will pull you into that state.

My spirit team says that alcohol, specifically in high amounts, lowers your vibration. This does not mean that they are pointing their finger at you demanding that you stop drinking. Your choices to do, stop, dissolve, or reduce any particular life choices that drop your vibration is for you to decide. If you enjoy drinking a bottle of wine every night and yet you regularly question why you're not content with your life, and nothing ever goes your way, then this would be one of the possibilities as to what is blocking what you desire from entering the picture. Since alcohol in high amounts blocks divine communication and lowers your vibration, then you miss out on the messages and guidance from your own spirit team that would give you the missing ingredient you crave to achieve happiness.

Some connect with their Spirit team as naturally as you brush your teeth. Others struggle to pick up on messages or they express that they're receiving nothing. Your spirit team never disappears and stops communicating with you. When you feel you are receiving nothing, then there could be a block you might be unaware of. Blocks can be something trivial such as a particular food you ingest. It can be any negative feeling you're experiencing.

You pick up on heavenly messages when your ego steps out of your higher self's way. Meditating and being in a still environment in nature is a great way to access Spirit much easier than when you're under stress or any other negative emotion. Meditating in nature raises your vibration and opens up your communication line with spirit.

Raising your vibration is a lifestyle change that needs to happen over time for your soul's benefit and not for anyone else's. There are things that need to be adopted or modified daily to reach a centered place that helps one to be more connected and at peace. In *Raising Your Vibration*, we'll look at how to identify some of the basics on what raises your vibration and what will lower it.

Chapter Two

RAISING YOUR VIBRATION
TO A HIGHER LEVEL

All human souls desire the same goal regardless of their interests, values, or lifestyle choices. They want to be consistently happy more than anything in the world and to have their dreams come true. When you live in a perpetual state of unhappiness with the way things are in your life, then you reach for an addiction. This is a time waster that provides false temporary comfort. It is peculiar that you would feed your body and your soul toxic garbage. What is the point of living if you're not enjoying the moment focused and clear minded? You will justify it and make excuses for your poor choices. You will tell others, "I'm not going to be made to feel guilty. I'm just going to do it this one time." Yet, you end up doing it more than once. Before you know it, six months have passed and it's become a regular habit. When you look back on those past six months, you discover that you accomplished very little if anything at all. You are exactly in the same place that you always were. Once this truth is presented to you, then you grow negative and despondent. It feels like a heavy weight closing in on your soul and

206

body. To escape this nasty feeling, you reach for an addiction.

One of the reasons it is important to fine-tune your body and soul is that you open up the portal to receive Heavenly messages and guidance. You have more energy during the day to accomplish what you want, not to mention you look and feel incredible. This assists in attracting in wonderful circumstances, jobs, friendships, and relationships of a higher caliber to you. This positive energy enhancement shoots outwardly into the universe brightening up the aura within and around you. This is hypnotizing and magnetic to others while becoming a recipe for tremendous situations to enter your life. When you live a joyful life, then you are more compassionate and loving to be around. People are not drawn to miserable drunks with a pessimistic attitude problem. When you take care of your body and treat your soul with the utmost respect, then the universe and Heaven returns that energy back to you tenfold. It raises your vibration closer to God. He has all of the answers you seek to navigate through what might feel like a rocky existence. Your life does not have to be treacherous, because you can experience tranquility now. Only when you have reached the place of peaceful contentment do you witness the gifts and miracles you desire.

When you grow and evolve you raise your vibration. Raising your vibration to a higher level takes work and discipline. It is adopting an entirely new way of living. It is viewing the planet, your life, your surroundings, and your soul in ways that you would not have noticed in a lower vibration state.

Some examples of necessary lifestyle changes that will raise your vibration are cleaning up your diet, eating healthier, breathing deeper, frequenting nature, and partaking in regular exercise. It is also avoiding alcohol, drugs, the media, and people who are toxic, drowning in stress, depression, or poor life choices. This is not to say that you should abandon family members or loved ones who are under stress. There is a fine line between getting too involved that you fall into a dark hole with them, or choosing to remain detached from their drama. You do not want to grow emotionally drawn into someone else's whirlwind of consistent upset. It does nothing to help you and nor will it help by feeding them the same vibrational words they're exuding by agreeing with their chaos. This is like sprinkling lighter fluid on a burning fire. This energy expands causing more of that same substance. It is not your place to live someone else's life for them. Saying no does not mean you are coldhearted. When you say no, you are saying yes to you.

Alcohol should be in moderation or eliminated if you have an addictive personality. I understand this being a former addict myself. Even when I was no longer addicted to drugs and alcohol, I still went through a period of what is called being a *dry addict* or *dry drunk*. This is someone who is no longer addicted or using drugs and alcohol, but is still behaving as a dysfunctional addict. The dry addict has made no positive changes within themselves and therefore is likely to go after the initial addiction again. This is not to say that angels and guides preach that you give up alcohol if you're a moderate user. They are merely saying that alcohol in regular quantities blocks the communication line with Heaven which essentially blocks awesome abundance. Choosing to reduce or eliminate alcohol is a personal choice.

For some, it's effortless to reach for an alcoholic beverage or more to decompress after a long day. This may relax you for an hour, but then as the effects of the alcohol wear off, you begin to feel lethargic, edgier, and worn out. Some have pointed out the negative effects they experience as the alcohol begins to wear off. They feel gross with a heavy dense pressure that surrounds their body. An array of negative blocks is created in this process. These blocks can be dangerous as it prevents the flow of positive energy, light, and manifestation to you. Alcohol has adverse health effects on your body and health in the long run. It attracts in lower energy and circumstances to your aura and soul too. It's important to avoid heavy alcohol or other negative addictions for escape as much as possible. There is no secret that regular use of large consumptions of negative vices cause future health repercussions. It also lowers your vibration and blocks the flow of positive abundance. Know that you have free will choice and that there is no judgment if you are a regular drinker. Please don't feel as if they're pointing the finger like a scolding parent. They are relaying messages to me on things that contribute to lowering your vibration. These are also things that prevent you from picking up on their messages while blocking in good stuff.

Instead of reaching for that drink, I am more inclined to exercise. I'll jog up a mountain trail, or on the beach, or anywhere in nature. It is less stressful than jogging through the busy streets. I bike regularly along the beach coast as well. Exercise centers and elevates your spirit. You have more energy in the process while appearing and feeling better too! Others notice a brighter glow around you. Your entire aura and being attracts others to you. You have more time and energy during the day to accomplish important tasks. These tasks are geared towards your life purpose, spending quality time with loved ones, and more time for healthy rest. Relaxation is a luxury as well as a necessity. Get away for a couple of days and head to a place in nature, such as a park, the desert, the mountains, or the beach where it is quiet and serene. I use those surroundings as an access to re-center myself if I am feeling out of sorts. If I'm at home and unable to get away for any reason I'll put on a melodic chill out or uplifting CD album, then light some incense and candles. I will create a safe calming sanctuary where I live.

BREATHING AND STRETCHING

Breathing is vital to your health and in raising your vibration. When you are stressed or upset, you hold your breath without realizing it. Take some time daily to sit still, pause, and breathe deeply in and out. This is stopping what you are doing, taking a huge healthy breathe in for three to five seconds, and exhale out all of your worries, stresses, and toxins. As you exhale, imagine the pressures and tension bottled and locked up in your body and aura exiting out into the air. Give those worries and stresses to your Spirit team and Heaven. Notice how relaxed and clear minded you begin to feel. You might experience lightheadness as your body, mind, and soul re-centers and re-aligns itself.

Doing this breathing exercise regularly sends and feeds oxygen to all of your organs and cells. This awakens your soul that often feels trapped and confined in its body. Those who suddenly have restless energy with an urge to take off, make drastic changes, or uproot their life in an impulsive manner feel this soul entrapment deeply. Their soul does not feel the freedom that would come naturally to them in the spirit world. Your soul suffocates in your temporary body when you feed it toxins. Your ego pushes you to make changes that will not usually bring the joy and love you crave. You might be happy once the initial change takes place, but it will not be long before you discover that you're suffocating again and the rise of restless energy is dominant. You're chasing a happiness that you will never find by running away. This is a search for something substantial that already lives within you. You need to access it and bring it out.

Taking time to partake in breathing exercises is essential to centering yourself. Yet, many human souls would rather hold their stress in. This leads to health complications by trapping in all of that unnecessary negativity and stress energy into the crevices of your body. This is an ugly breeding ground for health issues. Centering your soul helps you achieve wholeness. This adds clarity as well as a euphoric feeling of joy. It connects and merges your soul with your physical body. This helps you become aware of who you are in truth. You learn that the current functioning of human life is on the trivial side.

Incorporate body stretching into your routine. This improves your circulation and relaxes the muscles that tense up under daily stresses. Lie down on the floor and stretch every part of your body in various ways. Perhaps lay a beach towel down next to your bed and do the stretches there. If you are able to bring the towel to your backyard or a park is even better. It provides a cheering environment that ultimately relaxes you. You might not be aware that the wear and tear of your day can easily tighten up areas in your body and remain there indefinitely. All of the stresses compounded in your day become trapped into the crevices of the cells in your body. Partaking in daily breathing exercises will get a lot of that gunk out, but sometimes there are remains of it wedged into hard to reach areas that can later cause long term health issues. This also blocks the flow of good energy and vibrations throughout your body, mind, and soul. This is why stretching is beneficial to your overall soul and higher self. Talking to friends who are bubbly, upbeat, or positive is another way to lift your vibration. Suddenly everything shifts in and around your world. Feeling those good vibes from optimistic people, coupled with stretching and breathing exercises contributes to re-centering your being.

CUDDLING, HUGGING, TOUCHING

If you are involved with someone in a romantic relationship, then make love, and love each other up regularly. Put in frequent efforts to shower one another with supportive words. Those that are in healthy long-term, committed, love relationships are physically healthier and happier than those who are not. They are more productive and tend to live longer too. There are powerful healing benefits for couples who experience joy together and who are loyal with one another. When you are in a relationship, you need to hug one another often. This includes cuddling, making love, kissing, and giving each other massages especially after long stress filled days. Do this with one another regularly no matter how ridiculous it might seem to you. If you shun or shy away from this type of physical expression, then you need to let your guard down and open your heart up to your significant other. This is important for your long-term health and your relationship! Human souls were not born closed off and unreceptive to physical expression. This is behavior that is a block grown from the outside human tampering in your life.

In this cold love relationship world, there are many human souls who are single, so these activities are not always an option. However, equally harmful is being in a relationship where there is no love showered between the couple in any form. Let your guard down and hug a friend hello when you see them. Hug an animal or a tree! This may be more of a challenge if someone is male. Men tend to reserve displays of friendly affection, but I've noticed a growing trend where the newer generations are more open to those forms of hello than the previous generations. They are a newer generation of souls who chose to enter this lifetime to spread love and joy. Love and joy are two feelings that have been lacking for centuries due to societal influences.

Sharing in the cuddling, hugging, and touching activities with your mate lowers both of your cortisol levels and blood pressure. You are less stressful after a day that is compounded with negative strains. Cortisol is a stress hormone in your adrenal glands above your kidney's that shoots out to your brain when a sudden panic or attack in your life happens. This can be something as basic as feeling stressed when in traffic trying to get to work. A higher dose of this is damaging on your brain chemistry. When the nervous system is shot that high abruptly, it's not that easy for it to drop down. For some it can take as long as a day! You've likely noticed this with yourself or others who experience an alarming situation. You are also aware with how long throughout the day you or this person carried that alarm state within. This is what this cortisol hormone is. It can cause adrenal fatigue as you may have experienced following a stress filled situation. Hours after the stress event, you feel worn out. Some might cry out, "I cannot wait to have a drink!" Adrenal fatigue is also when you receive the recommended seven to eight hours of sleep a night, yet you feel tired and sluggish all day.

If you find that you are always tired no matter how much sleep you get, then there are an abundant amount of possibilities of what could be causing that. It can be that you are unhappy in any area of your life. Maybe it's your job, relationship, or home life. When you are experiencing daily doom and gloom feelings due to one or more of these areas, this drains you of life force and vitality! Just one of these areas can leave you perpetually tired. This tiredness is disguising a form of depression. If there is more than one area of your life that brings you down, then double or triple the energy of this feeling to understand the impact. Overtime this will take its toll on your body, mind, and soul. Naturally, the most obvious thing to do is get a physical with a doctor to rule out any potential health issues outside of being unhappy with life. Once that's ruled out, then the answer is in front of you. It is poor diet, not enough exercise, or dissatisfaction in one or more areas of your life. Identify where the root cause of this tiredness is coming from. Get happy now by making positive adjustments with the areas in your life that cause you daily grief. Doing this in steps won't make it feel so overwhelming.

Cuddling, hugging, and touching have immense healing properties as discussed. These acts are able to bring down your cortisol levels more rapidly than anything else. When you engage in these activities with someone, or your romantic partner, it will assist in lightening the load of unhappiness in your life. It will raise your vibration and boost your Oxytocin levels. Oxytocin is known as the love hormone. This calms your entire body and helps your soul brighten and shine. It blasts away any potential health problems. This will also open up your clair channels to receive clear accurate messages and guidance from Heaven. The guidance you receive is transparent while in this state. It contains the answer to your prayer that pulls you out of the darkness you were previously experiencing.

Touching relaxes you and lowers your blood pressure. Hold hands and touch your partner often. When you touch your partner, it merges your souls with one another. There is the emotional impact that reassures you both that you are protected and comfortable. This elevates both of your vibrations to a place of contentment and satisfaction. Touching has great benefits for the physical and metaphysical heart. Shaking someone's hand in a warm and friendly manner merges your energies brightening up both of your auras if even for an hour.

There isn't enough reaching out and expressions of love in this world to begin with. When someone is exuding negative traits and directing them outwardly towards anyone in their way, they are masking an inner despair. Grab them and hug them up to melt those wasted toxic feelings that do not help them or anybody around. Can you imagine that instead of war you hugged your enemies? The vibration of this entire planet would rise to a phenomenal degree. It would create a beautiful loving place where all human souls live in harmony and joy indefinitely.

EMOTIONAL EATING

Health and diet are crucial areas of focus that need to be adhered to in order to raise your vibration. You were not meant to consume chips and hot dogs on a regular basis! You were not meant to cause harm and destruction to your body, emotional state, and each other. There was once a time in history when humankind was living to be hundreds of years old. The food that existed then was what you were intended to consume. Eventually food grew to be complex and interesting. It would be injected with hormones and chemicals. Now you are fed a poisonous diet of processed foods and fats. America alone prides itself on the fast food diet. This is what some people raise their children on because it's fast and cheap. This is simultaneously programming the upcoming generations to become addicted to food that is lethal to your body. In a strange way, they are preparing you to die early by slowly poisoning you with bad foods. You become addicted to certain deadly foods and carry that with you throughout your life. Eating this way lowers your vibration, weighs your soul down, and causes a dark array of future health issues. Some of the highest obesity rates exist in the world today. Even if someone is not obese, they are living off food filled with lard, saturated fats, and cholesterol. Only select groups read the ingredient labels on the back of food packaging, and understand what they're truly putting in their body. These foods are made with an abundant amount of ingredients that contain words that most people cannot pronounce. These words are all different names for sugar, food coloring, and chemicals. It's like pouring water into your car gas tank and attempting to drive. This is essentially what is being put into your body. It's another disguise for controlling the masses. They have everyone move around dangerously pumped up on chemicals. This causes them to function severely sluggish or under stress.

The mantra that says you must do everything in moderation is important, however, eliminating negative substances altogether is even better. Unfortunately, human ego gets in the way convincing you that you need that piece of chocolate cake! The bad foods and

214

drinks that you consume are emotional eating and a result of something bigger going on underneath.

There is an underlying emptiness and cause going on within you that prompts you to have repeated cravings for something like Pizza or Ice Cream. God, the angels and spirits in Heaven do not say any of this to ensure you feel miserable. It may seem like that when they urge you to clean up your diet and avoid bad foods, soda, alcohol, or drugs. On the contrary, by cleaning up your diet you grow to become more focused and happier in the long run. You experience longer lasting feelings of pleasure and enjoyment, rather than feeling blocked and weighed down by sugar or alcohol. You attract in at higher positive levels while awakening your spiritual connection line to Heaven. You are more readily able to hear, see, feel, and know the messages and guidance that your own Spirit team wishes to relay to you that can assist you on a joyful path. If you do not make these changes and life modifications, then you are likely to stay in the same place you have been in your life to date.

HARSH ENERGIES

The energies around the world are harsh everyday and that is just the sad reality now. Despite this, everything is slowly shifting in a more positive way thanks to the many evolved souls who have incarnated from the Realms and Spirit Worlds that exist. With those shifts comes the tantrum throwing by lower evolved human souls. This is what you are bearing witness to around the world. Before the harsh energies came at you once in awhile, but now it is out of control and happens on a daily basis. The internet, technology, and phone apps that exist have positive uses, but most do not use it for positive purposes. Technological devices spit out toxic energy at your aura and latches onto your soul. If one is using the devices for selfish reasons, such as to spew negativity, or for ego stroking, then you and the person they direct the energy to will be a magnet for some of these harsh energies.

Do not continue down the path of living in turmoil. This

causes you to display agitating energies that the Universe rejects entirely. When this happens, you are denied great abundance and instead find the agitating energies to be mirrored and reflected right back to you.

It is important to make certain lifestyle changes that include avoiding harsh situations and people as much as possible. Steer your soul away from all drama that exists. It is all "noise", which is energy that you do not want to be a part of. There is no love or benefit that exists in that area.

Due to the energy being intense on Earth, you need to ensure you keep your life balanced in all areas that exist, such as your personal and professional life. Your life is balanced when both areas have equal attention. Unfortunately, most human souls work more than they play and relax. Balancing your internal energies can be done by taking quiet retreats or spending quality time alone. Get away for a couple of days to do nothing, but relax and enjoy yourself. You do not have to go away out of town if you do not have the money or time. You can go to a park and unwind for fifteen to thirty minutes. What happens when you are alone in nature amidst trees, grass, plants, and flowers? You feel a relaxing calming effect on your aura. I've walked through gorgeous parks to see people alone sitting near trees with a half-smile on their faces content with the energy that is overcoming them. You certainly do not relax sitting in your car in traffic, or trying to cross a busy street with horns honking, and people shooting harsh invisible daggers carelessly in the air.

There is great emphasis for you to take these nature retreats. You need regular stretches of time off. Get away from the noise and balance the energies in your often stress filled life. This gives you the opportunity to clear your mind of all that debris that latches onto your aura with its claws. Ask your Spirit team to help by giving you the time and resources to incorporate regular retreats and time outs. You can ask them mentally, in a prayer, or out loud, and even in writing.

EXERCISE AND FITNESS

The Earth's atmosphere is extremely heavy and compressed. This adds additional blocks that can make it difficult for many to connect to the Spirit world, even though your Spirit team connects with you on a daily basis. The stuff you put into your body contributes to these blocks including things such as cigarettes, alcohol, drugs, violence, anger, revenge, and dysfunctional relationships. Negativity and gossip as well as poor diets and lack of exercise are other factors. This is why it is demanded that you take care of your body and be mindful of your life choices and habits.

I'm a strong advocate for health and fitness no matter what age someone is. Since I was a child, my Guides and Angels have been sharing with me that exercising and taking care of ourselves physically is our #1 obligation to do while here. You have to take care of your body! It is a gift enabling you to function and accomplish your goals and manifestations while you are living here. You have to care about it and your soul.

Heaven considers certain things a sin, although the word sin isn't in their vocabulary, but the meaning is still the same. One of those sins is: Lack of Exercise. You are urged to take care of your body. You must take the vessel you are living in with incredible seriousness.

Some souls have elected to come into this lifetime where physical exercise may be impossible. Know that when they say exercise and take care of your body, this is to do it in the best possible way that you are able to. Not everyone can run up a mountain, but there are light cardio exercises one can do. There are stretches one can do or lighter forms of exercise movement. There is a difference between whining that you don't feel like it, or that you have other things to do and are too tired, or that you physically cannot do it due to a life health circumstance that prevents it.

Before computers, cell phones, and even television sets, how did humankind get through the day? They spent more time outdoors! The bigger cities were not as busy and congested as they are now. You could go for peaceful walks right in the middle of the largest city. Now thanks to the greed in human ego, this spawned an indefinite need to over develop where nature once existed. This self-indulgence produced the over population of humankind on planet Earth. You have to search for a nature preserve or a park unless you live in such a location. Before the days of electricity, light, or clocks for that matter, people did not obsess over the distractions that exist today. We would be outdoors and head to bed when the sun went down. The next morning, there was a full day packed with more energy to accomplish what is needed. The enhanced physical energy was due to having a full night's sleep and being outdoors partaking in physical activity. The foods were not full of chemicals and toxins in the way that they are now.

If I am on a large amount of caffeine, then hearing my own Guides and Angels is difficult. As a Clairaudient, it is as if the sound has been turned down low. Caffeine speeds up your heart and therefore your anxiety levels. Anxiety and stress block heavenly communication. In order to turn up the volume of your Guides and Angels, remove negative substances such as coffee, sodas, and other heavily caffeinated drinks. Are you addicted to energy drinks? They tend to be consumed mostly by teenagers, young college adults, and busy professionals. Imagine the toll this has on your heart over time. Pouring sugar, chemicals, and way too much caffeine into your system on a regular basis like that is a bomb waiting to go off. I have been guilty of consuming energy drinks in abundance. At one point in my life, I was doing it daily without a care in the world. I would say, "Oh there's a ton of B vitamins in this." Yeah, and add to that the list of sugars, caffeine in large amounts, and other chemicals no one can pronounce.

Many of the toxins I mention, I have been guilty of consuming like a fiend at one time or another. It was only after my Spirit team consistently warned me about the repercussions did I realize that I had to work on making healthy life changes. Take caution and pay attention to the consumption of toxins you ingest on a regular basis. Aim for dissolving or reducing these harmful products when possible.

Your body is an instrument designed to receive messages from

God when you are operating at a higher frequency. You are unable to do that efficiently when you are consuming high amounts of caffeine or alcohol. Heavy stints of caffeine increase anxiety and hypertension, which can cause long-term health problems as well. When I'm doing something that will affect me negatively, my left ear rings loudly at times. This is my Spirit team's way of getting my attention and downloading information to assist me in dissolving my cravings for these more dangerous, addictive, substance behaviors.

Water is also a critical necessity you need to consume lots of. Your body is compiled of water. God created tons of water in and all around human souls for a reason. This is to ensure that you keep your body in operable condition while you are using it. One of the ways this is accomplished is by drinking water. This hydrates and fuels all of your organs flushing out all of the toxins you breathe into your body. These pollutants and waste stay in your body causing damage to your kidneys if they are not rinsed out repeatedly with water. When you drink plenty of water you have more energy, a clearer complexion, and not to mention you look better too! I have been drinking over eight glasses of water since I was a teenager. I carry a huge missile of water with me every day and have been doing that since I was seventeen. One of my many secrets is having a disciplined exercise regimen that includes consuming at least eight glasses of water a day. Your water consumption needs to be done indefinitely.

Exercise is significant in maintaining your body, mind, and soul. You do not need to be a hardcore body builder or world-renowned athlete. My Spirit team has explained to me that some body building lifestyles fall surprisingly into the realm of addictions. These people pump themselves up daily with chemicals before they spend hours working on their body. Some of them view their bodies with a distorted view not realizing when they are doing too much. You may have likely heard of cases where prime athletic and fit people have had a sudden heart attack. This isn't because they were fit and athletic of course. The cause was all of the harsh chemicals they ingest on a regular basis to pump them up to exercise. This sounds much like a catch 22. You're feeding yourself these chemicals in order to take care of your body. Doing this on a daily basis can actually cause the opposite effect such as heart failure or other health complications.

The other form of exercise addiction is when you work out purely for vanity reasons. Your frame of mind is in the wrong place causing an unhealthy obsession connected to body image. This lowers your vibration.

I enjoy cardio more than several times a week. I head to the gym to use the weight machines or the free weights at home on a weekly basis. I will randomly drop down to do pushups. I am always active and keeping my body as healthy as I can. Exercising and being active has always been like oxygen to me. There are days where my energy level is low, but I push myself to get started with some cardio if even for a short bit. About five to ten minutes of jogging and your blood starts pumping through your organs. Exercise fights feelings of anxiety and depression prompting you to be more alert and energetic. It also releases endorphins, which make one happy giving them uplifting feelings.

When you head for a jog, start out by walking briskly for about three to five minutes to get your joints lubricated, and then move into your jog. If it's a short jog, then after about another fifteen minutes give yourself an additional five minutes to cool down at the end. Avoid stopping abruptly and sitting down immediately. This is not good on your heart. You'll want to have a cool down process where the jog slows down into a walk for a few minutes. There are lighter forms of exercise you may find more suitable for your sensibilities and body chemistry such as Yoga, Pilates, or Tai Chi. Do anything besides sitting on the couch all day, in your car, or in an office chair. Get at least fifteen minutes of brisk exercise everyday. Do it several times a day if you are able to. Get moving!

I carry my gym bag everywhere for those days where I know I will not be back home for awhile. If you head straight home before you go to the gym, you might talk yourself out of going. When you arrive at home, you are comfortable and just want to relax. Stopping at the gym on the way home has many benefits like giving you a break from rush hour traffic!

Chapter Three

REMOVING ADDICTIONS AND NEGATIVE SUBSTANCES

It was not easy or immediate when I was brought to a permanent healthier space in my life. I was a compulsive addict as I discuss in my book, *Reaching for the Warrior Within.* I was addicted to drugs, alcohol, over the counter prescription medications, cigarettes, coffee, sugar, dysfunctional relationships, and people! One by one, my Spirit team started dissolving or reducing my cravings for those addictions. I did not go through any professional therapy. I accomplished this with the power of my mind and the help of my Spirit team. I was surprised to find that I was happier and more energetic when not using any of those vices.

Coffee blocks and dims the communication waves to Heaven. My Spirit team said I didn't need it. Naturally, I argued as I do with anyone who is pushing me to do something I disagree with. I was not a big coffee drinker to begin with, but I did have one cup of coffee every morning. The rest of the day I would be drinking a huge bottle of water. I fought with my Spirit team on this. Others were far more into their coffee than I was, and those people were drinking tons of it. Researchers have said that one-cup a day has shown no negative adverse health effects. I always showed up to battle or to debate by having done my research.

Every morning I would get up at 7:30am tired, even after sleeping my mandatory minimum eight hours a night. I would head over to my fancy French press to make that perfect cup of coffee. As I was getting ready, I'd continuously hear my Spirit team say, *"You don't need it."* I'd ignore them and grumble. "Yes I do." I would need concrete proof that I don't need it in order for me to quit.

One day after the nudges persisted, I slammed my hands down and said, "Okay if you don't believe I need coffee and I think I do, then I give you full permission to assist me in reducing my cravings for it. That's the only way I see this working. If I'm craving coffee, then there's no stopping me. I'm going to have it, unless you can help me with this then too."

They agreed in succession.

The next morning, I woke up feeling unusually alive as I went into the kitchen. I thought, "Hmm, I'm not craving any coffee this morning. That's odd. I might try and do without it today. Let's test this out."

About one month later, I discovered I was having one cup of coffee a few times a week instead of every single morning. Over the course of the months that followed, it was one cup of coffee once or twice a week. This moved into once or twice every couple of weeks. This pattern continued until by month six I was no longer drinking coffee at all! After twenty years of drinking a cup every morning I no longer craved coffee. I discovered I had more energy and less stress. I have the coffee bag in my house, but the same bag has been sitting there unused for emergencies or guests. I haven't found the need for an emergency. Even if I did, I would not beat myself up over it. You take it one day at a time. Do the best you can as you dissolve unhealthy substances gradually and safely. The way they removed coffee was the same way they removed cigarettes, hard drugs, and heavy drinking. They were all gone just like that. No urge. No craving. It was miraculous as the change happened after I made my official request to my Guides and Angels for assistance.

The world spends billions of dollars on coffee daily. Some buy that fancy cup of coffee every day at whatever coffee franchise is on the way to their work. Imagine spending about $3.00-$4.00 a day five days a week. You're spending $80.00 a month on a coffee drink that has no benefit to your health or bank account. Other than waking you up for a couple of hours, it exasperates your stress and anxiety levels throughout the rest of the day. Please know that it is not advocated that you stop drinking coffee. This is a personal choice that you decide on with your Spirit team. There is no judgment if you enjoy your coffee. They're merely stating the repercussions and negative side effects that lower your vibration and block or dim heavenly communication.

There are parents who pump their kids up daily with caffeinated sodas giving them repeated injections of caffeine and sugar. This is what you do with the soul you allegedly love? Granted it's not done with malice, but out of naivety and society's influence. I was one of those kids who would revel in the occasional soda. Luckily, my taste for dangerous foods and drinks were in adolescence. Even while consuming this stuff, I was "claircognizantly" aware that this was not good for the body. You have one body and you have to take care of it. You have to care about it and yourself. I do not have a sweet tooth or have a craving for desserts. I can walk past a buffet table spread to the gills with cakes, cookies, ice cream, and yet there is no temptation.

The painful issues you focus on are self-induced by yourself, your ego, and those you surround yourself with. You can eliminate the pain and issues as I did with the assistance of your own team of Guides and Angels. You do need to formally request their help since they cannot intervene with your free will. They can only intervene when you make a request. Ask God, or whoever you equate God to be, to send you a health and lifestyle angel or guide. This is one that will work with you daily on making the shift into a stronger self. After your request, you will need to pay attention to the signs and messages around you. They will place these signs around you, or nudge you to make positive adjustments in your life. For example, they may guide you to a certain gym class by consistently dropping the flyer to this class in your path repeatedly until you finally take notice that it is divinely orchestrated.

My Spirit team worked with me to change my life one-step at a time. I have never felt as great as I do today. I had more energy, stamina and optimism at thirty-five than I did at twenty-five. I was more physically fit at thirty-five than I was at twenty-five, which means you can do it too!

Instead of coffee, I juice one cucumber in the morning with a juicer machine. I might add anything from Maca powder or parsley. Sometimes if I want a real kick, I'll juice a clove of garlic with it and add a splash of Cayenne pepper spice. This healthy alternative gives me just what I need and in better ways than a measly cup of coffee that would only exasperate my stress, anxiety, and depression. I would later crash from the coffee, but the cucumber juice keeps on going. My mind is clearer and the messages from Spirit are opened up wider. Before this change, the messages were dim and faint. Cucumber juice is also great for your complexion. It cleans and clears out the toxins built up in your organs. It's fantastic on your lymphatic system and far less costly than paying for a daily cup of coffee.

In those days when I was guided to eliminate coffee, my Guides and Angels nudged me to reduce and eliminate sugar. Granted, I would sprinkle a little bit of sugar in coffee, tea, or cereal to begin with, but did I really need it? I wanted to test it out and see if I could do without it. I stopped sprinkling granulated sugar on anything after that and never went back. Instead, I use a healthier alternative such as a spice like cinnamon or nutmeg. Coincidentally nutmeg has its own healing properties. It is great as a brain stimulant and relieves stress and depression among other things. Cinnamon is high in nutrients and lowers cholesterol. Both are a much healthier alternative to sugar, which has zero benefits and is toxic to your body and health. I was surprised by how much I loved the taste of cinnamon after that. It far exceeds that of granulated sugar. The same goes for salt. I never used salt in all of my life, but the rare occasions where salt is needed for myself or a friend, I offer Sea Salt or Himalayan Salt, which is not damaging to your body the way processed salt is. In fact, it detoxifies and assists in balancing the energies and cells in your body.

When I quit cigarettes at age twenty-five, I had a box hidden away in case of an emergency, even though that day never came. It is preferred that you throw away whatever it is you're trying to quit. The reason is you have some of that energy hanging around the house. There is no temptation if the product is not there. I later stumbled upon the cigarettes in a box and ended up throwing it away realizing I was no longer a smoker. I never had any cravings for cigarettes after the age of twenty-five. Ironically, I'm unable to stand immediately next to someone who is smoking around me. Friends that are the occasional smoker will not smoke around me, or they will disappear somewhere outside down the street away from my vicinity. It's not polite to force others to breathe in the air of cigarette smoke. Even when I was a smoker in the early days, it was rare that I was seen smoking. I never did it around a non-smoker out of respect. Whereas hardcore smokers would run through a pack a day, it would take me several weeks to a month before my pack would run out. I was a casual smoker, but have been cigarette free since 1999. It's hard to believe I smoked at this point since I demand fresh breathable air around me. I found it easier to walk past a window with marijuana smoke wafting out into my lunges, than cigarette smoke.

As a former addict, I can tell you that most of the people using drugs, alcohol, or any other toxic vice are running from something that includes some form of emotional or mental trauma. There are human souls who use these vices because they enjoy the way it makes them feel. If they enjoy the way it makes them feel, it's because they don't like how they feel when they're not on anything. Why don't you like how you feel without being on anything? The inadequacy inside you is a false reality. Everyone is too busy fixing their outsides so people will find them attractive or like them, but they are not bothering to correct the core problem, which lies inside you. You are more attractive when you exude that from the inside out.

Ask your own Guides and Angels to steer you towards a healthier lifestyle. All you have to do is say the words, *"Please help me with…."* And then pay attention to the signs and messages that they put in your path.

225

They also assisted me in removing my need or hankerings for anti-depressant and anxiety medication. I started using it after one of my relationship break ups, and then ended up staying on it for three years. It was not easy waning off the drug as I had become dependent on it. I attempted to dissolve the medication through repeated attempts on my own with no success. Another relationship ended in the process as I was attempting to wane off it again. At that point I said, "Oh forget it, I need to stay on this a little while longer." I also discovered the anti-depressants helped me with my social anxiety. I did not want to be on it forever and preferred to function as clear minded as I possibly could.

I asked my Spirit team and Archangel Raphael to help me find healthy alternatives that are superior for my body, mind, and soul. Nothing was going to stop me from dissolving it. They guided me to the right vitamins that were deficient in me. This isn't to say that everyone should dissolve their anti-depressant medication. This was a personal choice that I wanted to do. You should always discuss dissolving your prescribed medication with your Doctor first. I know what it's like to struggle with lifelong anxiety and depression symptoms.

I was determined to live as naturally as I could while trusting that I would be okay. I was on the anti-depressant drug Effexor for several years. After I asked for heavenly assistance, they guided me to a reduced anti-depressant in Wellbutrin. They do not abruptly take you off something, but instead gradually wane and reduce you off of your addiction much like a Doctor would. After six months of the Wellbutrin, I took the last tablet in the pack. I agreed with my Spirit team, that I would take it day to day from that point. Granted I was slightly nervous over how long I could go before I faltered. I would not push myself any further that I didn't think I could do. In the end, I haven't had a prescribed anti-depressant medication tablet since that day.

It is more than cutting all of these toxic consumptions out, but I personally had to cut many things out of my life as I shifted into becoming a Warrior of Light. This included the biggest culprits and cause of my addictions: Certain people. Toxic, negative, and abusive people were all out and gone! Those around you contribute to one succumbing to a pill or vice to begin with. The insufficient and uncomfortable feelings that lead you to the drug were not there when you were born. I had joked with a friend once that people are on medication...because of other people! It's others that should be on medication. Don't give them that power. Tell them no, go away, and get lost. It was Archangel Raphael that helped me off anti-depressants without any support from anyone around me. He altered my entire life into something positive. He cleared the debris and toxins from within and around my body.

CLEAR THE CLUTTER

Simplify your life by eliminating the clutter in and around you. This will help bring any hidden positive energy out and moving. You accumulate clutter everyday from material things to other people's energies. The angels have shown me that this clutter is similar to a drainpipe in a sink. When hair and gunk gets stuck in those pipes the water doesn't flow freely. This same concept goes for your bodies and the life around you. It blocks good things from flowing easily to and from you. This includes good energy streaming through the organs and cells in your body and soul.

You do not realize how stagnant the energy in your life is when stuck in a rutted routine. Educating yourself and becoming a lifelong student of higher learning is another additional way to raise your vibration. Your diet and what you consume has an effect on your overall well-being and energy level. High vibrational foods are fruits and vegetables, especially organic foods, which are free of pesticides. Avoid sugar and alcohol, along with foods and substances filled with preservatives. Drugs are a definite no, as it has detrimental effects on your vibration, health and the relationships around you. It blocks messages from Heaven while opening up the portal for negative energies to attach themselves to you. You'll know this has happened to you when your life spirals out of control. You might experience one poor circumstance after another or feel eternally lethargic and moody.

I have seen many rave about soy products, which does have positive benefits, specifically the whole fermented soy. Then you have the other soy products that exist such as, Soy Lecithin, Soy Protein Concentrate, and Isolate to name a few. These are all names for chemical preservatives. It's appalling to know how much food is manufactured and eaten that contain harmful forms of soy. Human souls are more or less being slowly poisoned by the masses.

Men should avoid soy or reduce it when possible. This may seem impractical considering that the food industries have chosen to infuse some form of soy in their products. Soy increases estrogen levels in men. The nutrition and diet industries have been feeding the health benefits of soy to the public, but the problem is they are not mentioning the repercussions on men specifically. Kids have been raised on soy more than ever before. The boys will hit a hormone drop in their mid-thirties instead of the expected mid-forties because of this. Soy suppresses a man's sex drive because of the immediate drop in testosterone along with other side effects.

Besides waking up the next day with a hangover from alcohol or drugs, do you ever notice that it takes a great deal of effort to get yourself and your body back up to standard? It takes longer than a day to get there and some don't even survive the week without consuming another drink or drug. The older you get, the harder it is on your body, which is why many quit altogether. If they don't, then their poor bodies just give out and stop working resulting in death. They exit this life long before their time.

Retreat often and take vacations to decompress the built up stresses you've added onto your soul. A time out is necessary even if you don't have enough time. Make the time! Eliminate people from your life that drain and suck your high energy dry. Abolish those that consistently lead you to partake in activities that are not healthy for your soul and body.

I've always been a firm believer that having a drink or some bad food in moderation is okay. Moderation means once in a blue moon. Yet, many souls slip out of that moderation and it ends up becoming a regular habit.

You are here to fulfill your life purpose, learn soul enhancing lessons, gain knowledge, and to enjoy this life and have some fun.

This fun does not fall into the category of toxic. You are not asked to stop these poor ways of living for anyone's benefit, but your own. Heaven wants you to live at your fullest potential while experiencing euphoric feelings of joy. When you participate in healthy activities, exercise regularly, and have some measure of discipline about what you put into your body, then the fun and enjoyment you experience is beyond cosmic. If a stressful situation hits you, then as a high vibration soul you are able to take on that stress in exhilarating stride. You are equipped to allowing the stress to roll off you without tampering with your energy field. The stressed situation evaporates rather quickly, than it would if you had not asked your Spirit team to intervene and work with you.

Your individual blocks need to be identified through personal self-analysis. You can do this by being as truthful with yourself as possible in order to extricate those blocks out of your life. Be objective during this process and get your ego out of the way. Blocks are what prevent you from achieving happiness and your wildest dreams of abundance from Heaven.

AVOID GOSSIP

I don't watch regular television and nor do I have it hooked up. I do watch movies on DVD though. I stay away from the news because it's mostly always spun in a negative way to get everyone riled up or to bring them down. It also prompts others to gossip and argue their beliefs and opinions back and forth. This does nothing to help them, the other person, or the situation they are arguing about. Yet, it is impossible not to notice the headlines at times when you are checking your email for example. When you read the negative headlines, or absorb that energy, then you have invited it into your vicinity to hang out. It tampers with your aura and darkens your energy. Your self-esteem plummets and your soul grows dark and muddy. It also blocks Heaven's wonders from entering into your life. Once you plunge into the dark depths of the abyss, it is difficult to climb back out of it.

Work on reversing any negative effects built up by being considerate and thoughtful with your media and lifestyle choices. Be mindful of how you communicate with others and who you allow into your world. When you express compassion towards someone else, the energy lifts you and the other person as well. You are no longer burdened by the weight of that darkness. Allowing yourself to be affected by someone else in a negative way erodes your self-esteem. Your energy and state of mind becomes messy and full of confusion. You grow agitated and feelings of low self-worth permeate through your body. Do not fight against the current by being affected by those around you. Recognize this when it happens and start treating yourself a bit better. Do not worry about the news headlines or what others are saying. All of that is noise that does nothing to bring people together. Give yourself a time frame such as a week where you avoid the news and gossip. Notice if it lifts your state of mind into optimism. You might find that your life is indeed in a more peaceful space than it was before. Optimism is a powerful attracter of your Universal desires.

REMAIN OPTIMISTIC

Millions of people around the world acknowledge holidays, their birthdays, or even the end of the year as a guide to see how far they have improved or progressed. They look at it as a time out to celebrate with optimism in hopes that the future will be brighter for them. It is when people will often say, "Next year will be better." If you keep saying tomorrow will be better, then you will always be one step away from happiness. Feel peacefulness today and then your challenges will lessen.

You are being asked to examine your life in a deeper way in order to make significant positive changes. Many human souls have been waking up in the process. This transformation you have been going through will make someone's ego unhappy, because change is something different than what you are accustomed to. You get uncomfortable whenever there is a drastic adjustment that forces you out of your comfort zone.

There is often fear energy talk surrounding new diseases or an end of the world. These are all false fads that are beat upon society by human ego. There is never going to be an end of the world, but the negativity and the obsessive focus on that sort of talk amplifies the darker sides of the world's character.

Get unstuck so you can be at a place that benefits your soul. Evaluate your beliefs, values, and ways of doing things. Make significant changes in your life immediately. Shed all of that garbage from in and around you. This will open you up to be receptive to the wonderful circumstances headed your way. Be open to receive those gifts in the right spirit and start living fully today.

AWAKEN YOUR INNER CHILD THROUGH JOY

Inviting laughter into your life is crucial to your well-being. It opens up your heart while awakening and unleashing your inner child. It has profound health benefits next to love. Love and joy are two of the highest energy vibrations in the universe. The entire Spirit world is bathed in the wonders of exuding those powerful feelings eternally. These are some of the biggest most recurring messages I receive. The messages they give me are sometimes repetitive if they are not being followed. The messages sound easy enough, but why is it so hard for some souls to live in that space 24/7?

Many lives are full of stresses, toxins, and disappointments. You have no problem living in those conditions and choosing grief instead of harmony. This way of living is thrust upon you by others. It is a learned trait because you certainly were not born that way. You come into contact with someone who is negative or toxic and you absorb that energy. You end up taking it out on someone else and they pay that forward and so forth. Your aura and soul darkens along with your state of mind. Soon you are behaving like that too. You pass it around to one another like contagion. This is what gets passed around when it should be lightheartedness, optimism, love, and laughter. Many choose a path of deep anguish where they allow that distress to drop to a level where no one can reach them.

I sense every range of energy in the air without escape and we are indeed stressed globally. There are evolved souls in this lifetime spreading humor and joy, but it's not enough to get the tides moving fast enough. Get everyone to join in!

It can be challenging being around others who are permanently mired in negativity and you cannot get away from them. They may be a romantic partner, family member, roommates, or the worst offenders, which are colleagues. The reason they are the worst offenders is because many human souls spend most of their days with those they work with. You cannot escape them. If that one draining apple exists in the bunch, they have the power to shift the entire mood within the work environment. Typically, that one sour grape is keen on spreading it around to others who are not interested. This causes a decline in productivity and morale. It takes great effort to raise it again. This is carried over into your daily personal life when you head outside, brave the streets, and eventually head home. You pass that energy to your friends and loved ones. You suppress it or feed it by getting your hands on a toxic addiction.

A friend sent me one of those social media tests that allow you to check to see what your mental age is. I scored the lowest in our group showing that my mental age is nineteen. I joked that I am either immature or young at heart. This is an example of keeping your responsibilities and commitments balanced, but also remaining young at heart. Take some time out daily to see the humor in life. Make light of situations that would otherwise be distressing. You might have put your body into a tense position, or perhaps you are stuck in a rut without realizing it. You can get unstuck if you remember to have fun and unleash your inner child. You remember that kid when it was little. You saw the wonder and joy in the smallest things. When you laugh and have fun it opens up your heart Chakra, which not only invites romantic and loving situations into your life, but enables you to manifest your glorious dreams.

DANCING AND SINGING

Dancing raises your vibration! So get up, move, and hit the dance floor! This is a quick way to awaken all of your cells at once. Dancing prompts you to feel alive. It opens your aura and soul right up. Your inner light blasts wide open and radiates when you dance. It does not matter where you do it. Take some time to crank up your stereo at home. Dance in your living room or in your bedroom. Sway your body and get into it. Do not feel ashamed. The spirit world is bathed in the fun of singing and dancing for a reason. They do not place the kinds of shameful or embarrassing burdens on their backs the way a human soul's ego might.

When you dance you experience joy, gratitude, and optimism. Some of our greatest entertainers throughout the world's history whose specialties have been dancing on stage or screen agreed to a human life to bring this wonder to the masses all at once. Their goal is and has been to liven up human souls who get stuck in the mundane unable to break loose. It took a long time for human souls to become aware of the joys of singing and dancing. The spirit world agreed to send souls to enter into human form and display what they have been doing on all spirit planes for eons. And that is dancing and singing! Your thoughts and feelings are uplifted when you dance. Who cares if you feel you have two left feet and are tone deaf. To God, you are perfect in every way, so do it anyway! This is for your own long-term health benefit.

Society has established so many ridiculous rules that hold human soul's captive. This includes restricting each other from opening up and releasing. There was once a bigger stigma with dancing when it came to men specifically. Men were trained by society to remain withdrawn, the rock, unemotional, yet strong. Men were trained to not display emotion or feelings, let alone dance. To do so would make you weak. It's the opposite in fact. It takes strength to reveal feelings and emotion. Expressing yourself through dancing and singing releases your soul from the trappings of human life!

Statistics have shown that women live longer than men. Why

do you think that is? For one, women tend to be more expressive with their emotions and feelings. They do not typically hold this stuff in. They are receptive and nurturing by nature. However, a shift has taken place over the last few decades where the life expectancy for both men and women are relatively similar. This is due to men being taught to be more open, feeling oriented, and expressive. They get out there on the dance floor and do not care what others think. They're not afraid to move to the music. In fact, even though there are still some traces of stigma in certain areas around the world with dancing, the newer souls coming into this world now are defying those absurd stereotypes that once held the human soul prisoner. European cultures such as Italy or Spain tend to radiate their love for dancing and expressing joy full time. Other cultures are slowly moving in that direction in a bigger way. Let's crack it wide open!

Dancing and singing releases those rigid blocks that later cause health concerns. You live a longer more prosperous life when you get into the groove.

One interesting dichotomy my Spirit team has shown me is that some partake in drugs or drinking tons of alcohol and then they get out on the dance floor. The reason this is contradictory is that even though they are at the clubs or a party dancing which raises their vibration, the alcohol and drugs soon drop your vibration to a great degree. It's counterproductive where your vibration is not rising at all. There is nothing wrong with alcohol in moderation or that it is kept to a healthy minimum of two glasses, but the dancing and singing they're talking about is the natural kind when you're not on any mind altering substances. The dancing and singing is what will raise your vibration and overall view naturally without the need for a toxic substance. Alcohol releases inhibitions, but a human soul with a high vibration releases these inhibitions naturally without any harmful vices. Crank up your stereo or music player and move that body! Not only does your vibration rise, but these movements tone and strengthen your body with regular bouts of dancing exercise. Dancing and singing raises your vibration and releases your higher soul from its body confinement. This prompts your entire aura to feel alive!

Chapter Four

PURIFICATION KEEPS YOUR WORLD CLEAR

As you make positive life changes and adjustments that include modifications to your diet and your exercise routines, it is vital to be aware when antagonistic energies are in your vicinity. Most human souls head to work on a daily basis only to be met with a colorful array of personalities. Some are good and some are shooting invisible daggers at you. If clairvoyance is your opened *clair* channel, then you may see this energy. If you are clairsentient, then you are feeling what others are pouring into you as if you are a drainpipe for their pollutants.

There are techniques you can partake in that can minimize or eliminate the effects the damage causes you at the hands of others. You will need to keep an open mind about some of these methods described in this chapter. Have trust and faith it is real. These methods do and have worked for me and countless others. You need to be disciplined about it. You can always test my Guides and Angels hypothesis before you discredit it. Hearing my Spirit team repeatedly instruct me to do these things, I folded and decided to try it out. Granted at first I was grumbling as I was doing it: "This is ridiculous." It wasn't long before I noticed the positive changes and improvements in my life.

CORD CUTTING

It can be challenging making the transition into a worker and warrior of light. Sometimes there are people in your life who hold you back from evolving. They get in the way, have zero support, or cause you grief. If there are certain people you wish would go away, then you can do so by what is called *cutting cords* or *cord cutting*. It is almost like magic in the way it astonishingly works. With some suspects, it can take awhile to remove them out of your life, but you need to cut cords to them every single day. Do not give up or stop cutting cords until you feel the circumstance has improved. I have witnessed incredible results over the course of my life doing this for myself or I would not continue with it.

Anytime you connect and form a relationship with or to someone whether that is a family member, friend, colleague, or love relationship, then you form an etheric cord of attachment to them. Clairvoyantly this looks like an etheric gasoline hose coming out of the other person and hooking itself onto you. If the person is needy, negative, or always stressed for example, they are pulling high vibrational energy out of your soul. This feels as if someone is sucking the life force right out of you. This gasoline hose is a dark etheric cord that clairvoyantly looks like spider webs wrapped around this tube strangling it.

Whenever someone in your life affects you negatively, you can be sure you have a toxic cord attached to them. You will feel drained, stressed out, or uncomfortable whenever they are around you. When the thought of them approaching you makes your stomach turn, then you can be sure you have a tough nasty cord connected to them.

This cord attachment is placed between romantic partners or

potential dates as well. Let's say someone is chasing a guy or girl who is not romantically interested in them. You start to check that person's social networking page daily for weeks. This is followed by a negative cord of attachment to that person. You grow to obsess over it to the point where it has taken over your life in an unhealthy way. Married couples, roommates, and anyone who lives together form cords of attachments. This is why some couples are so in tune to how the other is feeling. Both of the lights around your souls have connected and merged. Even if one of you is living in another city - the cord is still there. This is why you need to make sure that you and your partner are aiming to practice living a life of joy in your individual lives. If one of you is experiencing constant negativity, then the other partner will absorb that causing your cord between one another to become polluted. This is draining and can even cause you to have incessant arguments or to ultimately break up! One of the many points of a relationship is that you support and lift your partner up when they're experiencing discord.

It's important to cut cords regularly to certain relationships due to the buildup of dirty energy. This doesn't mean that you are cutting them out of your life necessarily, unless this is what you choose. You are removing the dysfunction or toxic part of the relationship.

What I have discovered while cutting cords is that my Guides and Angels will either remove and eliminate that person out of my life or improve the relationship. They eliminate them if they know there is no additional purpose or lessons needed to happen with that particular connection. Your Guides and Angels will remove the person in question if the lessons you need to gain with them are completed. They will also remove them if that person is still hanging around causing you turmoil. This can simultaneously hold you back from moving forward. Your vibration has risen while the other person remains buried under a lower vibration. They are not intending to deplete your energy, but this is what is happening regardless since you are made up of energy. If you are a sensitive person, then you are especially susceptible to the repercussions of forming an attachment to a negative and toxic person. I cut cords to certain people as part of my daily morning ritual. I mentally cut cords throughout the day if I need immediate cord cutting intervention with someone hostile or draining around me.

Sometimes when you work with certain people who are toxic it may be difficult to get rid of them. This is where some of the uninvited contamination in your aura happens. The second place is at home if you are living with others. This is why it important to do your best to ask that you be guided to work or live with high vibrational people. If you are unable to live alone, request to live with similar higher vibrational people who are peace loving souls. You will need to raise your vibration and keep that energy in your vicinity in order to attract in someone of a high caliber. High vibrational people can sense someone who is not of integrity or who is going to be a problem from a mile away.

If you are in a loving, committed relationship with someone and you are living together, then you have formed a cord. If the relationship is based on 100% pure love and compassion, then the cord will not be as dirty, but there will be a cord. You still need to keep some form of detachment so as not to fall into a position of co-dependency since the cord can get a little dusty. Those that you have formed a cord attachment with are not purposely attempting to drain your energy or spit toxins into you. They are unaware they are doing this. You are your own barometer gauge to know how certain people affect you. Do not forget that this is your soul to protect and it is up to you to manage it. You have the assistance of God, your angels, guides, and archangels within reach for this process. All you have to do is ask for their help. You don't need to chant some complex invocation. Saying something like this has invited in heavenly help: *"Okay, Archangel Michael I need your help with this…"*

As you begin cutting cords, then you will find methods that you're comfortable with that work for you. You can think the word *"angels"* and you are heard and have invited them in. One way I say it is: *"Please cut the cords between (so & so) and I."*

List the people that you find to be toxic and draining. Say one person's name at a time. Take a deep breath in and exhale after each name. Do this by visualizing Archangel Michael taking his light sword and slicing the cord away between you and this other person.

The people you list are those you know you will have to deal with or face that day and you definitely do not want to. Sometimes it might just be one person, while other times it's a few. There are some whom you will have to cut cords with every single day until they are gone from your life or the connection improves. When you find a connection is putting you in a repeated negative place, then cut the cords immediately. There are those you love and are close to, and you do not want them to go away, but you do not want any pain or dysfunction in your world anymore either.

For those cases you could say something like this:

"Please cut the cords between (the person) and I. Only remove the toxic, fear, and dysfunction from this relationship, but keep the love and lessons."

When I've requested that the dysfunction be removed, I have found those relationships drastically improve or they elevate into something better. I hear Archangel Michael cutting the cords with one slash of his light sword. If it is a difficult cord that's hard as cement, he will continue cutting every day until it is removed. This can work with someone you're involved with romantically. If you find yourself not trusting them, and yet you have no valid proof to be reacting this way, then you will want to cut the cords with them. Some are afraid to do that because they fear that the person they love will be taken away. Having the cords cut does not necessarily mean they will be banished from your life. Your Guides and Angels will take care of the when and how. They will make the decision that benefits your higher self's path. All you need to do is ask for assistance. There is no reason to endure negative insecurities with anyone including a romantic partner.

I have had cases in the past where I was stuck having to deal with someone I did not want around me. This might have been an acquaintance or colleague that was toxic, negative, or a gossip - all of which I will have no part of. It was pushed to the point where I was done with them. I had no interest and they offered nothing to me in the way of progress or growth, but merely contributed to heightened negative feelings. For those special cases I am quite firm in my cord cutting and even angry if nothing has been done about it. The angels are egoless and see your true light and nature. They do not take anything personally such as you stomping your feet in aggression. Not that I'm advocating that you do that, but there have been times where you are pushed to the edge and scream out for help.

"That's it! I want you to cut the cords between (the person's name) and I. Remove them from my life in all directions of time. Thank you."

I will immediately begin to see that our connection is elevated to a level that I can tolerate or they are removed from my life permanently.

Sometimes it's a process to extricate some people out of your life. The improvement might not be right away. I have witnessed changes and shifts happen over a period of time for some cases. Suddenly that person is let go from their job, they decide to leave and move on, or you have been moved away from them. The angels are maneuvering obstacles in the way. This is in order to bring about the changes you wish for that benefits your higher soul. They might be working behind the scenes with the other person's guardian angels to enact positive changes that benefit all parties involved. In the meantime, continue cutting those cords to that person every day until they are gone, or you are seeing an improvement in your connection with them.

Working lower energy jobs, while attempting to grow your light and become spiritually evolved can be challenging. You might have to deal with someone who can be disconnected from the real reality and living in full on arrogant ego mode. They are extremely deadly to you, your environment, and well-being. You could be working at the greatest place on Earth with wonderful colleagues, but there might be one or two bad apples who you might love to toss out a window. Every time you turn around they are standing there. They might be pushing your buttons in a negative way or getting under your skin. This is where cutting cords works beautifully. These are people you have to cut cords to every single day. They may not always be extricated from your life immediately, but you will start noticing them become a bit more tolerable and eventually off your radar. You form a cord of attachment to anything that is made up of energy. This means that cords can also be formed with material items such as your home, car, or any other material items that you hold dear to your heart. You form cords to your feelings and

240

emotions too. Cord cutting is a positive lifestyle trait you're adopting and incorporating regularly. Be aware of what you are attached to, as that is a clue where the cords exist.

SHIELDING

I am a sensitive who grew to have immense social anxiety due to a volatile upbringing. With the help of my Spirit team I was able to bring my social anxiety down to a manageable level. However, at the time of this book, I also function in an unpredictable and somewhat soulless city. You take unstable people and give them a machine to roam around in and control, such as a car, then you have a full-blown battlefield on the streets. The energy is worse than the anger of a murdering terrorist. This is why it is important to shield yourself. Shielding is another beneficial process to incorporate especially if you are a sensitive person. Sensitive people absorb energy emanating off of others like a muddy kitchen mop.

Take a deep breath in and exhale out. Call upon God and Archangel Michael. Ask him to shield you with bright white light for protection. Visualize a cocoon of white light surrounding you. This will keep out those nasty pests that insist on entering your field. The people you work for, or whom you are around regularly can be the greatest people, but even great people get moody, agitated, and out of line. You sense this energy and vibration and it suddenly lowers yours. See the innocence and humor in other people, and do not let their drama and moods affect you.

Be wary of over shielding yourself or your business to the point where all are invisible. To avoid that from happening, ask to be surrounded by a *permeable* white shield of light allowing only the love to infiltrate.

You can request and envision different colored shields of light around you. These heavenly lights can be layered together or on its own. Your soul and aura is six feet tall, which is why your soul is literally too big for your body. It is important to be aware of it, sense it, and take care of what enters your auric field. The shields of heavenly light last up to 12 hours so you will need to do it daily as needed.

- ❖ *White* – Strongest light that protects you. Nothing can penetrate this shield.
- ❖ *Rose/Pink* – Offers protection while allowing only the love to enter your auric field.
- ❖ *Emerald Green* – Heals you in all ways such as physically, mentally, or emotionally.
- ❖ *Violet* – Assists in raising your spiritual gifts and psychic sight.
- ❖ *Gold* – Powerful. Brings in God's love and light. Blasts away and repels all traces of negative thoughts and your lower self from your mind and body.

Remember to ask for help from your Guides and Angels. Even if you've been asking for help, you haven't seen results, and are losing faith – keep on asking and putting that energy out there. They are not ignoring you. If it is not happening right away there is a reason, but it will happen. There are obstacles and barriers being removed that are in the way to get you to that place you want to be in. Pay attention and listen for the signs that they might be giving you as well. They may be answering and advising you, but you are not paying any attention to it as you're expecting the answer to take a different form. If you are receiving a repetitive sign that happens more than three times and benefits your higher self, then you are receiving heavenly messages. They want you to be at peace. They want you to have enough time and resources to be able to focus and work on your life purpose. They do not want you to feel stuck at a dead end job struggling to make ends meet for all eternity. Start working with God and your Spirit team today to improve your life one-step at a time.

DISENGAGE FROM ANGUISH

Steer clear of everyone else's irrelevant drama. It doesn't do you or anybody any good to get involved with someone's ego.

Someone else's stuff is not yours to absorb. You cannot learn other people's lessons for them. If a hostile person is continuously unloading their drama on you, stop responding, ignore them, and walk away. You are the manager of your soul and life.

Human souls do not take enough breaks. The few holidays they are given the time off, they spend it tired or wasted in a toxic haze. When everyone is back to what they consider to be the grind or mundane, they are reminded of how unhappy they are with some part of their life. *(i.e. job, relationships, finances)* The edgy, angry feelings they had surrounding their current lives and in feeling stagnant rise once again. The slightest issue can be blown out of proportion and you might be caught in the line of that fire. Remove yourself from the racket if you find yourself being a target of someone else's blow up. Always revert back to focusing on you and your higher path. Become the calm in the eye of the hurricane. As for those acting out, they are discontent with where they are at. They are receiving nudges from their own Spirit team to make long awaited adjustments to their life, but are ignoring those messages. That is not anyone's problem to solve, but their own. You want to disengage and detangle yourself from other people's misery. This doesn't mean you are to be cold hearted. You can still be supportive and compassionate by not attaching yourself to their drama.

ETHERIC CREATURES
GNAWING ON MY LIGHT

The same way that spiders are sensitive to vibrations on their web, I am equally sensitive to the vibrations in and around me. If you are a sensitive or in tune to Spirit, then you likely know what this is like. I cannot be in crowded environments or stand obtrusive noises such as traffic sounds or garbage cans banging around. Naturally I assume no one is a fan, but my not liking it borders beyond what the average soul seems to tolerate without issue. I have to close my windows for a few minutes, or cover my ears when a siren is going by or a super loud plane is flying overhead. Being a clairaudient heightens every sound around me beyond the norm too. It's much like a dog or animal that perks up at a sound that no one else can hear. The only loud sounds I can tolerate are music. Music is the sound that connects you with the Other Side. Positive uplifting music raises your vibration. The Other Side enjoys riding on the notes of the music. This is where the greatest message input is found next to being out in nature.

When my spiritual sight re-opened up wider after I had rid myself of negative ways of living, I found that I had a steady link and connection to the Spirit world. This was also when I began hearing what sounded like chattering. I knew it was not Heaven as the sound was creepy and uncomfortable. It would cut in and out as if it were a bad static phone reception. It wasn't long before I clairvoyantly saw these dark insects in my peripheral vision. My Spirit team wanted me to know that due to my sudden increase in psychic activity that I was attracting in a number of skittering little etheric creatures that nibble on positive energy. The more you study and grow your psychic abilities, the brighter the light that you give off becomes - both in your aura and as your soul footprint. These etheric creatures feed off random positive energies. As your light grows they are attracted into your vicinity. These creatures make a little skittering noise like squirrels chattering. They were distracting me on a level that I wasn't fully aware of immediately and this caused a subtle change in my focus. These annoying little pests would break up my concentration. They would keep my subconscious mind from working on the walls and barriers I erected to protect myself from emotional damage. My Guides and Angels explained that I had full knowledge of suitable aura protection methods, but that I was not using them consistently enough. This allowed these little pests to get in.

I used to be lazy when it came to shielding and protecting my soul. That was until I had invited in an army of negative pests. Don't underestimate the value of soul protection, because if these little pests can penetrate your armor, some bigger bad bods can do more than just distract you. This is in no way meant to scare you. No one is in immediate danger from anything on this level. As you continue to study or grow your psychic abilities, and raise your

244

vibration, you can become the target of larger entities that require bigger feeding stations, and this can get to be pretty draining.

A certain level of my consciousness was distracted by the ebb and flow of the spiritual work that I was doing more of. Combine this with the annoying little pests that were nibbling at my energy. I was not quite aware of who or what is and was coming into my immediate path during the pivotal spiritual transition. I could hear the little skittering noises of these psychic pests, which can be likened to that of a buzzing bee. When you hear them it will confirm their presence for you. If you choose to take action without the confirmation, then you need to bump up your protection visualizations morning and night. This can be as simple as envisioning an armor of golden light of protection around you and make that absolutely impermeable. Visualize yourself completely surrounded and utterly sealed off to anything except 100% positive energy. Believe that you are protected against all incoming energies that try to drain your psychic, mental, and emotional energies. Affirm three times each session that you are protected and armored against these intrusions. See yourself as unbreakable!

The heavenly white light energizes whatever is in it. If it's an entity made up of negative and evil darkness, then the white light will literally cause an explosion when it meets its opposite. The entity will disappear and leave. I had experimented with this by pushing a few of those little mosquito-type chattering annoyances into it as you would push something in the water away from you. They would pop like popcorn to demonstrate their change in polarity.

If you are going to grow your light and expand your consciousness, awareness, place and work in this world, you will attract those who will try to stop you from doing this. It doesn't mean you're in danger. It just means you need to be aware of this and practice safe psychic study. Nothing is free as there is always an exchange of energy for energy. The more light you give off the more darkness you attract. The more you know and grow, the more attractive you and the light you give off becomes. It's like putting a low watt bulb on your porch and having a few moths attracted to it. It is that versus putting a 100-watt bulb out there and having every

245

single insect of all varieties within a 10-block radius coming to gobble up the heat, light, and any other food they can find there. You're drawing in more of those energy eaters.

My higher self and soul grew to be so bright and intense with blasting white light that the darkness was extremely attracted to it. Think of it as mosquitoes buzzing around a tasty human wanting to take a drink of the yummy blood. They are dark bugs drawn to a blazing flame. I was dinner and those nasty dark beings wanted to get in and drain my delicious positive white light energy from me. This is why it's important for you to cleanse yourself with white light and seal your aura with gold light. Having the intention and visualizing this can do the job. You can find various instructions online on how to do this. Ask for guidance on the right way to do it. You'll know it's the right one when you experience positive vibes about what you've stumbled upon. Once you build that better suit of armor around your soul, then you will be able to concentrate on your own interior work, knowing that you are safe from all nefarious incomers.

Regardless of where I, or you, came from, you are here in your body now. The brighter your light shines, the more you draw in negative energy. If you are in the middle of a spiritual awakening or transition, then you are at the beginning of an important journey. Don't rush it because it takes years and lifetimes to master. You have been truly blessed with your own gifts and abilities whether you are aware of them or not. What you do with them in this lifetime is up to you. You have the opportunity to do great good in the world in the subtlest of ways. This is by allowing your light to shine in a way that is not harmful to you or anyone else. This light can infuse everything you do. By learning about it and yourself, you will allow more light to come into the world. The world is always in need of more light to keep the balance between the light and the darkness. If you never do anything else, but let your loving energy shine through to the world, then that will be enough to help combat all the evil in the world.

DIVINE TIMING

Heaven wants you to experience contentment and to not suffer, but they can only help you achieve this when you invite them into your life and begin working with them regularly. I began testing them out as I was growing up. I received incredible results in the process and was wowed becoming a true believer. Some may call it coincidence, but how can you call something coincidence that happens consistently every time you ask for something over a period of decades?

The more you work with them, then the more your life begins to change in positive ways. You find that your friendships and relationships begin to shift and improve. Those that were toxic and negative to begin with start exiting your life or you drift apart. It is not that you are repelling them, but they are repelling you! What once attracted you to them is no longer the case. You no longer feel a rush out of gossip, negativity, addictions, or destruction anymore. This process can take what seems like a long while, but know that it is all happening and in motion. The angels are working with you on eliminating these people that no longer serve your higher purpose. Your vibration rises in the process. As that happens, you find that you are living the life you always wanted or you're heading towards it rather quickly.

There is always some measure of turmoil or tantrums whenever change happens with human souls. Trust the changes have a greater benefit to you in the end. Have patience and faith that it will. Everyone wants things now-now-now and I'm certainly no exception. You can make things easier on yourself when you know there are good reasons for things not happening right away and trust that it will come on its own time.

Sometimes there are lessons that you need to learn before you are shown the next move. Take a step back and pause. Move within for the answer. This is also known as your intuition. Notice what answers come to you on the situation you are questioning. Request that your Spirit team remove your ego as you tune into the messages being relayed to you. You will discover why there has been no change in your life yet. You may find that your lessons have been learned and there is nothing more to gain, but the delay in movement is because your Guides and Angels are working diligently behind the scenes to make it happen for you. There are circumstances that need to occur first on the other end before anything can happen.

An example might be, let's say that you are unhappy in the apartment you are living in and have asked for help in finding a new place of residence. You can't understand what the delay is in receiving that help. What you may not realize is that you have an idea of what apartment you're going to move into, but your Spirit team sees an even better scenario. They see you in an actual home of your own in an area you have only dreamt about, but brushed off as impossible. Yet, you deny this possibility because you do not believe you could ever own a home in this current market and with your financial status. They see something bigger entirely up ahead for you. They see a big sell with a project they have been assisting you with for some time. You do not see the potential financial gain, but they do which enables you to purchase that home. They may see you moving in with a potential love partner you've been dating or will be dating soon. This move takes place in an entirely different part of town. If you jump towards something out of impatience you could potentially throw your path off course and cause an even greater delay.

Your ego is fixated on nabbing something immediately and talks you into jumping. It sounds like a great idea to you at first. You later wished you had exercised more patience for the real excellent stuff. Delays are for good reason so that other pieces of the puzzle can be put into place and maneuvered into something far greater than you imagined.

When you meditate, take pause, or move into a daydream as you connect to your Spirit team. You can discover what they are currently working on for you in this state. Your Guides and Angels always see you as being more capable than you see yourself. If you are receiving messages that seem far-fetched, then it is important that you remember to have faith and trust in it. You have abilities that you might be discrediting as impractical. Heaven knows what you are capable of. Your soul was born into this life with the capability of wonderful magnificence.

THE WHITE LIGHT

White light is the color of spirit, purity, transformation, and completion. All human souls have been changing whether they recognize this or not. They have been bringing their previous lives to a close by shedding anything and everything that has blocked or prevented them from welcoming in new and brighter circumstances. Some do not have a choice. The universe is forcing it on all of humanity. There are some who may stomp their feet, or sulk, since change can feel uncomfortable. Your Spirit team is assisting you more than ever to make this change. They are also bringing souls to you in human form to enlighten and change you. The answers you need are coming from the source and the white light within you. Tune into it, embrace it, and follow it. It has always been there and it has always been this way since you came to being. This white light has been kicked up a notch and is targeted globally. Many souls are looking and longing for answers. Some of them are seeking out some form of spirituality since it is more compassionate and open hearted. You cannot wander around oblivious in your life anymore and nor can you can ignore it. This white light is growing around the globe. More people of this white light are being born to usher it along so that it will be spread like wildfire. We are banishing the darkness in humanity. It is no longer acceptable behavior to be cruel or to be operating from pure ego.

Chapter Five

LAW OF ATTRACTION

Successful people have at least one thing in common. They are optimistic when it comes to what they want to achieve. They fixate on their desire with unwavering strength and focus. Heaven does not want you to suffer, but your ego will do whatever it takes to ensure you experience downfall. Heaven and your team of Guides and Angels understand that you have basic human needs. When you are happy and fulfilled in all areas of your life, your Spirit team knows that you are more apt to focusing on your life's purpose. The daily choices you make can block the flow of abundance without you realizing it. Sometimes it can be a perpetual cycle of negative thoughts that run through your mind. Perhaps you sit in traffic every day to and from work with anger or stress. This negative mindset constructs a block on your road to abundance. Your words and thoughts have a powerful energy vibration. It effortlessly brings you something of equal value. If your words and thoughts are mostly negative, then this is what you're going to bring to you. You either bring in more negative circumstances to you, or you bring in nothing. These are the human souls that complain that it feels as if they've been stagnant forever with little to no movement. If you spend your entire day doing nothing or partaking in time wasting activities of a low vibration, then you have made a choice. All of your choices have a cause and effect in what is to

250

come to you. Take note when you made a decision in your past that potentially altered your intended course. You may be able to recall how this choice caused a preferred or undesired effect. The goal is to be aware of your thoughts, words, and the choices you make throughout your day. This is how to stop yourself from making a decision that you know will set off an entire array of unwanted results. When you connect and tune in with your own higher self, then you become fully conscious of the choices you make. If you make a decision that you know deep down is going to cause unhappiness to yourself or someone else, then re-consider your approach. Notice how unnecessary the choice might be when compared to the ultimate outcome. Your lower self and ego makes choices in haste, or in an impulsive burst of suffocating energy. It is bathed in overwhelming negative emotion and then this is what you bring more of to you.

Allow any damaging baggage in your life to fade away. Carefully plan the next few years of your life. When deep in thought or meditation, focus in on what it is you dream of or desire. For example, say a positive affirmation such as, "I'm going to buy a home that will be the foundation of my life." Ask your Spirit team for help with this. Tell them what you want and give them an area, "I will buy an affordable Condo in this area and here's how much money I have." Sit down with your Spirit team and visualize what you want with them. Envision exactly how you want your life to be in a year. Before you know it, it will be the end of the year and it will be exactly that. Human souls need steady, stability, and calm. This state of mind is the perfect breeding ground to raise your vibration and attract in positive abundance. Love yourself and all the good that you have within you, because you are awesome!

VISUALIZING YOUR REALITY

Visualize how you want your life to be. Even if it seems impossible, do it anyway. Feel it in your gut and in every cell of your body. Believe it as if it is already happening. This can be from the career you want, relationship, home, or anything you desire pending it is not harmful to you or someone else. Aligning it with your higher self's purpose is the way to create good Karma. Visualizing circumstances that are harmful to you or someone else is dangerous. It will backfire and become part of your Karmic thread, even if it is initially a success. Eventually it is a debt that has incurred on your soul that must be paid back. When someone's ego wants something with great veracity, then it is not in a high vibrational state of mind to understand the consequences until it's too late. Never discredit the power of your mind. You have the power to create your reality. You are creating your reality whether you're fully aware of this or not. You can have anything you want as long as you hold the intention with positive thoughts. Allow your mind to wander into a daydream visualizing the life you want. Remember that if a thought has any doubt in it, then this can negate or delay what you want from happening. Therefore, it is important to catch yourself when distrust creeps into your mind. When this happens and you are aware of it, then mentally say, "Cancel that thought and replace it with this." Modify the negative thought with something positive in exchange. Some of history's immense talents, leaders, and CEO's are in the positions they're in because they do not allow insecurity or negative self-talk to stop them from accomplishing what they intend to. They set intentions without negative interference. They know exactly what they want with unwavering excitement surrounding this desire. They go after it with enormous gusto and they get it! If you witness successful leaders in action, you will find they are precise, focused, and optimistic.

THOUGHTS PRODUCE CIRCUMSTANCES

Negative thoughts cause the majority of human unhappiness. It is true that challenges happen for a reason. If you do not have challenges, then you do not learn, grow, and overcome. When you are aware of the challenges, then you are able to shift them into something positive. Being aware of them is to have an understanding of why a challenge took place. Avoid losing sight of what is important on your journey here. It is easy to veer off track when functioning in this material based world on a regular basis. Take a little bit of time out daily to detach from the chaos around you. This is to avoid permanently drowning in the ego based noise of the world. Days pass by and you discover you are going through the motions. Your thoughts move into words of a lower vibration, thus bringing more of this to you.

You are always creating your own future reality. When bathed in negative thoughts, it will soon make it seem as if nothing is going your way. Suddenly you receive a parking ticket, or you get into a car accident, or you are pulled over. Next thing you know you are running into one person after another who is making you feel even more miserable. It turns into a domino effect that continues forward without any hope of escape. You become immersed in it to the point where you're oblivious to the fact that you created this reality. This consistent negative reality persists for weeks. You complain about it with anyone who will listen from friends, family, to colleagues. This lowers their vibration in the process. Those around you soak up this energy since it latches onto their aura. They begin to exude this same behavior and spread it around to others as well. You can see how this can get out of hand. A movement of this negative outbreak infects the entire planet. For some, this carries on for years and even decades! They do not believe they are the cause of this and therefore are unaware that they have the power to stop this cycle. This is why no one can deny the planet is in complete chaotic angry disarray. Turn on the media or visit a social networking site. Most of it contains a diatribe of complaints.

The words are easy to detect because they can be negative, judgmental, critical, and abusive towards yourself or others. The reason that we use the word vibration or energy is because they are invisible particles in the air that many might not be accustomed to understand. Human ego believes something to be non-existent if it is unseen. You have more power than you realize. You have the power to manipulate this energy in your surroundings and bring forth to you that which you desire. Keep your thoughts and words high vibrational in order to attract in abundance.

If you find you're buried in negativity, then it is time for a soul time out. Escape from the noise around you and retreat to somewhere quiet. Close your eyes for a moment and relax. Take a deep breath in and exhale. Change the negative sentences, complaints, or worries, which your mind is repeatedly stating. Shift them into something positive. You can do this by starting your sentences with, "I love..."

"I love myself. I love who I am. I love that I have a car that runs. I love that I have a job that pays all my bills." And so forth.

Practice shifting your words to those of gratitude. If you find you're moving back into negativity and destructive thoughts, then be conscious of this and shift it once again. Re-word your sentences to more positive uplifting ones. It is work re-training your mind to get to that place, but with practice and over time, you will get better at it. The results will be astounding when you find that great things begin coming your way. You discover that your life has become less stressful. Negativity is a learned trait. Most of it stems from childhood conditioning. You unknowingly adopt it as second nature. This is why breaking those bad habits down or diminishing them can take some time and work on your part to bring your soul to the high vibrational space it was when you were first born.

The Archangel Michael vacuums away all dark energy. Visualize him holding an ethereal vacuum hose. He takes this hose and inserts it into your crown chakra above your head and down into your body. Imagine that he turns the vacuum on and sucks out any negative, dirty ion debris lodged within and around your body. Some of this negativity hardens if you've been harboring it for some time. Allow him to remove all traces of this toxic negativity within and around your body and soul leaving you feeling uplifted and optimistic. Let go of all burdens and concerns and hand it over to him for transmutation. Once you release the need to control the outcome of your worries, the more likely it will resolve itself in a rapid fashion. If you have been hanging onto tons of negativity, then do this clearing daily until you know or sense that it is gone. At that point, you will be much better at managing it and extricating it from your vicinity when it happens again. It is advised to do a routine cleaning once in awhile if you live in a heavily populated area, since this is where negative energy expands on a daily basis.

DAYDREAM

Avoid getting caught up in the noise and drama of the world's nasty behavior. Human drama flies out from all angles on a regular basis. It is erratic and unstable. It does nothing to help you or anybody. Take regular time outs than necessary, and relax and smile more. Shun going to places where you know it is going to be taxing on your system. Go for walks alone *(or with a love interest)* and daydream. Do this in a nature setting if possible. Daydream about beautiful, wonderful circumstances and feelings. Think about the amazing blessings you currently have, and then daydream about what you would like to see manifest next in your life. If your life is where you want it, then daydream about that more. Take walks in areas where you know it will not be crowded with people. I've witnessed others attempting to go for a stroll in busy cities only to dodge restless and reckless drivers nearly running them over. You're on guard and your heart rate shoots up on high alert every time you have to cross a busy street with impatient drivers. This is no way to relax and center your soul. Venture off into a nature setting whenever possible for strong effectiveness. Find a quiet place to focus or meditate on anything that is not man-made. This can be something like a sunset, a plant, flower, or mountain peak.

The moon phases and cycles have a larger energy power behind them. Check online or a planetary calendar for the dates of the New Moon and Full Moon phases. Most calendars tend to have those two transits listed for each month. The New and Full Moon transits add extra manifesting energy to your thoughts. Be careful with your thoughts more than usual during those moon phases. Keep them positive and upbeat. If your mind goes into worry or something negative, you are going to bring about more of that to you! The New Moon is a great time to start a new positive activity or regimen. This can be beginning a new relationship, job, or sending out your resume. The New Moon symbolizes new beginnings. The Full Moon has immense manifestation power as well. The Full Moon is typically a nice phase to release bad habits or people, while aligning your focus with what you truly desire.

Do whatever it takes to get you to that place of feeling happy and content. This can be anything small from watching a funny, uplifting movie, to hanging out with a cheerful friend who always makes you laugh. Place your work and worries aside and celebrate your life. Be grateful for what you currently have. See your soul and where you're at in a positive light. See the blessings that you have in your life right now. Do not think about or worry over what is coming next or what is not here. Put that all aside and let loose and enjoy yourself. Learn to celebrate this life and insist on having more good times.

It is inevitable that you will hit a rough patch in your Earthly life. This might be where your soul feels lost, overly emotional, or lethargic. Sometimes these feelings signify that you are on the precipice of grand changes needing to happen in your life. It is a transformative period prompting you to be more introspective. What matters is how you work through the issues that this energy is bringing out of you. What it creates within you might be uncomfortable as it is asking you to examine where you are at in your life. This can be in any area such as career, relationships, or health.

Learn from your current circumstances, choices, and experiences. Avoid remaining mired in negative feelings and thoughts. Heavy emotions force you to be hyper-focused on where you are at. This prompts you to feel stuck as if you are trapped in an eternal prison. Yucky feelings stall your progress and forward movement. It becomes difficult to reach a place of happiness while in that state. In order to work through these feelings and thoughts, you have to examine them with a fine toothcomb. Look for the underlying cause and message that continues to prompt you to obsess over thoughts which have no basis in reality. What areas in your life are provoking you in a negative way? Those are areas which require a necessary change. Ask your Spirit team for assistance and follow their guidance, even if they push you out of your element. Know they do this for your own higher self's good. It is a sign that it is a time to move on to the next plateau. See only the love and lessons in the experiences you are asked to modify or leave. Make your peace with it in order to move to a brighter, content life.

MONEY, SUCCESS, ABUNDANCE

Everyone deserves to live comfortably without worry. Even if you're twenty years old, create supplemental and retirement income today. Before you know it, you will be forty years old and wonder why you had not started earlier. When you take one action step at a time towards your goal, you will be that much closer to seeing your dream happen. One of the positives of the modern day world we live in is that everything is at your disposal. It is not like earlier history, or the 20th Century, where everyone had to rely on corporate greed to have the opportunities to express their talents. Those days are no more and thank God. You are able to go out there and put it together yourself at any age. The plusses of the digital world are that it allows one to successfully work for themselves.

All human souls want to live comfortably happy. This is in knowing that your bills are paid on time without any struggle while having more time to pursue personal luxuries and focus on your purpose here. Sometimes it might feel like you are taking a step forward and then a step back. This is much like the image of a spiral staircase. You are not going backwards or having a setback. Rather you are going around and then up.

When you focus your sole attention on obtaining money, then you shut off the supply. Do not believe that money is your security. Look to God as your source of security. This is how abundant manifestation flows freely. You work for, "God, Incorporated." When you need supplies, then you ask for it. It is only when you say the words with intent that it soon takes form. Success is not always financial. It can be a state of mind where you feel grateful and are optimistic with what you have, where you are at, and how far you have come. It is to take note of the great progress you have made to date.

Understand that money is only paper. Back around the B.C. ages, humankind created money by using things like sticks and stones. This was in order to obtain certain living essentials. We were not paying for these necessities, but rather exchanging it for goods. There is an exchange of energy. You're giving something to receive something. Soon the sticks and stones were manufactured into paper with dollar amounts and symbols on it. Human ego placed great emphasis and need on this paper. This pushed it further away from them. The real moneymaker is your higher self, the YOU of all you, God, the source, whatever you want to call it. Your thinking and limited reasoning mind is not. Let that all go and focus on the source for your abundance. Say affirmations such as: *"All of my needs and supplies are met in every way and in all directions of time."*

MANIFESTING

The key to manifesting is having an unwavering passion for a desire. You can have anything you want and can cause anything to happen when you have unbending passion for it. This is where you feel this passion for your desire all over you, within you, and around you. You feel and know it in your mind. You feel and know it in your heart. You feel and know it all throughout your body and soul. You know without a doubt that it will happen and that it is here now. It's allowing this feeling to build to the intensity of an erupting volcano. You feel this desire continue to rise with positive excitement from within. There are no negative feelings associated with this passionate feeling. You visually see what you want happening in reality with great optimism. If you are having a passion for obtaining something, but you have doubts circling that, then the doubts will overpower the desire and you will receive the doubts instead of the desire. Experience inner peace and uplifting joy that you're living this vision as if it is real time. It is seeing this vision as if it is here and happening now. Hold this intention everyday and avoid negative thoughts from taking over. It is not enough to visualize something you want, but to also take action steps to get there. When you have a passion for something, you naturally want to dive into that passion. Having passion is a joyous feeling. It's the key to manifesting positively.

Once this is complete, the most difficult step is to then let it go. It's to release this vision and desire of what you want to your higher self, God, or your Spirit team. It's completely letting go of this desire and not caring about it. It's releasing and surrendering it to a higher power. The reason this is a challenging step is because most people find it difficult to let go of something they really want. They fixate on it heavily never letting the desire go. This then moves into obsessive doubts and concerns that it will never happen. However, if this last step is not followed, and you do not let this desire go and release it, then the manifestation connection is not fully made. It may push the outcome further away from you. This gives you an idea as to why your desire is not coming to fruition. You must let it go and move onto the next manifestation. Do not concern yourself with the how or when a manifestation will occur as this will block it. If you obsess over a desire, then you will block it from manifesting. Instead, you will receive negative manifestations or you'll find that you're in a stagnant position where there is no movement at all.

I've always been manifesting, as everyone is manifesting whether they're aware of it or not. I've been manifesting since I was a teenager through this process I describe. When I was sixteen, I knew I would be an author, but I also knew I would have to obtain a regular job first. I needed a steady income. If I were attempting to work on my dream as an author while worrying about not having a paycheck, then this would block me from achieving this dream. My Spirit team revealed the film business to me. They let me know that I would get a job in the creative side of the business, where I'd incorporate my love for storytelling and writing. I knew I was going to get into the entertainment business and nothing was going to stop me. When I was sixteen years old my mantra was: "I'll keep trying to get in until I'm 80." I studied books about the business and then went after notable production companies at full force. I got in the door right after my 23rd birthday. This was when I started working for one of the top ten most bankable and popular actresses at that time. Not surprisingly one of my main roles for her was to read scripts and provide written coverage or a synopsis on the work. I graduated from that particular class after she dissolved her production company. I then made a move into coordinating film production shoots for the major studios. This was followed by me making the transition into work as an author. This is the quick cliff note version, but hammers home that I knew what I wanted with a burning desire, I went after it and got it.

Many struggling to get into Hollywood have always asked me what my secret was to getting in. I was passionate about it. I knew I was going to get into the industry. I had a steady, calm, euphoric positive energy surrounding what I wanted. I use the word passion to describe this process. If you don't have passion for something, then it will show. It doesn't matter what your expertise is or what kind of degree you have. None of that matters. If you have no passion and it shows, then you can forget about attracting your desire in. You need to passionately want it, but then let go of knowing how or when it will happen.

When I first started out in the entertainment business, I had no skills or experience to warrant getting a job in that industry. All I had to sell them was my personality, drive, and passion. I walked in there and conveyed how much I wanted it and how right I was for the gig. There was no acting needed, because I genuinely wanted it with incredible veracity. I went after every job position with this same passion and I was hired. This same manifestation process was the same process for how I became an author. I knew I was going to do it. I clairvoyantly saw it up ahead. I've been following my own Spirit team's guidance, messages, and steps relayed to me from as far back as a teenager. This same process was also the case with all of the relationships I was involved in. I knew without a doubt that I would be with a particular person. Granted, I'm sure in hindsight, I might have paid bigger attention to the red flags presented, but the point is to be careful what you wish for. If the

260

wish is felt with great positive veracity, passion, and steadfast intensity, then you will get it!

LIFE PURPOSE

Your life purpose is an interesting dichotomy in figuring out what it is. It can be what you love doing more than anything in the world. It can also be whatever makes you angry or riles you up. For example, someone who is always getting upset or angry when people throw trash in the ocean. They were meant to come here to do something about it such as joining in with an environmental organization, start a blog, or mobilize to clean up the oceans. This is their life purpose.

To turn your hobby into a career, take action steps towards it daily. You can do this in baby steps. Spend at least thirty minutes a day diving into whatever it is you want to accomplish. If you are working on a book, then spend at least thirty minutes each day writing a page. The universe will meet you tenfold in manifesting your dreams. When you are working on what you love, then it doesn't feel like a drag. You may be working at a job you're not happy with, but when you have something to look forward to at the end of the day, then it raises your vibration. This opens up the door for the universe to step in and meet you half way. You'll be that much closer to having your dream come true. It may feel like a struggle at first, but you will eventually notice the positive changes that are revealing itself to you in trickles over time. If you keep at it, then eventually that love will be your career! It will bring in enough financially that you're able to quit the job you're unhappy with. Ones hobby or love is often connected to their life purpose. However, a new human soul experiencing their first Earthly life may have a purpose that requires they learn patience or forgiveness. It might not be a specific "work" oriented goal, but it could be. It is up to them to discover this on their own.

When you are not at your job, what do you enjoy doing on your off time? What is your hobby? Is it painting? Is it singing or playing the guitar? Your hobby is not surfing the internet, heading to the bar with friends every other night, or shopping for clothes. Those are called distractions, time wasters, and addiction feeders. Your hobby is an activity that you enjoy doing on your own. It's one that gives you an added skill or knowledge around a certain area that gives you and others pleasure. Your hobby is what you want to turn into a career.

Let's look at a couple of well-known entertainers in music history. Bruce Springsteen has been playing his guitar since he was a teenager. When he was playing the guitar in those days it was his hobby and something he enjoyed doing. He was able to transition that hobby into a full time career that lasted a lifetime. When Madonna was a teenager she enjoyed dancing. This was her hobby. She took classes and looked for work that would enable her to incorporate her love for dancing. She was able to broaden that into an even bigger career that has also lasted a lifetime. Music entertainers bring joy to the world and Heaven applauds this.

Many who work jobs that are not surrounding their hobby or passion are more likely to be unhappy than those who are. I have been shown that those who are unhappy with their jobs tend to reach for addictions like alcohol, food, or other toxic vices more than those who are happy with their work. Some of them reach for addictions like a caffeine fix mid-day. They will pop pills to tranquilize themselves to sleep at night and then ingest high doses of caffeine for an energy jolt to get them started every morning. You take something at night to calm down and sleep, and then you ingest something to infuse you with energy to get you going. The days where they are not at their job, like the weekend or a vacation day, they are less likely to reach for these substances. This is a clue that you are unhappy at your job, but are convincing yourself that this is just the way it is.

What don't you have that you wish you had? Is it a great career, love, or great health? Are you at a job you enjoy, but wish you were working at your dream career? Take time each day to work on your career while you work your day job. You will be that much closer to obtaining your dream. You will also have something to look forward to at the end of the day when you leave your job. When you spend at least thirty minutes a day diving into your hobby, then you are devoting time towards your passion.

If you keep making excuses that you're too tired or that you never have enough time, then you push your dream that much further away from you. The right time may never come unless you take control of your life by working this hobby into your schedule. I've worked two full time jobs that include my regular job and my career. It can be done if everything in your entire being loves this hobby. You can turn this into a career if it is work that you are interested in doing. Another clue is that this is work that you would do for free if you had all day to do it. Your finances are taken care of and you are completely settled and secure in every way. You are then able to spend time on this hobby because it gives you joy. The money that comes in from this work is just the icing on the cake.

How would you like to get paid for doing work that you love and have fun doing? It does not feel like work if it is something you love. This is also a sign that it is your life purpose. You should never quit your regular job until your hobby has turned into something lucrative enough that you know you will be able to survive financially.

Chapter Six

TRANSFORM YOUR WORK LIFE

One of the biggest complaints and grumblings I hear others protest about is how tired they always are. Feeling tired even when you are getting an average of eight hours of sleep a night can partially be a symptom of depression. You might not even realize you are depressed because you equate the 'depression' word to be associated with feeling down or someone prone to crying in despair. This is not true. Many work at jobs they hate or are unhappy at, while others are unemployed for a great deal of time. Some work at jobs that pay just enough to survive. Weeks, months, and then years of this pass and the weight of these effects start to take its toll on you. Terribly unhappy with poor diets and lifestyle choices coax you onto reaching for bad foods and addictions in hopes of instantaneous comfort. The opposite is ego driven exercising, which is a form of addiction. This is when one merely works out to look desirable to others. When one is unhappy with their work life, it pushes them to reach for an addiction to keep going. Being unhappy in a relationship is significantly different. Those who are unhappy in a relationship will dive more into work or they leave their mate. When someone is unhappy at work, but their relationship is fine, they rarely dive into their relationship. For one, most people unhappy at work are working 40 hours a week, which is more time spent than anywhere else. The irony is that those who are unhappy find it easier to walk away from their love relationships in an impulse, but will stay at an unhappy job for years simply because it's paying the bills. You allow your job to rule you. Your job is paying your bills, but in the end when your soul crosses over, it becomes obsolete. What matters are the relationships you had with others that have more of a profound impact on your soul in the end. Your relationships are worth saving over an unhappy job.

More people resort to some form of anti-depressant or anti-anxiety medication than ever before. While there is nothing wrong with any form of medical treatment, you do want to make sure you are not on medication for the sole reason of shutting life out permanently. On the flip side, those who might be against anti-depression medication may be the ones who are abusing an unhealthy addiction to *numb the pain*. This would come in the guises of food, drugs, cigarettes, or alcohol. No one around me knows more about numbing the pain than I do. I used to consume anything and everything that was bad for me in order to feel bliss if even temporarily. Often it was on purpose just to cause my soul harm. As much as there are benefits to taking anti-depressants for those who absolutely need them, the down side is that is what contributes to a zombie like emotion-less state of mind. I am not advocating that you stay away from anti-depressants, because they do help a great deal of people who absolutely need them. Life has been tough for so many that they may be unable to pull through. Anti-depressants under the care of a physician can help restore and re-train your mind. The challenge is when you wane off the medication and attempt to forge on in life anti-depressant free. I was on anxiety medication for several years at one point in my life. They did help me get through two relationship break-ups with those who were emotionally unavailable. Those connections coaxed me to take back control of my life and not rely on someone else for my emotional comfort. It also prompted me to discover what I do not want in a love relationship. I would not accept anything less than stability, compassion, love, and trust in a romantic potential.

The average person works full time. This means they are working 40 hours a week, which is roughly 160 hours or so a month.

A large chunk of your time is spent at a job every day with no end in sight. Ensure that you are participating in meaningful work that makes you happy. Couple that with you working with people that you have a positive synastry with. If one or either of those things is not in place, then you will fall into a stress-filled depression. Those unhappy at their job are afraid to leave. They fear dusting off their resume, getting back out there, and taking a chance in a new work place. They have bills to pay and they find some comfort in the security that the job they are at provides.

Perhaps your job is paying the bills and you appreciate that, yet you are still terribly unhappy inside. You are unfulfilled in your life. You're working at a job that you do not enjoy. You find you have to convince yourself to love it just to get through the day. There are several factors, which cause you to feel despondent. One of them can be that you hate the work you do. Perhaps you are stuck in a cubicle and would prefer to be working somewhere in the outdoors in nature. What is a redeeming feature is that you enjoy the people you work with and love the company. You have just enough to keep going, but is it enough?

What if you not only despise the work you are doing, but you also experience discomfort about one or more of the people you work with. You can be working with one person who you find antagonistic or pessimistic. They are toxic and negative in numerous ways. They can be abusive, which is the worst kind of person to be around. Not all abusive people are aware that they are this way. They are unhappy about where their life is too. This spills over to the rest of the staff. Then there is the narcissistic abusive colleague or boss. They are the ones that are aware they're abusive and yet they do not care. They believe that instilling fear is how to be powerful and exert their dominance. Exerting one's dominance through aggressive behavior comes from fear, which has zero power. This is the same trait that a bully has. It overcompensates in an attempt to cover up the real weakness they hide. Assertive and compassionate people have the highest vibrational power. They come off diplomatic and strong while winning respect and a team player attitude from others in the process.

You despise going into work and do not look forward to it, and

266

yet you do it anyway. You do it because you are responsible and you have personal responsibilities to take care of, but inside you wonder if the horrid cycle will ever end. This downtrodden aura around you shows when you are at work, and then you bring it home to infect others you live with. You're the one the others in the office consider to be the unhappy camper. People who feel joy and contentment will shine and radiate. They are self-assured and lovable while still running an ordered ship. Find work that you love and avoid selling yourself out for a paycheck. Spending years at a job you despise will crush your spirit. This is heartbreaking and will keep your soul feeling trapped. Perhaps you work 160 hours a month at a job you despise, and on top of that you work with someone toxic. It is one thing if it is a colleague, but if it is your boss, then that adds an additional amount of issues weighing your soul down. Working at an unhappy job lowers your vibration and keeps it there until you break away from it. Breaking away from it can be through force, such as the company lays you off or fires you. You finally leave the company, or your soul gives out and you leave the Earth plane to head back home to Heaven.

Every morning the world sits in traffic attempting to race to work. You cannot race to work when you have endless cars in front of you moving at various speeds. For the most part, they are all riding with each other, but then you have the one person who is driving too slow or too fast. Everyone is a heart attack waiting to happen for many reasons. It is not just the obscene traffic. It must be stated since this is a common complaint among the 9-6 working class. They are either too tired from not enough sleep or they are fueled up on an abundant amount of caffeine and sugar. All of these exasperates and confuses your state of mind. When you are too tired, then you function in a haze. Your judgment is off and so are your thoughts and emotions. Pumping yourself up on high amounts of caffeine and sugar raises your blood pressure and causes hypertension, not to mention high levels of anxiety. You react erratically to every tiny little thing. This causes more unhappiness and blocks the communication lines from Heaven. The communication lines to Heaven are where the answers are to pull you out of this human designed trap.

The majority of people work in jobs they hate, or work with antagonistic and toxic people. You deal with at least one personality that never jives with your own. This is what your life has become. This is what dominates your world since your job is where you're physically at most of the week. It is difficult to shake it off. You know you fall into this bracket when you leave work at the end of the day and you're too tired to do anything. Instead you head straight home to collapse while shielding yourself off from the noise of the world. If you are not going home, you are heading to the bar with colleagues or friends to decompress. While there you vent or complain while drinking alcohol. Even the media perpetuates this ritual in entertainment where friends head to drink together at the bar to find bliss. This temporarily masks the issues and unhappiness. It does not permanently remove it. The next day the hole that has become your life is in plain view in front of you. If you are not meeting up with friends or colleagues for drinks after work, you are drinking at home to take the edge off. If you are in a relationship, you might take it out on your mate. However, if you are in a healthy love relationship, you may talk it over calmly. Couples in healthy relationships know about balancing the good with the bad. You retreat to each other feeling safe from the noise. Long term healthy love relationships raise your vibration just by being in each other's company and presence. Unfortunately, in this modern day progressive world, many complain they also find it difficult to find a long term loving relationship to begin with. Loyalty and commitment are lacking more than ever in history. This is what happens when your ego rules the roost. It wants to do what it wants you to do without any consequence or regard for others.

The ones that have it down are those who live in areas where there is a low population of people, living in or close to nature, and/or who work for themselves, and/or are in healthy long term love relationships. If you've got all of these, then you're likely in that space of beautiful contentment. There are those that love their job in the big city, but you do not love your job if whenever it is a workday you stress over the slightest disruption. It shows when you love your job. You are the one who is the calm within the storm. You are peaceful, centered, and happy. All of these traits radiate

268

around this person on a regular basis.

Tyler found that working a 9-6 job for someone else doing menial tasks only bored him. It was depressing and crushed his spirit little by little until he was permanently dejected. He would pump himself up with caffeine all day long. He did not drink soda or coffee, but he would use sports powders and B vitamin-energy powders so that he was at least getting some amino acids and vitamins. Although this is slightly better than soda, there are still other chemicals in there that should not be. They contributed to boosting his energy levels in some unnatural way. He would do this to pump himself up with excitement in order to gather enough energy to pretend to be into his job and get through the day. By the time the day was over, he would crash and collapse at home before he tranquilized himself to sleep at night. He would repeat this mantra the next day and so forth. Can you imagine the brevity of this behavior over the long-term?

The self-made prison he created was for a paycheck. He was grateful that he had a paycheck, but this Monday thru Friday ten hours a day drained him. He would wake up at around 7:00 every morning, fight traffic for a half an hour when it should be fifteen minutes. By the time he was back home and settled in, it was 7:00 at night. Sometimes it was eight at night or beyond if he made a stop at the gym or the store. He did not always feel like jumping in the shower to head out with friends. There was zero motivation for much else. He would have an hour or so left to eat and relax before he needed to wind down to get to bed at a decent hour. This is a minimum 8-hour sleep cycle requirement that everyone should aim for. Imagine how tired Tyler would be if he also had chosen to start a family with children. He would likely have to nix the strict 8-hour sleep schedule.

If you find that you are sleeping at least eight hours a night, and yet you are still tired, then you might have adrenal fatigue. This is that no matter how much sleep you get; you are still tired throughout the day. To get through each day, you stuff yourself with caffeine in any source you can get. This only masks an even bigger problem that includes you not being as happy as you think you are in your life. When you are happy, then you experience a natural uplifting high. It is an alert energy you access from God or Higher Power. You crave very little caffeine if any. The stresses of each day are hard on your system and this causes this type of fatigue. The depression symptoms are still there, because unhappy people have some measure of depression. Check with your doctor to make sure there are no potential issues within you beyond feeling tired and depressed around the clock. If you check out fine, then depression and adrenal fatigue may be the common ailment causing this low energy within you. Either way your doctor can adequately diagnose you. It is equally important to examine the trouble areas in your life that could be the underlying cause. When you ask for heavenly assistance, your Spirit team can guide you to the remedies that are beneficial for your case.

Americans specifically and some other parts of the world have this work and no play attitude. They have created a five-day work week when it should really be a four-day work week. Most people who work this type of schedule are not productive on Friday's. Some companies release their employee's mid-day on Friday. Many European countries do not observe the work them into the ground mentality. They have the four-day work week utilized. It is second nature to human souls to work five-day work weeks like dogs. This was programmed by the human ego.

Do you want to go out Friday night? Forget it. Many professionals have little to no energy for that unless it is work related and they have to. By the time the weekend rolls around, most of the working force spends Saturday running around playing catch up on practical matters. Sunday you cannot do much either since it is truly your only real day off. If you have families, then you know the demands of that time as well. Children see their parent or parents moping around the house exhausted and moody. When the uneventful weekend ends quickly, you dive right back into the unhappy work week angry and bitter. Years of this scenario pass by. You reminisce about what you wish your life could be like, and yet you never take any steps to get there.

Tyler wanted to have a career where he runs the show. He wanted successful self-employment, but he allowed negative thoughts to pervade him by asking questions like, "How many people actually get to do that?" As long as you have passion for it, then you can most certainly have that. Keep the faith and build your side business while working at your job. Remain optimistic and positive that the abundance will come in over time. When that happens, then you will be able to quit your day job and focus on your passion full time. You will be able to buy that house you have always wanted with an all cash offer. Home paid for and done!

Your future is changeable and psychically forecasted as probable. Due to your daily choices and actions, you might unknowingly alter your course with a decision or non-decision. You are the manager of your life. You are responsible for the choices you make. This is not saying that just because you find yourself in one toxic scenario after another that you are asking for it. It is a wake-up call to stop the cycle. The way to do that is to make different choices in your life. Break the pattern and make decisions that you might not normally make, or ones that might not be popular. Watch your life start to shift in a new, brighter way. Have faith that change is not only on the horizon, but that it is happening now. Accept that you will no longer be a victim of your circumstances.

If you are at an unhappy job, then start taking steps to change that. Schedule at least one day a week to explore your options for a new job. If you want to turn your hobby into a career, then start putting in some effort into it at least thirty minutes to an hour each day. Taking these steps and having a disciplined routine will start to raise your vibration and help you in attracting in the right kind of work for your temperament.

Ask your Spirit team on the other side for help. Tell them what you want and give them permission to intervene.

You can say something like: *"Please help me find a great job that is aligned with my purpose. This is one that ensures all of my bills are paid. And so it is. Thank you."*

Anytime you catch yourself feeling powerless or victimized, then strengthen the belief that you are the creator of your reality. No matter what is happening, how you are being treated, or how powerless you feel to change certain aspects in your life, you do have the authority. You have a choice and this is what you are choosing.

Even though you cannot imagine how you would be choosing what you are experiencing. Telling yourself this will help you take responsibility in understanding that you are the creator of your life. Take time to recognize the decisions you made that created the situation you are in. You do not need others to give you what you want. You and your higher self can create any life you dream of. The power of the mind can paint these wonders and bring it to fruition. Having one negative thought will negate and block it from happening. Quickly tell your Spirit team to cancel the negative thought you had and replace it with a positive affirmation. Keep your vibrational energy high!

Avoid getting caught up in depressing feelings surrounding where you're currently at. There are positives to every situation. If you're feeling dispirited, then look at the hidden blessings in your current reality. Okay, so you are not happy at your job and you want to leave or move into a position within the company that has more meaning to you. Change your thought vibrations to highlight something positive. For example, feel thankful that you have a job to begin with, and that your bills are paid. By shifting the vibration of your thoughts into something optimistic, you invite that energy in! It will not be long before you do get the job, career, relationship, or home you want. After shifting your thoughts into something positive, then take little action steps towards making your dream happen.

It is not enough to remain optimistic and positive. This is a vital aspect, yes, but you must also pay attention to your Spirit team's messages and guidance intended to lead you to your ultimate goal. You need to take the action steps they put in front of you in order to create a dent towards your dream. Investigate and research the areas of your interest, then dive on in. When you are healthy and clear minded, then you raise your vibration. Raising your vibration opens up the channels of communication to your Spirit team on the other side. They show you the next steps by handing you little opportunities that propel you one move closer to your dream. When you are dispirited, then you do not notice the messages of assistance. Be happy and optimistic in believing that you have everything you want now. This positive view opens your world right up. Many of the Archangels can assist you with this. Call upon Archangel Raphael to elevate your mood when it takes a dip into pessimism. Call on Archangel Michael when you're experiencing fear. Call on Archangel Raziel to assist you in manifesting your dreams.

Chapter Seven

DISCONNECTING AND ELIMINATING

Are you putting more focus and attention into your professional life leaving your personal life neglected? If one area in your life gets more attention than the other, then you have created an imbalance. When this happens, you are more inclined to remain stressed out, tired, and irritable. My Spirit team emphasizes on keeping your life in balance. Do this by honing in on the two most popular areas of your life: Home and work. This is the personal and professional.

Disconnect from the world as often as possible to clear your mind. Running your body into overdrive causes an array of health issues that are not limited to daily burn out. Disconnecting from your computer and phone for a few hours at a time is a great way to start. An even better way if possible is doing this for an entire day at least once a week. Use that time to interact with yourself or a close one such as a friend, your family, or relationship partner. Hanging out with someone who is negative, toxic or feeds an addiction is not using the disconnection wisely. If you are going to use the disconnection time to put in quality time with a loved one, ensure that it is someone who is optimistic, joyful, and makes healthy life choices.

Avoid bringing your work home, or your personal life to work.

You manage your soul and body. Only you know what area in your life is lopsided or receives little to no attention. Take charge and personally manage your day. If you are working too much, then take some vacation time off, even if it is a day or two a month. Focusing heavily on your interpersonal relationships and home life causes strain. Find a hobby or activity you enjoy doing that is productive. Make sure you keep your home and work life balanced otherwise you will experience symptoms of burn out.

STAY AWAY FROM NOISE

I do not pay much attention to the news, media, and gossip sites. It is typically days after a major story has hit the news when I hear about it through the grapevine. By this time, it has already been going on awhile. I discover that the world is in an uproar over something ridiculous or gossipy. I say ridiculous because all is always well. No one truly cares about the story since it's not long before they've shifted their focus onto the next attention grabbing headline. The uproars and the lynch mob mentality behavior are products of human ego. They serve no one and benefit nothing. All it does is add negativity and suppressed, blocked energy onto the planet. Human ego loves to create drama and issues out of a story. This goes for those that soak themselves into a story reacting to it negatively in some manner. Other responsible parties are those who work in the media feeding it to the masses like poison. The stories have a design intended to get a rise out of you and work you up into a panicked or angry frenzy. When in the end everything works itself out the way it's intended. There will always be something new in the media that pops up to suddenly divert everybody's focus onto the latest scandal, end of the world talk, or court trial. Yet they have ironically forgotten all about what they were upset about a week before that had meant so much to them at the time. How do so many live their lives donating so much of their energy into useless noise? There is no point to that existence. This exhausts your energy and keeps you from doing something that benefits you, the planet, and its people in a positive way. Stay away from all of it and focus on what makes your heart sing and brings you or others joy.

If you notice that you are feeling agitated, then the best thing to do is to make immediate soul enhancement steps. Think of what relaxes you or brings you joy. Head immediately to your nearest nature locale where there is little to no people. Breathe in all of that beautiful nature, the trees, grass, flowers, and ask God to surround you with angels creating a healing love cushion. Ask that they extract any negative ions that have latched onto your loving spirit.

If your days have been particularly intense, you may say something like this: *"Dear God. Please surround me with a hundred angels today creating a cushion of love. Thank you."*

When I have said those words on a particularly severe day in the past, I would find that my day would alter from intense to breezing effortlessly through it afterwards.

Are you procrastinating? Are you feeling like you are running around in a circle heading nowhere? This is a clue that it is time to work on breaking away from the self-imposed prison you have constructed for yourself. Break away from running around in a circle and find another path to go down. Break away from anything that is holding you back from moving forward. You may need to go back and re-examine what it is you want and how it is you are going about in obtaining it. Look at what needs modifying in your life. Take that new enlightened information and run with it. Shine a light on specific areas in your life that you are not paying attention to that need some revisions. Those adjustments will lead you towards the Sun and the happiness you crave.

CHECKING AN EX-LOVER'S PAGE

More people than not have admitted to spying on their ex-lover's social media page. If you're obsessing over an ex-lover who is no longer with you in your life on a daily basis for months and beyond, then this is a block which lowers your vibration. This ex has left you, moved on, or perhaps blocked you on social media, email, phone, or phone app with no explanation. Yet, you cannot find a way to let it go and move on. It's a natural reaction to feel immediate hurt, but the goal is to move past this upset over the breakup or separation. You will not be able to if you wonder about them indefinitely to the point where it puts you in a funk. This negative state lowers your vibration. If you're in this state everyday for a year, imagine how stuck that might make you feel. That is until you move swiftly through the negative circumstance by making important life changes and adjustments to reach a place where you're content again. Somebody who is not a part of your life anymore is no longer your higher self's priority or interest.

You might find that you are checking their social media pages from time to time to see what they're up to. You're looking for signs that they might be interested in you again or perhaps you want to see who are they talking to. How about what photos they post online with other people in them? Could they be romantically or sexually connected to any of the people in the photo? What about those who comment on your ex's page? This is an example of your ego desperately curious to know or find out some clues about what's going on with this ex-lover. This lowers your vibration and creates a block in your life. There are no exceptions to this. If someone is no longer interested in communicating with you, then that is your cue to work on moving on. If you feel there is still a connection with them, then message them how you feel once. If they have blocked you, or they do not respond to your message, then that is your answer to begin the process of continuing on with your life without them.

The moment you go to this person's social media page to read their posts in order to find out "information", then your vibration drops. A low vibration is what is a result of being depressed, miserable, angry, or agitated. When you focus heavily on this ex, talking about them, focusing on them, and wondering about it, then this drops your vibration. Your vibration continues to drop every time you obsess over their every move. One sign you are not over them is that every time you read their posts you experience some form of upset, distress, or uneasy feeling. After a year of this you might find that it has ultimately destroyed your life force, work, friendships, soul, and creative life among other things. It stalls your forward movement, until you begin the process of re-raising your vibration again and getting back to that place of perfect contentment. And you will get there with effort and discipline. It's a steady process as you deal with the death of what no longer is in your life to make room for what is. Your interest in the coming and goings of others will decline and you'll notice improvement and positive changes happening gradually as a result.

FULL MOON RELEASING

Release that which has been delaying you and holding you back from positive progress. You likely already know what you need to let go of, but are procrastinating out of fear or indecision. It is anything or anyone that brings you down or prompts you to experience consistent inadequate feelings such as depression, anger, or stress. This also includes foods and substances that are not good for you and cause your body to react negatively such as giving you low energy or irritability. This delays you from taking positive action and in moving forward. Release anything negative so that you can truly be free and soar upwards to where your higher self lives. When you release negative stuff, then you are on your way to obtaining your dreams. Your dreams come true as a result of this release, but you have to do the work. You have to release negative thoughts, patterns, lifestyle choices, and people.

The Full Moon transit happens once a month. It is a great time for releasing, re-aligning, and then manifesting (positively - so watch your thoughts!) Many use the night of the Full Moon to release that which no longer serves them or their higher self. Release anything or anyone that you know is toxic and causes you to experience uncomfortable feelings. The energy of the Full Moon is potent, intense, and powerful. It brings up all sorts of feelings and thoughts. It has the power to magnify and direct your energy in large ways. This is why it is important to be crystal-clear with your thoughts in general, and especially on the night of the Full Moon.

Simply having intention can make this release happen efficiently. One way is by meditating or gazing upon the Full Moon for 5-15 minutes. Take a deep breath in, exhale, and repeat until you are fully relaxed. Breathe in and connect with the Moon so that you are one with it. You can do this longer than 15 minutes if you choose. Sitting underneath the Full Moon outside in order to make contact with you is even better. Sometimes this is not realistic if it is a cloudy or rainy night, but as long as the intention is there is all that matters. Mentally visualize what you would like to remove from your life. Follow that with what you would like to see come to fruition. This brings in your Spirit team by your side notating the work you are putting in to make healthy life changes. Archangel Haniel is the hierarchy angel who you can benefit from working with. Ask her to be with you through this Full Moon releasing process. She awakens your third eye chakra which opens up clairvoyance.

FLOWERS

Flowers raise your vibration, so fill your surroundings with flowers. Purchase flowers or put up photographs of flowers. Having the real thing is the most beneficial. If the only option is a framed picture of a flower due to severe allergies or other circumstances, then that is better than no flowers. If you have allergies, call on Archangel Raphael and ask him to reduce or eliminate the severity of the allergies. Pay attention to the guidance he places in your path where other alternatives to having a flower can come into play.

Lean into the flower and breathe it in. If this is a photograph of a flower, then envision that it is real as you lean in to breathe it in. Notice how wide open the flower is with its arms outstretched. Take it all in allowing it to awaken and open up your mind and senses. Meditate on the flower or image and take a deep breath in. On the exhale release any negative thoughts or lower vibration words that you have been using. The flower's arms expand wide giving you a big hug.

The flowers, trees, grass, and all of nature are gifts from God to help you relax and connect with your Spirit team. God created flowers for numerous purposes. One of them is to surround you with beauty. Beauty and flowers both raise your vibration. It's a double whammy! It is not okay to destroy nature and this world through greed and naivety. Flowers keep this planet alive and to keep you feeling alive. Flowers are little reminders of the beauty that exists in the Spirit world, which is abundantly ripe with flowers. Nature is a powerful sense awakener with immense healing properties. When you take in a huge inhale of a flower, you feel invigorated. Your mind opens up becoming clear, focused, and stimulated. Absorbing nature regularly prompts you to experience the natural uplifting feelings of well-being.

Placing flowers around you can invite positive circumstances into your life. Each color tends to bring in specific energy into your vicinity. The darker the shade of that particular color, then the more intense it will be. The lighter the shade of that color, then the softer the energy will be. If it is a pink flower, it can bring in more love into your life. If that pink is a deeper rose color, then the love will be heavier, more intense. The lighter the pink is in that flower, then the softer the love is or subtle it is.

Here is an example cheat sheet of the healing properties that the color of a flower can give off. Place these flowers around your space if you would like to invite in a higher energy for a specific desire:

- ❖ **Red** – passion, romance, sexiness, deep relationships and commitments
- ❖ **Pink** – Love, beauty, attractiveness
- ❖ **Yellow** – Joy, optimism, success, ideas, thoughts, friendships
- ❖ **Green** – Healing, releasing, cleansing
- ❖ **Violet** – Spiritual awakenings, protection, third eye opening
- ❖ **White** – Harmony, Purity, vibration lifting, hope
- ❖ **Orange** – Growth, empowerment, expansiveness, career
- ❖ **Blue** – Strength, courage, calming, honor, creativity

There are books available on the market devoted to flowers that can offer more detail and insight into the healing properties that exist. Do an Internet search and type in something like: 'flower therapy'.

YOUR LIGHT IS POWER

Show your best self by sharing your light with others on a daily basis. Let it out and let it shine bright. This inspires a mighty movement of peace. The hardness and toxicity that has plagued humankind for so long is outdated. The light exists inside of you. You must allow it to take back the control of your surroundings. Be a warrior of light. Do your best to stay in that space even when you stumble upon a roadblock or a difficult human soul. Demanding people are merely acting out from their ego, which has no power or validity with anything real or long lasting.

The ego lives in fear and acts out in fits of temper much like a child having an outburst when it doesn't get what it wants. You find peace, joy, strength, and love when you remain centered in the light. When you lose your way, ask for heavenly assistance to get back on track. The more you ask for help and work with your Spirit team to reach this space of contentment, then the easier it gets. What can work for you might be lighting a candle and meditating on this light. Call in your Spirit team to begin the process of re-aligning your soul. Empty out your negative thoughts as you focus on this candlelight. Close your eyes and envision that the flame of the light is taking over any negative thoughts and blasting it away while lifting it off your body. Make room in your consciousness to receive the messages coming in from Spirit to help you be at peace and feel encompassed by love.

I have crossed paths with a wide variety of people who have different belief systems and values. I have witnessed those who might disagree with any of this or who find it to be ineffective. Yet, these are the same people that struggle in a constant uphill battle. Or they might be the ones who have been stagnant with no hope for escape. When in those states, your ego dominates your life big time ensuring that you never progress. Within you is the knowledge of all lifetimes. Within you is the knowledge of why you are here. Pay attention to your intuition as that is one of the many barometer gauges that exist within your soul that accurately receives heavenly messages. All human souls receive heavenly communication everyday without exception. It is irrelevant what the soul's personal values and beliefs are, and whether they're aware that it is indeed their Guides and Angels. Pay attention to the messages in order to help you navigate through life much easier than if you were not aware of them.

Keeping your vibration high takes daily work. It's a lifestyle and view change you're adopting. One day you are riding on cloud nine with joy, which raises your vibration. Your vibration remains high until a negative thought enters your mind thus causing it to take a dip again. The next day you go on a drinking binge. This drinking binge prompts your vibration to drop astronomically. It can be a struggle to raise it than it is to drop it. Raising it back up can feel like pushing a huge boulder up a steep hill. Those privy to this knowledge can raise their vibration much easier than someone unaware of what to do in order to get it there. Having an interfering culprit like the ego is what gets its kicks out of double-crossing you and ensuring your vibration stays low. It makes sure that you do not succeed. When you make a commitment to incorporating higher vibration methods into your life every day, then you will notice the changes in your life shifting in a more positive direction.

Chapter Eight

THE POWER OF THE MIND

It is true that having the great relationship, career, and home will not necessarily make you happy, but you might likely be happier. It's a human need to desire the basic materialistic necessities in this Earthly life. It's important to remember that genuine contentment comes from within. Focus on adjusting any ongoing upsetting feelings and thoughts inside you and then work your way out. Unsettling feelings are the ego mind creating something out of nothing. It restricts you from moving forward. You have the authority to free yourself of the prison that is formed by the power of your mind. Both your higher self and lower self are in constant struggle over who is to be the driver of your life. Often times your lower self or ego insists on dominating. It dictates and instructs you on how you will feel or react to something.

If your mind can create this restriction, then it has the power to undo it. The power of the mind can cause you unnecessary harm, but it can just as easily break the heavy chains that latch onto your soul. Your mind digs these holes to bury you in and stop you from progressing. It will do this by prompting you to reach for addictions and time wasters. It will do its best to lower your energy and mood. The false reality your lower self creates has the intention of stopping you from experiencing joy. Ignore that voice and choose to be free!

Re-center and align your mind by taking some quiet time out. Do this preferably in nature where Spirits power is heavy and therefore the healing qualities more powerful. Avoid choosing to needlessly suffer. Wrestle your inner ego demon to the ground. Decide to stand in the power of your high and most magnificent self.

Why does it sometimes feel like a job to get happy? Your thoughts can either cause damage or bring in magical manifestations to you. Which would you like to have? The irony we notice is that it feels so easy for you to think about the things that you're upset about. Instead think about the things you appreciate and love more often. When you're angry or negatively critical, then this adds unnecessary burdens to your aura. Your ego passes it around to those around you bringing them down in the process. They do the same and so forth. You notice how unsafe this makes the planet as it creates an endless pay it forward domino effect.

This dangerous energy that comes from your thoughts expands destroying anything in its wake. You do this by running into other souls and complaining to them. You call up your friends or run into a close colleague and gossip about the negative happenings in your day and life. There is so much energy invested in placing hyper attention on the negative circumstances that you perceive to be throughout each day. The additional danger is that nothing good comes of it. Not only does it darken and lower your spirit vibration, but it also brings more of that negative stuff to you. You are manifesting that which you don't want simply by talking and thinking about it. You can be an innocent soul who puts in the work to keep their vibration high, but by watching or reading any negative media force fed upon you will lower your vibration.

Think happy thoughts, feel grateful, appreciative, and move into the zone of inner stillness. Your vibration will rise and you will manifest at higher levels. Suddenly you will notice everything going right. It's one good thing after another. For instance, you receive a check in the mail you weren't expecting. This is followed by obtaining a job you were dreaming about. You head on outside and take a walk basking in the wonders of your higher self and run smack into your new love soul mate. This soul mate is experiencing the same vibrational rush too since like attracts like.

One soul is plagued with negative thoughts and is terribly unhappy experiencing one hindrance after another. This person finds sudden aches and pains in their physical body that doesn't seem to go away. They're late for work, get a flat tire, and their love partner breaks up with them. This is all in the same week!

You have the power to bring in anything you desire through the positive utilization of your mind. The gifts of manifestation live within you. It starts with your thoughts. You have free will choice to choose how you are going to use those thoughts. This is followed by your feelings. When your thoughts and feelings are balanced, aligned, and radiating with optimism on an equal level, then positive circumstances enter your life. When your thoughts and feelings are negative, then the opposite effects take place.

You might say, "That person I'm attracted to and desire will never be attracted to someone like me. And I'll never get that job."

What do you think you're going to get out of that thinking process? No love mate and no job.

It is understood that as a human soul something will throw your day off. It will spiral you into a negative mood. The challenge is then to be conscious of this when it happens and pull right back out of that before those negative thoughts cause additional catastrophic events to happen. The real reality of what you are experiencing at that very moment that has thrown your life for a loop has no basis for being. It is not real in the way that your higher self and soul know it. You are here in a physical body at this time, but eventually that body will be no longer. The things you fret over cease to exist and yet your attitude still sticks until you realize the truth. Just because others have said that this is the way it must be, does not make it true. This is their reality and the one they choose to live in. If someone is unhappy with you because of who you are and the way you choose to live your life, then the odds are that they are unhappy with everyone and everything around them. This is not your soul's concern to fret over someone else's challenges by making it your own.

Chasing physical interests only pushes it that much further away from you. Those who have an understanding of certain spiritual practices may find from time to time that when things go wrong, they might affirm positive words in a harsh angry manner. "I am happy! I have everything I want! I love life!" You are saying it fuming and irritated. The vibration that is being directed out into the ethers is an angry and irate vibration. The energy darted out is the feeling and your intent. When you feel this angry, it is best not to state anything at all until you've relaxed and calmed down a bit. Cry out for assistance to your Spirit team of Guides and Angels, or whomever you feel most comfortable with. You can cry out: "Angels! Help!" You are immediately heard. If you're going to cry anything out in anger, then scream out for heavenly assistance, since that's the positive help that will be forthcoming. You may need to have patience for any intervention, but have faith that you are indeed heard and help is on its way. This is far more efficient than immediately crying out positive word affirmations in an angry manner. Since it is the tone and feeling behind them that resonate with the universe.

When you are angry or upset, give yourself permission to have a time out and sit alone away from others. Allow the angels to lift the negative thoughts and ugliness off your body. Visualize these eons being lifted high off your body and soul until they are nowhere near you. Take deep breathes in and exhale out any negativity and ugliness. Find a space of contentment and allow it room for your positive manifestations to take flight.

Someone who displays high vibrational traits is a happy person. They feel immense joy and this is outwardly directed. They're optimistic and kind, which is not to be mistaken for weakness. On the contrary, they are strong, yet diplomatic and compassionate. They're calm and peaceful people who show love to others. They guard themselves from harsher energies that might surround them. God gave human souls an ego and free will to act how they please even if it sinks their spirit and lowers their vibration. It is up to the individual soul to discover that the way they've been operating has not been successful.

Communicating with your team of Guides and Angels is praying to God. The billions of prayers that come from human souls look like varying shades and sizes of lights being shot into the ethers. Clairvoyantly it may look like magical white light finger painting. When angels see the lights that come out of human souls during a prayer or affirmation, they see their true higher self banging around somewhere in that dense body they inhabit.

It doesn't matter if you're an atheist, or if you believe in God, or whatever your beliefs are. It doesn't matter if you call it a prayer, a positive affirmation, or just a thought. It doesn't matter if you don't believe in any of it. Heaven has heard you the second a thought has entered your mind. You have put it out into the universe. Your thoughts are prayers and affirmations. All thoughts are heard including the good and the bad. Regardless of the nature of the thought, you will likely get it. The response to your request is matched to the vibration of the prayer or affirmation you are putting out into the universe. There is no set time frame on when your desire comes to fruition. You may get it tomorrow or in six months. If you believe in obtaining something with powerful intention, then you are heard. The stronger your intention is, and the good nature of this intention, the more likely it will come to fruition.

The rays of light darting out from individual souls are in varying shades of light and sizes due to the intention and vibration of that prayer. If someone is praying or saying a positive affirmation, but yet there is no feeling behind it, then the light being shot out is dim. You are heard, but the way the prayers and affirmations are answered is much like an assembly line. Say your request with positive uplifting feeling behind it. It's possible you've grown frustrated and this energy vibration is picked up on in your prayer. Seeing no movement has caused your faith to be shaken over time. The tone behind your prayer or affirmation appears weak. The light of that prayer and affirmation is not seen as strong as others.

In the past, when I've cried out in frustration or anger demanding assistance with something, I miraculously see it come to fruition. The angels do not see your ego stomping around in a fury, but rather your intention. The reason my desire came to realization was it was seen that I wanted it with all of my heart and soul. The energy of the desire is so great that it was matched and returned right back to me.

New born souls in a human body are left at the mercy with

those older than them who do not always know any better. An adult can deal with life's repercussions better than a human child. A mother, father, parent, or guardian's prayer request for help with their child is therefore heard first. Sometimes caring for a child that needs assistance beyond what a human soul can help with results in a cry out for help. This is heard and responded to sooner than later. The bottom line is to watch the nature of your thoughts, feelings, affirmations, and prayers. If you feel your faith is waning, or you're reaching the boiling point of throwing in the towel, ask Heaven to boost your faith and patience. Continue to ask daily if you're not seeing any movement. Some people ask for help once and then weeks later will say, "Well I asked, but nothing happened." It's important to continue to put that positive energy vibration out there regularly. You're also developing a connection with your Spirit team in Heaven. This is rather than only contacting them when you want help or need something.

When I've asked for heavenly assistance, I always get it. Sometimes it's right away and other times it's eventually down the line. I found through experimenting with prayers my entire life that they do help. After you've requested help, you must pay attention to the signs that are being given. When you're bathed in negative emotions, then that blocks your clarity from seeing how the assistance is coming. Express gratitude along with your desires. It's important to include appreciation with your communications with Heaven. Whenever I head down to the beach near where I live, I say blessings and gratitude. I do this silently every time I'm there. I do not take the gifts handed to me for granted.

Sometimes the answers you're looking for come in ways that you do not expect them to. Other times there is a delay as Heaven maneuvers certain pieces of the puzzle before what's needed to know is revealed. There are also the experiences you have to endure in order to reach enlightenment on your own. Never give up communicating with your Spirit team and God. Have patience and faith that the answers will be forthcoming even if it's not on that given day.

Chapter Nine

FIND THE LOVE WITHIN

When you're faced with circumstances that do not jive with your higher self, examine how you arrived at that place. Look at the underlying cause that has prompted you to feel negative when this happens. Identify it, and then dig deep into understanding why it has upset you. There are circumstances that no doubt have made you angry or prompted feelings of discomfort. Maybe you ran into someone at the store who was rude to you. You being a sensitive absorbed that like nobody's business. It ends up putting you in a funk. For some sensitive's, they'll be angry for a minute, others for hours, or you could be one of those who immerses in the energy for the rest of the day. Avoid beating yourself up over it. It just means that you're a hyper sensitive psychic sponge. You have compassion and love within you as all souls do, even though this might be difficult to grasp. Whenever you witness ugliness in someone else, remember that they were born with the deepest love and compassion beyond measure. What you're observing with them is the darkness of ego at its best. This soul has given its power away to their lower self and ego. The ego cannot be reasoned with or convinced of anything, but of what it wants. The ego seeks to sabotage themselves or others. It can be someone who slanders a product they did not care for. A high vibrational soul who is not pleased with something does not waste its time resorting to negativity or in giving it any attention. It only focuses on the products it enjoyed.

When you witness aggression or disrespectful behavior flying at you, then you will absorb that energy. It seeps into your aura and soul. It causes an array of negative circumstances and moods to assault you. What is important is that you find positive exercises that can assist you in releasing it and letting that go. It might feel easier said than done, but when a slight happens in your world, your ego has trouble letting go of it. When you understand this concept of separating yourself from the troublesome ego, it becomes simpler to manage and temper it.

When you have a higher degree of sensitivity than other souls, then you are more likely to be affected by someone else's ego. You're a psychic sponge who easily absorbs the negative or off putting energies in others. It is a gift, but at times it can feel like a curse when you enter environments with human souls displaying low vibrational behavioral patterns. You absorb that negative energy which drops your mood affecting your inner and outer world.

When you grow negative, moody, or agitated, then this is a sign of two possible conclusions. One is that you've ingested a low vibrational food or drink. Or you may have absorbed this energy from someone toxic you crossed paths with.

It can even be a stranger on the sidewalk who walked passed you. If they're displaying low vibrational behavior, then that energy is lodged in their aura. As a tuned in sensitive psychic sponge, you've absorbed that into your aura sometimes without knowing it. Although, the super tuned in psychic sponges are typically aware they just absorbed this energy from someone in passing.

The souls you absorbed this energy from do not always intend to have a low vibration. It's usually done innocently and naively, or sometimes in other words not knowing any better. Some souls have not evolved enough to be more in tune to something outside of themselves. This is partially why that particular soul is living an Earthly life.

Those in tune with the other side, the soul, and spirit, are turned off by harsh people and energies. They steer clear of those who perpetually display low vibrational traits.

This coldness and reserve has grown in others thanks to the technological age. Newer and future generations are being raised on devices that train you to be lacking in honest face-to-face soul connections. For those that have gone out on a date, you've probably noticed some of the typical preliminary questions. They want to know what your job is or what kind of work do you do. What kind of car do you drive? These ego driven questions are externally based. Your job does not define you in real reality, but the human ego has set their life up in a way that their whole world revolves around what kind of job you do. Who cares what you do for a living. Unless you're working in a field that is your passion and it brings you joy, then it is irrelevant what kind of work you do. This passion is your life purpose, but many do not work in jobs that are their passion. For most, it is a paycheck that squeezes the life force out of that soul. They're usually under stress and grumbling about life in general.

When you absorb the ions of negative and cold energy around you, then this can put a damper on your spirit until you address it. You can sit around and hope that something amazing will happen around you that suddenly raises your vibration, or you can address it and do something about it immediately.

Detaching and releasing this energy is easier than one might believe. It can be going for a walk in a nature setting. This is followed by taking deep healthy breathes in and requesting that your spirit team release any and all negative energy that has latched onto your soul. It can be getting together with an optimistic friend who observes healthy life choices, or someone who always lifts your aura just by being in your vicinity. You can throw on a funny movie or make love to your relationship partner. What you're trying to do is re-raise your vibration. Taking basic soul enhancing steps when an assault has attacked your aura can do the trick.

A Vibration Raising Exercise

Everyone has experienced some hard times at one time or another. You have negative things to say about it. The ego fixates on the horrid that came out of that. Rise above your ego and ask yourself, "What greatness did I get out of that experience? What was awesome about it?"

The soul's experiences happen for a reason regardless if they're challenging or not. It is not because you did something to deserve it, but because your soul is destined for greatness. You're here in this Earthly life school to find ways that suit you in order to enhance your soul and spirit. You're not here to find out the latest sale on jeans or rip through relationships selfishly with no care in the world. In order to improve, you have much to gain. When something negative happens in your world, work on looking at it from an optimistic perspective.

An exercise you can do is to pick up a journal or a notebook. Use that notepad as your diary to put in only optimistic viewpoints in your life. When you find that you're buried heavily in negative thoughts and emotions unable to break away, take a moment to pull the notebook out. Devote a page or more to whatever it is that is upsetting you. If it's a person, then write that person's name in your journal entry. Instead of focusing on what they did to upset you or whatever circumstance has upset you, shift that into something positive. Think about all of the qualities you love about the person that has angered you. Remove your ego from the equation and look at that person through the eyes of an egoless angel. List everything that is positive about them and how that affects you in an optimistic way. I know some may grumble when reading that, and believe me I understand. I have an ego too! When someone has hurt or angered you, of course it's going to be difficult to see them through the eyes of love. Know that when you're looking at them through the eyes of love, you're not condoning their behavior and nor do you have to remain best friends with them. You're doing this exercise as a release. It's for your benefit in order to remove that old, tired, angry energy you're carrying around that surrounds the person or circumstance. You do not need that energy, but in order to release it, acknowledging it with love is what raises your vibration. When your vibration is raised you are more apt to receiving clearer communication from the spirit world, which in turn assists you on your path towards abundance in all forms.

Your mind may begin to wander to all of the things you feel this person has done that has hurt or upset you. However, you will not write those things down. Remember this is a positive journal. You will immediately adjust your thoughts back to the positive things about this person. Let's say it was an ex-lover who cheated on you, was abusive, or left you and the relationship. You will not write any of those things down, but rather will focus on their good qualities. If you're only able to come up with one good quality, then write that one down. It is an exercise that takes much effort in this case, because you're holding anger towards this person for doing one or all of the things I suggested. Your ego refuses to see the goodness in someone who has upset or hurt you.

If it is a circumstance that happened to cause you upset, then you will write down in this journal the optimistic features that have come out of that. For example, you receive a traffic ticket. Instead of focusing heavily on how you have no time to take care of the ticket, or no money to pay for it, write down the positive benefits that you've gained from the ticket. You might write something down like: "This has taught me to drive more carefully." That statement feels far better than saying, "I have no money. How am I going to pay for this! It wasn't even my fault!"

This exercise may not immediately change your life, but it will gradually guide you into positively changing your life. It will assist you in getting into the habit of bouncing back from upsetting situations much more quickly. It will help you to view circumstances and people in a more positive light. The key is if you're going to play this game, then you have to play objectively. Putting all things positive and optimistic in this journal is the exercise. Only write your blessings, appreciations, and gratitude for situations and people in your life. This absolutely includes everything and everyone that causes you to feel negative emotions. This might be challenging, but in the end it will be rewarding as you are re-training your mind to think positively. This raises your vibration in the process, which assists with attracting in positive circumstances and people to you over the course of time. Because it raises your vibration, it also clears out the debris that accumulates in and around the communication line to Heaven and your Spirit team. If it doesn't do anything, but allow you to start shining your true loving light, then that is all that matters in the end.

The ego is a wretched problem seeker. It might appear to be louder than your higher self and your Spirit team of guides and angels. This is due to a couple of factors. The atmosphere of the Earth plane is extremely thick and dense that connecting to the other side through all of the toxic debris makes it challenging. Your guides and angels are louder and more powerful than any ego. Yet, when the soul is in the Earth dimension, the communication lines are heavier and dirtier. The ego rises through the dirt. It already rises as soon as your soul enters into this human life. The ego is activated in a big way. When the soul is in the earth plane it's like roaming through life with ear plugs on. Anyone who has put ear plugs on to sleep at night may point out how they can sometimes faintly hear light sounds with them on. The higher self strains to hear Heaven through this muffled sound. When a human soul lives in a higher vibrational state, this allows light in, which gives rise to the higher self. Suddenly that soul is hearing their guides and angels more clearly than usual.

You are not alone as you are surrounded by at least one Spirit Guide and one Guardian Angel from your human birth until human death. They assist you down the right path in order to fulfill your purpose while here. When you are in your higher self's state you connect with your Spirit team on the other side with greater efficiency. When you are in your lower self's state or ego, then you block heavenly guidance and messages that keep you on the right path and assist you in achieving your desires. In my connections with Heaven, I've discovered that all are loved and seen through the eyes of love. Do your best to keep the darkness of your ego in check and exude love full time!

Chapter Ten

PATH TO ABUNDANCE

$\mathcal{I}$t's true that having the great relationship, career, home and car won't necessarily make you happy, but you may likely be happier. It's a human need to desire the basic necessities of life. However, a great many people who obtain these things still protest to not feeling happy and satisfied afterwards. I run in many circles that include those who are obscenely wealthy, as well as friends and acquaintances that are well known publicly due to my previous work in the entertainment business. I can tell you their problems are not any less important than anybody else's. They have money, a great career and popularity, sure, but they still have internal personal issues they are battling that have to be addressed. They have endless flowing money and are not completely content. This is because true happiness comes from within. You start there and then work your way externally. When you are experiencing joy and contentment inside, then the other needs manifest more quickly.

The fine print needs to be stated because often in some spiritual contexts it is taught that happiness comes from within and that craving a great relationship or career will not make you happy. If you are always feeling miserable and then you obtain the great career, it may still leave you feeling empty, but it could possibly offer you added fulfillment that will elevate your vibration. If you're miserable, it is highly unlikely you would attract and obtain a great relationship or career to begin with anyway. A wonderful fulfilling love relationship will enhance your life that is already enhanced. Bottom line is find that space within you that helps you to feel satisfied now, and then the rest will follow. The abundance of wealth, love, and home will be an added bonus that enriches your life even more. You are then able to put more focus on others, help those in need, and change things that need shifting in this world. When you are lavished in abundance, you are in a brighter mind space to focus on your life purpose without the added need of personal worries like paying your bills or finding a love relationship.

The key to abundance is feeling it before you see it. You feel it by believing it. It's in the way that you think and function. You can get there by saying affirmations to yourself daily until its part of your life and part of your soul. I am exhilarated. I am love. I am joy. I am in a place of perfect contentment. All my needs are met. All my desires are met. I sit back in awe at the wonders around me. I am taken care of in all ways. I have no needs because what I require as a human soul flows to me effortlessly. Abundance flows to me like water. I don't need it, but it is there and keeps on coming. I feel bliss. I am uplifted. I am always laughing. I am always seeing the humor around me. What I need is here with me now. I sit in peace and notice the abundance and love flow to me and around me like a spinning wheel. The more content I am, then the more the abundance flows. When I am resistant I am not there. When I am emotional I am not there. When I stand strong in confidence I am there. When I am sure of myself I am there. When I give love I am there. When I allow myself to receive love I am there. When I have compassion I am there.

These are examples of the thoughts that need to dominate your less than stellar thoughts in order to bring more abundance to you.

Let's say you were laid off from your job and you want to pursue the career of your dreams in opening up an art gallery. You know this will cost at least twenty grand in a good area. The devastation of being laid off from one's job depending on the scenario can be a blessing in disguise. It's a great sign to take you out of your comfort zone. It's understood about the ramifications that come out of being laid off or leaving a job in any form. The angels also understand that as human souls we have to survive, we have groceries to pick up, and we have bills to pay. The flip side is that it's almost a blessing in disguise giving you the freedom to choose what you are going to do next. Going after work that is your passion takes some orchestrating and maneuvering.

When I was sixteen I knew I would be writing books. I knew that I wouldn't start writing books out of the gate. I decided to first look for a job where I could incorporate creativity, writing, and storytelling. The entertainment business came to mind and I went on a huge hunt and fight to get in. When I turned twenty-three years old, I was hired by one of the top box office actresses at the time to read scripts and write coverage on it for her production company. It had the best of all worlds I was looking for to incorporate writing in some way. I was doing some writing work while getting paid. This led to the next thing and all great things came down from that.

If you wanted to open your art gallery, then consider pursuing obtaining a job in an art gallery. You're not going to start your own studio tomorrow, but perhaps look for work that is somehow connected to that world and genre so that you're inside. Accepting work as an assistant in an art gallery puts you in the arena of your interest. Be the receptionist if it gets you into that world. Take whatever work position you need to take that gets you in the door of the genre that is your interest and the rest will follow.

We're all teachers and have much to learn from one another. Everyone is important. Everyone has the ability to communicate with Heaven, God, Archangels, Saints, Angels, and so on. No one is more special than anybody else in that regard. Wise Ones help others improve themselves and their life by having a crystal clear communication with the other side. The main messages are of joy, peace, and happiness. Prepare to make leaps of change that you desire. Transformations are positive and life changing. It's like the caterpillar changing into the butterfly and freed from its prison on the ground. It soars out of its protective skin to greater heights. Happiness and contentment comes with change even if the change is unwanted initially. Everything is well in the end.

Chapter Eleven

MASCULINE AND FEMININE ENERGIES

$\mathcal{A}$ll souls have both masculine and feminine traits and energy within them. When you exude one trait over the other, then you create an imbalance that can eventually lead to complications or challenges. This is the same with giving and receiving gestures, which are both masculine and feminine energy. This doesn't have anything to do with what gender someone identifies themselves to be in this lifetime.

Masculine energy is external. It is about giving, action, security, and protection. It's putting outward energy into something or someone. It can be promoting yourself and your work. It can be putting effort into a relationship.

Feminine energy is internal. It's about receiving, nurturing and caring. It's being open, compassionate and receptive. It is kindly accepting praise, compliments, or monetary payment for your work. It can be accepting gifts of any type graciously from spirit. It's receiving love with joy from your significant other and showing compassion for them.

Selfish and self-centered behavior isn't masculine or feminine at all, but one's ego and lower self. If there is too much of either a masculine or feminine energy trait in someone, then the scales tip creating an imbalance in your world. An imbalance blocks the flow of positive abundance to you.

Keys to successful relationships sustaining the distance beyond basic attraction, compatibility, and values are balancing these giving and receiving energies. A successful couple is happiest when they exude both masculine and feminine traits. This is regardless of the genders involved in that relationship.

If you have two love partners who are both "yang energy", or both "yin energy", then issues can arise. It helps when one is more yang (masculine) and one is more yin (feminine), yet at the same time both know how to incorporate an efficient amount of masculine and feminine traits. This applies to all couples regardless of their sexual orientation or gender.

American men have the stigma of being previously trained not to show emotional vulnerability. It was insisted by society that they behave in ways that are considered all masculine traits. Their life expectancy ended up being shorter than women since withholding emotion can cause health issues later in life. Now it's become more on an equal footing where the life expectancy for both is relatively similar. This has become less common over the newer and future generations of souls. The younger generations of men display and express more emotion and feeling, than the generations of long past. This is creating a more optimum balance within the composites of many men. In fact, there is more emotion in younger men than younger women. Some European countries and other cultures never had the odd stigma of how a man needs to behave and how a woman needs to be. They are more evolved in that respect.

Everyone has the masculine and feminine traits within them. The traits are perfectly balanced when you are born into an Earthly life. Once society, your peers, and communities get a hold of you with the wretched ego domination, then they can cause future issues within you that can be difficult to reverse. This is through human ego tampering. Other human souls insist on how you must behave and live your life. They ingrain it into your psyche on what activities you must partake in. This luckily shifts when your soul leaves the Earth plane and crosses over into the next room. Your soul is restored to optimum levels before human tampering entered the equation. This is why it's important to be focused as much as possible now.

Avoid falling into the trap of believing what society and your peers say you must do or how you must act. Refrain from following the herd just because everyone else is doing it. Avoid being influenced by gossip and negativity. Just because a large percentage of people follow and believe that something needs to be a certain way, it doesn't mean it's true. You are a full-fledged thinking human soul and have an accurate barometer within you on what is right for you.

DIVINE MESSAGES FOR HUMANITY

Channeled Communication from the Other Side on Death, the Afterlife, the Ego, Prejudices, Prayer and the Power of Love

Chapter One

HELL AND THE DEVIL: THE REAL MONSTERS OF SOCIETY. THE EGO.

𝒾 receive many questions and inquiries about all sorts of topics that range from dating and relationship advice to what happens when we die. In this book are some of the things that my Spirit team of Guides and Angels has shared with me throughout my life. This particular chapter contains words that my hierarchy Spirit Guide, Saint Nathaniel, has relayed to me with his team of disciples who reside in another dimension in the spirit world. His words essentially come from God, as do all words that come from hierarchy Saints, Ascended Masters, Archangels, and Angels. He has played an integral part in contributing the tough love messages that I voice in improving humanity. He is someone who does not mince words as I state from time to time. He scolds in the way a stern Father might. It is not cruel and abusive, but firm and out of love. He is from the Realm of the Wise Ones and with that comes the nature of a strong spiritual adviser and teacher who knows all. I have interpreted and worded the messages as best I can, even though pronouns may be confusing at times. Grasping the concept and ultimate message is most important.

As a Wise One, I'm surrounded by Spirit Guides who are coincidentally Wise Ones from biblical days. Saint Nathaniel has been around me for a good chunk of my current adult life. He spearheads messages and guidance intended to improve the state of humanity. The former toxic and hate filled ways of life no longer work anymore. One of my roles has been to act as a vessel and translator to relay these messages. As I was growing up, the messages were always there and infused in my work and dealings. They gradually opened up with a more spiritual perspective as I grew older. I have close ones around me who have pointed out that they can decipher the difference between when it's me saying something and when it's a higher guide. There's a broad or profound distinction surrounding the intent, message, and language.

Saint Nathaniel's message
interpreted by the author:

Prejudices towards other people who are different from you have been going on for centuries. Someone's skin color is a different shade, their features appear much different than yours, they have a different religion or sexual orientation than you, and they are lambasted, criticized, attacked, and at times killed! You would think that after all these years on Earth and the progression of civilization that you would have learned something while you have been here. Instead, you allow other human souls and their surroundings to influence you causing one to form a false reality. You are placed here to teach, learn, experience, and give love. You are all here for this reason. Why has this most easy and wonderfully uplifting task been so magnificently difficult for some of you? Working on these attributes accelerates your soul's growth.

You are given a body as a protective shell to function while on Earth. Your Spirit and soul is your true higher self. It is who you are at the core and in all reality. Your body is a vessel you are renting for a short amount of time in order to live and function in the Earth's dense atmosphere. You came into this world for a purpose and it is your goal to find out what that is and master it. It can be something as simple as learning to forgive others or to control your anger. You must discover this purpose on your own.

Your body will not last eternally, but your soul will. Your body was designed to age over a period of time. There is no avoiding this. You can have all the plastic surgery you want in an attempt to keep your outer appearance appearing young. This will not stop the process internally. Your health and organs that keep your soul alive in your body will eventually falter, fail, or stop working. This is nothing to be afraid of. The sooner you realize this, then the quicker and easier your transition will be into the next world.

The average Earthly existence is one day long in comparison to life in the next world. When you cross over into the next plane, your body is left behind to disintegrate on Earth. It is no longer needed as you head back home and move on to paradise. This presents many challenges for those in this lifetime. The ego has become a wild and unruly monster crippling millions of human souls. You force feed negative images and stories to one another on a daily basis off of the internet alone. This ranges from salacious gossip sites to antagonistic news sites and sources that only feature the worst press worthy information provided specifically to control your ego. They blow it up and sensationalize it easily enticing the dark side of your ego. The planet and its people are hypnotized and succumb to its allure. They take pieces of this behavior and incorporate, and imprint it into their personalities. They then impose it onto friends, family, and communities who do the same to others. Suddenly you have this wave of negativity and gossip that has taken over the planet. This energy magnetizes it back to one another tenfold. It causes a flurry of anger and toxicity that plagues your body, soul, mind, and all of your surroundings.

You venture to the comment boards on the Internet, or wherever those who have too much time on their hands frequent. While there you discover criticisms and negative statements about someone else. The destructive tendencies of the human ego are alive and well. This was not what we intended for your soul. You did not agree to this when you chose to live an Earthly life. You forgot who you are my child. We do not say any of this to punish or judge you. The only judging that takes place is the one you produce in your lower mind.

You take everything personally and react negatively mirroring it back to one another. Soon you have a minefield of bickering and snide energy that is unleashed on the Internet and social media alone. This is transported into the heavens and reflected back to all human souls who absorb this into their auras. Some of you do this callously and naively. In this state, you rule your life by your lower self. Many are not learning from their mistakes, and nor are you aware of how you treat others, while the rest of you do not care at all. You are lost in a field of ugliness that you perpetuate daily. You feed off this brutality and off each other's ego. This is done in order to one up the next person and make sure your opinion is the one that is gold.

There was a story in the news featured about a brave fourteen-year-old girl activist from Pakistan. She posted a blog about women having the right to an education. She continued on her crusade despite threats from the Taliban. As a result, the Taliban stopped the school bus she was on and shot her in the head and neck leaving her in critical condition. This is the difference between a girl with no choice and one in America who has several choices.

The media and their peers are training and leading the youth of today. They are more interested in attracting sex or looking desirable than fixing this world. Still – they are more spiritually inclined than any of the previous generations. They have been chosen to bring peace and love into this world as long as they do not follow the path of the ego. These are spirit souls who have made the agreement to enter a human life for this purpose.

Some religions preach about a Hell and a Devil. The real Hell is on Earth. The Devil resides in you and is unleashed with great magnitude. The impact is greater than the largest tidal wave, earthquake, or meteor rock threatened to smash into Earth. Those who stand in front of a pulpit to deliver fiery sermons are not protected or exempt from this. They are given a platform to reach many responsibly and are not encouraged to misuse that position as some do. Younger human souls pose provocatively online craving love. They are naive and heavily influenced by the mirage of the internet's fictitious attention. The photos show where their self-esteem is, at which is not in a good place to begin with. This is what some of you feel the need to do to receive instant validation, which is not honest confirmation at all. They learn this message from their parents, peers, communities, and media. It is a vicious cycle of mythology that has no truth. Your beauty shines through regardless of provocative poses. Many of you tend to put up these photos for various reasons. Sometimes it is just for fun and other times it is an attempt to feel validated and loved. This opens up a bigger can of worms and another plethora of issues that need to be addressed in the world by your media.

There is a rush that some of you get from what seems like positive attention. It is not positive attention as it is false devotion. You are not being loved for who you are, but how you look, and what you have. This is a product of the ego, when in truth you were born with God's holy light regardless of your belief systems. You have discovered that when you post hyper-sexualized photos that you receive more attention. No one is paying attention to you or your true soul dear one. You are blinded by what is not real. Nothing you do can take away God's love for you. These are good children who are misguided. It prompts them to seek out love through unhealthy sources that lower their self-esteem in the end. It makes us sad to see people agonize and suffer for attention that is all a hallucination to begin with. Who you are in spirit and what you set out to do is who you truly are. How you treat others and the love and compassion that you display for others is why you are here. Stay away from gossip, negativity, hate, or institutions that persecute others. You are to be a role model of peace and love. Allow God's light to shine within and around you.

When you pass on and head back home to the next spirit plane, your body is left behind, but your soul is intact and healthy in all ways again. What we in spirit see is a glow around us and around you. This glow has a varying brightness depending on one's spiritual evolvement and growth on Earth. On the other side, your glow is looked upon with the love and attraction you crave. On Earth, you are attracted to the physical look of the body your soul was born into. This attraction is removed as the body ages and dies. Your soul then becomes a light and that light is the main attraction to other souls. If you are inclined to be an attractive soul, then focus inward and work on your spiritual growth. Become who you truly are and always have been. Peer within and ignore the rest of the noise around you.

A dark fog layer has formed around the Earth's atmosphere. This is due to things like the high amount of toxins that human souls consume into their bodies. They consume this in order to feed their emotional states. They consume these toxins to mask the venom that other human souls emit at each other around you. This dark fog layer of thick smog particles appears as heavy tar. It separates the Earth plane from the Spirit plane. It cannot be seen by the naked eye. If you are in a big city such as Los Angeles, you can see the brown dirt that envelopes it looking like a dirty run down mess. This is smog and no one pays any mind to it. They freely breathe in those deadly particles every second and strangely do it without concern. You cannot see it unless you climb up to the top of the Hollywood Hills and look down on it, or if you are on an airplane landing at Los Angeles Airport. This tar is far worse than that as it is made up of dangerous energy. You are all made up of energy. When someone gets angry around you, then everyone in that vicinity soaks that up ruining everyone else's day. It can incite unnecessary anger or sadness out of that soul. People are not accustomed to function on top of one another, as the energy is too intense and not conducive on Earth.

People are having Children that they should not be having. They give many explanations for this, such as God has asked them to multiply. This was not what God intended. Man has taken it upon himself to decide what he expects are best for him and his surroundings while allowing his ego to dictate. This includes those that pick and choose from your holy books on what you want to believe in and follow. Most of the time they pick and choose the content that they believe gives them an excuse to cause destruction, wars, pollution, or any other manipulative energy and harm. They use it as an excuse to suppress others and as a reason to justify their criticisms as if they are high and mighty and the rest have no business with life. This was not what God intended. He is wondering why all of the content on love and compassion, the most important parts of your holy books, have been ignored.

Those that do not have babies for the sake of multiplying have had them out of ignorance. They have had them in poverty or to satisfy the ego and to fill up the hole and void within you. Others have children to save their marriage, relationships, or to prevent their partner from leaving them. The only ones that suffer the most are the children. This creates a domino effect that causes additional suffering in society.

Some non-believers of God contribute to the mass hysteria by allowing their ego to give them free license to function as an animal might. They are irresponsible towards themselves and others by behaving without consequence. Who are you more likely to believe? Someone headed towards a path of love or hate? Those who choose not to believe do so in order to have an excuse to treat others or themselves unkindly. Now the planet Earth is overcrowded causing an overloaded array of toxins that are magnified beyond a human mind's comprehension. If all human souls comprehended this, then this would not be the case. You are in a critical state that needs immediate attention and change within every human soul. It is up to you as an individual soul to enact change. No one else can or will do it for you.

There are those that have been called out into the open to usher human souls down the path of the Spirit. They are here to improve this world and fill it with the love and peace that God intended it to be. They are around you now, or they are the souls prepping to be born into a human body for Earth's future. They are easy to recognize as some of them are ushering in peace while others are spreading love. They are working to clean up the environment and the surroundings on Earth. Some of them are teaching tolerance and love. You can easily recognize them as they have purposes that all lead to the same target: Love, peace, or joy. You feel euphoric joy when you are in love, experiencing love, or giving love. You do not feel this when someone is seeking to harm, hurt, or hate. These are the three "H's". You label each other with derogatory words. Those words are born out of rigid Earthly beliefs. They come from human souls who are blocked from love. The words are construed as values when it comes to your man-made political beliefs by the human soul. This is a waste of time as what is destined to happen is already set. Inciting anger and hostility towards others will not sway this change. Some will rejoice with the outcome, while others will be forced to adapt to it. The rest will fall into more anger and hostility.

The Devil sees you as disposable as he is what you have become. Your lack of love and compassion for your fellow man or your fellow brother has humiliated yourself. I am God. You are to love with all the compassion in your heart that I have given you from the moment your soul came to be.

One of your greatest challenges is that He gave you all egos. There is no way to run from what might feel like a prison, but in essence is instilled within your soul to help you grow and evolve. Even the nicest most spiritual being has an ego. This was God's plan since you are all here to learn lessons or to teach these lessons. You cannot learn specific lessons if everything is made easy for you. The decisions you make everyday make up your character. Your ego tests you as the Devil would since they are one in the same.

Here is a scenario: You are broke and living check to check, but one day you find that your bank made an error and deposited $75,000 into your account. Do you notify the bank of the error? Or do you assume it was for you to spend it and you do? This is where someone's ego might dominate. It is where the more civilized human souls were taught the differences between right and wrong. Be kind and accepting of your neighbor. How many live like this? How many teach their kids these concepts? In the example of the bank error, your decisions will eventually catch up with you and so will the bank and your authorities. Now you have committed an Earthly crime. You had not done anything like that before. This split decision happened when your ego jumped in the way and dictated a false move on your part.

Because you are born with an ego, it is God's will for you to rein it in and keep it under control. The most spiritually evolved uses the least amount of ego. Where you hear threatening and harmful judgment from others, then this is the ego at its worst. The ego is the reason you have witnessed the destruction of God's planet. You were meant to take care of His gift and not destroy it.

312

It is the reason there is abuse, violence, wars, anger, murders, ugliness, and negativity. You have had centuries to improve and yet although progress has been made, boy, are you slow! It should not have taken you thousands of years to get nowhere. Why have so many human souls not caught up with the program? The energy of the world is a loaded gun and a ticking time bomb.

There are angels that alternate surrounding the Earth with angel light wings covering the entire atmosphere to keep the energy contained 24/7. Earth is the most volatile, violent, and hostile planet in all galaxy's and planes that exist. Earth is where souls are firing harsh energy bullets at once. The Earth's atmosphere is like a pressure cooker that can destroy the entire planet. The energy emanating off the angels' wings looks like stardust particles in a massive meteor shower. Only the sensitive or intuitive are able to sense it and see it. They are the ones that are on Earth saving you from emanating destruction. The other human souls, including the abuse of power, and yes even the self-righteous that are delusional into thinking they are good, are contributing to permanent damage. This includes those hiding behind false collars preaching erroneous and harmful information. Those that fall into ego and attack back are no different. Peaceful interaction or no interaction at all from both sides is insisted upon in Heaven.

I am one in millions who serve humanity and Heaven to contribute to the improvement of a place to prevent it from rapidly dying. We gave you things like the Internet and cell phones to be able to connect and communicate positively with one another, and look what you have done with it. It has grown to be devices for narcissism and cruelty. Thank God there are warriors of light who use it for good. The media and gossip channels are the worst offenders using the devices to lure in the most fragile souls who succumb to operating from the lower self full time. There is something we find eerie about strangers pasting their thoughts about what other people are doing. This is perversely sick and contributes nothing to improve your soul.

You turned Earth into a Hell since your environment is what human souls create for themselves and others like them. The sooner all human souls accept this truth, then the quicker your consciousness will finally be raised to stop this from continuing to spread. This will bring peace on Earth. It is time for those who are on the receiving end of this nonsense to put their foot down and say, *"I am not going to take responsibility for you, because you are not doing your job. Your heart is closed. I will no longer be punished because of your indifference. I will not take responsibility because you have chosen to be unhappy and are thrusting that upon others."*

After centuries of evolution not only have you forgot how to love and spread joy to others, you have deluded yourself into believing that one man, a President or ruler, will pull you out of your difficult and struggling lives. The difficulty and struggle you experience lives within you as part of your ego. Religion and Politics are two belief systems you have created through Free Will. They cause wars, anger, and hostility towards other human souls. Two belief systems that become obsolete and irrelevant the second your soul leaves your body. You are in the midst of grand chaos and it is time to wake up and snap out of this design. It is efficient and effective to have compassion. Accept everybody's differences in personalities and interests, rather than trying to force them to change. This brings on peace and harmony for all.

Most human souls are struggling and suffering. They believe that someone in your government or in authority can change that. You are your own authority! It does not matter who is running things. You have all had the same issue decade after decade throughout history.

After September 11, 2001, the U.S. saw the economy collapse as they went to war. This was followed by the loss of jobs as businesses closed or downsized. Many human souls lost a great deal of money in the process. Human souls passed away into the next life over the stress of unable to find work, or due to the loss of their homes and families. You are arguing over triviality, over who should be allowed to marry who, and who should be killed and hurt. Where is the love? What happened to helping those in need? What happened to healing your neighbor and saying one kind word to someone else? Why are you not mobilizing to improve those living in poverty, the children, your economy, and way of life? Why have you allowed your concerns to be misguided?

314

Politics, religion, bullies, and your gossip media are the biggest and loudest ego offenders in the world causing the most damage to the Earth. The wounding done to others is at the hands of those operating from their lower selves. If everyone operated from their higher selves, there would be peace on Earth. Everyone would be experiencing joy and love.

We in Heaven see your flawlessness and your inner light. We know your most intimate intentions, thoughts, and feelings. You can never get away with a lie in Heaven the way you can with each other on Earth. If you put on the act with someone to manipulate and get what you want from them, Heaven knows your true intentions and will block you in the end. You might briefly obtain what you want out of manipulation, but ultimately it will catch up with you and backfire. We do not have your back if you have the intention to harm, hurt, or hate. You will never truly be abandoned as your Guide and Angel works diligently to wake you up. They do this knowing that you may never be awakened in this lifetime. We do not condone evil or assist those that seek to inflict pain or hurt on someone else. We want to work with you to improve God's Earthly paradise.

All souls are here to learn lessons, and many souls have to go through it the harder way if they are here for their first Earthly life. Some have incarnated repeatedly to gain additional spiritual wisdom, while others come into this life to help change, teach, or fix God's world in a positive way. If you are cut off from spiritual wisdom and in being good to your neighbor, and instead opt to do bad things, then you will have to repeat and repay that Karmic debt at some point.

Crises mode was hit as you entered into the year 2000's. Your economy started to tank, jobs were lost, companies were closing up, and then an abundant amount of your homes fell into financial ruin. This did not happen immediately so the average human soul might not have noticed. It happened in trickles until the energy around the globe grew to be particularly nasty. Adding to that, you have more people living on Earth than ever before. This magnetizes the energy put out there if you are operating from your ego. You are granted Free Will to set up life as you see fit. Therefore, human

315

souls have themselves to blame for the state of the Earth life.

Around the mid-1940's having babies and many of them became the thing that human souls decided was best to do. You call this the Baby Boom or the Baby Boomer age, which reportedly ran until the mid-1960's, but it actually continued into the 1970's and 1980's as well. It was what was expected of you by each other. You would grow older, become an adult, then immediately get married, and start a family. You were programmed Stepford Wives. Looking back on this history, you can see how and where you have been conditioned and programmed as a whole.

The world is now the most crowded it has ever been and people are suffering in all ways because of this. With the decline in available jobs, many people around the world have been out of work. You have a rise in population and a decrease in available jobs. You have a rise in the cost of living in an apartment or house, while minimum wage and the average job pay stays relatively the same. This is one of many imbalances in your lives.

The population will gradually decline over the years, as the newer generations of human souls are not looking to get married and have babies. They are thinking for themselves as opposed to the bulk of previous generations. They are being born into new parents in order to stop this madness the previous generations have created. The shift will not be noticed immediately. By the time the shift is apparent, it will take about another hundred years. This will bring on a more peaceful and accepting world then.

This is the end of Earth's final Dark Age. Earth will one day be a place of massive joy. This is being ushered in by the evolved souls standing in line to be born in the upcoming human generations. You are evolving, finding joy, and are teaching it to many of your children, and so forth now. It is a gorgeous mighty movement uprising in the midst of this negative energy from others. You are all each other's brothers and sisters. Encourage everybody to act and behave responsibly with yourselves and with those around you. This includes not having children you cannot afford or never wanted. You put it in your minds that you are under the impression that this is what God intended. He intends for you to love and to give love to everyone around you. Bring forth children out of love and out of loving households and relationships.

It can be taxing on your soul having to soak up all that nonsense energy out there in the world child. Walk away from those that express coldness or hostility towards you. You are to melt all of their icy hearts. Coldness in someone is a learned trait from when you were children. Coldness in someone is due to someone who does not or has not received much love or was ignored by their peers. This started with one's parents or society being aloof and dismissive towards that person during their critical developmental years. Coldness is not to be confused with introversion, which is a shy social veneer that might make one seem cold, but is not once you delve deeper. Cold people lack love in their life and therefore need your assistance more than ever to see the light and joy around them.

One of your quests on learning to love is that you are tested repeatedly. This is done at the hands of those who may not be walking the talk, or who are not spiritual, but superficial. While you are working on your life purpose and contributing to humanity and your surroundings in a positive way, you may wonder what they are offering besides annoyance and grief. God, Heaven, and the Angels see the love and your true self including the worst parts of your ego. Your criticisms and judgments are wasted words and energy.

You have to share this world with those that operate purely from the lower self. Some of those human souls are to have their first Earth life. If they do not learn, grow, and evolve on the first round, then they will incarnate and have to repeat the same mistakes in another life until they get it right. All human souls evolve at different stages in their lives. Circumstances that might seem as if they are happening to you are actually happening for you in order for you to learn, grow, and evolve. Otherwise, you spend your whole life staying at the same level and not learning anything - which for some souls will do just that. They are unaware of the need to learn from the challenges and signs that life is giving them. Therefore, they stay exactly where they are, repeating the same patterns throughout this lifetime and future ones.

The generations of human souls have changed throughout the previous Dark ages. New parents have come into this world at this time in order to incorporate these methods and spiritual principles with their Children. This will bring about peaceful, harmonious and joyful lives. This is a far cry from the more rigid fear based ways of the past where certain customs had to be upheld and were passed on from generation to generation.

New crops of warriors of God's light are being born into this world to usher in this brighter shift of human souls. This is by teaching love concepts and passing it down the family lines. A mighty movement is being created. Those that are not on board are gradually dissolving out of the way.

FROM THE AUTHOR

The angry, negative, or bitter way of living doesn't work anymore, and nor does a lynch mob society. It is all just noise whenever people's ego and values are bruised. People want freedom to say and speak whatever they choose only if it jives with their values. It is the ego and lower self screaming to be noticed and heard. When you experience worry, fear, or unease over anything, you are giving it energy and attention, both of which expand into more of the same. Avoid conjuring up a self-fulfilling prophecy that will cause negative circumstances to hit you.

Do you ever notice that when something goes wrong, that it is followed by more of the same? You may say, "Why does everything keep happening to me?" It is because you are planting heavy focus on it. Sometimes it is difficult at first to not experience some distress over a negative issue, but it is important to take a step back and detach from it. Your ego can dominate if you allow it to. It gets a rush out of controlling you and creating apprehension or fear about things that are not based in reality. There is one way you can tell the difference between heavenly guidance and your lower self or ego. When you receive messages from heavenly spirits, you will never experience fear, anxiety, or dread. The messages they relay are full of love, even if they are warning you of something negative. There is still a sense of peace or an uplifting feeling that all is okay.

Chapter Two

WHAT HAPPENS TO YOUR SPIRIT AND SOUL WHEN YOU DIE?

There are varying theories and beliefs as to what happens when you die. I will explain what my Spirit team has shared with me over the years. They say there is no pain when you die. If there was a car wreck or someone was shot, your soul is pulled out of your body before that happens. Some worry that your loved one suffered a horrible death such as by gunshot or car wreck for example. My Guides and Angels have shared with me that there is nothing to fear or worry about as their soul exited the body unharmed. Your soul is designed that way. It is still possible for the body to be moving or jolting moments after the soul has left the body. It appears as if they are still alive, but they are not. They are alive in the sense that your soul does not die, but lives on. However, the body is no longer being used.

When your soul exits your body, you may hear a sound or a

pressure change through your clairaudience channel when it happens. When you pass into the doorway to the next plane, your spirit and soul moves through what appears to be a large tube or a gigantic tunnel that grows brighter the further into it you move. I found this process into the different soul planes ironically similar to our own human birth that we are accustomed to knowing. The tunnel is nothing to be afraid of and you will have never felt this incredible. You discover that all the burdens of your body and the physical world were merely a painful weight. You grow ecstatic with an overflowing sense of the enormous joy you were originally born with when in the human body. Your soul traveling into the other side feels perfectly natural to you as your prior memories before having an Earthly life begin to rise once again.

The brightest Light up ahead at the end of the tunnel grows even more as you approach it. You are moving towards a paradise as one might have imagined it in their dreams of how Heaven or the other side to be. It is ten times more stunning than in your dreams.

Depending on who you believed in while living in your Earthly body, whether it be Buddha or Moses, that would be who would be in the mix of souls to greet you upon first arrival. If you were a Jesus follower, then you would immediately meet Jesus who welcomes you with open arms. If you were an atheist and you head towards the light you will be greeted by angels, your guides, and past relatives and family from centuries back embracing you with a big party. Your atheism beliefs would soon dissolve, along with the rigid materialistic or egoic beliefs and values that you picked up on during your development in a human body.

There is no judgment before God, but there is what is referred to as a life review. You are brought through a process where the good and bad things you have done are replayed for you. The reason is so that you own up to what you have done if you had not made amends during your Earthly life. This is not a form of torture and you are not being judged. The only judgment that is happening is your own. You sense and know the brevity of how you behaved and towards whom. If you caused harm or hurt to someone, then that would be made known to you. Yes, even your ex-lovers will know what you went through when they hurt you. They will feel what you had felt with great veracity. The pain someone else felt that you caused is felt by you in a much stronger way than you would feel it as a human soul. Part of the reason for this is that as a human soul you have attributes of denial and indifference. This is shed as you exit the body. Your senses and clair channels grow to be incredibly heightened flying off the charts. This feels awesomely natural as it re-builds itself.

When you were in your human body and in the Earth's intense atmosphere, you had a larger ego than you do as you enter the spirit world. You have a much clearer mind and are aware and affected by damage you had done to others on Earth. You know, see, feel, and hear what you have done with great impact. You proceed from that point when you experience remorse and own up to your mistakes. This is part of your spiritual growth before you move on to the next step. You have to make amends for what you have done or how you have caused pain to others. You will feel both how you felt as well as how the other person did as a result of your actions. When you reach a place of forgiveness for yourself and others, then you move onto the next stage. You are shown the good things you have done and the impact that created as well. This is why it is important to examine your life now. Look at how you made it from point A to point B. You are going to have to do it when you cross over, you may as well get a head start. You do not have to publish a book, but you can write a timeline for yourself in a journal. I had at first wondered if people wanted to display their life story, but we do it anyway on social networking, reality TV, and gossip sites, don't we?

There are different spiritual stages in all spiritual planes, so you will not necessarily be in the same stage or place as other people are. This is the same as it is on Earth where everyone is at a different spiritual stage. This is witnessed in all the religions that exist on Earth such as Christianity, Hinduism, Muslim, Jewish, and even no religion or spiritual belief system. The only difference is everyone on Earth is in varying spiritual stages all together whereas in the spiritual plane you are around those who are in similar stages of development.

If you were walking the path of love, you will not be around someone like Adolf Hitler who has had to go through his own life review sessions when he crossed over. His sessions had gone on indefinitely as he was made to feel and experience the pain he caused in others just as you will do. Because he destroyed so many human souls, he is walked through each and every one of those souls feeling and experiencing what they went through. This is a ton of souls he has had to go through and make amends with.

Hitler also took his own life, which has its own repercussions. When you take your own life, you are doing this before your time. There are several things that happen. Many who take their own lives have to go through another kind of spiritual training to get them to a place where they can assist those on Earth who are suicidal. Some may opt to go back to Earth and incarnate again for another run or class while others are asked to go back. If you exit before your time, then the majority of the time you will have to repeat another Earth life. Your clarity is profound on the other side. You feel immense regret and guilt for having exited before your time.

Some souls have an Earthly existence to live a human life and this is their purpose. There are rapidly evolving souls who choose an Earthly life as teachers. Many of them are given an accelerated crash course of several lifetimes rolled into one for a purpose. Before you enter a human life, you discuss what your mission and purpose is with your Spirit team. This is discussed along with the kinds of work you'll take part in. You'll know who your soul mates will be and the kinds of relationships you'll have. Your memory slate is wiped clean to a great extent once your soul is born into the human body. The traits you carry that are engrained in your soul's DNA house the important data you'll need to function with while on Earth. Part of the reason your memory is wiped clean is because if you knew what your mission and purpose was immediately on Earth, then you may rush to complete it before your time. Since I am someone who wants to get the job done right away, they know I would no doubt complete it quickly. It is up to you to come to this realization on your own time.

When your soul exits your body, you are ushered into the Light, but you are not forced into the Light. If you as a departing Spirit are afraid of the Light due to fears of being told of Hell, damnation, and judgment when living, then you may choose to avoid the Light. Atheists may avoid the Light or not truly understand what has happened to them. They might choose to stay in the Earth's spirit atmosphere, which is no place for any departed soul. That spirit stays stuck in what some like to call purgatory or limbo. They roam the Earth plane attaching themselves to human souls. If the spirit was a drug addict or alcoholic they will glob onto a human soul who is on Earth abusing or using those vices. They make it worse for that human soul by doing this as they coax that person on to continue drinking, doing drugs, or any other harmful habits. These are the same spirits where people have reported "hauntings" or a negative presence. If you are experiencing a haunting or a negative spirit, call on God and Archangel Michael and his band of mercy angels to take that soul into the Light. They can do so on your behalf even if the soul had previously chosen to avoid the Light. You have the power to request their removal on your behalf. I equate it to making a *citizen's arrest*, except they are not going to a place that is similar to jail. They are going to a place they will later wish they had done so to begin with.

Many atheists immediately discover there is life after death and they love how they feel when they cross over. During that process, they no longer doubt moving into the Light. They remember who they were before they were born into a human body. Choosing atheism is a learned trait and a decision based on Free Will choice just as any other Earthly belief system.

The Light is nothing to fear, as it is all love where your wildest dreams can be conquered and felt. You can build that dream home you always wanted. You do not need money to buy it. Your Earthly burdens such as jobs and health worries are no more when you're in Heaven. You are who you were before you agreed to be born into an Earthly body. You experience God's love in ways you wish you had allowed yourself to be part of all of this Earthly life. All of the solutions and answers to questions you had are brought forth to you gradually on the other side. You come to the realization that the point to your soul was about pure love. You weep with tears of joy to know and understand that love in ways you wished you had known about to begin with. You discover that all of the things you took for granted were simple such as the trees, flowers, the oceans, nature's wonders, and above all love. You see how human souls have destroyed the Earth's habitat and you wish you had done something to contribute to its survival.

One of the things as you progress as a soul is you can choose any route you like from that point. This can be to train as a Spirit Guide or prepare the new souls that are arriving. You can also reincarnate and have another Earthly life. There are many different paths and choices you can make with your team on the other side. This will all be brought forth to you when it's your time.

You may choose to reincarnate at just the right time in history to contribute something that will continue to improve Earth life. Earth life progresses slower than any other habitat. It houses the souls that are the slowest to learn and grow. When you cross over, it is your inner light that is found attractive, and not your exterior looks. The brighter your light is, the hotter you are!

Many grieved in the year 2012 when a man shot his Mother multiple times. He then went to an Elementary School with a high-powered rifle to shoot many children, some adults, and then himself. It was added to history as a perfect example of true evil that exists in human beings. The children's souls that crossed over were extricated from their bodies before the bullets hit. The day this happened when many were grieving and upset, I was shown through clairvoyance that the children were doing great and were in recovery. This is not the kind of recovery you would have after a human surgery. It is a peaceful comforting and healing hyper-sleep. The souls were unharmed and surrounded by God and the Angels Light. Many angels nursed the souls to full potential. When the souls woke up, they felt immeasurable love and joy. They feel no pain or grief during the healing process. These departed souls are concerned when they see their loved ones on Earth upset. The children's souls soon visited with their grieving families not long afterwards. Days after the deaths, my guides had shown me visuals of the children at one of the most stunning gorgeous and vibrant playgrounds one has seen in Heaven. They were surrounded by Mother Mary, Jesus, and Archangel Gabriel – all of who are so powerful and unlimited they can be with anyone who asks. I found it interesting that they were the three that came through, because according to some religious beliefs, it was Archangel Gabriel who announced the coming of the birth of Christ and the new age of Pisces. Here in this visual, Archangel Gabriel was with Jesus and Mother Mary surrounding the children's souls with their light after their passing.

Some have asked that if there is a God, then how could He have allowed this shooting to take place. You are granted free will choice. This is in order for you to learn the difference between right and wrong. As you gain knowledge and grow from that knowledge, then you experience spiritual growth and evolvement. No one in the Spirit world can intervene without your consent. The ego mind of the shooter was wrecked with anger and pain from being bullied at the school beforehand.

The shooter's guardian spirits attempted to help and stop him from acting out, but if you are not listening or paying attention to the communication that your Guides and Angels are making, then little can be done. You have free will choice and his mind had blocked out the Divine communication that was coming in. His mind was filled up with negative wasted feelings of anger and pain. He was warned along with his mother repeatedly for some time, but both of them ignored the messages coming in from Heaven, as is common with many human souls. This is why it is crucial for all human souls to have a clear focused mind. Aim to live a healthy life so that you can pay attention to the Heavenly messages given to you to make your life easier. This is also why if everyone listened to their own Guides and Angels we would have peace on Earth.

When you cross over, your families from many of your previous lives, as well as your Guardian Angel and Spirit Guide, greet you in the spiritual plane. You meet your Spirit team and the ones you were communing with all through your life on Earth. This is regardless if you were aware that you had a guide and angel with you. I often wonder how there are human souls who move through their entire Earthly life without noticing the slightest hint that they have a guide and angel with them. After crossing over, you will immediately know that you are truly home and showered with

God's impenetrable Light of love. This Light of love is so powerful that it can become so overwhelming that your soul feels as if it will explode.

You will know who the people are who greet you in the Spirit world even if you did not know of them while on Earth. Your memory of who you once were as a soul before entering a human body grows to be fully whole again. You meet your Twin Flame if they are on the other side waiting for you too.

People often ask if they can have sex or eat when they cross over. The answer is yes. All of your senses are awakened when you cross over and you are brought to peak form. If one wants to partake in certain pleasures they enjoyed on Earth, then they most certainly can. What they do tell me is there is a difference between that and someone who is obsessed by carnal desires. Satisfying carnal desires stops your spiritual growth because you are feeding the ego and/or emptiness within you. This is not to be confused with having a healthy sexual appetite that is kept under control. When your soul is whole and healthy, then your sexual appetite is also in that natural state as well.

If you are reuniting with your soul mate or twin flame on the other side, and you both had an active sex life or love together on Earth, and you want one in the spiritual realm, you may choose to continue. Only this time it is better than any other sex you have ever had because all of your senses are heightened to a great degree. You are not burdened with the physical problems that plague your human bodies and psyches such as daily stress, depression, or impotence. If you have those issues while on Earth, they are lifted and left with your body when your soul leaves its human vessel.

I have had others ask me if the spirit world watches us have sex on Earth. The answer is no. They see us all as varying lights and have no interest in spying on you during fornication, unless it is harmful to your Spirit in some way. They are around to guide you down the right path and steer you away from dangerous mistakes. Whether you listen to them while in the heights of passion is another story. They know your thoughts and feelings even if you think you're withholding it from them. They know what is to come for you up ahead in your Earth life if you continue on the path you are on.

There is knowledge you need to gain before you reach a place of knowing your mission. For some people they may have known immediately what their mission was as a child, but might not have known how it would apply to them until later in life.

When you cross over, you will be brought to peak form. This means any health issues you were having are no more. If your human body had gained tons of weight, you slim right back down. If you used a wheelchair, you would not need it when you cross over. Any deterioration you might have had happened to your body is rejuvenated. You can appear to others however you choose. This can include appearing in the image of the age you were when crossing over. However, most souls appear around the ages of 27-34 in human years. If a loved one on Earth has heightened clairvoyance able to see Spirits on the other side, you may not be entirely recognizable to them immediately. The reason is if you were overweight at that age or had a different look, you do not exude that look. It will look like you, but slightly different and more beautifully profound and strong.

You are a soul temporarily inhabiting a body that you came into this Earthly life with, and then the body will be of no more use. The body is allowing you to have life on Earth, and to learn how to love and experience life lessons. This is so that your soul may grow and prepare for the next plateau. In order to be on Earth your soul has to inhabit a physical body. The body is formed within a female human being whom you chose to enter this life from. Even if the woman gives their child up for adoption, you still chose that particular person to enter this life from knowing that she would not raise you.

If you live a long life, then the body you inhabit will grow old as an indicator that your life run has been complete. Actual Earth age years have no relevance to anything beyond that. This certainly contradicts the Media and society's ageism discrimination that they have created and taught the public. This is a product designed by the ego and is not based in reality.

CLAIRGUSTANCE

One night I jolted awake to the smell of an exotic flavored sandwich. It was so potent as if someone was cooking it in my bed. This is a form of what some call *clairgustance* or *clear tasting*. This means that person can taste or smell something that is coming from the spirit world. The sandwich I smelled and tasted was seeping in from a spirit on the other side who was hanging around me temporarily at that time. When this spirit lived an Earthly life in the early 1900's, he loved ordering these sandwiches everyday at his local deli for lunch. My light is so bright that these spirits are drawn to it. The light grows even brighter at night due to the fact that I am in a more relaxed state and away from the stress of the busy streets. I naturally inquired as to why he was eating when I was under the impression that you do not need food on the other side. One of my guides said, *"Your soul does not require food here. You are able to manifest the things you want or once loved when you were living on Earth."* This is true pending it is not harmful to your soul. In this case, this spirit wanted to continue eating those sandwiches he so enjoyed when living an Earthly life. Of course, the sandwich is ten times better than the deli made it where he is now. The windows were closed and it was in the middle of the night. There was no one cooking anywhere in my vicinity. Even if they were, those smells never reach my room.

ABORTION

I have been asked about Heaven's views on abortion. There are souls in Heaven who want to have an Earthly life for the purposes of growth, learning, teaching, or for a specific purpose that will benefit humanity in a positive way. Those souls choose the people that will become their parents beforehand. Some people might have a difficult time accepting that they chose their parents, but it is for the objective of immediate soul growth. Sometimes before the soul comes into an Earthly life, they may play a hand at getting the two specific people already on Earth to come together in love and marriage or at least to consummate so that they can be born into an Earthly life. They know beforehand which way it is going to go.

This same case applies to a woman who chooses to have a baby or wants one. If that woman goes to a sperm donor, the same process applies where that soul is choosing to be brought into an Earthly life by that mother. If the mother is a surrogate, the soul is fully aware that they will enter this life through that mother, but someone else will be their parent or guardian. They will know who that is as well, but they will not have memory of this once born. If a woman decides that she wants, chooses, or needs to have an abortion, then she is essentially preventing the soul from having an Earthly life. Someone once responded to my statement, "So then you're pro-life?" I am not either. I do not make the choices for an individual and nor do I pass any judgment on either side. I merely relay what I am told and you take and do what you will with it.

The mother that is having this abortion is not technically killing the child, as the soul experiences no pain. For the soul, it is more like, "Okay, back to the drawing board." The mother that is making the free will choice to have the abortion is in a sense preventing that soul from having a chosen Earth life. However, the soul that is aborted will have priority dibs on choosing another set of parents to enter this life with. They might also choose to stay in the Spirit world and perform other functions and duties.

If a woman has a miscarriage, then the same scenario still applies as well as if it were an abortion. If the mother who had a miscarriage or aborted a previous pregnancy is pregnant again, then that same soul is allowed to be first in line to re-enter the Earthly plane through that chosen mother. For those that have miscarried and eventually had a baby this can be comforting news to know that it is likely the same soul from before. The soul may choose not to re-enter, but may choose to be the Spirit Guide or Guardian Angel of the next child the mother has. They might also assist the mother with not miscarrying at a later date. It's always important to exercise safe sex practices and be responsible when creating a baby.

Chapter Three

THE SOUL, SPIRIT AND POWER OF THE LIGHT

God created everything that exists in the Universe and all of the parallel Universes. Some say that you are born in the likeness of His image. They are not far off because you branched out of Him. There are sparks of Light that shoot out of His presence. It looks like the kind of white sparklers that you might see in a firework, but there is an abundant amount of this Light shooting out of Him. These sparklers of Light are the individual souls born and formed out of God. This is why you are born with the greatest qualities of God. Those qualities consist of 100% pure, unconditional love, joy, and peace. You are born into a human body in this complete state. Unfortunately, all human souls house the human ego. The human ego tampers with your development as you age in a human body. It teaches you to hate, harm, and hurt the planet and each other. It teaches you to experience negative emotional traits such as fear, guilt, stress, depression, anger, and low self-esteem. This creates a wide array of issues that wreak havoc on your existence in this life. It is the biggest cause of turmoil and upset on the planet.

God is magnificent beyond human comprehension. His Light

is vast spreading like a gigantic blanket that fills up every atom and cell that exists in any spiritual plane. He resides within every living thing, person, planets, or organism. He is in the trees, in the mountains, in the beaches, and deserts. There is no escape from Him. There are Archangels, Saints, Spirit Guides, and Angels who reside in other dimensions as well. They know everything about you from your thoughts and feelings, to what is coming up ahead for you. Many of them can be everywhere at once. Imagine what God is like if He is more powerfully prophetic than any other creation or entity in the Universe? There are ten core spirit dimensions. The first seven are the numerous stages of where human souls go to. Most move into the fourth after the Earth dimension. The higher the number of that dimension, then the closer God is. God is everywhere, but He is even more powerful and present in the higher dimensions. Dimensions eight through ten are filled with legions of Archangels, Saints, or Ascended Masters.

God would never hurt a soul. They are His Children after all. He would never ask you to hurt or harm another soul either. Those who do this and protest that it is in the name of God do not know God by this act. You know God when you exude love. All souls must develop, grow, and evolve. They do this by going to school. This is similar to how earthly souls go to grade school as a child in order to learn something and make something of their lives. This school is on a much larger scale than this. This particular school or class begins when your soul is born into a human body to live an Earthly life. Human souls are on Earth in human form for countless reasons. One of them is to learn lessons in order to develop and grow their individual souls. There are also higher evolved souls born into a human body in order to act as teachers. Many of them come from various spirit realms on the other side. They are the ones teaching humanity about love. Other evolved souls who elected to live an Earthly life are the ones teaching others about love and compassion. They are the ones righting a wrong. If those souls did not choose to incarnate into a human body for an Earthly life, then life on Earth would blow up into an even bigger chaos than it already has. They contribute to keeping it somewhat contained and on the straight and narrow. There are also souls born into human form who take care of God's planet. This is part of how some souls contribute positively in the name of God. He expects everyone to display His best qualities, which are what you already have within you, even if you have forgotten how to access it. This includes love, joy, peace and compassion. This is what a high vibrational state of being is. In my book, *Realm of the Wise One*, I discuss how to recognize some of the higher evolved souls that exist on the planet. They are the ones making positive contributions to the betterment of humanity or the planet in some way. The Wise Ones are typically the teachers. They have an inner sense of knowing. Part of this is due to the many lifetimes they've lived on Earth.

All human souls have an ego which expands once your soul enters a human body in the Earth's dense atmosphere. The reason for this is much like a test. You are not taking the kinds of tests you would take in school, but you have other kinds of tests to take. These are tests where you learn lessons that enhance and grow your soul so that you can be a most magnificent soul. When your soul enhances and grows, then your light grows big, bright, and more powerful. This is what attracts positive circumstances in your Earthly life too!

The brightest lights in human souls are those who display high vibration traits. They are also the Children around the world. That is until some Children develop negative traits learned from their peers, community, and adults. This dims the light within their soul causing them to exude negative traits that have repercussions throughout their Earthly life. Some of those repercussions include attracting in a continuing array of challenging circumstances. Karma is built up due to bad behavior and must be paid back. No soul is going to get away with murder in the end. This Karma is paid back in this lifetime or future lifetimes when you are asked to incarnate repeatedly until the Karma has been balanced and your soul has evolved to a great degree.

The human body you occupy will reach a point where it will expire. This is no secret as every human soul is accustomed to this reality. It might be one of the few things that all human souls can agree on. There is no real death and end. It is only the beginning.

Your soul exits the body it was born into. The light of your soul expands as it crosses over to the other side. This is also when your soul begins increasing and expanding gradually to perfection. This is where you remember the lessons you learned in your Earthly life which prompt you to become a brighter soul because of it. It is important to note that your ego will still be intact. What this means is that if you were an irritating nag on Earth, then you will carry this trait as you cross over. After you cross over, then you begin working on diminishing the negative traits you adopted on Earth. This is why working on all parts of you now is essential. Where you head to after this life has no space or purpose for any of the nasty habits that you adopted while living an Earthly life. Nasty habits are what your ego collects at this time as if it has value. It is corrupt and destructive aligning itself with the Devil. Your ego is the real monster and Devil at play here.

Take care of this planet and everything God created in it. Put a stop to the volatile destruction of your inner self and its surroundings. This cripples and harms other human souls merely to feed your ego, which has no worth or power in the end. When you head back home to the other side everything you attempted to gain disintegrates. Wake up and take your soul's existence seriously. Humanity as a whole has become a spoiled, greedy, materialistic movement. It is time to rise above this weakened ego driven mentality. This, *kill or be killed,* notion that there is not enough to go around, or that you are better than someone else will crumble when you leave the body you inhabit. Always remember to revert to love in order to experience peace.

Saint Nathaniel's message
interpreted by the author:

When you have fulfilled your lessons and life purpose, then you will get to go back home. Home is a much grander paradise than life on Earth. When you understand this reality, you learn that none of this ego based hate filled hunger matters. You cannot take anything or anyone you've crossed paths with for granted. They all

333

play an important part in the process of your soul's growth experience. It has nothing to do with the body you consume which enables you to live an Earthly life. You inhabit the space of the body in order to move around in what might seem to be an intricate design. See the false reality that this is not real in the way you identify your life to be. As a collective, all souls have advanced in the sense that they have made this Earthly life somewhat of a functional place to endure. However, it is not your home base in the end. It is merely one long adventure in a school. Once you've completed this Earthly life run, you get to go home and talk about what you were lucky enough to learn while on Earth. What your Spirit team of Guides and Angels on the other side will ask you is, how about love? Did you remember to love? Did you mend and forgive the Karmic relationships you intended to do? Or will you need to endure another long period of time before you both agree to meet up in a future Earth life to complete the cycle?

You created some wonderful technology to function with one another, but your lower selves have taken advantage of it by treating it with disrespect. This is done in the same manner a child would when it is newly in human form. It reacts to things innocently and naively stomps out of turn. This child grows up to exude that same personality trait acting the way it did in lifetimes past. We wait for you to break the cycle that your soul endures through one life after another.

There are other similar realities to the Earth reality running in other parallel universes. We know this might sound like science fiction. Science fiction is what you have put in your Earthly entertainment designed to bring you joy while you function on Earth. This science fiction is not fiction at all, but stems from what some souls have seen in your mind's eye. Those who do are what you consider to be a star child or person. They are souls who come from world's different from yours, and yet you discredit that this can be true. All souls are psychic beyond comprehension. Human ego takes over and diminishes those telecommunication receptors with us. Every now and then you receive what others call a hit of clairvoyance. You see in your mind's eye the lives you once lived in other dimensions. What you're really doing is communicating with us accurately. We communicate with you so that you can remember who you are as a soul, and know what is important on your Earthly journey. We made this challenging for you, yet so many of you are evolving rapidly and strengthening your soul in this process. Indeed, you have opened up to the other realities that exist beyond your current soul lesson. We watch many souls growing and teaching others about Heaven. Ignoring those who express doubt and remembering that you are not truly home. You will be home soon when you cross over. Remembering to walk the path of the light will assist you in many great ways. The Light will ease the burdens, turmoil, and grief you often experience. Call upon us to awaken your soul and assist you down the right path. Bathe in His love and strength, which wipes those negative troubles away. All is well we always say. This is to remind you that there is no reason to suffer when you are living in the Light. The Light protects you from the evil you sometimes face.

There are different levels and branches of souls living an Earthly life. There are advanced souls in human form sent to teach you a wide range of soul enhancing gifts. All of the teachings lead to the same goal, which is love. Love is the thought form that began when God consummated. His love is overpowering since He is in every molecule, atom, and cell. You cannot escape him. You cannot lie or cheat. You cannot deny Him. He is undeniable. He knows what you were thinking of yesterday and where you will be tomorrow. He knows when you will head back home to Heaven. He knows what you will be doing before that time. He knows what you agreed to do when you entered an Earthly life. He knows when you have strayed from this agreement. When you've strayed beyond comprehension or He sees you have given up, then He pulls your soul out of your temporary body. You are delivered back home to Heaven. You know in that instant what you neglected to do while living an Earthly life. You wish you had this epiphany when you were on Earth and are amazed at how effortlessly it comes to you in Heaven. While living an Earthly life, connecting with us will assist you on staying on the right course. This is so that you do not stray too far from your goal and purpose. This goal is where the true happiness you search for resides.

Chapter Four

SCHOOL FOR HUMAN SOULS AND THE HELL DIMENSION

Why would God create human souls to begin with? Why create Lights that are destructive and hateful to one another? The following chapter is what God, Saint Nathaniel, and his team of disciples have relayed on this.

Saint Nathaniel's message
interpreted by the author:

God knows all souls are highly spiritual at their core, even if they do not remember being in this state. He knows who your soul was before you entered an Earthly life. He knows those qualities were diminished due to society's conditioning. He sees your soul as pure innocence and love. This was the state you were born in. He understands that because He gave you free will choice wiping your memory clean when you were born into a human life, that you will do and say things that are not of God. It is intended that you learn to grow and evolve even if it takes many lifetimes. He knows human souls will act out in fear or naivety. This happens when you do not understand the concept of what and who you are in truth. You are taught and led by others on how to function on Earth. This is someone else's moral compass which is generally ego. It has no basis in real reality. You must reach spiritual evolvement by branching out into independence and figuring it out for yourself. Some will experience an awakening when they reach a certain human age. This awakening will help you remember who you were before you were born. Many human souls are blocked and embedded richly in the material world. They remain blocked at the same level they were when they were Children. They will repeat another lifetime until they come to the profound realization of spiritual reality.

Human ego convinces the soul that you are less than you are. When your soul came into a human life, you were perfect in every way. You become less than when you allow your ego full control over you. You move into this state when you allow your material world to influence your actions. This heavy attraction to material superficiality stunts your soul's growth. None of the gadgets and material items that have been created to entertain you will have any validity beyond keeping you entranced and pre-occupied in a timewaster. This contributes to delaying your soul's growth and purpose. It is okay to enjoy yourself pending that it is not in addictive ways that stop you from moving forward. This is not for anyone's benefit, but your own.

God created souls out of His Light. Your human body is a temporary vessel you inhabit for the sake of an Earthly life experience filled with lessons and growth. An Earthly life is the bottom of the barrel so to speak. It is the lowest level as far as spiritual advancement goes in all of the spirit dimensions. It was designed for brand new souls to go to "school" in order to learn and gain knowledge. However, God and spirit also send highly evolved souls to have an Earthly life in order to act as teachers, healers, and leaders. The evolved soul agrees to this mission, even if they temporarily forget while living an Earthly life. They incarnate in a human body in order to coach and inspire chosen souls who are ready to move to the next level on their soul's growth. These evolved or evolving souls agreed to come into an Earthly life for this purpose. The human souls that have allowed their ego to run their show and influence them poorly are in great need of these teachers. They may come into contact with these evolved souls, but may not likely be aware of it since their ego is in full control. They are lost in the chaos and negativity that their lower mind creates. Eventually there is a point with some of them when they reach rock bottom and are in desperate need of guidance or answers. They are ready to receive in this state and therefore the right teacher for their soul's growth will appear.

You witness negativity, darkness, and violence around you and ask why would God waste His time? His creation is not destroying each other as it would seem. Because that is impossible since your soul is eternal. The harm these particular souls cause are only harmful in ways that is understood on the physical Earth plane. He gave you free will so that you can learn what is right from wrong. The Earthly life is one made up of students. They are the new souls who are much like children that act out in a tantrum. The other souls are the teachers who enlighten and empower in a myriad of positive ways. There are vast reasons placed on each individual as to why they are having an Earthly life. This is one that must be gained on your own time.

This Earthly life school for souls is similar to how humankind has created schools around the world to educate you on the ways of functioning in current human life. Unfortunately, they rarely include spiritual or godly studies. The one reason humankind exists in the first place is exempt from these studies. There is little to no teachings of love and compassion for all of humanity. This is what spiritual and godly studies are. This is partly due to those who make decisions in the human school system have long forgotten who they are as a soul. Some human souls grow angry if the word God is uttered in the human life education system. This is also due to the rise of a belief of non-belief gained through society's programming and human life development on Earth. You are allowed to set up life as you see fit in order to feel comfortable, safe, and secure. These are humankind needs, but not real soul needs. It is much like chasing a mirage for comfort when the relief, safety, and security you crave lies closer than you would believe. These needs are achieved by connecting with the one true Divine source. This contentment lives within each human soul. It is a part of God who supplies all of your needs when you request. God allows humankind to act how they please. This includes using His name in vain, as well as causing hate crimes, destruction and violence. Those that act out in this manner cause negative Karma, which they will have to pay back. This might take them lifetime after lifetime until they figure out that their actions are harmful and not of God. God is all about love.

There is a dimension in existence where the souls who are buried underneath masses amount of ego such as eternal hate, destruction, anger, and bitterness reside in. It's a dense atmosphere similar to the dimension that Earth exists. It is no place for any soul to inhabit and we call it the 'dark dimension'. These souls are not cast there, but their soul moves into that plane willingly. Those particular souls are attracted to false desires and interests. They are the souls who choose to suffer over peace. They choose to be self-sabotaging or self-destructive while living an Earthly life. They are the souls that hurt others while living on Earth. This might have been done through violence or prolonged hate with no sign of remorse and rebirth. They might have been a soul who caused love pain to other souls they came into contact with. This could also be someone who repeatedly abandons a love mate for selfish needs and priorities.

The souls in this dark dimension have very little love in their hearts beyond what they expect in return from others. They have an insatiable need and desire for the toxic material comforts they craved while living an Earthly life. The dark dimension is the least evolved above the Earth plane. They are recognizable on Earth as they are also the ones who display negative traits on a daily basis. They consume themselves with greed and chase needs that have no love in it. They are the souls that murder, inflict destruction, and never see the error of their ways. They are the ones that are oblivious to their surroundings and out of touch with their own soul and spirit. They are callous, but do not think they are. They only have a desire to be filled up with unreal selfish needs. These are the ones that may latch onto a human soul for the sake of coaxing them onto drinking, doing drugs, or causing harm to another soul. They are the ones that cause pain in others on any level. Only this time the pain is mirrored back to them in the dark dimension.

The dimension is like its namesake in that it is dark and dreary due to their manifestations. It is made up of false mirages that evaporate out of the sands when you draw near it. They are the lost souls relentlessly intending on shunning any form of light. Their confused soul craves a perpetual escape and freedom that is non-existing. They design situations that are toxic by feeding their soul rubbish. They are destined to be stuck in the dark dimension until they come to true consciousness. This is by stripping away the selfish tendencies, greed, self-destruction, and excessive carnal pleasures. This is by exuding love in all directions. Only then can they truly move forward. This is a rare and difficult task as these are the same soul's that lived an Earthly life who refused such love when it was given. They do not change when they cross over. They resist the tunnel of light that would only free them of harsh circumstances and bathe them in love. When someone attempted to love them on Earth, they rejected that soul. They do the same in this dimension unable to be penetrated by the power of God's love. Know that the angels repeatedly attempt to bring the soul into the light and often succeed, but there are cases where it is difficult. Since all souls are granted free will choice, they cannot force a soul into the light, but merely guide them into the light.

God's love comes to human souls in many forms including the soul mates they encounter. When they enter a companionship with one soul in a love relationship, then this is the highest form of love lessons for them to experience. The love relationship is what teaches you to love and to compromise. It gives both souls companionship on their journey together. It is what is intended to teach you to give and receive equally in order to create balance. The love relationship teaches you to strip away your materialistic needs and grandiose narcissism when you allow it. It helps you remember what is important. It is the love of another human soul. Your soul benefits greatly from this form of relationship. The reason it benefits more than any other is because you are joining forces with this person who is not like you. They might test you and bring out uncomfortable feelings that you must face in order to expand your consciousness. When you reject or ignore these connections that are divinely orchestrated, then you do not know love or God. This carefree nature is ego driven to satisfy what you want, which has no room for love or soul advancement. These are the souls that head towards the lifeless dimension as they cross over. They carry chains that hold them captive unable to break free of the padlocks of steel that formed from their materialistic and selfish desires. Learn about love while you are living an Earthly life now. Do not wait until your soul crosses over into the dimension that awaits you causing an even bigger delusion of who you are. Give love. Express love. Remember love. Do not treat others unkindly. Do not act out selfishly or recklessly with abandon. Remember who you are in truth and as a soul. Strip yourself of the toxic cravings you have that only weigh your soul down. Think of how you can serve humanity. You are not living an Earthly life to wallow in despair and pity, or to chase greed and cause harm. You are here for the reasons of love, which expand your consciousness. Take action steps to improve your soul today.

PAINTING WITH GOD

God and my Spirit team have explained that manifesting is much like painting. He says that you envision what you want in your mind's eye. You hold the paintbrush in your hand. You gaze upon the canvas and paint your desires on this surface. There will always be parts of the canvas that have yet to be painted. It is this way because you are painting and erasing on the canvas depending on how you direct your thoughts. Your thoughts shift, vibrate, and change throughout the day. When this happens you are painting over your previous image on the canvas, thus changing your reality in the process. You erase it and you paint something new. Sometimes you paint something bad and this is what you get. Sometimes you paint something good and then you back track. You think about what you want. When you do this you are picking up the paintbrush ready to paint this visual on your canvas, but then you take a few steps back. You stop yourself from painting the whole picture. You fear success and what might happen.

I asked, "Is this why bad people that do horrible things sometimes end up succeeding?"

God said, "That is correct, my child."

I felt my connection wavering. "Zadkiel connect me to God."

God replied, "I never left. You did."

"How do I stay with you?" I asked.

"You believe and it is done." He said.

He shows me an image of my soul on the other side as a Wise One and hunter. There is a bright light shining on vibrant flowers and the greenest grass. A radiant colored light shines out of my hands. Wherever I direct my hands, the light splashes images around me as if I am in my own painting. These images are the things my soul craves or desires. This is how you manifest. I asked God if this were possible.

He said, "You believe and then you doubt. This is how you disconnect from what you want. You forget who you are. You can create your reality. You do this where you came from before you took this current form. You did this effortlessly and never doubted. When you are home you will understand."

"Are you one person or soul?" I said, "Sometimes I have noticed that you refer to yourself as *we*."

"I am everywhere. I am in your Guides. I am in the Archangels. I am in the angels. I am in every planet, every cell, every tree, every mountain, every human, every cloud, every particle, every atom, every centimeter. I am in the best of your "self". I am in you. I am you."

"I get it." I said, "Can you tell me more about this painting concept?"

"I've shown you what you need to know."

"I was never painting the entire canvas. I would start to paint, but then erase some of it. I would erase the good. This is done by doubting."

"Now you understand." God said, "See the life you want and you shall have it. Never waver from this thought. If you negate

342

that thought of what you want, if you are indecisive about it, then that is what you will get. Nothing. When you doubt you will get what you want for one second, then you forget who you are and therefore receive nothing. As you are a part of me, you have the power to paint what you want and receive it. There is no class you need to take. You are the example. You are the Light. You are a powerful manifester. Paint what you want on this canvas. Never sway from the good you desire. When you sway, you forget who you are and where you came from. Paint the entire canvas. Keep it painted everyday or it will evaporate off the page."

Chapter Five

THE EGO

Every soul is on a spiritual path even if they're not a believer or follower of any particular denomination. They might not devotedly follow any belief systems, but they are still on a spiritual path. If your soul chooses not to follow any belief system with great discipline, then that is your belief system in this lifetime. If you're an atheist or agnostic, then that is your belief system. It is not uncommon for souls to evolve from one belief system to another while on their soul's path. These are souls who are searching for a higher meaning beyond what may feel like the mundane human physical existence. All souls are intended to gain necessary tools that expand and enhance one's consciousness while on their current path. The exceptions are those drowning in perpetual ego and selfishness. They are the lost ones refusing to believe they have anything to gain or have areas to improve on. It's much like being stuck in hardening mud until a circumstance comes about to knock you off kilter that assists you in looking at the bigger picture. It is the awakening moment where your higher self grabs hold of the reigns and smacks your ego and lower self out of the way.

There is always room for improvement. It's one of the reasons you're here in this Earthly school. You chose many of your experiences for your soul's growth. Perhaps you came into this

344

lifetime battling a drug or alcohol addiction. Maybe you lost your parents when you were young, or you grew up in a difficult and challenging environment. Much of this is not by accident, while the rest of it is what the soul is attracting in while on its journey. This is based on the laws of attraction, energy, and vibration.

The energy surrounding your feelings, emotions, and mood you put out is what will be returned back to you. For example, you could mentally say something positive such as, *"All of my dreams will come true."* However, if the feeling you're experiencing behind those words is one of doubt or sadness that your dreams will not come true, then it is the feeling behind the positive words that will soon come into your world, rather than the actual words themselves. This is in the same way where you cannot tell a lie or get away with murder with those in the spirit world or Heaven as your true feelings are always on grand display. It is as important to watch your thoughts, as it is to watch your moods and emotions. Keeping it all aligned positively and with great optimism is vital to your soul. This is the difference between what your higher self is ruling and what is your lower self or ego. Your ego will sabotage and coax you to feel pessimistic instead of optimistic. Your higher self is what guides you to a place where you're soaring high with joy, serenity, confidence, and love.

Your soul is having human experiences for a higher incentive. If the reasons have not yet come to you, then you can be assured it will come to you at some point. This is either in this lifetime or after your soul has moved into the next room. Discovering this enlightening information is one that your higher self will assist in uncovering as part of your individual spiritual path. No one can point it out for you.

Heaven, God, the spirit world, your Guides and Angels will assist you in attracting in your dreams and keep you on the right path, but they also do not live your life for you. It's your life to live and no one else's. This is why they are called 'guides'. It is to guide, channel, and steer you appropriately in a way that benefits your higher self's goal, but you make the ultimate choice or decision. This is where the ego comes in who will do everything, but listen to your higher self or any enlightened soul being in Heaven or the spirit world. If the ego is conducting your life, then it will do everything in its power to control and direct you down a darker path that is filled with misery, anger, and negative circumstances. Your ego will cause you to second guess the nudges and messages your Spirit Guide and Guardian Angel are giving you. When you raise your vibration through positive life choices, then the communication line to your Spirit team on the other side is clearer. This is what leads you to a much calmer and peaceful life full of abundance and positive circumstances.

The biggest cause of turmoil and conflict in one's life is executed by the human ego. All souls have an ego whether living an earthly life or in the spirit world in another dimension. The unruliest and destructive ego that exists reside within every human soul on Earth. When the soul enters into a physical human body in the Earth's dimension and atmosphere, the ego immediately compresses and then swells up. It is the human soul's higher self's goal to ensure it remains in check while living an Earthly life. The ego is what tests each soul along its journey. It is how one learns right from wrong. The experiences and challenges that the soul has while living an Earthly life contribute to the soul's growth. When a soul learns lessons, it is intended and expected to grow and enhance from the experience. Yet, there are a great many souls who do not learn lessons and remain in the same spot making the same mistakes over and over. The worst of the bunch are the ones wreaking all kinds of destruction and heartache in its wake. They operate from the most ego. They are asked to be re-born again into another Earthly life school in a far worse circumstance than the one they're currently in. This is for the benefit of teaching that soul some basic proper etiquette of behavior. Good people operate from horrid ego as well from time to time. It is common for those who are typically good people to be hit with challenging circumstances that test them by bringing out the dark shadows of their ego. Their basic human nature is good and they're able to effectively position themselves back into positive alignment. This is much different than someone who operates from nasty ego full time.

Many human souls have entered into a human life for the first time. They are known as a 'baby soul'. When the soul is birthed on the other side, it immediately moves into an Earthly life for its first class run. Earth life is essentially a school for these souls. This is similar to life on Earth where you are sent to grade school to hopefully learn how to be a functional and compassionate human being. As most have likely witnessed, this is not the case. What is taught are skills that one can eventually utilize in a human job of their choice, but that is where the teachings end. While this is an important component in gaining skill building qualities for that soul's growth, there are crucial elements that the human ego ignores. Compassion and love are two words lacking in teachings in the human school system. It is also lacking with the way parents raise their children. It's no wonder that Earth life is so chaotic, stressful, and devastating. This lack of compassion and love has been present all throughout Earth's history, and yet it is the answer as to why you are here. It is what all souls subconsciously remember and desire.

Among the baby souls are souls who have lived an Earthly life before. They might be the ones who never gained specific knowledge or balanced out Karma from their hate filled wicked ways in another lifetime. They are asked to have another Earthly life after they've passed on. The soul mostly wants to have another Earthly life at some point. Their perspective on the other side is much clearer than when they were living in the Earth dimension.

Advanced souls in various levels of evolvement have also chosen to incarnate on Earth for important or specific purposes. One of them is in the role of teacher or leader type. This can be someone such as a compassionate spiritual healer, to an author, or lecturer, to someone running important charity companies designed to help heal the world. Earthly life mirrors a school where you have students and teachers. The teachers enlighten these baby souls on the civil ways of functioning and behaving on Earth. You have good students and you have bad students just as you would in any human school on Earth. There are also teacher souls that incarnate into an Earthly life for the purpose of tempering the horrid negative energies which saturate the planet every second.

The teacher souls are usually the ones who enact positive differences, changes, and benefits to Earthly life. Other souls are spiritual teachers whose role is to teach about love and compassion.

There are teachers who might also be scientists, inventors, and even entertainers. These are the ones that positively contribute to bettering humanity through key areas such as bringing joy, love, and compassion to others. Then you have the task mastering teachers who slap a soul away from bad behavior that will harm themselves or someone else.

The chaos, harm, and discomfort that have pervaded human nature for eons are executed by human ego. There is little light that exists in the ego, but there is some good that exists within the compartments of the ego. When you pull away the cobwebs, debris, and dark fungus away from the blinding ego, glimpses of the light within the ego attempt to break out. Having a healthy self-esteem and drive to accomplish and succeed is the lighter side of the ego. Running others over in your wake to succeed is the dark side of the ego. It's crucial to identify, know, and understand when the ego moves from the light into dark.

There is light within a healthy ego that reacts angrily to an important cause, but the anger comes from a place of love. For example, this is where one heatedly reacts with assertiveness towards an injustice or cruelty that was inflicted upon another living soul, animal, or the planet. Although understandable to be infuriated when situations such as this take place, it is more so crucial that one tames the ego keeping it under much simmering control. This is by moving one's logical reaction from aggressive anger and into composed assertive diplomacy. There are different layers and levels as to which the ego operates from. For some it may move up and down into the varying shades of light and dark depending on what upsets it throughout any given day. While others perpetually reside in the dark side of ego, there are some who use very little ego and operate from the lighter shades of self-worth. They are easy to identify as these human souls are typically good natured loving souls who just want everyone to get along. They have a healthy self-esteem, which is good ego in action.

The ego is not something that a human soul can see via the human eye. Clairvoyantly it's no bigger than a pebble or kidney stone. It resides within the soul between the third eye and crown chakras. Not surprisingly it's black with a ring of yellow or orange

348

tinge around it. This reminds me of what a Solar Eclipse looks like. The ego is invisible within the chemistry of the human brain. It's amazing that something so tiny can cause so much harm to oneself or in others beyond immeasurably large proportions.

It's no surprise that life on Earth is challenging and tough for so many human souls. These challenges are spearheaded by one's ego. Having an understanding of the basic functioning nature of the ego and the havoc it wreaks is essential as a human soul. The ego is greedy and wants to dominate. It is power hungry desiring to be number one at any cost. The ego sabotages that human soul and its relationships through poor decision making. The ego destroys anything and everything that it can. The list of destructions and darkness it causes is endless. This is can be with circumstances surrounding relationships, jobs, humanity, nature, property, and people. There isn't anyone who has not witnessed the ego in action. It's especially impossible not to considering that it's in your face wherever you go. Every human soul is given an ego in order to test them for the benefit of their soul's growth. When you display a healthy ego, then you take two steps forward. When you showcase an unhealthy ego, then you take two steps back.

An unhealthy ego would be someone who criticizes someone who is doing well in the world. They would be a terrorist who murders another, to someone displaying road rage while driving a car because someone moved into their lane in front of them. Granted those two examples are vastly different ways the ego functions. A murdering terrorist is not the same as someone who displays road rage. Someone who displays road rage can essentially be a good person, but once their ego is provoked while behind the wheel you witness the monster in control. They're suddenly tailing the other person aggressively to intimidate and instill fear. This is the darkness of ego in action! Next the car ends up flipping over in the process causing a major accident. The ego has done its job, which is to see that soul make errors in judgment that cause a chaotic mess.

An unhealthy ego would bully an innocent person. A healthy ego is someone who believes in their talents and gifts to achieve and make magical manifestations happen. This type of high self-esteem is the light of the ego. This is not to be confused with someone who treats people unkindly in order to reach the top and excel. That is someone consumed by greed and a type of grandiose self-importance, which is the dark side of ego in action.

Spirituality is not only living in the light, turning the other cheek, and pretending that all is okay. It is essential to remain in that loving space, but to also not be naïve to the dangerous waters that ego churns up. There is a darkness that pervades the planet and it is crucial in identifying its source. Targeting the ego's destruction on humanity is what's up in the next chapter.

Chapter Six

HUMANITY'S DESTRUCTION

Why am I here? There's very little that's pleasant about this place. Oh wait, the natural wonders are magnificent and awe-inspiring. This includes the beaches, the deserts, mountains, and all of nature, but none of that is human created. The most blissful pleasant features on Earth formed at the planets conception. It is the reciprocated love between two souls in a committed union working together. It's walking through a garden paradise breathing in clear air and experiencing unadorned contentment. It's having radiant physical, emotional, mental health.

There are billions of human souls on Earth with one third of them called to duty to enact positive changes on the planet in desperate need of it. Every soul is assigned at least one Spirit Guide and one Guardian Angel who is with them from that person's human birth until human death. If the Earth's population is estimated to be around 7 billion and every one of those 7 billion people have two spirit guides with them, then that's 14 billion Spirit Guides and Guardian Angels in the different dimensions working away with that soul they've been assigned to. This is to give you a frame of reference as to how busy the spirit world actually is! Those beings are then working with other people's Guides and Angels to help them in a myriad of ways. Some will assist human souls in connecting in a love relationship, friendship, colleague setting, or other purposes. This is with the goal that benefits the soul's growth in both individuals. Other times it is to assist the soul in reaching feelings of joy, peace, and love. The angels know that when a human soul is in this original state, then they are able to attract in positive abundance. They are more apt to conquering their life purpose, helping others, or the planet in a positive way. They do not enjoy seeing human souls experiencing misery and unhappiness. You can see how complicated this gets when you break down what they're all up to in the spirit world.

Human souls sit in jobs they hate to make money to spend on "things". This hard wired, materialistic, struggle is a product of programming from previous generations. Many want to see a positive shift in the world where peace reigns on all, but that's challenging to shift on a global scale. There are too many opposing sides and opinions with no happy medium or balance. It's that soul's way or the high way. The ego acts out in a tantrum fury on another soul who doesn't believe or follow the things they do. They often do this without having been asked for their opinion.

A stranger reads an internet comment they disagree with. This comment was posted on their social media account. The message or comment comes in the form of a negative, critical attack. The human ego wants to dominate and have power and control. This most primal way of reacting has been going on for centuries. It's barbaric, animalistic, and a poor use of time and energy. Human souls as a whole are unable to wrap its mind around the concept that this way of life serves no one. The human ego is to blame as it prefers to keep you and your higher self suppressed. One might be aware of this when it's pointed out, but it's quickly forgotten as they drudge on with their day-to-day activities. Human souls function like cattle due to societal programming. They are miniscule and insignificant from the grander perspective.

Human ego does not want to listen to a "know it all", because then it feels inferior or secondary. A well-adjusted soul is not threatened by someone knowledgeable or one who owns their life. The ego is all about power therefore it denies guidance and wisdom that is intended to improve and enhance one's soul. The ego wants to be #1 and will not listen to ways it can progress. Its role is to push the human soul down, and prompt them to act out negatively. It wants to sabotage that soul, which the human soul allows. Everyone wrestles with a nasty human ego, however those with an elevated consciousness, or who are spiritually evolving, use less of this human ego than say a criminal who has been tormenting and harming others in some form their entire life. The levels and the degrees of which others use the dark side of the ego are vast and complex.

The media and political arenas contribute to a great deal of the negativity that plagues the planet. It's typically the negative news stories that gets picked up and talked about through social media, news sites, and water cooler circles. This is what gets spread like wildfire. News outlets are known for resorting to gossip instead of accurate reporting. What does this say? Humanity as a whole globally is not interested in anything good. They are lost in the thud of gossip and distraction. If something good is suddenly blasted and picked up around the world, there would be enough people to find something negative to say about it. This is the state of humanity. To not believe this is the case is to function in denial. It's not getting any better despite what some optimists might believe. If it were getting better, then the majority of the stories that would get picked up and spread around the world would be positive stories. Positive stories do not excite the human ego. Ones lower self receives a nice drug high from gossiping and turning everything in their lives into drama or negativity. This pushes the mass majority into feeling miserable and stressed out. They might have blips of enjoyment, but the overall unhappiness that exists within them shines through in what they perpetuate out into the media. They have not come to the conclusion that the way things are in this world do not work. There's nothing good about any of it. To be disconnected from anything outside of your self is detrimental to your soul.

Before the year 2000, journalists went out into the trenches to find a story. After the year 2000, as the Internet and social media took off, journalists rarely went out into the field to report on a story. They scoured the blogs and other less than news worthy websites that had a huge following and basically re-worded the information. It is more or less a cut and paste job to get the same news filtered out and as quickly as possible on any given day. Whether or not the original information reported is accurate or biased becomes an irrelevant factor. Fact checking is no longer on the list of requirements before posting a story. There is little to no journalistic integrity involved in reputable news sites. The real danger is the kinds of media hungry stories that are propelled out into the atmosphere from these sources. This is on the list of what has and continues to damage humanity. It feeds toxic energy out into the Earth's atmosphere that the lesser evolved would deny. There are those who succumb to the allure innocently and naively because it's all they were taught growing up to know. It is that soul's higher self's intention to break away from the monotony of media toxicity.

Gossip media is one of the many leading the pack. The reality is they stay in business because enough of the public's ego is transfixed on it. If there is no interest in something, then it will die off. This has not happened with the gossip media since too many human souls get their fix from it. This is predominant in the United States where celebrities are elevated to the status of royalty as if they are Kings and Queens.

Conduct a thorough examination process within you to discover what is missing in your life that would cause you to be driven by negative talk about someone. What influences dominated your life in adolescent years to grow attracted to gossip and negativity? There is no real reality when it comes to the media and gossip. All human souls will eventually reach this conclusion when they pass on, but why wait until that day? Have you asked yourself: *"What is the point of my existence? This most certainly cannot be it. It has been pure drudgery fawning over what strangers are up to everyday. I need to attack them in order to feel better. I need this rush as my life feels pointless otherwise."*

You cannot watch trash television regularly and be that in tune with the other side. Negative entertainment in abundance is a block that prevents heavenly messages from sifting into your consciousness. The activities that you partake in, which include the

354

media you read and watch, seeps into your perception often without realizing it. Therefore, those that spend their daily lives watching reality TV or reading gossip sites regularly have the least heavenly spiritual connection with the other side. It is a dangerous, toxic addiction to be fixated on the superficial. A high vibrational soul might find themselves reading a negative story once in awhile, but this is about those who fall into its trap and remain there. It's a daily drug fix high to read it, gossip about it and comment on it. For the most part, a higher vibrational soul is turned off by negativity and typically avoids it like the plague.

News sources used to be balanced covering both sides of a story in an objective way. Now whoever runs the particular website or cable station is only interested in manipulating the truth so that it favors that company's personal views. This further divides humanity thus fueling the case of starting a culture war with one another. When these human souls have passed on, they will realize they put so much energy into something that is immaterial and without validity.

The Internet gave voice to those who are in no position to have one. This is apparent on all comment boards that exist on news worthy and gossip sites. This is where the unpleasant side of humanity shines through. This hyper technological world has damaged personal relationship connections. People discover the ugliness that lives within human souls through these avenues. They are not of love or God regardless of one's beliefs or lack of beliefs. It's 100% toxic and there is no room for any other kind of energy to grow beyond mold. The comment boards, forums, blogs, critical review pages, and social media platforms attract more negativity than positive. It's instinctual and human nature to attack while hiding behind a computer screen. No one can physically harm you so you're free to be as nasty as you want to be.

Instead of writing one's thoughts in a diary on a matter, they want the world to know how much they hate a person or group of people featured in the media. It is a form of bullying and bullies act out of repressed rage beyond what they are truly upset about. Their ego needs to be stroked and they need to feel as if they're in a position of power, otherwise they'll have a tantrum. The negativity that exists in the comment boards and forums alone is a mirror of the ugliness that currently exists with human souls. They can pour out all of their repressed or damaged inner feelings out and no one can stop them. This stems from what they've been taught, from their upbringing, and peers. They easily believe this is the way, because they haven't been shown anything else. Comment boards should be banned as there is no real positive benefit to it. They are devices to hide behind a safety net and attack others. It is negative noisy energy that does nothing to help anyone.

Chapter Seven

MASS HYSTERIA AND SPIRITUALISM

The top baby makers continue to be those lacking in a primary elementary education and those living in poverty. They bring masses of Children they cannot afford into the world and resort to abusing them. The children end up homeless, unloved, and without basic education. The wise tend to be more responsible when they have a child ensuring they are indeed evolved enough, strong enough, and with enough resources to raise a child. Those who do not hold those qualities have the baby anyway out of a selfish desire, or through society's programming urging them that they must procreate. It is an egotistical decision to bring a child into conditions which are harmful and unrealistic for the raising of a child. If you do not make enough financially, then you should not be bringing a child into your environment. If you are emotionally unstable, then bringing a child into your surroundings is not wise. There are egos that believe it is what God wants - which is an untrue myth. There are over seven billion human souls all around the planet at this time. Human souls have procreated enough. They've created mass hysteria globally in the process. Many of those babies grow up uneducated and living in poverty as well. When they grow older, they repeat the same cycle multiplying at a dangerous rate. Only this time the reproduction of human souls is too great to control. They have not reached a full level of awareness to see the concept of this poor design, nor do they care. When someone cares, it shows through their actions and life choices. The ego is at the helms in these scenarios as it is more interested in riling itself up dramatically over petty issues rather than facing and correcting the real problems that exist within the confines of humanity.

There are wise human souls who have been brought up in poverty and without education. There are also great deals of privileged educated human souls who lack in love, compassion, and common sense etiquette and intelligence. It is important to understand these are generalities and not specifics. *Warriors of lights* are being born into challenging conditions of poverty and a lack of education in the human school system. They are naturally connected with the soul, spirit, a higher purpose, and cause. They are the rare breed breaking away from the cycles of being brought into a challenging environment. It is a smaller percentage compared to the overall number of people being pushed out into the world in horrid unlivable conditions. The souls gain essential qualities while in those circumstances, which they soon apply towards their life purpose.

There are more people in the world than ever in Earth's history. Newer souls entering an Earthly life are more evolved than the previous generations while purposely opting not to reproduce. The world will gradually notice a drop in the astronomical seven billion population number. This won't be evident until the year 2150 and beyond. One of the main issues is those below the poverty level line are the ones reproducing by the masses. Much of this is due to the rule of the ego, which prompts the soul to make poor life choices. This isn't a matter of scolding or pointing the finger as all souls are living an Earthly life for the purpose of growth, learning, or teaching. The intent is to wake others up to the damage being created. Those who are a part of this design will never see these words. If they do, they will likely deny it, not understand it, or respond with insult. This would be an admission of guilt by the soul's ego. When you're in school and you make a healthy array of mistakes on a project or test, a good teacher likely writes on the paper: "See me." A teacher displays concern to discuss the errors made in order to correct them. It is for the student's benefit in the end. This same concept applies to the *Earthly Soul Life School System*. Only this school has a much greater impact since it lasts lifetime after lifetime and beyond.

One day far out in the distance, there will be no government in the United States. The White House will become a landmark museum for tourists in the later centuries. Anarchy began its rise in the late 1990's and into the 2000's just as the Internet and social media rose simultaneously. The Internet and social media gave birth to anarchy. The anarchy and lack of government will blow up into chaos down the line. Many who are self-aware and in tune notice the signs of this happening currently in small bursts. The masses do not see it, because if they did they would make contributions to stop it. Change starts within every human soul. The change will not happen from a ruler, the government, or President. You cannot change on a global scale without first opening up the minds within every individual soul.

The mass majority has set the way others must live. It is all about others succumbing, folding, and agreeing with that point of view. The ego stomps around screaming about what isn't being done for them and how unhappy it is. It is interested in being heard, supported, and loved. Ironically those are traits that come from within the higher self, yet the ego and lower self disconnects from the access of the higher self and searches outside of themselves to find it. You'll be searching forever until you discover this truth on your own.

Organized religion will diminish and move into the bare minimum as spiritualism rises. The future generations want peace and quiet. They will aim to conquer this goal over time. There is less anger, judgment, and hate involved with someone who operates from a high vibration. Souls in the spirit world, different planes, and realms are standing in line to be born to usher in this change. Many of them are moving in the direction of unity more than ever in Earth's history. They are moving away from what they consider religious dogma. Instead - they remain open and connected to God or a higher power and force in a bigger way. Some of them are getting lost along the way by believing in nothing. This is that soul's particular spiritual path. There is and will be a rise in the upcoming souls who retain their spirit connection from the point of birth. They are able to do this through a diminished usage of the dark sides of their ego. They will remain believers in something grander than the human body. Many human souls want peace and love in the end. They are over the old, tired, argumentative, hate-filled, critical, and violent ways. The latter has got humanity nowhere fast. You're still fighting for the same power and dominance you were fighting for centuries ago. Are you done with your tantrum yet?

There has been a shift taking place where advanced souls on the other side and from the various spirit realms are being born into a human body. They are easy to spot as they are highly connected to the other side. There are more being born now than ever in history. This is partly due to the massive outburst in population that has plagued the globe. When you have more people on the planet, then you need more soldiers of the light to counter balance this. The advanced souls that incarnate into an Earthly life have to drudge through a human experience with challenges that get in the way of their life purpose. Luckily, these souls will pick up on this inner calling that is connected to an improvement of humanity and the planet at some point in their human life. They are the ones who contribute to this positive shift of making the planet a more peaceful and harmonious place. Some do this through peaceful activism. While others shine their inner light on all those they come into contact with. Love is contagious and enough of it will stomp out the darkness on the planet.

When human souls are born, they are operating at top capacity. They are 100% connected, psychic, and in tune. That is until society, their peers, and surroundings quickly influence them. This causes an array of blocks which prevents the input of heavenly guidance and messages from reaching them. Since they are receiving no input or are unaware of where it's coming from, they come to the conclusion that they must indeed be alone. It is the belief that there is no afterlife, spirit world, Heaven or God, and all psychics are scams or frauds. This would mean they are a fraud since all human souls are born psychic. This is part of where the rise of Atheism or Agnostic beliefs has come out of. This was innocently picked up on during one's upbringing. While some have converted to a no belief system preceding a non-stop array of challenging circumstances that hit them. They might have grown up in a household where it was never discussed, or they asked for help and felt they received none. This is where faith comes in to empower you.

Science and spirituality should work together instead of trying to oppose one another. Opposing gets you nowhere. Being open to all possibilities gets you everywhere! Scoffing doubts are a lower energy and you do not want to remain in that space marinating in it for too long.

As spiritualism rises, religion moves into the bare minority. This is currently being seen as Churches attempt to attract in members. Other Church congregations are evolving and altering their services to be more open minded and inclusive of all people in order to bring in members. They are also seeing the love in all of God's creations instead of pushing the Hell and Damnation card for all eternity. That was man-made superstition instructed to the masses during the deep dark ages when man was afraid of everything and full of fear of the unknown. To still be playing that card stunts your spiritual growth possibilities. Fearful superstition comes from the darkness of ego.

Human souls are finding out the answers for themselves. They are tuning in like they used to in centuries past. They will tune in more instead of relying on what their friends or peers are feeding them. As other souls move away from the hardcore religious establishments that have been more judgmental, the world will also see a decline in atheism. Atheism was birthed out of its Mother, which was hardcore religious dogma. It's ironic that one extreme side is responsible for creating another extreme side. Many who are atheist have admitted that their reason for becoming so was due to their upbringing and the harsh brainwashing at the hands of a religious fanatic. If this wasn't the case, it was by being fed this negative perception of religion by the dominating media. The unfortunate side to this was that both sides spawned out of some form of judgment and hate. This causes those blocks which prevents someone from remembering or being in touch with their true nature, or something outside of themselves. There is no big man in the sky instructing orders that cause destruction to humankind. This is also not the end when your body has officially reached its current human death.

Being too extreme causes the most friction and unhappiness in human souls. With no room to breathe within the harsh confines of one's mind creates an array of walls difficult to scale. It's the biggest cause of anger, stress, hate, wars, and hostility. This is by being too Democratic, too Republican, too evangelical, too atheist, too left wing, too right wing, and the list goes on and on. Being too rigid and on one side of the fence doesn't bring people together, but rather separates them even more. It creates antagonism instead of peace. This is taught by the ego in one's peers, society, and surroundings. It's not something that is developed on its own. You were not born rigid and unloving.

It is important to have room for movement and an understanding of others. Avoid forcing engrained harmful beliefs on those who are choosing a peaceful path. This is when someone volunteer's information to someone that says that they're going to Hell. It's when a stranger retaliates against someone for having a different opinion or belief system. It is against God's law to enforce and demand that someone follow your personal belief system. To angrily attempt to debunk something you do not believe in comes from the dark side of one's ego. There is no love or God for that matter in that space. Souls have been granted free will to choose how they wish to live their human life without interference from other human souls. This is in keeping that they are not harming or hurting themselves or someone else. The free will law causes so many mistakes in this world, but you are granted that freedom for a reason. You need to make mistakes to learn and grow your light.

There are human souls who have no real connection to the other side. Some have no belief in anything except making money. They're not living a life of joy, peace, and harmony. They're working 9-6 jobs that are cutthroat. They are in their cars driving under stress with aggression nearly running over pedestrians and other cars. They're not extending kind words when someone does something nice for them. They are not saying thank you when someone holds the door open for them. They are miserable and unappreciative while deteriorating at a rapid pace without realizing it. It saddens Heaven to see this pain and loss of love in so many souls. The nature of how life on Earth has been designed by human souls has been constructed in a way that kills that soul gradually over time. Hostile human souls have risen to the surface. They are prevalent in great numbers unable to effectively navigate through the intensified energies. Human souls are the number one greatest contributors to unhappiness and misery in themselves and in those around them. Who else do you think is causing this? Someone's cat? God? No. The human soul's ego is to blame for the agony and suffering that exists.

Earth has unfriendly energy flying around in immeasurably dangerous ways. It makes you feel like you have to be on constant guard. You move about ready to fight off all those that come at you with their antagonistic energy. Perhaps you have the stance of always having to defend your territory from those that attempt to enter your vicinity without your permission. When this happens on a severe scale, Mother Mary says she comes into your life to say that this requires silence. She says when this happens it is a sign that you must disconnect and turn it off in all areas you are able to. Shut it down and go completely still and dark. Disappear and extricate yourself from anything hostile around you. Avoid getting involved with others if possible at that time. It's understood that you might have obligations in your life where you have to face others. This might be at your job or you have to go to the store where you know it will be crowded. Mary urges for silence whenever and however possible in the cases of hostility. Escape to a quiet location if you can. This is preferably in nature or you can create a calming sanctuary at home. Take a break from returning calls from those where you know you'll have to absorb their negative energy. It's too burdening on your souls back to take it in day after day. The negative energy from others is that soul's ego acting out. It's best to steer clear of the line of their unnecessary fire. It's essential to disengage and disappear to gain perspective. This means disconnecting from world technology *(phones, computers, etc.)* Take a sabbatical or trip into nature. Go with a love interest or a friend you enjoy. Read a book!

If you question whether or not you are peaceful inside, then this cements that you're evolving more than you might believe. Being evolved is asking the tough questions. It's examining who you are and how you act and react. This is how one continues to grow. It's being able to take a good hard look at yourself from time to time. When you notice areas where you feel you need to make adjustments, then you take action and make those modifications. Someone who has not evolved stays relatively in the same place. They believe there is no room for improvement. It's always about them, their needs, and what everybody owes them, or isn't doing for them.

Others have purposely placed themselves in neighborhoods where they knew it would be taxing on their equilibrium. This prompted them to question what they were doing. It also made some of them question their sanity. Eventually they left those areas once they realized the work they needed to do while there was complete. The role you agreed to take on when you came into an Earthly life is going to at times put you in a position where you will feel challenged. This includes circumstances such as being in neighborhoods that you would typically feel uncomfortable to be in.

How many more of God's Children must suffer until humanity wakes up and sees the light and error of their ways? The streets of many countries are attacked by the worst kind of demon and horror you can imagine. This is the same demon that has been destroying this planet for centuries. It is the one that lives within the mind of every individual called the ego. When it grabs holds of the steering wheel, then there is no telling of the destruction it will cause.

In Gaza, Children were killed, losing limbs, dragged in blood half alive, and going hungry. While American children are lucky enough to be playing with "Lego's" or their cell phones, the Children in Gaza were playing on tanks or they're being used as human shields. While Palestinian Children pretend to be soldiers holding toy guns to reenact abductions. This is what human ego is teaching newer souls. It's a cycle that perpetuates going around in a circle with no real destination.

Mobs mock the deaths of these Children. They are allegedly doing this in the name of God. God would love to know which God they're talking about. God - the one true source of light creator calls them godless, inhumane, and not of His word, so who they are talking about? Heaven can use some illumination on this Godless God they speak of. Anyone who kills and harms with malicious intent is barbaric and will have a huge load of debt to pay back. This could not be wished on your worst enemy. It is someone with no conscious who seeks domination and power, which is not real reality. The terrorist group ISIS is a perfect example of the darkness of ego in action. While those affiliated with ISIS might believe they are acting out in the name of God, they are in fact acting out of the darkness of their own ego. God is all love and it is considered a sin to speak or act in any manner that is the opposite of love. Whether they are actually a terrorist group is debatable depending on who you converse with. The bottom line is that the heinous atrocities they commit on humanity are equal to that of a serial killer and not aligned with God. Humankind just came up with a fancier word for what they do such as terrorist. As it stands, ISIS is growing and will continue to expand and dominate for eons to come before they are overthrown and conquered.

A peaceful prayer:

"Dear God, thank you for ushering in your warrior angel soldiers to infiltrate your light into the ugliest heart in all men and women responsible for wreaking unrelenting and pointless havoc in others. Do whatever you need to do in order to bring this to a swift resolution of peace for all involved. You have full permission to bring in the big guns. Take your light and crack open and shatter the darkness that plagues those who know not what they do."

Chapter Eight

PRAYERS, AFFIRMATIONS, MANIFESTING

*W*e are in a critical state as a human race. Many are unhappy with where they are at in their lives reaching for a miracle or an answered prayer. You wake up in the morning and your mind immediately moves into worry or something negative. You know how this makes you feel and it's not pleasant. This is how you have set the tone and theme for your day. I have certainly had those moments in my past. Every morning my eyes open I move into a channel and communicate with my Spirit team. I may ask them, "Is there anything I need to know right now?" and/or "Is there anything you would like to discuss?" I will also let them know what I am grateful and thankful for. This is followed by positive affirmations. Positive affirmations have a higher frequency vibration when you say them.

When you say this line: *"I'm broke and never have any money."*

How does that feel to you? It feels yucky doesn't it? I felt that just writing it. Well, guess what you're summoning? You're bringing in more of that broke stuff to you. How about instead you say something such as: *"I have plenty of money. I am taken care of and my needs are met in all ways."*

Notice how saying that makes you feel.

Your lower self, which is the imposter self, will chime in at about this moment. *"Yeah, well I don't have a lot of money. I wish."* Or, *"I'll never get that job. I'm too old. I'm too fat. They want someone younger and better looking."*

When your ego and lower self take control, it seeks to undo the greatness that you were born with. Your lower self does not want to see you happy or succeed. Your higher self knows there is plenty to go around and makes sure you are taken care of.

"I'm never going to get that job."

This feels as if there is a heavy weight of an elephant sitting on you. You suddenly feel low and worthless, and begin attracting that same energy in. What spirals in is a domino effect of more things that only increase those feelings of low self-worth.

Now firmly say believing it, *"I WILL get that job."*

Much better.

Now say, *"I HAVE this job and all is wonderful."*

Even better!

Say it as if you have it and mean it. Even if you don't have it yet, say it every day as if you do. Never stop saying it or believing it. This is what a positive affirmation is. It trains your mind to be in that space more than when it's not.

The three main aspects where people struggle the most are career, love, and health. These are the areas that people often want to look at when they get a psychic or angel read. When you fight needlessly against the current, then your circumstances grow worse. This is due to the energy you are putting out there. Because your soul often feels trapped in human form in this heavy and dense atmosphere, your lower self and ego rises and becomes attracted to material and superficial things. Your soul is limited in its body for a reason, but the angels, guides, and spirit souls are unlimited. You lose yourself in outside events forgetting who and what you are.

If you use negative affirmations, then through the law of attraction you bring more of that negativity to you. You are always manifesting whether you like it or not so you may as well manifest what you want. Use positive affirmations and words when you speak, think, or write so that you can attract that same energy in. Try it out for a week and observe how things improve for you. You will discover that this will take practice. It isn't long before the ego grows angry attempting to take over once again. It doesn't matter if your ego fights you on it. Because you can train your higher self to take it right back! Always revert to seeing things as working out positively in your life in amazing ways.

Perhaps you've experienced a situation where your work life is on cloud nine, while another part of your life suffers, such as love and relationships. It may feel like one area of your life is mastered while the other areas are lacking in positive vibes. If you excel and shine with confidence whenever you are at work, then this is a great example where it comes to you naturally. This state is a positive form of manifesting. Your lower self does not question it or think about pulling you down. This is the same as creating a vision or dream board. You are saying the magic words without realizing it. Look at how self-assured you are at work. You can do it effortlessly and blissfully. This is the state where you manifest positive circumstances in other areas of your life. You have the positive visions in your head and know how to accomplish what you need to when you are at work. This is how I obtained the things I wanted in my work life. I saw it in my mind's eye beforehand, even though it would seem impossible to someone else. I didn't care. I knew and felt it in my gut and every cell of my body. I paid no mind to anything else including my lower self and I obtained what I envisioned.

Never discredit the power of prayer. I've spoken to others who do not believe in prayer, as they do not believe in God or that there is a higher power. Or they may not pray because their prayers had never been answered before so they gave up. However, those same people may suddenly call out to God when something detrimental happens to them or to someone close to them. God notices that you will cry out for him suddenly in a panic. He wants you to always communicate with Him, and not only when there is a dire circumstance begging for His intervention. He will of course intervene, but wishes to have a closer relationship with you beyond only needing help.

Prayer has provided miracles over the centuries to millions of people. I have witnessed the marvels and wonders that have taken place by praying. It is not enough to pray, but to keep an optimistic mindset. If you pray, but continue to fall into deeper despair, then pray for help with your emotional state. Once your emotional state is back to full power, then you are in that space where you can pray with detachment for the outcome of your desires.

Pray with intention. This is where you experience it everywhere such as your heart, stomach, and mind. I have noticed great changes within and around me after I prayed.

Prayers are also positive affirmations. It does not matter how you pray or whether you recite positive affirmations. It is all the same intention. God, the angels, and your guides are with you hearing every word. There is no wrong way to pray. Traditional religions have shown one often depicted as kneeling down by a bed with their hands clasped together while others may bow. It does not matter how or where you do it. It can be done anywhere. You can communicate with God mentally in prayer as you are walking to your car, driving, or sitting at a spotlight. Of course you won't have your eyes closed and hands clasped together in those cases. The point is that it does not matter how you are doing it. Just do it!

Prayers are communicating to God out loud, mentally, or in writing. Prayers are asking for help or thanking God and your Spirit team for their assistance. "Praying" is praying for other people too! You do not want to be slacking in that department either. If someone is cruel to you, it is easy to want to lash out or become negatively affected. As a Wise One part of the rough and tough Indigo generation, I'm guilty of that too. Try praying for that person instead. Request that they receive intervention and assistance to operate from their higher self. It does not matter how or where you pray, but that you do it. I would not continue with something if there were no results.

Atheists have protested that they do not believe in prayer. They may however sit with their own thoughts and ponder about their life at some point. They will feel grateful for what they have, what is to come, or what they would like to have. Without realizing it they are praying. They are reciting or conducting positive affirmations and prayer. It is the same concept and intent regardless of what title you use to describe your belief systems. All of these thoughts, affirmations, or prayers are heard and answered by God

369

and your Spirit team depending on what it is.

There is often a bad rap from atheists also with respect towards certain religions or people that pray to God. They may say something like, *"How can they talk to someone in the sky who does not exist?"* To them He does not exist, but to others He does. I do not blindly know that He, my Guides, or Angels exist. I have experienced great circumstances firsthand by being connected to them since I was born. I have tested them. I have requested specific assistance only to witness it come true. I am always communicating with Him daily and subsequently receiving results. If I never did, then I wouldn't bother with prayer.

It is important to remember that prayers are not always answered in the way you expect or hope. Sometimes they are answered in another way you never thought of. When it comes to God and Heaven, it is important to keep an open mind. Nothing has happened where I have not asked for it. I have mentally asked and then I watch it eventually come true. Sometimes it is immediately and sometimes it is far off in the distance, but I never stop praying or believing. I know that there are reasons that nothing is happening right away, because there are certain pieces of the puzzle that have to come into place first.

Let's say that you are wondering why the right partner has not come into your life yet. It may be that you are ready, but perhaps your love partner is in a place where they are not ready to meet you yet. They may currently be involved with someone that will not last. This is why you must keep an open mind and consider all the possibilities.

Always say thank you for being helped as well. Not just, "I need." The angels love it when you show gratitude and express thanks for what you do have. You do not want to become a spoiled child of God who takes and asks constantly. You are blessed in many ways so take time out to say, "Thank you." Every morning when I'm getting ready for the day I'm communicating with my Guides and Angels. There is not a day that goes by where I am not. Some of the things I say to them are things like, *"Thank you for my health, thank you for the place I live in, etc."* I move down the list letting them know how grateful I am for the blessings I currently have. I

370

feel more alive and alert when I start my sentences with, *"Thank you for...."* Those words have ferocious power!

Focus on being grateful and saying thank you for what you have and watch how much lighter and happier you start to feel. You'll find that your life starts to feel less tumultuous in the process. Being grateful and saying thank you raises your vibration to the level where positive manifestation occurs. Your prayers will be answered in ways that benefit your higher self. You may need to get knocked around off your high horse a bit before you can see how your prayer is indeed being answered. It seems challenging to break out of a cycle of negative thoughts and words used. It feels far easier to think and speak negative thoughts and worry. *"Oh I'll never get that job."* or *"No one will ever love me."* How about saying something positive? Oh forget about it! Choose not to live your life in misery. Choose to live happy and grateful. Choose not to allow your lower self to have control over you dominating your thoughts and mood.

You can pray for other people and send angels to intervene with someone else, but that person has to want help. The angels will definitely be by their side. They will give them love, offer assistance, and nudges, but if that person is not paying attention or wanting it, then there is only so much that can be done. God and the angels will stay by that person's side continuously trying to get them to notice. They do not give up on you, but do you just give up?

Here are some examples of positive affirmations and high vibrational phrases:

"I am worthy."
"I have strong health."
"People like me."
"I have a wonderful successful career."
"I live in a beautiful house in the countryside."
"I have a loving and loyal relationship partner."
"My opinion is just as valid as anyone else's."
"I am taken care of in all ways."

371

Don't short change yourself or be embarrassed as if you are not deserving of a great life. Heaven and your angels know you deserve it. They want you to be at peace so that you can fulfill your life purpose. You do not have to be on this planet to suffer.

Make a list with your own positive affirmations and recite it every day either mentally or out loud. Do it before bed or when you wake up. Keep doing it until you have obtained your dreams. God, the angels, and spirituality are like vitamins. You have to keep at it daily before you begin to notice the much needed improvement and changes shifting in your life.

Everything you desire will not happen right away. Sometimes for certain things there are life lessons that you must go through and be enlightened about on your own before the next step is shown. If you are feeling stuck at a dead end job and nothing is moving forward, then look at the lesson that is surrounding where you are at and acknowledge this. To do this you have to be completely unbiased and remove your ego from the equation. Look at this dead end job in a positive light and ask yourself, *"What have I learned while I have been here?"* What positive trait or traits did you gain while working this particular job that you did not have before? This is your answer to absorb and learn from. Acknowledge it so that you are open and ready for your next step.

You can write your angels anything you want in a prayer. Tell them about your fears, issues, and circumstances you would like to change. Remember that when you pour your heart out to them with great purpose that you are truly heard. Then release it and move on with living life graciously and positively. Have patience with the outcome. Watch the miracles and changes happen in the coming months that follow as you continue with this positive mindset.

When you pray or recite positive affirmations, I will conclude it with: *"This - or something better God."* Because they may have something greater than you imagined in mind and you don't want to limit yourself. Your dreams and wishes come true, but sometimes not the way you requested. It will be in an even greater way than you expected. It can be a major change or it can be subtle. Sometimes you will find you're still at the place you complained about, but then you realize that you're perfectly content there. They are keeping you somewhere for a reason and to fulfill a purpose such as getting along with a particular colleague. The delays can be that they have much to maneuver beforehand or have a grander plan that you cannot see yet.

Once again, remain optimistic and open minded to the outcome of your prayers. Know that there is a reason for everything that is happening for you in your life at any particular time. Know that you also have the power to change that simply by adjusting the way you think.

Praying for others has therapeutic effects. When you send positive words about someone else whether in the form of a prayer, affirmation, or a statement, you are raising your soul's energy vibration. This process not only results in additional healing light sent to the other person, but this same light is magnified and re-directed back onto yourself as well. This only solidifies the theory that your thoughts do produce things, whether those thoughts are of yourself or someone else. When someone upsets you and you find yourself complaining about them, you are not only sending negative energy to that person, but that energy you're toying with acts as a mirror reflecting the same energy right back onto your soul. This is why it is important to catch yourself when you discover that you are spending more time using negative words about a situation, then quickly modify the words to be optimistic. Sending prayers or positive words to someone else is a win-win situation because it not only has the added benefit of elevating the other person's soul, but it also improves yours.

Sending positive prayers and affirmations to others will help as much as the other person allows it to. They have free will choice to go against the prayers and override any heavenly assistance offered. If they are choosing to stay in a negative space, or they're making choices that their ego insists on, then there is little you or Heaven can do. When you send prayers for another person, the angels will continue to uplift that person's thoughts and nudge them in the right direction continuously hoping that person will notice.

Sometimes you pray for change with little to no instant results. When you notice that nothing has happened, your ego kicks in and causes you to worry. The ego wants things immediately. You start to lose faith when you notice nothing has changed. Your unanswered prayers sometimes have other factors that need to come into play first before you notice changes.

There are times when your prayers are answered. The way it is answered might not be in the manner you expect it. You fail to notice the blessings that have indeed trickled into your life. There are the repeated signs you ignore that your Spirit team is asking you to do. It could be something as simple as signing up to take a particular class or go to a seminar. They put the signs in front of you. You continue to notice the same seminar flyer, but you never act on it or equate it to Divine orchestration. Sometimes your Spirit team has to maneuver certain pieces of the puzzle before you notice the changes. Other times they want you to endure a particular experience as part of your karmic thread, life lesson, and growth. The insight you gain in what appears to be a less than stellar situation carries over into your new situation. You have the revelation of why the experience was necessary. "Oh, I see why it didn't happen right away." It all eventually makes sense.

RECAP:

Ask and you shall receive. Pray about the changes you'd like to see happen in your life. Have faith and believe in it. Focus only on what you desire to see happen and not what you don't want. For example, say something like, "Please guide me to friendships with likeminded interests." Also add in, "Thank you."

Be grateful for what you have. "Thank you for keeping my body healthy in all ways. I'm grateful that I have shelter, etc."

Shifting your outlook can take practice and time, but before you know it, you will start noticing the positive changes happening in your life. Ask Archangel Michael to surround you with white light protecting you from lower energies when you pray.

A Prayer

"I'd like to thank God for creating this planet and its entire habitat, plants, wildlife, animals, and the beauty of all of the nature surroundings. Help me to take care of it and never take it for granted. Thank you for providing me with all of the necessities I need to survive in a human body such as food, clothing, housing, and money. Help me to align perfectly with my higher self and its purpose while here. Thank you for assisting me to always express love."

Chapter Nine

JESUS CHRIST

Jesus Christ is one of the most powerful benevolent and compassionate beings in the Heavens that I felt compelled to mention him. It is important that I include him, since he has had a huge significance in my life at times. I knew who Jesus was and had learned about him going to Bible School as a child. The images of him are everywhere around the world in Churches and people's homes. I have been privy to the negative words by those who claim to speak the word of Jesus. I have heard those same negative words coming from those who do not believe in him too. It can be rattling that one man can create such harmful thoughts in themselves and in others.

I had avoided him at all costs until he entered into my space during a spirit reading I did for someone one day. Jesus moved into the room where I was with immense force. He flushed through me and awakened every pore and cell in my body. I felt lightheaded and was prompted to pause as my head fell over. When I adjusted to his energy I experienced an incredible feeling of love than I had never felt before. I didn't want it to end. I knew him as if I knew a friend without question or suspicion. I discovered the person that I was reading for was praying to him daily for healing. Jesus was coming in to reassure her that he is hearing her prayers. He was working on healing her ravished heart.

You have likely had a love crush on someone at one time or another. You know the feeling of that crush where it's a roller coaster ride of excitement and immeasurable happiness. Now magnify that feeling by a million and this will give you a good idea of the feeling Jesus Christ conveys when he is with you. He is a magnificent love light and you experience it all over and around you. You feel a vast greatness of love that prompts you to be moved to tears. The tears you form are tears of joy, since he has the power to blast away any negative emotion or block just by sitting next to you. You are overcome with emotion as if all pain has been dissolved from your soul and body. The weight of your entire life is lifted off of you.

I learned two things about Jesus that I was previously unaware of. He is all about love and healing in a grand way that I never knew or understood. No one ever talks about that aspect of him and it bemuses me. What I have heard or noticed were statements condemning and disapproving of other people. I have never received that impression when I have connected with him. In fact, the Jesus I know is someone other than how others have described him to be. I wonder if they know him at all.

Jesus is a powerful healer and can work with you to have trust and faith in the miracles working for you in your life. His healing is done with an overflowing feeling of love that you may become dizzy or lightheaded. It is as if you are soaring above the clouds with joy. His presence is intense and massive that it is impossible to forget. He leaves an indelible impression on your soul.

Jesus said that his messages have been mistranslated over the centuries. It reached a point where they have now been so poorly interpreted that it is no longer his message. His message of course is simple and on par with all of Heaven and that is *love*. His main goals are always revolving around love, compassion, and healing. My Guides and Angels continue to tell me that this Earthly run is all about learning to love and express love. Jesus only emphasized this with me, as he is the King leading the pack.

Jesus Christ is a Wise One who is profoundly psychic and was as a man on Earth. He was one of the biggest healers and prophetic teachers we have had in history when he was living as a human soul. Jesus was and is giving, compassionate, otherworldly and full of love.

There are good people in every group, but in my research and in the media, I've only been privy to the negative words that others vocally shout when it comes to Jesus. This is why so many get uncomfortable when I say the word *Jesus*, because of the negative connotations associated with the name. His name has been so inadequately portrayed in the media by both sides of the debate that I have no idea who they are talking about. I have found that others I have met shutter at his name. When I speak of him, I speak of him because I know him personally. I have met and communed with him on occasion. He has the most astonishing presence as a spirit that ever graced the Universe and the Heavens together. I admire and adore him. His presence and power is indescribable.

There are religions that believe your soul will be trapped in your body when you are buried if you have not accepted Jesus Christ as your personal savior. There are people that believe that some souls will burn in Hell and bonfire. None of this is true to what Heaven has shared with me over the years. According to God's law they are free to live and speak as they choose even if it is not true. No one has had any experiences to report back regarding this alleged damnation. Whereas there are many who communicate with the other side who have received and reported countless accurate information regarding a stranger's loved one. They relay information to that person about their loved one that is accurate and confirmed by the other party.

I have spent my entire life experiencing first hand of what the truth is by conducting my own communications with the other side. The helpful information being fed to me ends up coming true. This was how I grew up and there is no other belief system that can or will ever sway me. Discover the answers for yourself by doing the work and stop living in false fear.

Jesus wants you to work on being a good person always striving to improve yourself. He wants you to do the best you can to operate from a place of love. Anything less than that is unacceptable. I don't respond to any other source no matter what they claim. It has no bearing of truth to me and nor will it ever. I do not act purely on faith and trust, which is why Heaven had to spend so much time in my life convincing me. When I started seeing and experiencing results, I knew that they and it were real.

You have heard stories from others that have said that Christ is coming or that they are the Coming of the Christ. Christ is not coming and nor is that person the coming of the Christ necessarily. Jesus Christ is one of the most powerful spirits in the Heavens now. He can be with every human soul at the same time if you ask him to. What I have been told by him and my Spirit team is that Christ is not coming because he is already here. Due to the fact that he can be with so many people at the same time, he is also living in many of us. He is unlimited in that pieces of his soul exist in certain people. These are the people who do the work of bringing others together, who teach about love, who teach about humanity and compassion. These are the people who live in this space and are doing his work because they are channeling him often unknowingly. He is not coming in the way others have depicted where a hole is formed that swallows up mankind taking only the believers. He is already here in many of us doing HIS and God's work.

The coming of the Christ is already here and we are all around you. Some of you may not even be aware that you are doing his work, but you agreed on it before you arrived. Live as Jesus did. Love yourself and your neighbor. Work together in healing one another and this world today.

Whether or not you are a fan of Jesus Christ, you cannot deny the impact he has had on humanity and the world. He is not an Archangel, but he does fall into the category of what some consider an Ascended Master. This makes some religious followers uncomfortable, but an Ascended Master is a spiritually enlightened being. Jesus is absolutely this and so much more regardless of the title you prefer to give him. His messages and intention are about all love and all healing. He is not about anger or judgment. He is not about living your life in stress or greed. He is all about the uplifting joyous kind of love. This is why he was sent to Earth in human form. It was to teach that and spread it around. No one is going to listen to a spirit being. If they did, then we would not have the drama that exists all around the world throughout history. This is why many souls come to the Earthly plane in human soul form. They do this to send heavenly reminders and do the work for the Light. There are millions of human souls wandering off their path and forgetting how to love. They have grown to be indefinitely lost with no hope in sight.

Jesus is not typically the light I call in, although he has come in to visit by connecting through my clair channels on occasion. Those are the moments where I feel the indescribable kind of love that does not exist on Earth. It is a powerful euphoric feeling. It's as if you're soaring and floating above the clouds with immense eternal joy.

Before I entered this Earthly plane, Jesus was one of the final spirits to approach me before I came to be this lifetime. He said that love would be what I would retain from the spirit world. He whispered in my ear, "Remember all that matters is love. You will forget at times, but you will find your way back to that essence. At that moment, you will remember who you are and the purpose of your agreement. *We* will immediately connect with you when you are born into a human body, but it will take some time before you fully remember."

He said I would be tested in unimaginable ways in order to know what human suffering was like. I watched others on Earth suffer while on the other side, but I felt nothing. I was detached, but this was a detachment with love, and not a cold indifference. There are different levels in the way spirits feel and perceive things. As a warrior hunter on the other side, I had some measure of disconnection to the pain that human souls suffer through. All I knew and understood was taking care of business. I have incorporated that into my purpose here as a human soul.

GOD HAS A PLAN FOR ME

Some have used the phrase: "God has a plan for me." There is some truth to this statement. Those who have used that phrase have forgotten that it is your plan too. You made the agreement with Him before your soul entered this life. You know what His and your plan is. It is up to you to discover what that is. No one can tell you what it is. It was removed from your memory bank on purpose so that you can stumble on your way to discovering this plan. If you did not stumble, you would not grow and evolve. What matters is how you glide over life's challenges and become a stronger soul because of it.

There is much selfishness, rebelliousness, and ego on the planet. This comes from those who are not seeing the real gifts that exist in their life. Count your blessings on a daily basis. The *'poor me'* or *'I wish things were different'*, way of thinking will only make you feel more stuck. It blocks positive manifestations and you dig an even deeper hole into a bottomless abyss.

MOTHER TERESA

This huge burst of shining white light wanted to live in the trenches on Earth in order to make a difference. She never wavered from her quest, which was solely focused on reaching out to the poor, the hungry, and the destitute. Her light was so bright to begin with, that it gave them all hope. Tirelessly she forged on even when faced with doubts that God existed. As a human soul, she had at times forgotten where she came from. Visiting those that are ignored by the world, she witnessed the conditions they lived in and could not understand how God could abandon them. How could He not intervene and help them? She would only entertain this uncertainty once in awhile. When that happened, Jesus lifted her up each time she expressed reservations. It is understandable to feel like your fight is worthless. It may seem like you are at odds with the world, but what you are really doing is fulfilling your mission. Your human life is sometimes faced with challenges in the process towards your life purpose.

Known to human souls as Mother Teresa, she crossed over back home to the other side and works as an Ascended Master once again. She is now a guide for those who tirelessly work on their life purpose in ways that help many people. She's with those who express doubts of God and wanting to stop their mission from time to time. You can call on her to work with you when you feel like throwing in the towel and giving up on your quest. She will strengthen you as she has come through for me. She visits you to lift those qualms off your body making your soul strong and whole again, so that you can forge on as a warrior of light. She radiates a light of love so magnificent it would astound you. Her work continues on the other side, as it always has. This is to help those in need. She does not fall into ego and instead adopts the mantra that all of Heaven lives in, which is pure love and joy. When Mother Teresa, also known as Agnes, came into an Earthly life, she immediately got to work and did not waste any time absorbing pettiness. She was on a mission that would carry on throughout her entire life and beyond.

What have you done lately? Do not forget who you are and why you are here. Never give up or throw in the towel. Forge on with your purpose and mission. Life on Earth is always critical due to the overpowering domination of the Devil, the Ego, and the lower self. They wrap themselves up into one and exist within you. The ignorance and blindness of the cancer can no longer be. Stomp out all of that darkness within and around you. Remember to love and fight in the name of the light.

Chapter Ten

WHAT DOES HEAVEN SAY ABOUT HOMOSEXUALITY?

It would be remiss of me to not reveal information on one of the most controversial topics that exist in present day. I did not intend to, but my Spirit team had urged me to considering that it is playing a significant part in the darkness pervading the planet. Someone who does not understand another, or who hates another they don't know with immense venom is a product of the ego and fear. There are many who want to see death against homosexuals while others attack, condemn, and harass them. There are those that hide behind the words of false prophets who claim to speak the word of God. I know the word of God and have been with Him long before I had this Earthly existence. No human soul is any more special than any other. I discovered that the words *homosexual* and *gay* are not in Heaven's vocabulary and therefore nor are they in mine. I will put down as best I can what God, Saint Nathaniel, and his team of disciples have relayed to me on this.

Saint Nathaniel's message
interpreted by the author:

We attribute no labels to your souls in the way that you have trained yourself to. You choose this act on your own volition of Free Will. You are all created in the likeness of His image. Things such as judgment, maltreatment, and murder are what is considered a sin in the eyes of God. Homosexuality is not a sin in the way you define it. We have to use words that you are accustomed to understanding. The world is experiencing a transforming shift organized and set out by God. This shift is part of the evolution of His creation in order to bring it back to the grace and beauty intended from its inception. You are responsible for it and how you set up your own lives. The world is at a place where there is as much good as there is bad. Dark energy pervades half of this world dictated by human ego. The other half is filled with the light of God. This is the dawn of the new age upon us. You witness this darkness in the constraints you have created such as politics, government, social media, and those in power. These branches seek to interfere with others in how they live. They persist to obstruct how others choose to set up their Earthly life as a human soul.

The Light in you is growing in numbers. They are the newer Earthly souls electing to come into this Earth life to work in making significant changes to the planet and its habitat. They are what you consider the new generations of people. They are peaceful loving and in tune to their surroundings with limited ego. They are more privy and conscious to how they and others behave with others. They are stripping away unnecessary toxic ways of living from addictions to poor behavior patterns including escapism.

Many organized religions are broadening their teachings. Others are using their placement to condemn and curse certain human souls who appear differently to them. Those souls elected to arrive in ways you do not understand in order to awaken your hearts so that you may grow spiritually. This is a way to accelerate the planet as a whole in reaching a place of love and compassion. Some of you may have a tantrum or want to stop what you are afraid of. You cannot stop what God has intended.

You have had same sex marriages centuries ago during what you call the medieval times long before you made it a current issue. These same sex marriages stopped around the 340 AD period due to the rise of Christianity and the Christian Emperors who passed laws forbidding it. They were infused with fear and instilled this same fear into the public. Because they did not understand the true nature, they called it a crime and punishable by their own new laws that they saw fit. This was all man and ego created, not God created or inspired. Eventually the punishment was to be burned alive in public. This is still happening in third world countries. They have carried out with hangings as if it were 400 A.D. Some of these countries continue to stone them to death by bashing them in the head with bricks. They attribute this to the Devil. What is unseen is that the real Devil is how they choose to react. Your ego makes excuses so that you can justify causing others grief and harm.

You are witnessing the destruction towards homosexuality being reversed hundreds of years later where you have progressed becoming more compassionate and loving towards one another. You are all of God's children and loved equally. Why do you not show any love my child? Why do you fret and experience so much pain and anger so? What offends your fragile ego that someone has another path that is not like yours? Do not lose sight of who you and your soul truly are and will become when you have completed your Earthly life.

You are not going to Hell for French kissing. You will not go to Hell if you are in a committed love relationship with someone of the same sex. There is no Hell in the way that you know it. The only Hell is the one you create for yourself. The shivers you feel are a product of living in fear and the unknown. Do not be afraid my child. The only fear that exists is the false reality your mind tricks you into believing. We understand you do not fully comprehend what Earth's existence is about. To hear this may seem like you have had the rug pulled out from underneath you. You are always safe and always will be. Some of you react in ways that have been taught and trained by other human egos. You must stop what you are doing and the way you have been thinking to date. Eliminate all of the noise of the human egos around you and focus on the

385

stillness within you. When you let go of all the burdens you carry on your soul by others, will you then see the truth of who you are dear one. The obsession some have with homosexuality, race, and religion diverts the world from love, joy, and their life purpose. You have a preoccupation over a breed of God's creation that you do not understand. Your ego allows this to happen. It is pushed to uproar out of fear and misguidedness.

God, the angels, and Heaven see no distinction between heterosexuality and homosexuality as long as two people, two souls, are in a loving committed relationship. We are always happy to see love being observed. Your souls are attracted to one another. Your genders are irrelevant and not based in your current reality. When you leave your body, your body does not come with you. Your soul is left intact along with its ego. You must realize this as part of your lesson and growth.

Some have allowed their ego to feel uncomfortable with homosexuality. You have allowed it to control you into forming warped thoughts into your minds that it is perversion, pornography, and sex. This exists regardless of the human soul's attraction to one another. Two souls born of the same gender who experience similar love for one another know God by this act. They are no different from any other soul who craves the love and companionship of another. They have elected to come into this life as a homosexual knowing they will put up with tough lessons at the hands of newly developed souls. They know they will put up with it by those who have had their ego guided by another.

You are here to set up life and provide for yourself regardless of who you choose to do this with. Those that seek to condemn homosexuals often do not know others who are homosexual. The truth is they do. Those who have an attraction to the same sex surround you. They are forced to hide their true identity for their safety or to avoid ridicule or punishment from their communities.

Many use the holy book as justification to revile others after having misread and abused the text to give them license to conduct harmful acts. God does not support a justification of evil, anger, or hatred even if you have decided that your holy books do. You added text to your holy books at a later date to condemn homosexuals. These were men with human egos who experienced living in limitations and were misguided by fear. It is a danger to use God as your reason for your harmful justifications as God only sees the innocence in your soul. These men had no knowledge of homosexual relationships. They feared homosexuality and anything that appeared to be different than what they were accustomed to in their communities. What they were accustomed to was self-taught by the society they lived in. It was not and is not God's word. God's word is simple dear one. Love. Learn to love all of His creation and you shall know God. If your ego seeks to find ways to explain why you condemn, harm, and judge others, then you do not know God or the Holy Spirit. You can only reach God by experiencing love, joy, and peace. You can reach him by keeping your mind clear of the addictions and toxins you escape for. Do not act out aggressively towards another because they are different. This is a product of fear and not the love you were born with.

Men of the cloth, and those who are similar, have chosen to set up and run organizations that support human laws where countries may place rules on their unholy books to harm others. These laws seek to put homosexuals behind bars and even death. They are perpetually foolish and disconnected from the Divine Creator. They are dictated by rules that souls from thousands of years ago claimed to be receiving from God. Yet, there was no more input from God afterwards? Did God stop communicating? He can never stop communicating child. It is you who have stopped listening.

You have men donning as preachers speaking for God that you publicly assassinate the homosexuals. You have been doing this act for centuries persecuting anything or anyone who was not like you. You have done this with the Indians, the African Americans, Asians, and all of God's races. You have done this with others who do not practice the same religion you do. You have done this with all souls who are not like you. God did not create a world where everyone is the same. You must stop allowing your ego to control you into experiencing fear and anger because you have met someone who is not like you.

Some of you will say that you love everybody. We wonder who

would befriend one who disapproves of them. You misinterpret holy text. You pick and choose what suits you for your life today while ignoring the rest and giving no compelling reasons why. God knows your actions and what you are up to. You may deceive another human soul yet you cannot cheat God. You live erroneously and savagely as if you are doing right. You are not doing right when you condemn and harm one of God's creations.

You have Free Will laws made by God where you may set up your life however you choose. We cannot intervene unless you specifically ask for our help. If you have come into this life as a homosexual, you would do well to remember your divine heritage and pray for God to assist you in making this world brighter for you and those around you. This will speed up the process to peace on Earth.

Many homosexuals and the newer generations lack in faith or do not believe or buy there is a God. This is understandable considering that growing up as a human soul all they heard and read were stories of sermons from churches or their community calling them sinful and the Devil. You are not sinful. It is your unruly ego that is the Devil. There is no sin when it comes to love and who you choose to love. The rules apply to you as much as they do with all human souls. Treat yourself and the people around you with compassion, kindness, and love. Do not choose the role of a monster. We watch over you and guide you away from a state of mind that chooses suffering. When you feel empty you reach for harmful pleasures out of hoping to fulfill a void. We do not condemn how you choose to live. We hope and urge you to do right. We cannot cease to love you.

We do not push you to need several partners whether homosexual or heterosexual. This need you desire acts out to temporarily fill a hollowness within you that demands carnal pleasures of the material world you have created in order to escape from your inner unhappiness. You are seeking to fulfill an absence that you believe to be missing in you. This desolation that grows into loneliness is God's love you desire. It is the only love that can fill you up whole and help you remember your Divine soul heritage. It is your ego that takes over convincing you of harm. There is a distinction between two people in a loving and committed relationship forging an alliance regardless of their human genders. The discrepancy is wide when compared to a relationship that chooses to have more than one partner. This speaks to your sensual urges that are satiated by the ego. There is a difference between a man who is in love with another man in a committed relationship and a man who is lying in bed with many different men. This same concept applies to a married or committed man or woman who lies in bed outside of his commitment with others. There is a difference between being an upstanding hardworking soul and one who is not. We do not talk about one man and one woman. We speak to you about two souls who join together to express love and a cherished commitment with one another.

There are millions of souls who agreed to come into this lifetime as a homosexual understanding the repercussions that will come about. There are some who say that you were born this way when this is not technically true. You might have chosen to come into this lifetime as a homosexual. Your attraction and feelings are not chosen. As difficult or incomprehensible as this may be for some, the truth will be revealed to you when you are ready. This is why it is imperative to do the learning and growth work now. You do not need to wait to do it when you cross over. There is no fire and brimstone expecting you. The only judgment that you face when you cross over is your own.

There are homosexuals who feel the entire world has turned against them. Imagine what happens when you believe that you are hated. You are not hated in Heaven's truth. Your ego functions at full force when you crave attention and love seeking it out through destructive relationships, sex, or any other toxic addictions. Be clear now and invite in God and the Holy Spirit to fill your soul up with the love you require.

God knows what is to come on the planet. He has known this trajectory for centuries. He knows what His creation would do and how they would behave. He knew the souls he created were naïve and innocent in their anger and actions. He still loves you regardless and wants you to feel inner peace. He wants you to grow and learn. He does not want you carrying around these unnecessary and unhelpful burdens and emotions. You have allowed your material world and human ego to overpower and control you. This has weakened your communication with God. You can resurrect it and develop it back with focus, practice, and study. When you do this you will discover the same truths of where you came from. You will discover how to improve your way of living. This requires a lifestyle change some may not welcome. This new existence will be more inviting than you have come to know.

You have been abused, you smoked, drank alcohol, did drugs, slept with more people than you can remember. You never found what you were looking for, did you child? You come face to face with misery and your self-esteem plummets further into a deep abyss. You used these manufactured outlets as ways for you to quiet the noise of your ego. They were ways to feel loved and wanted. Release the need to continue abusing your soul. Allow your world to open in ways you have always dreamed of. The unnecessary outlets of escape harm your soul, your body, and yourself. You desire the almighty's love. He will give it to you no matter who you are and at no cost.

FROM THE AUTHOR

To give you an example of the brevity of what young people are going through, a sixteen-year-old guy writes me: "My whole family thinks liking guys is a disease. They make me sad."

His family does not know any better. It's not a disease. Anger and lower feelings are a disease. Some human souls are on the lower end of becoming an evolved spirit. This is why they're experiencing an Earthly life. This is to gain knowledge in terms of their own soul, before they can graduate to a higher spiritual plane. If they do not get it right or learn anything while here, they will have to come back to Earth again repeatedly until they have mastered it.

You cannot reason with someone who does not know any better and believes what they were taught by others. They have to figure it out for themselves. If not, they will when they cross over. Often human souls are poorly influenced and advised growing up by those around them. They believe certain things are wrong without knowing anything about it. They follow the cattle believing what they were taught instead of rising above that and doing the work to uncover the real answers.

A good Christian woman walks the talk and lives in His presence. She never judges and has a 'live and let live' attitude as long as no one is being harmed, but is exuding love. She lives in goodness. Another woman lives in His presence except she fumes with judgment and negativity. She does not live in His goodness, but the wrath of her own ego.

Jesus absolutely loves and accepts you as I've discovered through my connections with him. You have to be completely removed from both sides in order to connect to anyone in Heaven. You are not removed if your views are set in hatred. It is learned behavior and your ego has set these views. These same human souls were the ones who crucified others into slavery. They are doing the same thing to homosexuals, those who are of a different race, culture, or belief system. Do not allow your ego to control you into believing that those who use the Jesus or God name to attack you as being accurate. They cowardly hide behind His name and use Him so they can have an excuse to misbehave. God accepts and loves all that He has created despite what some religions teach. It is easy to deceive the lower evolved.

Whenever you do something good or bad this is filed away in what some call your Akashic Records. Archangel Metatron holds these records and stands near the throne of God during your judgment life review. All of your Guides and Angels are highly developed psychic entities that know your probable futures, your map, thoughts, feelings, and life purpose. They work to keep you heading in the right direction. You must tune in, pay attention, and communicate with them regularly, so that you stay on course and do not experience anger or sadness.

The Archangels are the managers of the angels with profound and powerful psychic perception. God's abilities are beyond what you can comprehend. He knows what's up ahead backwards and forwards. He knows what you are going to think before you think it. He knows how you will proceed even when he hopes you will choose wisely.

God saw the technological age that would bring everyone to connect more efficiently. Now you can easily find out what someone in China is doing if you are in the United States. The Internet was created to bring people together, but it has magnified the anger and the noise. Human souls are flawed and have predictably abused what it is given. People follow each other and pat one another on the back when they are doing wrong. Human souls have such capacity for greatness, but they refuse to budge. It is not God or Heaven that takes issue. It is sections of society that take issue. They are afraid to embrace all people, unless all people live as they do. When you do not understand something it is important to take the time to understand it before you can draw a conclusion. It is important to walk in your fellow man's footsteps and understand what it's like to live in their shoes. I do not subscribe to traditional religions that promote low self-esteem, fear, and guilt. I believe in the power of prayer and Heaven.

Growing up I continued going to Church because I enjoyed it into my teenage years. I felt secure and safe by those who were seemingly good hearted. I was not at any Church that was screaming fiery hate words, but they were speaking of love. The reason I stopped going was because I received all I needed to. I already knew the real truth about humanity and Heaven, because of my regular communication connections with Spirit. I was ready to move to the next level rather quickly. I continued moving through each level as they kept my class lessons and growth accelerated to reach the place I'm currently at in teaching this. This does not mean I had it easy, but far from it. This is a world that shakes its fist in anger, "Hang him!" This is without knowing if there is guilt or not. Even if there is guilt, it is not your place to pass down judgment or punishment. Mistakes are made in this lifetime to be corrected. Nothing has changed from the days of hanging witches that were not witches, hanging someone because of the color of their skin, feeding Christians to the Lion's because they had different belief systems, assaulting homosexuals because they love someone of the same sex. Human souls have much to learn and have not grasped their purpose here, which is as Heaven has said: Love. You are asked to live with and be with those that are not like you to build up your tolerance to learn to love. This is non-existent on the planet.

The highest reported rates of hate crimes in the world are racially or anti-gay motivated. There are officials who do not report every crime as anti-gay motivated even when it is. We live in a country and world where there are crimes acted out on another human being because of where they are from or whom they fall in love with. These are people who have to suffer because someone doesn't understand it or is uncomfortable with it. Identify the real lower self in that passage. All of the souls on this Earth are here to share it amongst one another regardless of their interests. No one owns this planet, as it is God's creation and world. No human soul has the right to dictate to others how they choose to live.

My Guides and Angels have told me that Same Sex Marriage will one day be legal throughout not just the United States, but the entire world. They would not tell me when, only that it will be coming in the future. At the time this is written, there are less than ten states in the United States that allow Same Sex Marriage. The Supreme Court will do what they did with interracial marriage by knocking down the ban in the United States. The number of countries to come on board in legalizing and allowing Same Sex Marriage will increase in the years to come. God allowed human souls to set up shop here as they see fit even if they are instilling rules that are incorrect such as denying others an opportunity for love. It is not how your soul entered this life to begin with, but was rather molded by the communities and influences others had on your souls growing up during the human development process. The main reason human souls have agreed to be here is for the purpose of love, which I will hammer down until the end of time. All of the rest of the nonsense is "the noise" as they call it.

Chapter Eleven

LOVE BIG AND LOVE ALWAYS

Human souls often choose to live in fear and obsess over power and control. In this state they infuse their lower self into the Holy print in the name of God. They paint false pictures to control others through guilt and fear. This is what they consider to be a moral way to live at any given time in history. The only ethical range that exists is your own character. You are here to make your own choices and decisions as to the best course of action for yourself. When you make a poor decision you pay for that consequence. Every time you get knocked down you are experiencing a lesson. Each lesson you learn helps you to grow to be a smarter and stronger soul.

God and the angels will never stop loving you. It only pains them to watch you suffer needlessly. They see no need for you to exude anger and other wasted emotions and feelings that have no positive power over anything in the end. Those feelings are reactions that your ego objects to. The only true power that exists is God's LOVE

Keeping your ego quiet is up there on one of the most difficult tasks for you to do. You're human after all and born with an inflated ego that you wrestle with daily. The human ego is the worst ego that exists, but it is there in order for you to learn necessary lessons that assist your soul in growing and evolving.

How many times are you going to allow yourself to get knocked around before you wake up? When are you going to grow up and be fully aware of your actions, your thoughts and how you treat others? When are you going to learn right from wrong? When are you going to learn to love unconditionally? When are you going to learn to treat others with respect?

The best way to quiet your ego is by stating positive affirmations that all is as it should be and everything is taken care of for you. Even if you do not see your desired outcome yet, you need to act and believe as if it is already here. You need to live in a state of gratitude and feel joy for this life you have been given the opportunity to have. Do not let someone else's ego stop you from your purpose and goals.

When you look back on your accomplishments you may have noticed they came to you when you were not struggling for it. It came to you naturally and effortlessly. There are reasons that your desires are delayed or are not instantaneous. Some of the common suggestions the angels urge you to have are patience, trust, faith, and love. Try living in this state every second if you can. Practice it regularly and especially when you know you are being tested like when you get a flat tire and you're late for work. Take the roadblocks and challenges with calming stride. This is someone in complete command and control.

Do you ever notice that when you push for a relationship to happen with someone that it ends up back firing and doesn't go as planned? This is because you cannot push for anything including love. As far as love and relationships go, those that merge with one another blissfully are when both parties are patient allowing it to evolve on its own course.

In order to improve your life, the first thing you will need to do is reduce or eliminate your addictions, bad habits, and even some friendships! When you ask your heavenly spiritual guides for assistance you may be prompted to make crucial life changes that you may not feel ready to make. They have you do this because you are being prepped for something greater up ahead. Before that can happen, you will have to strip away all of your toxic baggage. You may be absorbed in it to the point that you might not be aware that it is poisonous. They do not ask you to do this because they are against the fun you have when you have several alcoholic drinks. They do it so that you can live a more blissful life full of happiness, success, and love. They know that vice is only a temporary high that is not long lasting and delays you from moving forward. You're too busy battling the side effects from your addiction to have enough energy to focus on what's important. When you continue on with your former toxic way of living, this gets in your way of success and holds you back. You may remain stuck at a dead end job you do not want to be at. When you have all that poor energy around you it blocks good things from entering your life.

This is about stripping down to your soul core and eliminating particular behavior patterns and lifestyle choices that are disruptive to your soul's enhancement. It can take some time dissolving these things, as the changes do not happen immediately. They will be met with some resistance or unhappiness. You are shedding all of the bark around the tree that is part of your life experiences. This is so that your true inner light can shine outwardly as bright as the sun. Once this is done then you will be shown your next move. This can be digging up those projects, ideas, and anything you have always wanted to do, but were stopped by procrastination or negative self-talk. You will attract in friendships and relationships of a higher caliber on your new improved level. You will stand in your own power with great strength and there will be nothing that you cannot do. The floodgates open for you as you tackle and accomplish your dreams. When you begin to take steps, then the universe will meet you tenfold!

I connected with Mother Mary and Jesus Christ for any messages to incorporate in here. The message they gave me was to experience joy now. I know for some that might seem like a difficult place to get to. There are things that you can do to elevate your feelings into a happier state of mind. Do something fun with a friend. Surround yourself with other people who lift your mood. Watch a comedy or a lighthearted feel good movie. Blast some good music. Stay away from negative substances that will only bring your vibration down. These are things such as news headlines or going out to places when you know it's going to be crowded. Those activities tamper with and lower your high vibrational energy.

I've been out there in the trenches with the crowd's everyday so I get it. I previously placed myself in a part of town that borders soulless on purpose. You could call it research or just plain crazy. I witness harsh energy regularly. I conduct frequent sessions of shielding every day because of this. I am careful with the places I go to, what time of day it is when I go out, and who is around me as well.

The morning before Christmas Eve I witnessed many rushing around frantically unhappy. They were pushing and shoving each other aggressively. Some were getting into fights that were taped on cell phones of onlookers and uploaded on video websites. Others waited until the last minute to shop since their heart is not in it or they are functioning with no time and energy. A friend of mine who was out there as well called me to ask, "What's going on with everybody?" People have lost sight of what is important. They are hurrying around doing what they feel is expected. The only thing you should be doing is getting back into the joy of your life. Regardless of your spiritual beliefs, it is unavoidable to know that the Christmas word is meant to be a time of joy. It is the kind of joy you should be reaching for daily. You should be celebrating! You should be celebrating this life and each other.

Remember what is truly important to your soul and why you are here. It is to love, to give love, and to spread love. This mantra should be adopted everyday and every minute of your life. Deep down your soul knows what you can do to bring yourself back. Know your light. Know your power. Know what you were born here to be. Be one with the Light and one with Spirit. They are waiting to walk beside you, in front of you, and with you. They see you holding the hands of your neighbor no matter what they are into or what they are like. If you treat your neighbor without love, then you don't know God. When you see yourself and others with disgust, then you only know the ego and the Devil.

Love is who I am. Love is the source of all that I wish. Love is the source of power. The more that I love, the safer I am. The more that I allow myself to love the more powerful I am. Sending God's light and love is not enough. It is powerful and necessary. Some of us have a soldier nature in the name of Heaven and we do have to fight. When I say fight I don't mean with violence, but by being assertive in your stance. You have to stand in your individual power. Think and speak for yourself even if you stand alone. All of our goals are to unite as many people as possible in peace, love, and joy.

Have zero tolerance for anger, violence, and hate, which gets everybody nowhere. Yet, you cannot be a doormat either and nicey-nice all the time. There are some souls who are specifically here to exude the characteristics of love, which warms the coldest of hearts. We are an army of workers of the Light who all have varying and specific gifts to contribute to ushering the world gracefully into a new age. This is why we elected to show up at this time in history. This is how we all found each other. It's all connected. We are all connected. We are soldiers and fighters of the light. We are warriors in the name of God and Heaven. I am a warrior of light and I exude the honor that God desires. Join me in teaching these messages so that we can shift and change this world for the better, one person at a time.

CONNECTING WITH THE ARCHANGELS

Connecting with the Archangels

$\mathcal{T}$he Archangels are powerful, benevolent beings of God present to assist you along a higher path. They are the managers of the angels and are non-denominational, which means they do not belong to any religious establishment. It does not matter who you are or what your beliefs are. Like God, they are available to anyone who asks for their help. There are legions of Archangels residing in other dimensions. I will focus on sixteen of the more popular Archangels in order to assist you in understanding what their basic roles and specialties are.

Several of the Archangels have been featured in the different holy books. Others have reported sightings or visions of an Archangel when they needed the help most. There have been devout religious followers who I have heard say that you are not supposed to worship Archangels or angels. No one is advocating that you worship or pray to the angels because all exaltation goes to God. The Archangels are gifts from God to help you experience love, joy, and peace in your life. In order for one to hear and communicate with God you must be completely at peace. You must be feeling and exuding joy, love, and compassion. You have to be living in your higher self. You need to be in this state and stripped of your ego. God wants to communicate with you, but you do not hear God unless you are in that state of higher consciousness. This also means that those who condemn and harm others in the name of God are not communicating with God. They are instead operating from their lower self and ego. You cannot communicate with God in a state full of blocks.

The Archangels are God's gifts to help you reach that place where you are fully able to communicate with Him. The Archangels are His messengers who deliver God's messages and personal guidance to you. Everything the Archangels communicate is God's word. They raise your vibration so that you can indeed hear and communicate with God Himself. Although God is always communicating with you, you are not listening if you are experiencing negative feelings such as anger, stress, hate, or even sadness and depression. This is why the Archangels and angels come in to lift those unnecessary emotions. They assist you in diminishing your negative ways of thinking.

The Archangels names end in '*el*', which means "of God". The exceptions are Archangel Metatron and Archangel Sandalphon who were once highly evolved prophet men in human form.

I am always communicating with several of the Archangels every day. I correspond with them everywhere no matter where I am. I may commune with them while I am in the shower, walking to my car, driving, riding in an elevator, and the list goes on. I call each in as a reminder that I appreciate all they do for me and others. Since they are God's arms, you are communicating with God too. He wants to have a relationship with you. He wants you to talk to Him. It does not matter where or how. It is not necessary to do it in a church, but it does help to do it in a calming environment. You can communicate with Him mentally while you are brushing your teeth, while you are driving, or jogging. It does not matter how or where you do it, just talk to Him!

Calling upon God, any Archangel, Angel, or Spirit Guide can be done at anytime and anywhere. They are all powerful and unlimited which means they can be with anyone and everyone simultaneously. This is the same way God is everywhere at once. The Archangels each have specialties that they can assist you with on your journey here. They are magnificent Lights, and like God they know your thoughts, feelings, and desires. They show up before you have finished your sentence! You do need to ask for them in order to help you since they cannot interfere with your free will. This is God's law. The only exception is if there is a life threatening moment taking place that may result in your premature death. They will appear in your life to attempt to stop it. Many around the world have witnessed and professed stories of their encounters with an Archangel.

One of the more efficient ways of connecting to any Archangel or enlightened spirit is by creating a soothing atmosphere and environment. You can do this in a quiet room that contains soft music playing, a candle burning, and the smell of incense. Breathe in deeply and exhale out any stresses or thoughts until you are fully relaxed. Call the Archangel by name and pour your thoughts and heart out to them. Do not push or attempt to receive any communication otherwise you will block it. Remain open while allowing any messages or guidance being communicated to you to sift through your *clair* channels *(seeing, hearing, feeling, and knowing)*. You do not need to create the perfect ambiance in order to communicate with them. However, you may find it will relax you and bring you to a blissful state where your connection is made. These beings are highly responsive to the light of a candle and a calming environment. The light of a candle is much like the light of an evolved soul, in that it is bright and white!

There is no greater feeling of freedom than connecting with Spirit. You can do this anywhere, but in nature or a peaceful locale is ideal. Only then do you experience the weight of your burdens and worries being lifted off your soul. You realize that nothing else matters. All of the restrictions that the human ego forces upon other human souls are not real. They are a product of the lower self, which is born out of fear.

Archangel Michael

Every morning after I wake up, I connect with my Spirit team and ask them to keep my thoughts aligned and positive for the day.

"Dear God, please surround me with a sphere of powerful, brilliant white light six feet tall all around me. I ask that my Spirit Guides and Angels guide me, guard me, and keep all negative influences away from me."

I envision white light shoot out from all around me followed by a jolt of positive energy. I call in some of the Archangels that I work with by name to my side. I light a small piece of Sage and smudge it around my body to clear any negativity as I begin making my contact with the Archangels. You may develop your own way of connecting that works for you the more you practice. I take a deep breath in and exhale so that I'm fully relaxed. I call on my right hand man through all good things and bad. He is my daily protector and invincible warrior, the powerful Archangel Michael.

"Archangel Michael I call upon you now. I ask that you cut any cords of fear and anxiety that drain my energy and vitality. I ask that you cut the cords between (name of person) and I. I ask that you cut the cords between myself and (substances/negativity)."

I take a deep breath in and exhale out after each person or substance if there is more than one. I allow Archangel Michael to cut any cords of dysfunctional attachment to myself.

"I ask that you surround me with your permeable white light shield (protection), violet light (spiritual sight), rose light (allowing only the love to penetrate my aura and being)."

Archangel Michael is one of the most powerful Archangels in the Heavens. He has been by my side everyday for a good part of my life. He has appeared to me visibly over the years materializing as tall as twenty and sometimes thirty feet! He can be as big or tall as he needs to be to get his point across. Some have reported to have confused him with Jesus. This is because they both sometimes appear with a similar golden glow. The difference is Archangel Michael has a violet glow with tinges of white and gold. Jesus appears to me with gold and white light.

Archangel Michael carries a shield and a mighty sword made out of bright light. This light is extremely vigorous able to cut through anything. He is a tough protector, fierce one, nightclub bouncer and bodyguard for myself, and for you if you ask him to. I communicate with him every single day more than any other being. He is the loudest entity in the heavens. He is the only being I have come to know that is louder than the almighty God. One of his roles is extracting anything that should not be around you whether they be living or dead. He takes his light sword to cut, remove, and dissolve things like your fears or addictions. He cuts the cords and webs of your worries or other negative feelings that accumulate around your body. Someone who is clairvoyant may see the effects of your toxic emotions as cords and shades of dirty, dark, cobwebs both thick and thin in size.

Old paintings often depict Archangel Michael as a warrior wrestling a demon to the ground. The demon Devil is a metaphor and can be a negative entity, negative energy, your fears, or your ego. He cuts that stuff out only when you ask him to. If you do not ask for his help, then you remain in that state. Since I had invited him to be by my side permanently, he has never left. I have witnessed profound life changes take place in my life thanks to him being around me. I would never continue with something where I was not experiencing positive changes. I am someone who questions and tests every hypothesis before I follow or adhere blindly.

Archangel Michael is the Archangel who often leaves feathers around. He will do this when you ask for a sign that he is around you, or when he wants to remind you that he is with you. Other ways he does this is by turning up the volume in his colors so that you witness a vibrant display of fireworks. For me, he will usually show off when I have been discontent for a prolonged period of time. When I hear him speak or when he is warning me of danger, I hear his voice loudly in my left ear. It sounds as if a man is standing next to me speaking to me. As someone who has been plagued with social anxiety in the past, I have felt comfort and safe knowing that he is right there with me around the clock. He lets me know whether it is okay to proceed with anything or anyone. He will warn me if someone has honest intentions or not. He has jumped in when I have had technical issues with an electronic device as well as with past car problems. He has rectified what is broken after I have specifically asked for his assistance with it.

One Summer I had been driving around in one of my previous cars. It endured a bad car accident when a driver plowed into the front of it prompting my car to smash against the sidewalk. This was long before I had asked Archangel Michael to stay in my life permanently. My car had suffered endless car issues every couple of months for years after that accident. It was exhausting for me to be driving a car to and from work five days a week only to have to shelve out hundreds of dollars in sudden repairs on it. Friends would comment on this every time my car was at the mechanic again. "Wow it seems like your car is always having problems." I had wanted a better car, but did not want to waste the money, or go through the hassle of the transaction.

This particular Summer, I was driving from Hollywood to the Valley in Los Angeles. I took the infamous Laurel Canyon Boulevard, which is a long, winding road that crosses over the Hollywood mountains to get you to the Valley on the other side. There was a ton of moving traffic as if it were rush hour, except this was a hot, weekend day in July. I arrived at the top of the hill where Laurel Canyon intersects at the Mulholland Drive stoplight. My car suddenly stalled and all the lights on the dashboard flashed with all sorts of emergency warnings saying that the transmission is out. What?! I couldn't believe it. I went into a panic as the Summer sweat dripped down my forehead. I attempted to start the car with no success. It was completely dead and I had a sea of cars all behind me with no way to get around me. I paused, took some deep breaths, closed my eyes and lowered my head. I had my hand on the keys in the ignition and I said, "Okay Archangel Michael, I can't do this anymore. I can't keep going on like this. Please help me start this car and get me out of here safely and to a trustworthy dealer in the valley now. Don't let me leave the dealer without the transaction going through effortlessly. Please get me out of here."

I took a deep breath and opened my eyes. I heard a male voice loudly say, "Start the car." I turned the ignition on and the car started! I immediately said, "Thank you Michael!" The traffic light turned green. No one realized I was briefly stuck on the road except myself and Archangel Michael.

Although the lights on the dashboard continued to flash with its warnings, Archangel Michael got me and the car safely to a dealer. Everyone at the dealership was fantastic, upbeat, and friendly. We worked on a smooth transaction for a new car that the angels picked out. I say they picked it out because the dealer and I had combed through the entire lot with the representative and found nothing that caught my eye. I was defeated and didn't know what to do. I did not want to buy just any car, but I felt I had little choice. I heard a voice urge me to go back down a particular aisle again. I came upon the perfect car I envisioned in my mind. It was like new and affordable with only 15,000 miles on it. Even the car representative seemed stumped and commented, "Interesting. Where did this one come from? I'm sure we came down this aisle." I smiled to myself, as I knew where it came from.

The next day I walked out to my new car outside my place and there was a huge white feather sitting on the driver's side floor. Archangel Michael leaves feathers around you, so that you know he is there working with you.

One day that following December, I went into a channel. I called in any who wanted to communicate with me to come into the channel. I fell into a deep trance and a Spirit being came in on my right slightly behind me. I noticed the dark shadow in the corner of my eye. I asked him who he was and he said he was Balthazar. I experienced a rush talking to this Spirit that I wanted to know more. As he began to speak, I lost focus because I was in shock at how potent the energy was. Archangel Michael came in visibly on my left side and he rose up 15 feet tall from the ground lighting up the entire room. His right wing went around me like an arm as he stood and towered over me. It broke me out of the trance. I stood delirious watching Michael point away telling the Spirit, "Go now." I was trying to explain to Michael that it's okay. I'm fine. Then I wondered, "Who is Balthazar? And why did Archangel Michael jump in?"

Archangel Michael has made himself my protector on my journey here. He apparently did not like Balthazar's energy and blasted him with white light to see if he would stick or leave. There was a lesson in there and here it is: Any time you sense any entity that is not a person or other living being on the material plane approach you or any type of non-corporeal entity whatsoever, if you are not comfortable with that energy command it to go into the white light. You will know if that entity scares you or makes you nervous instantly. If so, visualize an open doorway with blinding white light beyond it. Demand and require that the entity go into the white light. What happens next will tell you if the entity is positive or negative. This is sometimes good or evil and a question of intent. This is how one can test it out with Archangel Michael to make sure that he is not an imposter. Ask Archangel Michael to demonstrate for you by stepping through the door into the light. What you see will astound you as Michael will become the most gorgeous light show of colors and warm light. This is while radiating so much loving energy as to almost overwhelm you. Archangels are like that. He'll probably laugh and then show you his colors and then laugh again. Archangel Michael isn't arrogantly cocky necessarily, but he knows he's the bomb. He's similar to a tough alpha male who struts around like a male peacock showing off his feathers with a smirk.

Most of us have come across a constant complainer. This is another form of toxic energy. There may be circumstances where you find it difficult to get away from that person. It is one thing if you seek it out, but it is another if others seek you out to unleash their complaints onto you. What you want to do is visualize a shield of white light around you when they start at it. As this is visualized, mentally ask Archangel Michael to extricate them away from you since the energy is too harsh. Once that has happened, the person suddenly stops talking and wraps it up abruptly wanting to get away from you. If they don't budge and are sticking around you, then continue to get firmer with your request. I continue to be amazed at how it is almost like magic the way it happens at every turn.

Because Michael is with me every day, I might notice an odd sketchy character heading towards me on the sidewalk with fixation. Right about the moment where that character hits the white light that is around me, I notice the person suddenly shifting uncomfortably and then dart away. Before Michael was with me, I would face head on towards danger or into a character you do not want to cross paths with or have to engage with. This is one of the reasons I see Archangel Michael as my own personal security team.

Archangel Michael makes himself known and stands behind me when I am upset. I see his wings outstretch into oblivion and then curl up and envelope me in them when I have experienced past pain or depression. During my initial introduction to him when I was doing my typical questioning and asking for proof, he started dropping feathers everywhere in my path. There was one floating by itself outside my window. On the same day, another feather floated out of nowhere past me while I walked on the sidewalk. If you tell that story to a skeptic they will say something like, "Well how do you know it just didn't happen to be there?" It is a waste of time trying to convince someone of something they do not understand. Human ego is not used to a reality beyond the material concrete existence they have created on Earth. It takes more than a conversation to re-train someone's mind that is set in stone due to their upbringing, or a mind that is permanently closed. Your senses need to be finely tuned to have any sort of connection with the other side. If your senses are not used, or you are unaware of anything besides what fits into your hands, then you will be oblivious to the wonders that exist beyond this planet.

Archangel Michael has prevented near accidents from happening with me. Every single time I get into my car, I always ask Archangel Michael to shield it.

"Archangel Michael, please surround my car with white light. Don't let anyone hit me and don't let me hit anyone."

There have been several occasions where other drivers were inches close to ramming into my car. They seem to skid to a stop or miss me as if a powerful Light hand placed itself between our cars. My heart would pound at the narrow escape while mentally thanking Archangel Michael profusely. Once at a stop sign, I pulled behind a car that backed up into my car without realizing I was there. We both felt our cars hit, but when we looked at the damage on my car there wasn't even a scratch. The car that backed into me however had a little dent. This is thanks to my daily shielding with Archangel Michael.

There have been occasions where I had attracted negative entities into my light. I would clairvoyantly see cockroaches and dark insects crawling on the ceiling from the spirit world. They are attracted to dark energies and/or negativity. Call on Archangel Michael because he is a great bug extinguisher too! I can see these energies at times around other people with my peripheral vision. Other times I clairvoyantly see them around someone who is heavily intoxicated, on drugs, alcohol, or experiencing potent negative emotions. I see it around those who are over the top angry or depressed. Negative spirits and insects feed off those souls like vampires feeding on a victim. This makes you feel worse prompting you to reach for another drink, smoke, or any other toxic vice. The negative spirit receives a rush by pushing you to continue down a bad cycle. You become appetizing food and no one benefits except those ethereal insects. You and certainly the people around you in the line of this fire do not gain either. This is why we call these wasted emotions. It is pointless energy when you outwardly direct negativity. This affects everyone around for no purpose except to lower yours and everyone's vibration.

One Halloween night, I headed out to a major street festival with some friends. Even though I did not dress up or drink anything, there were varying energies and spirits latching onto me. The veil to the spirit world is the thinnest on Halloween. My light is so bright the negative entities made a beeline to me without me realizing it in time. Before bed, I noticed the spirits being extricated by Archangel Michael. They had their claws in me and this kept me on high alert. When they were removed, others like them entered my vicinity throughout the night. Archangel Michael was flicking them off like a bee. He said he was doing a necessary clearing along with his band of mercy angels. I had absorbed so much bad, negative energy from others while out at the festival that there were etheric cockroaches, spiders, and termites crawling around me and dripping from the walls as well. It was the creepiest thing I had seen seeping in from the spirit world. They were gnawing on some of the light around me. Archangel Michael and the angels were doing a thorough hardcore cleansing that included blasting these things away, while re-elevating my vibration and Spirit. This is why I continued to wake up in sweats even with the air conditioner running on a cool night. This was an incident where I did not actually call in Archangel Michael, but because he is with me regularly to begin with, he went to work on me automatically. He has already had my permanent permission to intervene as he sees fit.

One morning I had woken up about ten to fifteen minutes before my alarm was set to go off. I mentally connected to my angels and guides as I always do.

Archangel Michael shouted, "Get up!"

I quickly rose and climbed out of bed. I mumbled complaining, "Why do I have to get up? I have plenty of time."

When I left the house there were several delays that prevented me from reaching my destination that took an extra fifteen minutes. If he had not warned me, I would have been late for my appointment.

On another incident, I had stopped by a relative's home one evening and felt a negative presence in her place that made me uncomfortable. I left within ten minutes. I later told her why I had to leave abruptly and suggested she Sage her place once in awhile.

She did not think anything of it until a friend of hers who is connected to Spirit as well informed her of the same thing. This friend walked into her place and told her the energy did not feel right. The relative texted me afterwards, "How do I Sage?"

I said, "When you Sage it's called 'smudging'. Light the end of the sage stick. Smudge it all around your body and all around your place. This is by waving the stick around the area. Make sure you get the corners of your home since negative energy gets trapped in those crevices."

She added, "My friend says to open the windows when I do that."

I replied, "Keep them closed for at least five minutes after you have smudged. The Sage is powerful as it grabs the negative ions. Give this process at least five minutes and then open the windows. The Sage smoke will float outside taking that negative energy with it."

She had a difficult time grasping anything beyond the physical plane. It had taken her awhile to come around enough that she later ended up going to get a psychic read from a Medium. This woman informed her that a negative female spirit presence was in her house. The spirit had a red color associated with it. She then added, "You are related to someone who knows about this and connects to spirit. Ask him about it."

She asked me, "What does it mean that it's red?"

I said, "In this case? Aggression. Rage. Vengeance."

She asked, "Is it safe to sleep in my room?!"

I said, "Yes, but it's attracted to your energy. Have you been drinking and smoking marijuana? Are your words negative when you speak?"

She said, "All of the above."

I said, "It's time to re-evaluate your lifestyle choices so they are more positively aligned. Right now, this spirit is attracted to your addictions and its feeding off that and feeding off you. Work on being more optimistic and using positive words when you speak. This means avoid complaining. Ask for assistance in reducing or eliminating your cravings for these unhealthy substances and addictions. Call upon Archangel Michael and say, *Please clear my space of negative entities and energies. Please throw a net of white light over this spirit and immediately take it to the light!'*

She naively asked, "How do I do that if I can't see it?"

I explained, "You don't do it. You ask Archangel Michael to do it. It is not your concern or worry to wrestle a negative spirit to the ground. Light the Sage as you call Archangel Michael and tell him what you need help with. You have to say the words or he cannot help. As ridiculous as it might sound to you right now, you have to say the words."

I had to re-iterate to her that she has to say it, as she was always skeptical when it came to Spirit in those days. She is not religious or spiritual.

She then asked, "Is it safe to sleep in my room."

I said, "Yes, you can clear it out now if you do the steps I've relayed to you, then you have to work on making changes to your lifestyle by making healthier choices. Use positive words when it comes to your thoughts and when you communicate to others."

Negative spirits are attracted to darkness and the shadows in people. This can be someone who is under constant stress, anger, or depression. Any ongoing negative feeling is nourishing food to this hungry spirit. They are not in the Light. They refused to go into the Light possibly due to fear of judgment. This will not happen when you cross over of course. The Light is all love, joy, happiness, and peace. The Spirit does not know that. If someone calls out to Archangel Michael, he will escort them into the Light and out of your vicinity. Archangel Michael is one of the most commanding beings in the Universe. During the days when I was experiencing an immense amount of life changes, which had tons of fear energy from others around me, he was popping in extricating people and situations out of my path. I was in awe and asked him to stick around full time. Nowadays there is not much fear energy around me so he does not have to step in for that as much as he did before, but he continues to travel with me regularly acting as my permanent brawny security in case. These were some examples of how Archangel Michael has helped me and how he can assist you in similar situations.

413

Messages from Archangel Michael

Archangel Michael is the Archangel to call on when you experience fear or apprehension. He can extract anyone out of your vicinity who is not operating from high integrity. If someone causes you uncomfortable feelings, then he will remove them at your request. He explains that some souls create self-induced fear that circumstances in their life are out of control. When the circumstance is examined from one's higher self or a detached point of view, it is apparent that the situation is unnecessarily hyped up to be bigger than it truly is. You witness this behavior in outlandish and dramatic human reaction by the masses to the latest media headline alone. The ego enjoys conjuring up unnecessary worry and drama. They will somehow come to the conclusion that an apocalypse is going to take place at any moment. There is never anything to fear when you have Archangel Michael by your side. Taking a step back you will notice the drama the mind creates is not based in reality.

The human souls that commit violent crimes attract in dark energies. These are souls who go against God and act on free will. They grew up heavily influenced by the people that raised them and the communities they grew up in. The human ego often goes mad from the nonsense of its surroundings. One half of the population is bathed in dark energy, while the other is in the light. The light has gradually been growing in numbers wiping out the darkness, but that does not mean it will not meet resistance. It helps to avoid anything and anyone that triggers negative feelings in you. This includes news sites filled with negativity and gossip. Human souls absorb that energy without realizing it. It seeps into your DNA, cells, and pores. Before you know it, you feel negative agitation that never lightens. Ask Archangel Michael to stand by your side and shield you with pink light so that only love can enter your aura. Follow his guidance to stay away from any and all drama around you.

Your thinking processes are the biggest culprit and cause of any unhappiness in your life. When you find you're moving into negativity, then adjust your thoughts into something more

414

optimistic.

Do you feel like you are running around in a circle going nowhere? This is a clue that it is time to work on breaking away from the walls you have constructed around your soul. Find another path to go down that works. Break away from anything that is holding you back from moving forward. You may need to go back and re-examine what it is you want and how it is you are going about to obtain it. Look at what needs modifying in your life. Take that new-enlightened information and run with it. You will be that much closer to reaching fulfillment.

Avoid getting bogged down in a power struggle with your ego. Do not allow it to drown you in negative emotions. This is wasted energy that tests your patience. It causes one to react and jump into dangerous circumstances and choices without thinking. When the ego is upset, it causes unpredictable behavior in you, in others, and in your environment. There is a domino effect of energy which takes place from one over reactive human ego. Imagine thousands of people obsessively overreacting over the latest media story. They weigh in their two cents on the comment boards or on their social media pages spreading that plague like nobody's business. It is a waste of time since all drama works itself out in the end. It fades away and everyone forgets about it days later. They move onto the next biggest drama to fixate over. The ego blames everyone else, but themselves. This behavior goes on with some businesses, companies, and even in the government. The public weighs in with their opinions and criticisms. All of that toxic energy is darted here, there, and everywhere like bullets from an aimless gun. Stay away from the gossip and noise surrounding negative stories, as it will bury you in the dense energy pull on Earth. It is one thing to be aware of what is going on in the world, but another to absorb it all into your spirit. Sometimes when you experience negative emotions or turmoil, it attracts accidents and tumultuous circumstances in.

Ask Archangel Michael to protect you and shield you from all harsh situations. He can give you courage and confidence when you ask him to. He will help you to keep on going with whatever it is you are at odds with. If you feel weary from struggle, then Archangel Michael sends a reminder that you are more powerful than you give yourself credit for. With Michael by your side, you will persevere. Your ego wants to convince you that you cannot do anything and are incapable of success. These thoughts have no basis in reality. You can do it and have anything you choose. You have to fight for it and put in some effort. Sitting on your couch all day drinking beer will get you nowhere. Dive into the battlefield and claim what is yours.

Archangel Michael is also there for the Dad's as well. Many souls have naturally exuded a paternal role at some point in their lives to either their own children, or to those in the world just when that soul needed it most. Whether you are male, female, or a single parent is irrelevant. The role of a Maternal Father is a psychological one. Society has evolved where Father's used to be seen as distant and emotionless. They were seen as the primary breadwinner and the harsh disciplinarian. This did not quite work creating issues in how souls were developing. Positive creative emotional expression is the innate nature of souls. Inexpressiveness is a trait learned from the Fathers of the past and at times with Mother's. This trait was ego taught and not God and spirit taught – since Heaven is all love.

The newer souls who chose to be born as male in this lifetime display both maternal and paternal traits. This is the same as souls born into this lifetime as female. Females are exuding masculine energy as well. This has stripped away what society has taught what a father should be. All souls when born share within them an equal amount of masculine and feminine traits as God intended. This creates more balance within your soul and ultimately in this world. Wear your masculine traits proudly regardless of your gender. Some have lost their Earthly paternal fathers, while other human souls had an abusive or absent father. They reached out to those who showed healthier father figure traits towards them. Anyone can be a father figure whether you are male or female. If you tend to be mostly receptive, then call on Archangel Michael to help balance that out with other masculine traits.

Archangel Raphael

Archangel Raphael is known as the healing angel. This is because he has performed miraculous assistance and remedies to those who have asked for his help. I have invited him in to assist those around me who have been ill or in need of healing. This can be any physical, mental, or emotional state. He has a bright emerald green light around him that emanates off his body. He uses this light to heal those who are in pain. A friend of mine developed a bad throat infection. I took the role of a healer and carried out a long distance reiki session. I envisioned Archangel Raphael pouring his emerald green light into my friend's mouth and down his throat. My friend experienced great improvement the next day and every day after that until he was completely healed. This was after days of the infection continuing to worsen. Raphael's emerald green light reminds me of the Emerald City in the Wizard of Oz. It is bright, uplifting, and joyful!

After Archangel Michael has cleared and cut my daily cords in the morning, I call in my pal, Archangel Raphael:

"Archangel Raphael I call upon you now. I ask that you pour your emerald green light all throughout my organs and body. Please pour this light through my crown and over my mind calming my thoughts. Pour it over my heart so that I can experience and exude love. Help me to be free of toxins that have accumulated within and around my body and soul in all ways and in all directions of time."

Ask Archangel Raphael to pour his emerald green light in areas that need healing, help, or as a preventative measure. Archangel Raphael assisted me in dissolving my dependence on anti-depression, and anti-anxiety medication. When I was ready, I asked him for assistance by locating healthy vitamin alternatives. This is while guiding me to make certain lifestyle adjustment changes so that the medication was no longer necessary. This would include cutting out anyone or anything that was prompting me to run to the medication to begin with. He worked with me to remove people in my life that were draining, toxic, or stuck in negativity, chronic depression and anger. It was not my job to be the dartboard or on the receiving end for other people's negative energies and issues to hit. There were people in my life that I would find myself feeling cornered by. I would be stuck on the phone with someone who would be tiring on my own energy. I would spend lengthy phone conversations listening to their endless train of neurosis, complaints, and issues. This is what it is like when dealing with a narcissus. I had enough of the one sided friendship and needed to stop the cycle of attracting those types of personalities in. The particular people I am talking about were living in a perpetual state of drama and gloominess. Archangel Raphael taught me that it was essential that I dissolve them out of my life. He said that it did not do me any good and that I was not helping them by being an enabler. They were not bad people or doing it intentionally. There was nothing positive or beneficial to have that constant negative energy around. They were takers and I was given the go ahead to add them to the axe list.

Archangel Raphael worked on the axe list with me as this process took anywhere from a few weeks to several months. I cut out roughly three to four hundred people off my personal social networking page that I had never heard of and nor communicated with over the years. No one should have that many people on their network page unless they are promoting a product. If you are promoting a product or service, then you need to set up a group/fan page for that. I have allowed people to subscribe to my personal social media pages, but I denied random requests unless I knew them personally. These were also people who do not know me, but

418

had a larger image of who they believed me to be through what some call the online persona.

Doing this cleanse during my spiritual transformation specifically was empowering and freeing in all ways as I cut out all of that unnecessary fat in my life so that it was more manageable and balanced. The majority of people today seem to rely on social networking as their means of a social life. It is a false reality because people only have a handful of close friends they actually know in person. It does not matter if they are a celebrity or the President. In the end, the true close ones they have in their life can be counted on their own hands. If you have more people on your social networking page that you do not know, than you do know, then you have created an imbalance in your world. Everything and everyone is all energy and there is a cause and effect. If your world is lopsided, then you are going to bring more of that unevenness into you. It is another form of an addiction as it feeds your boredom or loneliness preventing you from obtaining your dreams.

Since Archangel Raphael is the go to healing angel, he can also help you get your physical body into shape. You can ask him to motivate you to exercise. I do not need much inspiration to work out, because I love being physically active. It is like oxygen to me. I have always been into health and nutrition since I was a teenager, yet there were moments after a long day of being sedentary where I would ask Archangel Raphael to give me that extra push to go for a jog or hike.

I ask Raphael to guide me to the right form of exercises for my body and to keep it strong and healthy in all ways. Being physically active is one of the most important activities I love to do. I am not good with sitting still unless I have something important to accomplish. I want to run, jump, and climb over everything. When I am this active, I do not crave unhealthy substances like bad foods or even an alcoholic drink. I am way too happy and that other stuff only brings that natural high down.

Archangel Raphael can pour his healing emerald green light anywhere from places like your prostate if you are a man, to your uterus if you are a woman, keeping it functional and healthy. Ask him to pour his emerald green light over all of your organs for that matter washing them with his energy light. The power of the mind and working with Archangel Raphael can benefit your health in ways you have never imagined. I have witnessed his miracles in action by working with him for myself and for others. I have asked him to guide me to a stress free lifestyle and to keep my energy high when I am lagging. I ask him to guide me to the right natural products that can assist in this. He always leads me to just what I am looking for not long afterwards.

If I have had a beer or glass of wine with a friend, then I ask Archangel Raphael to clear me afterwards. When I moved into my late twenties, my cravings for alcohol were sporadic and in moderation anyway. The majority of the time I do not crave alcohol or unhealthy foods, and nor do I have a sweet tooth. You can put out a buffet of cakes, cookies, and desserts and I am unaffected. I have no desire for it while others around me typically cry out in pleasure towards it. He can help you reduce those cravings and needs for alcohol or sweets, both of which are covering up an emotional need in you for something else.

Archangel Raphael has a graceful, upbeat energy and I always see him smiling and glowing with joy. This is no surprise considering that he wants us all to be clear minded, always laughing, and enjoying ourselves. When you are happy and filled with joy and love, then you attract and manifest brighter circumstances to you. You are able to accomplish your tasks and life purpose with amazing gusto. Raphael pushes you to get outside in order to receive fresh air and sunshine. All of this has positive benefits to your overall health and well-being.

During the dark winter months, he can guide you to the right indoor lighting lamps. He asks that you open your windows everyday at some point to allow the fresh air to run through your home clearing out any toxins and negative energy that has been built up. This is something you should do daily. When it is cold out, you should still open your windows if possible for ten minutes to clear the accumulated pollutants and energy out.

You can connect to the Archangels anywhere, but the connection is heightened when you are outside in the stillness of nature. It is calming and allows you to hear, see, feel, and know the accurate messages coming through from Heaven. Archangel Raphael is a major advocate for pushing you to get fresh air and exercise as that is an immediate way to balance your Chakras and raise your vibration level. Your Chakras are energy spots located in key areas throughout your soul. When your Chakras and vibration are working at optimum levels, you are happier with more energy. Sometimes the messages he gives you will be to change your diet, give up cigarettes, or to get outdoors. Know that this is all for your greater good. Your own angels, God, and Archangel Raphael will pour their light into your body prompting you to feel alive if you ask.

Please do this often: Take a walk in nature, or through a park, the beach, the mountains, or desert. Nature is filled with angels and environmental spirits around every blade of grass, rose, and tree loving it to life. They take care of God's creation, as you should be too. Do you ever notice that when you walk through a nature setting that the stresses of the day suddenly lighten or evaporate? As you breathe in the flowers and the fresh air deeply, your soul is livened up. It is important to get out in nature and fresh air as much as possible.

If you are at work, then at lunchtime or during a break, instead of eating at your desk, which I never advise because everything can wait, go outside and take a walk around. Head to a quiet area with trees and grass to regroup and realign your thoughts. Avoid the crowds as much as you can. You will notice your circumstances and overall well-being shifting for the better. You will have more energy to complete your work for the rest of the day too! When you leave work at the end of your shift, you will feel energetic and less worn out. This state can be achieved by making these necessary lifestyle adjustments to your routine.

I have always been drawn to nature since I was a kid and felt more at peace being active in a calm, beautiful setting. Archangel Raphael showed me images of the way it used to be in history and how others functioned. People were always outside in nature and much more in tune to their inner selves, the Spirit world, and in Heaven. Before electricity existed, they relied on the sun to know when it was time to go inside and head to bed. They went to bed at decent hours and woke up around the same time at sunrise. They had full days to be productive and get outside the next day. There was a sense of real community and camaraderie. People rarely consumed themselves with timewasters the way they do now.

Archangel Raphael explained that computers and the Internet are great inventions divinely guided to an extent. They have assisted us in connecting the world to one another, but Raphael points out that it is also severely misused in numerous ways. The flip side is that some souls get attached to it and lose their identities in it. As much as it was created to connect us all, many are not connecting to anybody and instead constantly look for the next best thing, which does not exist. The Internet is often used as a major time waster around the world. It's used out of boredom. It is one thing to use it in a positive way that benefits your business or someone else in a way that enhances their lives in a healthy way. It is another thing if it is used to play games on or spend day after day clicking on negative stories or gossip sites. Some do this only to post destructive comments and opinions that come entirely from their ego. The latter is dangerous energy and a major contributor to the downfall with parts of humanity. Many live in a false reality feeling truly alone. They want to be important and seek out validation from others. The media has force fed this hollowness that this is the way to be loved. This deception exists with those that you believe have it all. The only way to have it all and feel truly loved is by knowing who your soul is. You are loved entirely by God around the clock and free of charge.

There was one occasion when I was jogging through the streets exercising. On my way home, I felt strain near my ankle. I walked it off a bit and then started to jog lightly again. I felt this sharp pain around my ankle area. It would hit me each time my foot landed on the pavement. I slowed to a limp and felt the sting of the pain in my ankle every time I moved it. I had quite a way to go before I reached my destination and I wondered, "How am I going to get back on foot? I have too far to go." I heard a voice reminding me, "Ask for help!"

I called out to Archangel Raphael and he came rushing in. He asked me to stop walking and instructed me to rub my hands together. As I did that, I noticed sparks of emerald green light emanating between them. He guided me with additional instructions asking me to hover my hand over the pain on my foot without touching it. I saw emerald green light rush out of my hand onto my foot. I thought, "Well I'll be." I put my foot back down and started to walk it off feeling no more pain. I lightly jogged building up steam again. I was soon jogging my typical speed with no discomfort. It was removed completely and because I asked for assistance. I have not had an incident like that since.

Archangel Raphael is the physical fitness angel too. Ask him to strengthen your body physically, emotionally, and mentally. By asking him to strengthen your body, he will motivate you to take better care of yourself through exercising techniques and nutrition. He will guide you to the right foods and supplements that will benefit your overall well-being so that your inner self is strengthened and upbeat. He will prompt you to lose your cravings for the addictions you are always reaching for. Taking care of your inner and outer body are your first steps towards finding happiness and conquering your desires. Your life will go nowhere if you sit on the couch all day drinking beer, flipping the channels on your television or chatting online with strangers. Your life will go nowhere if you do not get up, move around, and watch what you ingest into your body. Your life will go nowhere if you are consuming endless addictions and time wasters, or if you hang around people who lower your vibration. Believe in yourself and take care of all parts of you and your life. You have to take YOU seriously. You have one body and one life here. Ask Archangel Raphael to work with you daily in making positive lifestyle adjustments.

Archangel Raphael can assist you in ensuring that when you travel it is a smooth one. This travelling can be anything from walking, jogging, flying, riding a train, or taking a road trip.

You can say something like this:

"Archangel Raphael please help me to get to work on time and have a parking space available when I get there."

423

I know for some new to requesting something like a parking spot seems ridiculous, but I would not continue something if I were not seeing results. If I know that I am going to the gym after being away from home for the day, I will give Raphael at least fifteen to twenty minutes to request that a parking spot be available for me. I will ask him to keep the gym as empty as possible or get me on the machines that are beneficial for my body. If I am taking a road trip, I will let him know this so that the trip goes off without a hitch. This is from safely arriving at my destination, to assistance with finding the right hotels and restaurants that are reasonably priced. You can say something like:

"Please ensure that there is as little traffic as possible and help me to get to and from my destination safely."

If I am going out to eat, I will ask him to guide me to the right restaurant with little to no wait. Often I would find that when I have asked for his help in things like this, that there would be no traffic at all and that the trip is smooth and peaceful. I would also be guided to a restaurant that has no wait. The days I would forget to ask or I am disconnected, I would be met with insane traffic and find one thing after another going wrong.

While I have Archangel Michael surrounding my car with white light for protection, I ask Archangel Raphael to make my trips smooth and as traffic and hassle free as possible. The days I would forget to ask for a parking spot or even a table at a restaurant I would find that I would be circling forever with no luck. You will be floored when you begin to witness positive results after requesting the assistance of these and some of the other Archangels. If this seems absurd to you, don't knock it until you try it. Give it a week testing it out. Watch what happens when you do ask for help and when you do not.

I miss the days when bookstores were all over the city. Now that most everything is found on the Internet, the majority of those stores have closed up shop due to huge drops in sales unable to make the rent. This includes regular big chain bookstores, which normally do not carry all products anyway. I would always end up having to order it online. The other stores that closed up were independent specialty shops that were of the spiritual variety. It was always calming to go into those particular stores feeling the good vibes in them wandering down the aisles and absorbing the book titles. I would pull out books on any topic that resonated with me. These were books I was guided to that opened up my worldview.

I was in one of those bookstores months before it closed down. I tripped over a wooden step and stumbled bumping into one of the bookshelves. A book fell off the shelf and hit the floor. I leaned down to pick it up and put it back on the shelf, but I noticed the title was on a topic I had been thinking about the week before. I thought, "That's strange. I don't need a brick wall to fall on me to take a hint." I ended up buying the book. Archangel Raphael is the Archangel that will drop a book you need to read in your path or anything that benefits your overall self. This is what he does when he is trying to get your attention. Never discredit divinely orchestrated events that happen in your life. Archangel Raphael is a powerful being that you will be grateful to have in your life on a regular basis.

Archangel Raphael can help you with things such as: diet, nutrition, exercise, addictions, anxiety/depression disorders, eating disorders, health, finding a great doctor, or parking space. He can help you find that perfect car or home. All you need to do is ask him for his help and to show you signs of his healing guidance and messages.

Messages from Archangel Raphael

Archangel Raphael asks that you get out in the sunlight at least once a day when possible. He also demands that human souls get moving and exercise outdoors more often. The sun has positive benefits like reducing blood pressure and decreasing feelings of depression. A healthy balance of sunlight is more beneficial than getting none. It is not necessary to spend all day in the sun. Get out in the morning hours, or towards the end of the day when the sun is not beating down as harshly. Do this for at least fifteen minutes a day. Granted there will be seasons when the sun is virtually non-existent all day or it's unbearably cold or obscenely hot, but getting outside in the fresh air as much as possible is vital to your soul. In the cases where weather is extreme, it is understandable that precautions need to be adhered to. He's more pointing out to not make excuses to get outside when one is perfectly capable of doing so and the weather is fine.

Do you often feel drained and burned out? Are you overextending yourself? Many human souls sleepwalk through life going through the motions exhausted around the clock. This draining feeling causes you to wish you could just go back to bed and sleep until it is over. Call on Archangel Raphael to help in restoring your energy levels. He can help you get a restful night sleep and to awaken with natural energy.

Crimes have been committed regularly throughout history. It seems particularly heightened these days because of the rapid way the media reports it across the Internet. It is in your face 24/7 with no hope for escape. This is still a Dark Age filled with many dark souls functioning in a human body. However, the Light has grown in many of the upcoming newer souls. This has brought the light in humanity to be equal to the Dark. Those living in the dark operate purely on ego and hostility. This is why the world is in terrible upset. If everyone was at peace, there would be no violent incidents, no hate, stress, or anger. What part are you playing in this equation to stop the madness? Are you a contributor to some degree on certain days? Are you teaching others about love, and to relax, or to stop complaining? The more that others step in to correct certain poor behavior patterns in others, the closer to peace Earth will be.

Archangel Raphael can help energize you and increase your personal power. Sometimes you might have a day where there is an overload of information and feelings within you erupting to the surface. You may have to endure some ugliness or even delays on your life's path. When you gain enough wisdom from it, then the next guidance step is revealed to you. This step might take you in a different and brighter direction. This new road leads you towards enlightenment and a richer life.

Sometimes you experience loss, victimhood, or antagonism. These are products of the ego and lower self. Even if you have felt pain or hurt, then it is time to let that go accepting defeat. This way you can move forward to awesome pastures. Ask Archangel Raphael to help you let go of any pain you're hanging onto for dear life. Circumstances will look up when you let go of the control or outcome of how things will improve. The door opens to reveal something better when you release this tendency. Make your peace with whatever abuse or ill will might have happened to you by others and bring it to closure. See the lesson meant to learn or gain. Release it by moving on into the light of happier times ahead.

Archangel Gabriel

Archangel Gabriel is the messenger angel who works closely with writers, teachers, and speakers of all kinds. Archangel Gabriel is front and center with me. She guides me as a teacher, communicator, writer, and messenger in this lifetime. When I was born, the planet Saturn was moving through the sign of Gemini in my 10th House of Career, Social Status, and Ambitions. The 10th House is where one looks in their birth chart to see what kind of career they would benefit doing. Gemini is the sign of communication, so it is no surprise that I ended up naturally heading towards a vocation as a writer, teacher, and communicator on some level. I've had Hollywood agents who have been on the phone with me suggest that I consider doing radio. They said I have a voice that is commanding, attractive, and inviting to others. Archangel Gabriel is there if you need a push in speaking your truth, even if others disagree. This truth is not in any way used to hurt others vindictively, but to spread positive messages that assist and guide.

Archangel Gabriel is the mother of all mothers' next to Mother Mary. She is there for all children, protecting, and taking care of them. She will step in and assist someone with conceiving or in adopting a child if they ask. If you are having issues or discord with your own child, then ask Archangel Gabriel for intervention and help. She can assist you in creating a calming and peaceful atmosphere to raise your child. All in Heaven work in miraculous ways. Sometimes just by requesting their assistance and stepping out of the way allows them to bring closure to a situation.

When I decided to make a full commitment with my writing work and career, I called in this magnificent Archangel to sit by my side on a regular basis. I write as an outlet for creative expression, to help others, for the sake of release, and because I love telling stories. It is work I would do for free as I receive pure enjoyment with it. Archangel Gabriel pushes me to sit down and write. When I am procrastinating and avoiding getting to work, she swoops in and motivates me.

The first week I asked for her help changed everything for me. I had a newfound enthusiasm to dust off my previous books and revamp them. She helped me take control over my career and re-ignited my passion for it. The ideas started to overflow in me. They have not stopped since I've been working with Gabriel. My work continues to improve and I love what I do. Before I had asked for Gabriel's assistance, I had lost interest in my lifelong hobby and instead focused on time wasters. I would procrastinate to no end making excuses. I would say things like, "I'll get to it when I have more time. I'll do it when I get over this relationship break up." I would make one excuse after another. As soon as I said the words and requested her help with great intent, the changes shifted immediately.

Because she gives your voice confidence, she taught me to speak up in my own life more than I had ever done before. I owe it to Archangel Gabriel for being my own personal author's Agent. If you are a spiritual messenger, she will open every door imaginable to help you get the message out there. All you have to do is invite her into your world.

I talk about Archangel Gabriel as if she is female. I know there have been books and others who have referred to the Archangel Gabriel as male. The Archangels are genderless and have no anatomy, however due to the nature of some of their specialties they tend to have more of a masculine or feminine quality to them. Archangel Michael displays typical masculine qualities so he appears how one might define male dominated traits to be. Gabriel exudes more nurturing and creative qualities, which are more aligned with feminine traits. If you are accustomed to associating Archangel Gabriel as male, then this is how he/she will appear to you. Gabriel is a name that is interchangeable where it can be attributed to a boy or a girl. Archangel Gabriel has been depicted as both male and female in literature, religions, and mythology, so this can certainly add to some confusion. The Archangels are genderless. They are neither male or female. They exude particular qualities that could be deemed masculine, while others are more feminine. This forms how the Archangels often appear to others. The Archangels will take shape in a way that is recognizable to you.

In history, the Catholic Church changed the Archangel Gabriel to a male figure. They wanted to leave Mother Mary as the only divine feminine deity. This was during the days when the world was more of a patriarchal society. Man pushed to keep things male dominated. Women's right to vote and for equality did not come to light until centuries into evolution. In some countries, women still take a back seat. As the gender lines grew to be equal, Archangel Gabriel's gender was shifted back to how she always appeared. Archangel Gabriel was previously known as "Archangel Gabrielle". This is no surprise that certain ways of life were changed to fit that period in history. This included making the Archangel Gabriel male. There is no such thing as either gender dominating the other except where your egos have made this so in human form. The genders of anyone in the end do not matter. What does matter is your light and how you allow it to shine. As it stands now, the church has confirmed that they see the angels as I see them. They know them to be genderless and pure spirit and light. The Archangels are often depicted as having a gender in artwork. This is all imagery in order for you to identify them. This, of course, is contrary to Gabriel's gender belief never being corrected back to female. It is because they are genderless in the end. Archangel Gabriel has been mentioned throughout various religious and holy texts. It has been reported that she announced to Mother Mary of the impending birth of Jesus.

Call upon Archangel Gabriel if you are afraid or hesitant to speaking up and owning your life. If you are in the creative arts such as acting, singing, painting, photography, or writing, then you will want Archangel Gabriel to be the overseer and manager of your talents. Ask her to open doors of opportunity for you in the realm of your gifts. If you are a struggling actor, she may guide you to a class or film festival where someone important hires you. Or you might gain additional wisdom to which you can apply towards your craft. If you are a photographer, then ask her to assist you with starting up your own successful studio. Whenever you are lacking in motivation in any area of your life, then Archangel Gabriel can help with this. Anything having to do with Children you will want Archangel Gabriel around for guidance and assistance. She is often seen carrying a copper colored trumpet that is so bright that the light around her is a magnificent copper and gold color. Visualize Archangel Gabriel showering this light over all of your creative pursuits or your Children. Prepare yourself for the grand miracles that Archangel Gabriel produces while working with you.

Messages from Archangel Gabriel

Archangel Gabriel explains that your soul suffocates when you suppress your emotions and dreams. It is a volcano waiting to erupt and can no longer be contained within you. This is a sign that there is bountiful creativity you need to unleash through healthy sources such as taking on a hobby like painting, gardening, writing, photography, or any other creative and artistic pursuit. Gabriel shows me a butterfly, which is a symbol of the great changes and shifts to look forward to when you unleash this creativity. This happens when you release any pent up non-action. Dig up those projects, ideas, and anything you have always wanted to do. Do not allow procrastination or negative self talk to stop you from diving into creative pursuits. If you have completed a project, then take it to the next level and market or sell it. Purchase some yellow flowers and place it close to where you typically hang out in your house. Yellow flowers awaken creative visions, intelligence, as well as positive new beginnings.

Gabriel pushes your soul to take immediate flight towards your goals, dreams, and career. Whatever it is you have been procrastinating with, she will remove that ego delay tactic at your request. Archangel Gabriel is the Archangel who inspires and lights that fire within you to take action. She is the one that faces you in the direction of your dreams. She plants the seeds in your soul which ultimately gives birth to your creative pursuits. She pushes you out on stage where you belong!

Gabriel is all about creativity and passion. She will assist you with your creative endeavors, or even spice up your love life. This passionate spark can be the push you need to ask someone out on a date or take the relationship to the next level. Even if you have a spouse or love partner, she will light the passions within you to rekindle the heat for one another. Gabriel helps you express love in grand ways while adding the seductive charm to any courtship. She awakens all of your senses so that you experience deep gratification in all areas of your life. She will take your wildest ideas and push you to take action and turn the ideas into a reality. Archangel Gabriel is the muse to call on for all of your creative, artistic, and passionate endeavors.

Archangel Uriel

As a Claircognizant, I often know things that are coming before they happen and do not know how I know. Claircognizance is the sense of knowing the accurate answers about something without being privy to this knowledge. Later the statement you've made turns out to come true and those around you are blown away by this accuracy. This knowledge and information is filtered through your crown chakra above your head by your Spirit team in Heaven. From as early as I can remember, I would pronounce things that would later come to fruition. Others would say, "How did you know that?" My response was and has always been, "I don't know. I just knew." Those close to me are never surprised and just expect it. The souls that are predominately claircognizant find that others always seek them out for wisdom and guidance on issues. This sense of knowing what someone should do or having the answer they need to hear proves accurate. Archangel Uriel is typically present in a big way with those who are Claircognizant.

Archangel Uriel works with me on a daily basis guiding the way, giving me advice, suggestions, and filling my mind with ideas and words. The way Uriel works is he infuses me with spiritual loving ideas where I am able to incorporate and thread them into my work. I use this for myself or to give to those who need specific guidance. The readers of my books may never know what hit them, but perhaps it prompts them to pay attention and see things in a greater way. The positive notes I receive from readers tell me about how they would read a line I have written and picked up on the hidden truth underneath that benefited them in a positive way.

433

I took a long break from writing books and instead wrote in journals and blogs. This was another lifetime ago it seems. I would even consider emailing a form of writing. When I email I can often be long winded, which is the mark of a writer and communicator through words and teachings. It also may point to someone who has incarnated from the realm of the Wise One, as well as someone who is claircognizant in a big way. Luckily, my close friends express that they love my lengthy notes. I was writing everywhere except in books. Archangel Uriel wanted me to get back on that wagon again as he urgently needed me to incorporate these messages for particular audiences who were ready for it. He was nudging me for quite some time trying to get me excited about it. I ignored the guidance and made excuses to avoid getting to work. "I guess so. Okay, I will do it soon. I know the time is coming."

While Archangel Gabriel is the CEO of my creative life pushing me to stop delaying my purpose, it is Archangel Uriel, who is the hands on Archangel through and during the creative idea and writing process. Archangel Uriel made it so that I could no longer temper the creative juices that were flowing within me. I made the deal with Archangel Uriel officially by requesting intervention.

"Archangel Uriel. I am ready now. Please show me the way."

It was within days of my asking him for help that the ideas began to flow the way water flows when it breaks through a dam. It gushed through all of the caverns in my mind with mighty force. This was how I wrote and published several books back to back in under a year. I have not been able to stop my productivity and creativity since.

I like to use the Michael Jackson "Billie Jean" music video analogy as an example of how Archangel Uriel (and Archangel Gabriel) works. In the music video, Michael Jackson is dancing on the streets. Every step he hits lights up including the one in front of him. This is the way Archangel Uriel is with everything in my life.

He played a huge part in the development and creation of my horror drama book, *"Paint the Silence"*. I had explained to him the tone of the story I was going for and that I had no idea what to do with it. He said that he would help by showing me each scene only after I had completed the previous scene. As I delved into writing one scene, he would immediately show me what would happen next and so forth. Blown away by this process, I had no idea what was going to happen until I closed the scene out. As I would reach the end of the scene, the image popped up for the next scene of what was going to happen in the story. He would wait to give me the next cue until I had completed the previous cue. I wrote the first draft of the story in under a month, which was a record for me at the time. Before that, the idea sat on a shelf for several years and I almost trashed it altogether. He understood the nature of the book as I am not just a communicator and spirit teacher, but I am also an entertainer. I enjoy entertaining and bringing joy with my stories. He said that he would help by giving me messages and ideas about humanity that I am to weave into my work. This made the story that much more meaningful or striking. This is an example of how Archangel Uriel can work with you in most any part of your life. He infuses you with a sudden light bulb idea that benefits you and your life in a positive way. He will then show you what to do with it. When you receive a sudden rise in clarity, you can be sure Archangel Uriel is nearby. Archangel Uriel and Archangel Gabriel would be a great benefit for writers to work with.

When Archangel Uriel is sitting next to me, I experience a blasting surge of joy as if I am on top of the world. It is the most uplifting and alive sensation conceivable. Imagine being deep in love or excited about something and multiply that feeling by a hundred thousand. Sometimes the feeling is a few minutes long and other times it goes on for hours! This is when I am my highest creatively open self. I receive an overload of urgent information that I am to do something with at some point. Uriel will give you confidence in your creative abilities.

In my earlier life, I made excuses that I was not good enough so I would hide instead or not bother at all. With him, I no longer doubt anymore. I allow his words and ideas to seep into my consciousness. I bring it all out to the forefront instead of keeping it bottled up. He works with me as a thinker and writer beyond what some are able to see or understand. My existence revolves around work as a communicator. I have my moments of feeling scattered or on overload in the process. He quickly diffuses that and allows me to reach a place of calm so I can easily know what my next step is. Archangel Uriel will unclutter your thoughts and help you focus if you ask him. He is great for students and thinkers alike.

He carries a lantern or light, which he uses to light the path for you when it's unclear or dark. Ask him to light the steps you need to take to reach where you need to be in your life. If you are claircognizant, then you would benefit to work with Archangel Uriel. He will shine his light on the dark caverns of your mind and all of your surroundings and world. If you are experiencing anxiety or clouded by judgment, then ask Archangel Uriel to blast that negativity and debris out of your mind so that you can see the truth. Are you a student or someone who is having difficulty with a test or solving a problem? Call on Archangel Uriel to be your guide. Allow his lantern to shine a light on your entire being so that you are thinking clearly.

Divine messages are passed onto all human souls every day. No one is exempt from the gifts of Heavenly communication whether you are an atheist or deeply religious. Your life choices have an effect as to how clear the messages from the other side come in. You might chalk it off to being your imagination or perhaps you're not able to decipher what is real or what is not. You will know it is the real deal if you are guided in a positive way that enriches your life or someone else's. If it helps you or helps others, then you will know you are receiving accurate messages. When prompted repeatedly to follow your passions and go after your life purpose, then those are messages from your Guides and Angels. It is no accident that you are being heavenly guided. If your singular goal is to be famous, then that is your ego in control. It is important to avoid deception coming from your lower self. What you crave is not always aligned with your higher purpose. The other side does not fulfill those types of requests. Ask Archangel Uriel for assistance when you need a burst of new idea energy and to open up your claircognizance channel, which is your sense of knowing the accurate messages coming in from Heaven.

Archangel Uriel & the Majestic Tree

Your caregivers instill your beliefs in you whether that is your parent or guardian. Society and your peers add that extra layer of burden onto you and then before you know it, you have forgotten who you are. Archangel Uriel shows me a clairvoyant image of a Majestic Tree. He says, "The way that a tree gets its rings and grows outward and upward is similar to what happens to you in human form as you age and mature." He has explained to me that you are a product of your environment.

If you cut a tree open, you will see the many layers that create the rings in it. There is a protective layer on the outer layer called, *'the bark'*. The layers are your experiences that have a profound and lifelong effect on you. If the experiences you had growing up and the molding of you were more negative, then your protective bark is that much stronger to break. As strong as it is, the negative side can be how much do you allow those that are good into the many layers that have defined you?

The inner bark of the tree is called the *"phloem"*. This is where the tree gets its nourishment and food drawn in from the leaves of the tree. The leaves of the tree are the many caverns of your mind. The inner bark is your basic chemistry. If your mind has been polluted by your surroundings, then you can imagine all of the toxins and debris that you have nourished yourself with. This is being fed to you all through growing up. Most souls will get out or break away from their environments especially if it was tumultuous. The problem is that it does not matter how far you travel or the new people you surround yourself with, you will still be carrying the baggage of your upbringing with you. You may not even realize it unless you do a serious self-examination of yourself and the things that block or hinder your progress while in this lifetime.

The next inner layer and the ring within the trunk of the tree is called the *'cambium'*, which is the cell layer that annually produces new wood. This is the good news for you as this is where you're able to start adding new and brighter experiences into your life. It is the healing source of your body. This is where you can correct what has been wronged.

437

The *'sapwood'* is the next layer in the tree, which is where the water flows. For you, this is the blood flowing through your organs. Keeping it clean with a good daily diet helps you detox and cleanse your inner and outer body. When you do this, then healing takes place quicker. You are that much stronger and faster able to communicate with God and Spirit with a clearer reception.

The center of the tree is the *'heartwood'*. This is appropriately titled, as it is your entire body with your heart pumping to keep you alive the same way the heartwood keeps the tree alive.

Cluttered with toxins and debris at the hands of those in your immediate environment are the rings that exist in you. By the time they are all finished, you will have no idea who you are anymore. Those that have deeper wounds from poor handling by those that raised you are for a reason. This is because you have a greater purpose to make significant contributions to your planet. A large percentage will deliberately break away from that mold of abuse. It is basic human nature to seek safety and shelter within groups and fads. This only perpetuates the fear you live in. Have no fear and go at it alone.

There are forest fires that do not always kill all of the standing trees, but they do scar it. As the years pass, new layers of wood cover up the scar by surrounding it. This is what happens to you. You become a new person and have better experiences as you grow older, but the scars from childhood stay buried underneath. The danger is anything can inflame this scar if it has not fully healed. In order to heal your past wounds, you have to face them head on. One of the ways of doing this is by going back into time and honing in on the source of the problem through an in-depth self-examination process. Take that opportunity to release it all in order to move bravely forward into a wondrous new life that awaits you.

Messages from Archangel Uriel

Do not lose sight of what is important on your journey here. It is easy to veer off track while functioning in a material based world on a regular basis. If you do not take just a little bit of time daily to detach from chaos, it can drown your spirit. Soon you find that days have passed and your thoughts have moved into words that are of a lower vibration. Uriel is the Archangel who focuses on improving your thoughts. He extracts the cobwebs that grow on absent minded words. He is also the one who infuses you with brilliant ideas as well as claircognizant hits of heavenly guidance.

Human souls have more power than they often realize. You have the power to manipulate energy in your surroundings and bring forth that which you desire with your thoughts. Do your best to work on keeping your thoughts and your words positive and high vibrational. It is understandable if you live in areas or with people that are predominately ego driven such as the big cities of the world. If you find yourself buried in negativity with no hope for escape, then this is a sign to give yourself a time out alone. Take a deep breath in, exhale, and relax. Call in Archangel Uriel to work with you in eliminating any low vibrational words you cannot get out of your mind. Ask him for intervention in modifying the negative sentences, complaints, or worry that your mind refuses to let go of. Shift your sentences to start with, "I love…" I love myself. I love who I am. I love that I have a car that runs. I love that I have a job that pays all my bills, and so forth. Modify your words to that of gratitude. If you find that you revert to negativity, then stop and re-word your sentences to more positive uplifting ones. It is work re-training your mind to get to that place of catching yourself every time you move into negativity. With practice you will get better at it. The results will be astounding in the end when you find that great things come your way. Your life is less stressful when you shift your thoughts into optimism.

Every thought that pops into your mind has an effect. This effect will determine whether you attract in what you want or what you do not want. Be careful of your daily thoughts, as you may not realize the power they have. You are always manifesting circumstances with the power of your mind, thoughts and visions. When your mind is plagued with worry, then guess what you are bringing into you? You're inviting in more of that negative stuff. This is why it is important that you catch yourself if you find that you are thinking negative thoughts. Quickly envision what you really want and ask that Uriel negate your harmful thoughts. Think about what you want as if it is already happening and you are living in that state. Even if what you want is not here yet, envision it as if you are happily living the life you want anyway.

Uriel works with those who daydream by allowing them to dream big. He pours wonderful ideas into these dreams. A child with an active imagination can create and attract beautiful circumstances over the course of their life. If that child has a hostile or naïve parent, peers, or teachers, they may find the adult saying, "Stop daydreaming and get your head out of the clouds." This is unfortunate as that child could suddenly stop daydreaming. They will instead focus on doing what they feel is expected. When they grow up, they are not manifesting great things in their lives. This is due to the stigma that daydreaming is not taking action. On the contrary, daydreaming is where the seeds of your dreams begin. Our successful artists in history are proof of this. Daydreaming is the beginning stages of attracting in abundance. Abundance is where the necessities you need to live comfortably in life reside. As an adult, you might have a hard time keeping your thoughts positive. This is because society and your upbringing surroundings have taught you that daydreaming or living in the clouds will get you nowhere. Ignore that negative voice imprinted within the DNA of your mind. Daydream, live in the clouds, and envision what you want without human ego interference. Since your thoughts are producing things, you may as well think of what you want. Avoid wasting time thinking of the things you do not want. If you continue to think about what you don't want, then that is what you will get. Take control of your thoughts as if you're the driver of this car.

You cannot sugar coat any of the negativity that might happen around you. Nor can you turn your head away and pretend that everything is okay. When you read media reports of violent acts one after the other, it shines a huge spotlight on the ugliness that exists in the world. There is good and light, but unfortunately the media rarely reports the good stuff because those who run the media tend to function from ego. They feel reporting the good will be boring to people. Therefore, they predominantly feed toxic horror stories instead of balancing it with the good stuff. The media is ego driven and only interested in manipulation to make their quota. The human ego is under the influence and control of the media. The media does this successfully, since the human ego willingly follows. Ask Archangel Uriel to keep your thoughts focused on what matters most to your higher self and ignore the noise around you.

Archangel Nathaniel

Archangel Nathaniel is enormously passionate, intense, and fiery. He is ironically a lot like my personality! There is a lot of heat and red around him when he shows up in your vicinity. He is an assertive no-nonsense bulldozer. He slaps circumstances, people and lower selves out of the way without so much as a warning. He is also tough and strong like Archangel Michael. He appears brawny and muscular in this similar way. Whereas Archangel Michael is a great protector, Archangel Nathaniel is more brutal in that he pushes you beyond comprehensible measures. It is not cruel, but for some new to working with him it might come off like that. The reason is due to the drastic and abrupt changes he enforces in someone's life. You might find that people who you are attached to are suddenly distancing themselves from you. Archangel Nathaniel is clearing your path of anything or anyone that he feels is preventing you from conquering your life purpose. The people he is extricating out of your life might be toxic on some level and hold no positive function for you. All they contribute to your life is delaying you from your purpose, while leading you down the wrong path. You may not immediately see how they are wrong for you, but in hindsight once the beautiful changes happen for you, it becomes all too clear. If you are unprepared for the way that he works, then it might almost seem ruthless or cutthroat. You have to remind yourself that it is for your higher good. What is coming for you afterwards will be even grander than you ever dreamed. He is helping you get there quickly by bouncing these people and toxic vices out of the way.

I had summoned Archangel Nathaniel not realizing I had done

so during my major spiritual transformation. Things were already happening and changing in my life and then he told me who he was.

When you invite him in, he clears the decks on the ship that is your life. People will go away, situations will go away, and things that do not serve your life purpose will fade away. Suddenly certain people you were once close to will stop calling. You might wonder, "Hmm did I do something?" No. Archangel Nathaniel is removing them whether you like it or not. If he feels they are not in line with your purpose and the higher path you are headed down, then he removes them. He does this with great veracity. He is one tough light! He does not apologize for his actions at all. This might make him come off quite harsh and forceful in the way that he works. Know that he is all good, but that he is simply direct in his approach. He was one of the main Archangels that pushed me out towards my writing career purpose with ferocious veracity. He lit that fire in me. I have not been able to slow down or stop ever since. I have had projects on top of one another and ideas that do not stop coming in. This is due to the combination and influences of the Archangel Gabriel, Uriel, and Nathaniel.

At one point, I found it ironic that the regulars around me daily have been Archangel Michael and Archangel Nathaniel. They are both *"bros"* hand in hand working together for me dude. When you have those two working together in your house there is no stopping them. There is no telling what great things are going to come out of your life. You have to be strong enough to realize you will have some losses. Situations, lifestyle changes, and people will fade away when Archangel Nathaniel is at the helms. You have to be mentally and emotionally at the point where you can have that happen before you ask for his help.

When you reach the point where you discover your vision or your life's direction shifting a bit, then that is when you experience an awakening. It can take about a year to re-direct that ship. It is like turning around a big freightliner down a new course as you are making an agreement and a pact with the Universe that the time for change is now. There is a sense of urgency in you where nothing is going to stop you from achieving your dreams. In this process, Archangel Nathaniel comes in to sweep things, people, and circumstances out of the way.

In a sense, it is much like the planet Pluto energy to a degree where the Pluto energy tends to wipe the slate clean. This forces you to make drastic changes in your life. Pluto can have an influence on you suddenly losing your job or some other devastation. The reason becomes clearer afterwards when you obtain an even better job where you are much happier. The way Archangel Nathaniel works is quite similar in that he is wiping your slate clean. He is getting rid of vices that hinder positive progress in your life. This is ultimately in order to assist you in obtaining the gifts you desire. He is removing situations and people in your life who do not benefit your higher self.

Archangel Nathaniel's work has always been invited and welcoming to me. I have never minded the abrupt changes, because he would inform me that it is to bring in brighter circumstances into my world. The old has no use or benefit. I am up to the task and right there moving along with him. He is quite empowering in the way that he shifted my mind and outlook to be receptive to the way he works over the years. I can handle that kind of intensity as if it were second nature.

Call on Archangel Nathaniel if you need assistance with your life purpose, but be prepared for the drastic changes that happen in your life. The shift can take about a year or so depending on you and your progress. After this has happened, you will start to notice the changes. You will be in a place to accept them with the right spirit. Initially, it might be met with some unhappiness as he removes certain people you care about or the circumstances and lifestyle choices you were used to. Change is often meant with resistance in human souls. Remember that this is happening for your own higher good. What will follow this process are grander events in your life. You will be much happier when it is complete. You'll be wondering why you were so attached to it at all to begin with.

Messages from Archangel Nathaniel

Archangel Nathaniel cuts people out of your life that no longer serve your higher self's purpose. This person he removes can be someone who is a constant energy sapper and yet you continue to keep them around. You do not owe anybody anything. You have to take care of you first. If someone is the cause of you feeling constant drain or burn out, then this may have detrimental effects on your health in the end. Not to mention it blocks abundance and delays you from achieving your goals. Nobody needs to live in stress. That way of life and thinking is over. Turn your back away from all of that and face the rays of God and Spirit flowing through you. Nathaniel helps you choose a better way to live by prompting you to move on and away from toxic people and choices. The connections have served their purpose. Do not think twice about it, but swim towards the light and leave those situations that are sitting in dark murky waters behind.

The planet Pluto is dark, cold, and icy. When negatively aspected its energy causes wars, corruption, and abuse of power. It also rips things out of your life without warning. It knows what is not working for you and eliminates it, yet it does this for a reason so that you can change, improve, and grow. When you're hanging onto something toxic and it is removed with force, then this opens the door to bring in something even better. It is like the *"Tower"* card in the Tarot where it feels as if your structure is unfolding around you. These experiences are happening for your higher good so that more improved circumstances can enter the picture. Good stuff has a difficult time entering your life when you cling desperately to the bad. The planet Pluto can feel like it is unleashing internal hell. It shines a light on the dark shadows of your needs and desires. It brings them out erratically in full view. It may cause you to act out and become unable to control your emotions over a specific issue. You grow to be hyper-focused on the issue giving it more power than it deserves. Archangel Nathaniel knows that your ego may throw a tantrum as he eradicates important people and toxic ways of living from your vicinity with force. He pays no mind to your upset, as he knows what will benefit your higher self in the end. Your ego desires and tantrums are irrelevant to him.

You might find that you become more vocal over areas in your life that you are unhappy with during this process. Nathaniel pushes you to do some deep examining of your psychological self. He yanks out the unpleasant parts of your personality for you to face. He prompts you to confront the dark sides of yourself and then forces you to deal with them in a big way. You have to do this in order to grow and wipe out any nonsense for good. This process will not remain upsetting since what precedes this will be followed by an immensely beautiful transformation. Purge anything and everything that no longer serves your higher self. Avoid getting buried in the intensity. The intensity you're faced with is your clue to what is going on in your life that needs serious addressing. This can be your own behavior, your unhappiness at a job, or a specific relationship with a friend or lover. If you do not address it, then Nathaniel will address it for you by removing what it is that you are holding onto as if your life depended on it.

An example might be if you lost your job unexpectedly. The immediate reaction might be devastation or depression. You might come to terms that it was a job you were never truly happy at to begin with and that it was likely a blessing in disguise. Still your ego does not take this ending lightly. It has a difficult time shaking it off wondering what's next. That is until you obtain another job that is even better and feels much like an answered prayer. You end up happier than you were beforehand. You come to the realization that the original crumbling of the previous job happened for a reason. Another example might be a relationship couple who has been at each other's throats for an unhealthy length of time, and that abruptly ends for good. Are you arguing with a friend and not seeing eye-to-eye? One or the both of you may have Nathaniel rip the friendship and connection apart. It is no longer serving a positive purpose on your higher path. These are examples of how Archangel Nathaniel works with you. It may feel like you have no control over what and who is exiting your life. Know that there is a broader purpose for this transition. Patience and faith will be needed during that process.

Archangel Jophiel

$\mathcal{A}$rchangel Jophiel is the beauty angel. She helps you with the rigid stubborn stuff you have a difficult time letting go of. If you are agitated, unhappy, or your self-esteem has plummeted, Archangel Jophiel is an excellent Archangel to call on and work with.

When I need assistance from her, I may say something to her like, *"Please elevate my spirit to the level of joy, the highest vibration."*

She raises your thoughts to a more positive, upbeat way of thinking. I watch and feel her pour her rose light energy over me and all through my surroundings. She will restore everything around you making it all beautiful with this light. This can be from your home, your career, your words, and your body inside and out. She can even get you dressed! If you are going on a date or on a job interview, mentally call on Jophiel to help you look good and radiate that magnetism inside and out. She will spark your inner light allowing it to shine attractively.

Archangel Jophiel is also known to some as the Feng Shui angel. She can certainly help your home get more organized by assisting you in clearing out the clutter. She can do this beyond your home and in all areas of your life. She can help with any unforgiveness you have in your heart so that you experience profound love and joy. When you want more enjoyment in your life, ask her to assist you with that. Is someone firing cruel words of hate or intolerance around you? Ask Archangel Jophiel to intervene and beautify their words. If your life purpose is surrounding beauty endeavors such as the fashion industry, landscaping, esthetician work, or interior decorating then you want to ask Archangel Jophiel to be your right hand sister. Ask her to make your work beautiful and striking. She is the angel that can help bring you happier times in your life. Allow her to uplift your vibration and thoughts to joy and optimism.

Messages from Archangel Jophiel

Archangel Jophiel is the Archangel who helps you clean house literally and metaphorically. She can help clear any clutter within and around your world. She will guide you to re-arrange your home so that it is conducive to your well-being. Living in a cluttered environment will cause all sorts of imbalances in your life. Jophiel nudges you to throw unnecessary items away or box them up. Human ego becomes attached to material items and necessities for a variety of reasons. It's understandable to have an emotional attachment to certain material items which have historical value for you. It is compulsive to save every little thing to which you have no use for. Pack rats are those who save every single item or piece of paperwork they're given. This blocks the flow of positive energy. You walk into an office or home that is piled sky high with unnecessary 'things' and you can feel the strangling energy. Call on Archangel Jophiel to help you function in a free flowing energy environment. She might guide you to remove files off your computer that you never use. You can move them to the trash, or transfer them to discs or flash drives, and store them away. She also helps you relax, calm down, and take it easy. Cleaning up the clutter anywhere will uplift the energy prompting good things to come your way.

Jophiel might guide you to detox from technology. This is by disconnecting yourself from the Internet and television on occasion. Heaven always recommends that you avoid sensationalized headlines, gossip sites, and time wasting activities online. When you feel as if you're having an 'off' day, give yourself permission to disconnect from it all. This will realign your soul with your body so that you can wake up the next day feeling refreshed and fantastic. When you ask for Archangel Jophiel's intervention, she will elevate your feelings and thoughts to the level of joy, which is the highest vibration. She will beautify you inside and out. This includes uplifting the energy in all of your surroundings including your car, home, and office. Archangel Jophiel beautifies the land allowing the energy to flow. The trees, grass, flowers, plants, and all of nature's preserves blossom into a glorious beauty. The same way that she does this with God's planet, she coaxes you to display your most magnificent self by pouring positive energy through your aura.

Archangel Jophiel says that all human souls must break free of negative fear energies. This energy grows when one is involved in gossip talk, or obsessing over the lives of celebrities, to the drama featured in media articles. These are time wasters, which delay you from your purpose. Free your mind from the isolation of fear and misery. Get outside in nature in order to get unstuck. Break free from any self-imposed chains that have bound you and prevented you from moving forward. Have some healthy fun that raises your energy vibration. Fear or upset energy does nothing to help you or anyone. When you break down the reality of what is causing you to feel uncomfortable, you discover that your fears are not real. Everything works itself out when you invite a heavenly being into your life.

When Archangel Jophiel shows up, then a glimmer of hope is about to reveal itself to you. She wants you to be the star that your soul has always been. Human ego allows negative thinking patterns, such as doubt, to creep in and stall you from forward motion. She asks that you shun this mentality and allow your soul to shine bright with confidence. Be receptive to the blessings and good things handed to you. She helps you think big and go after what you want without hesitation. You will get it!

Jophiel can also brighten up your relationships. She will help you ooze attractiveness to your partner. If you are looking to meet someone new, Jophiel will get you out there allowing your positive self to shine. Jophiel delivers the kind of cheery messages that circumstances are going to improve. She guides you to be brave and take risks in your endeavors. The universe cracks wide open ready to bless you with your desires when you are in a joyful state.

Dive right in to your dreams without waiting or second-guessing yourself. Make a list of what you want and take action steps towards each of them today. Keep the list handy in a small box and refer to it often to see what you can cross off your list once it has been conquered and achieved. This is what I do periodically. When I pull the list out at a later date, I have found that most of the things on the list could be crossed off.

Before you can bring in anything new into your life, you will need to clear out the outdated. Archangel Jophiel can help you release that which has been delaying you and holding you back from progress. You most likely already know what you need to let go of. It can be anything or anyone that brings you down or prompts you to experience inadequate feelings like depression, anger or stress. This also includes foods and substances that are not good for you. These substances cause your body to react negatively. When this happens you experience low energy or irritability. This delays you from taking positive action in your life and blocks the incoming flow of abundance.

Jophiel releases anything negative in your life so that you can be free to soar upwards where your higher self lives. She also focuses on the core chakras within your soul aura. These chakras govern all aspects of your life *(physical, mental, emotional)*. If a Chakra is dirty, then that creates an imbalance around that particular area of your life. When you release negative thoughts, patterns, and people, then you are that much closer to obtaining your dreams.

Archangel Jophiel is surrounded by a rose light with tinges of yellow. She is the archangel who will drop rose petals in your path. She assists with things like pushing you to have a good time with an optimistic attitude, to putting together a function, party, festival, or celebration. This is by beautifying everything she touches. If you find your absorbing negativity, then call on Archangel Jophiel and ask her to intervene and help you to remain positive and optimistic.

Jophiel brings people together including groups around the world with extreme viewpoints. She can help them find a common ground, but the trick is they have to ask for her help otherwise the friction will continue. She will assign specific warriors of light from these groups to instill them with some middle ground to connect and link everyone together.

450

She has talked about how the holidays that human souls have created lost its flavor. It has become all about shopping and spending frivolously. This rises during the Christmas and end of the year holidays. The United States is the biggest sufferer of this. She says they have lost sight of their true soul. It is all about gain, buying material things, and one upping someone else. People pack into malls, fighting traffic, parking spaces, pushing, and shoving each other just to buy a shirt. Stores are now staying open at unheard of hours, such as overnight on major holidays just to make another dollar.

What's important to focus on is your soul and why you are here on this Earthly plane. When you fall into superficiality, you lose sight of your purpose. You are here to love, to give love, and to spread love. This mantra should be adopted everyday and every minute of your life. Deep down your soul knows what you can do to bring yourself back. Know your light, know your power, and know what you were born here to be. Love is who you are. Love is the source of all that you wish. Love is the source of power. The more that you love, the safer you are. The more that you allow yourself to love, the more powerful you are. All of your goals are to unite as many people as possible in peace, love, and joy. When all else fails, remember: LOVE. Think and breathe the word always. Call on Archangel Jophiel to uplift your soul to this beautiful state. If you feel agitation, then take immediate soul enhancement steps. Head immediately to your nearest nature locale where there is little to no people. Breathe in all of that beautiful nature, the trees, grass, flowers, and ask God and Archangel Jophiel to surround you with angels creating a healing love cushion. Ask her to extract any negative ions that have latched onto your loving spirit.

451

Archangel Raziel

Archangel Raziel is what I see in appearance as a Merlin type wizard with large gorgeous wings that shine a varying degree of brightly colored lights. He is the magician and sorcerer angel since he helps you manifest your dreams. The big dreams you long for which he brings to fruition come about magically. This can be such as a home you never thought you would obtain or the career of your dreams. He works with you by guiding you in steps towards making these dreams come true. He pushes and prompts you towards that goal by dropping hints and opening doors you thought were closed. He will reveal the wonders on your path that will help you turn your dreams into a reality. He infuses electrical rainbow colored lights from his hands, which he places over your crown chakra and into your third eye chakra to clear and open up your spiritual sight if it is muddy or weighted down. This opens up your clairvoyance channel so your dreams become clearer. The next step for you to take is revealed in these visions.

Archangel Raziel is immensely superb in working with if you are doing intuitive and spiritual work. He will bring all of that effort into fruition. He downloads guidance into your dreams, which contain the answers to assist you in manifesting your desires. He carries a book of magic, which contains the universes secrets that he will pour into your soul. Raziel has passed this information onto Adam after he and Eve were expelled from Eden. He gave it to Noah so he could build his ark. Enoch received the book's messages before his ascension and transformation into Archangel Metatron. He can help you take a leap of faith in your life if you ask him to work with you. When you are clairvoyantly seeing rainbow colored lights you can be sure Archangel Raziel is in your vicinity.

Archangel Raziel has been around me since my spiritual growth and gifts kicked into higher gear. This was after I rid myself of addictions, toxins, and negative people. Once I was on the clear and healthier path, then Archangel Raziel appeared to me for the next step. He comes in strongly for me because I use much of my intuitive gifts for my writing projects. I write from the Spirit, not so much as the Soul. It is from Spirit and divinely guided. I write things down in a journal before I commit them to paper. He has said that I write about what I want, whereas I am envisioning what I want through the writing. If it is a fictional piece, then I am writing my intentions of what I want, but it's actually something that will sell too. He says that I write my dreams in books and then sell them. I envision what I want and I do it through the creative process. Then in my life, I find that I am manifesting what I am creating and writing. This I have found to be true. He is one of the manifesting angels after all.

Like a magician and like magic, Raziel can help you turn your dreams into a reality. Envision with him what it is that you want to see happen in your life and then step out of the way so he can get to work on it.

Archangel Raziel taught me to recognize that I have the commodity here and this is my God given gift. He has said, "Your intentions have manifested you to where you are today." I am using my gifts as directed from God, the Divine, and my Angels. Call on Archangel Raziel to assist you in opening up your clairvoyance and spiritual gifts. These gifts contain the answers to bring your manifestations to flight and reality.

Messages from Archangel Raziel

You are creating the reality you want with every choice you make. This is done with the power of your thoughts and mood. Watch your thoughts and make sure that they do not shift towards something negative. You will manifest the energy that pervades your thoughts. Archangel Raziel encourages all souls to be an individual and not follow the herd. Everyone has unique gifts to utilize to their advantage while here. You were born with it and therefore can easily access it. Do not allow your innate talents to go to waste due to doubts, procrastination, or fear. Raziel helps you become one with the entire Universe. When you are one with the Universe, you connect energetically to a higher frequency. Positive manifestation is what spawns out of this. Because you have the power to create your own reality, you also have the power to shift the bad stuff into something good. With Raziel by your side, you can magically conjure up the life you want by envisioning it with him, and painting the picture in your mind. He can train you to learn how to keep it there. He also acts as a great publicist coaxing the real you to the forefront and marketing it to the masses. He can help promote your higher self's face, your work or career to others. This naturally draws in financial abundance.

A lizard has the ability to act as a chameleon shaping and shifting itself into nature. The same concept applies to you when you work with Raziel. You can be whoever it is you want to be. He says you already have the tools and capabilities to conquer whatever you desire. He warns you not to sway from this God-given gift and use it without guilt. Do not fall into negative self-talk, or the imposter self that makes excuses so that you avoid bringing in the greatness you want. The gifts bestowed upon you are all encouraging and to be used in a positive manner. Raziel can also help you manifest great relationships by showering you with a magic that makes you magnetic to others. Envision the kind of love partner you want with Raziel. He will assist you in attracting that mate in. He advises you to be careful what you wish for, as you just might get it!

Archangel Ariel

Archangel Ariel heals animals, the planet, and all wildlife, but I call upon her to give me courage, confidence, and a fighting nature. I ask for her assistance in helping me reap what I sow. She can help you in manifesting your material and physical needs. Visualize big with Archangel Ariel for circumstances such as working in the career of your dreams, or by envisioning the home you have always wanted to have. In a sense, she works similarly to Archangel Raziel, although they are quite different. Archangel Raziel assists with manifesting your larger dreams into reality while Archangel Ariel assists with manifesting your day-to-day needs that ultimately lead to the larger dream coming true.

Your Earthly material and financial needs can achieve a nice boost when you invite Archangel Ariel into your life. Are you starting a new business? Request that Archangel Ariel join you during that process. Ask that she work with you in getting you all the right tools you need to make it a successful business. This can be anything from the right office space to business cards and even clients.

Archangel Ariel is nicknamed "Lion" or "Lioness" because she is often seen with a wild animal or Lion. She is strong and tough like the image of the Lion. If you say or think harsh words about yourself or others, Archangel Ariel can help you be more compassionate and forgiving. She will be present with you when you need strength and courage. This has to do with your inner spirit and that you can accomplish anything you want to do.

The Lion often seen with Archangel Ariel is also a symbol of the ego, while Archangel Ariel is a symbol of the higher self. She has complete control or domination over the Lion. She is relaxed in holding the reigns of this wild beast. She does not put up a fight because she is strong and powerful. She does not ever need to push against any resistance, but rather glides through it effortlessly. She does not fight or control the animal aggressively, but rather is assertive in her stance. She will remind you to own your life and be self-assured. Ironically, the *"Strength"* card in the Tarot is similar to how Ariel is. The *"Strength"* card in the Tarot typically shows a woman with a beast that appears to be under her magnetic control.

Ariel says to not be afraid to say no if you are not interested in someone or something if it does not feel right. This is your life and you need to be the manager of it. Sometimes you may not realize when you are being aggressive instead of being assertive. The difference is that aggression is hostile while assertive is standing up for yourself without walking over someone. You will reach a place where you and everyone else are respected and pleased with the outcome when you are assertive. It is far more effective than bull dozing over someone aggressively out of fear, anger, or worry. We all do it at some time or another without realizing it, but Archangel Ariel will ask you to be mindful when you are behaving aggressively. When you are aware of it and cannot seem to calm down or stop it, ask Archangel Ariel to come into your life and channel your energies more effectively.

Archangel Ariel is seen with complete commanding strength and at times long flowing hair that varies in its color. I think of her as the sister of Archangel Michael as she is tough in her own right and presence. She says that you have the power to accomplish whatever it is you choose. You must choose wisely of course, as vindictive power never garners Heavenly approval and support. Archangel Ariel can help you manifest your material and financial needs when you invite her into your life.

Archangel Ariel is a tough warrior female hierarchy angel. When you put in a request, she can come into your life and assist you with magically manifesting your desires in steps. Need to improve your finances? Ask Archangel Ariel to help.

You can say something like this to Ariel:

"Archangel Ariel, thank you for taking care of me in all ways and guiding me to the right home that is suitable for my temperament. Thank you for guiding me to a financially successful career. Thank you for working with me in ensuring that all of my material needs are met and that all of my bills are paid. And so it is."

Archangel Ariel is deep in our oceans, high up in our mountains, and present in the open desert. Anywhere in nature is the best place to commune with her although you can ask for her help wherever you are. She is so powerful and unlimited like all Archangels, that she is everywhere at once. She watches over all of God's creations from animals, pets, and our habitat. She steps in to intervene with those who harm any of God's creations while protecting this planet in the process. She does not take it lightly when human egos inflict destruction on nature. Archangel Ariel is a fierce and powerful soldier Archangel that can infuse you with a fighter spirit, and bring out your compassionate inner power helping you to obtain all of the wonders you have imagined in your dreams.

Messages from Archangel Ariel

Archangel Ariel is immersed in radiant violet and purple colors. The colors are a symbol of magical manifestations and serenity. It invokes heavenly spirit and raises one's spiritual vision and consciousness.

Ariel urges you to tame yourself if you have been on a recent kick of lashing out in outbursts, negativity, and upset. She warns you not to act or react impulsively, but rather systematically with bravery and self-control. Let go of the need to control things that get in your way. Refrain from taking other people's egos personally.

Ariel can also bring you positive new beginnings where finances and career related endeavors are concerned. Envision with her what it is you want as if it is already here. Remain upbeat, positive, and hopeful about what is to come. Do not allow any negative thoughts to take over. Ariel can bring in an increase in abundance and finances. Gifts may not be monetary based, but can be an improved relationship, or stronger commitment with your partner, or sense of self. It can be a long lasting spiritual joyful feeling. Call upon Archangel Ariel to work with you in creating this firm foundation where you can begin building the life you want upwards. She helps you to believe that you deserve it.

Retreat into a nature setting and call in Archangel Ariel and absorb in her powerful energy. Literally stop to smell the flowers as you take your time strolling through nature. Lean in to breathe in the flowers, plants, and all of nature. Hug a tree or sit up against it to release heavy toxic emotions. Nature is where spirits power is heavy. Take it all in allowing it to awaken and open your mind and senses. Take a deep breathe in and on the exhale release any lower vibrational thoughts and words. Nature affects all souls positively on a biological level. Flowers can brighten up a room, but they also raise your vibration. The different colors of a flower send particular messages to your brain pertaining to the flowers specialty. For example, green flowers can calm someone who is full of anxiety. Yellow flowers can brighten and uplift. Red flowers can awaken your inner passions and invite love into your life.

Ariel governs the changing of the seasons. The seasons changing serve as a reminder of how far you have come. You are aware that time is forging on and it is a new period in your life. Nothing stays the same and you must move with this shift in the right spirit.

Archangel Ariel works with you on obtaining material success. She knows that as a human soul, you have a need for certain material necessities. This isn't to be confused with a greedy hunger for material excess. She provides abundance by showering it upon you when you ask her to work with you in your life.

Ariel is ever present in all nature settings, high up in our mountains, soaring along with the wind in the deserts and surfing the waves of the oceans. Your concrete material needs increase when you invite Archangel Ariel into your life and follow her guidance. Success is not always financial. It can also be a state of mind in feeling grateful and optimistic with where you are at now and how far you have come. Be grateful for what you currently have. See the blessings that you have in your life right now. Do not think about or worry over what is coming next or what is not here. Put that all aside and let loose, enjoy yourself, celebrate, and have a good time. Living in the moment and enjoying it brings you closer to having your dreams come true since positive thoughts attract the same energy to you.

There is nothing wrong with believing in yourself and shouting what you have accomplished from the highest mountain. Graciously accept all positive gifts showered upon you and do it without guilt.

Ariel also asks that you make regular efforts to connect with family or close ones. When we say family, know that it does not necessarily mean your earthly blood related family. Family is a place of unity, hope, and gatherings with likeminded souls. Families are your friends, your close ones, the trusted ones. We are all family and connected as souls.

Ariel shows me vibrant images of people boldly wearing warm, bright colors to accentuate their state of being. They are outdoors basking under a beautiful warm day. Their personalities are rich with fulfillment. They bask in smiles and are having a good time. They are not gossiping or speaking negative words. They are laughing while feeling joy and relaxation. This is what Ariel wants for you. She wants to help you get to that place of being in this state around the clock. Get outside and rejoice in a private celebration known only to your soul. Call up a friend who knows how to have a good time. Let all of your cares go and have an awesome time in this life!

Mother Nature is the perfect place for spiritual and personal enrichment of the body and soul. There are more angels, guardians and spirits watching over every flower, every grass, rock, and mountain terrain than anywhere else in the world. Ariel rules the nature areas with her strong Earthly spirit presence. Many human souls stick close to other people in the bigger cities. This is where most of the negative energy is. This is where there is an immense amount of people, buildings, or man-made developments.

No matter what you are facing, Ariel can help toughen your inner self's resolve. Pull yourself up by your bootstraps and run over your challenges with great vigor and detachment. Take the rough patches in your life with stride. Being strong can be difficult when you are facing adversity. You can be strong by taking control of you and your life. Accept that some things have happened beyond your control and leave it alone. Know that it is all for a reason even if you cannot see the reason immediately. Ariel will help you be the calm within the storm. You handle your challenges the way Ariel tames the beast and lion. This is done with assertive grace.

Archangel Haniel

Archangel Haniel has a soft blue light around her, which she uses to re-center and ground your soul when needed. She communicates through your feelings and can assist you in awakening your intuition. Your intuition is where the true answers live. She will show up when you need to be urged to withdraw from the noise of your daily life. Her energy is delicate and gentle. When she moves into your room or area, it is often so subtle you might not notice it unless your clairsentience is running on high gear. If you are in tune to feelings and sensations of everything around you, then you will likely sense her presence.

Archangel Haniel works with artists and creative people opening up their sixth sense in order to assist them in producing exceptional work. When I am writing she moves into my vicinity filling it up with her bluish-white light. Her purpose is to keep me in a warm state of mind by having a crystal clear communication line to Heaven.

Archangel Haniel can turn the cruelest heart into something beautiful and loving. She tends to show up around those who are experiencing accelerated spiritual growth or who are super vulnerable in some way.

Haniel is connected to the Moon cycles and can help you manifest during the correct phases of the moon. Call on her for assistance during the night of the Full Moon and ask her to awaken your inner perception and release toxic energy, people, and substances. She will work with you in getting you to trust the

Heavenly messages you are receiving. She will help you to follow your intuition, how to believe in it, how to nurture it, and how to move forward with it. Awakening and protecting your psychic gifts are some of Archangel Haniel's specialties. She is a gentle Archangel for the sensitive and those with deep psychic gifts.

Messages from Archangel Haniel

Archangel Haniel works overtime during the week of the Full Moon transit which happens once a month. The intensity pull of the Full Moon begins to build 3-5 days before the day of the Full Moon and then 3-5 days afterwards. It affects so many at once which is why Archangel Haniel's work runs full time during that transit. The Full Moon can make one feel uncomfortable while bringing up feelings of anxiety, uneasiness, stress, and depression. It places a spotlight on what you are going through internally and pulls that out of you for you and those around you to see. Because it brings that stuff out, some souls may be prone to want to cover up those prickly feelings with toxic substances or addictions to cope. This will not make it go away, but instead will mask the cut like a band aid. You will wake up the next day feeling low again.

If there is anything negative lurking within you, then examine what it is and then release it. Some do this through Full Moon rituals. You cannot make a mistake when you are purging something under a Full Moon. It is about setting the intention that you want to get rid of whatever baggage or emotion you have been carrying around. Intention is feeling what you want with every fiber of your being. You feel it in your mind, your heart, and your stomach. Many use the night of the Full Moon to purge this baggage, because the energy of the Full Moon is incredibly powerful. You may want to make a list of the things you would like to get rid of on a piece of paper. On the night of the Full Moon, say each line mentally or out loud. Follow this by releasing it to Heaven. You can release it by mentally releasing it, by shredding the list, and then tossing it in the trash, or burning it safely.

The Full Moon tends to prompt the ego to shout their issues into the ethers or to anyone who will listen. The Full Moon loves drama and puts all of it out there on display. You want to be extra cautious that you do not express every single emotion that could cause some backfiring where personal relationships are concerned. If you are angry or irritated about something, wait until the Full Moon passes before acting if you can help it. I've noticed so many ignore this advice unable to control themselves. They eventually witness it backfire. They end up worse off than they were before.

The Full Moon brings up anguish, anxiety, and fears. All of that is a mirage, but the energy pull of the Full Moon aggravates your inner emotions lodged within you. Thoughts produce things so if you are marinating in constant daily worry over an issue, then that will expand and bring more of that to you around the Full Moon time. Release negative thoughts and get rid of it. It does not do you or anybody any good to hang onto that stuff. The thoughts are so powerful that you refuse to let them go. This is a burden of heavy weight on your soul, which can stall you from movement. It essentially holds you prisoner.

The Full Moon energy pushes you to fall deep into your psyche. It pulls out your most troubled issues in order for you to address, release, or correct the issue. Imagine the plaguing thoughts are sitting in your hand. Cup your hands together and lift them into the air. Follow this by opening up your hands allowing the troubles you have gathered up to fly out into the air up towards Heaven for transmutation. Perform this with intention and you are heard. Once completed, feel the release all throughout your body. Your spirit and light will expand upward to a higher level. You will look back in hindsight wondering why you were holding onto those negative thoughts, people, and circumstances so tightly.

When you are riding on a level of joy, the answers or insights you need miraculously appear. Archangel Haniel relays these insights to you. She heightens your psychic perception so that you receive profound insights that can benefit you in a positive way.

There is often talk about the dark energies in the world, but Haniel says your soul must meet challenges in this lifetime. This is how you grow, change, and evolve to the next plateau. However, these challenges do not have to be difficult or seen as dark. It is all in how your mind perceives them to be. As long as you remain grounded, centered, and keep an optimistic attitude, then you will be fine. You will be able to handle the challenges that come your way with poise.

Archangel Haniel works hard during any Full Moon week helping you have deep insight while awakening your own inner truth. During the Full Moon, your emotions will increase. This might make one cry out for help. Haniel hears these cries and moves into your space to ease you of any pain you're experiencing. The Full Moon and Haniel combined open up your intuition and sixth sense. It is important to understand the difference between what heavenly prophecy is and what your fears and ego are. The Full Moon energy unleashes all of that intertwined with one another so it might cause confusion. Ask Haniel to give you crystal clear signs of what you are intended to know. She asks you to remain positive as you purge and release any negativity in your life. As you release these things to Heaven and the Universe, be optimistic knowing that they will go through a transmutation process and in return bring you blessings.

When you work with Archangel Haniel, she reveals hidden truths and secrets. Some of this guidance can be the information you need to reap rewards from your endeavors and ideas. She shines a light on this truth. This may cause upset, as it is sometimes not expected or wanted news. The truth reveals itself so that you do not continue living in denial. Denial cripples your soul's growth and movement. You might be shown people or circumstances who should not be in your life to begin with and you have to face this truth. Ultimately, what follows is a positive transformation related to your growth. Those that will get through it effortlessly are those who already do the emotional work on a regular basis. Haniel holds a mirror up to your inner emotions and world. She does not allow anything to stay bottled up.

Archangel Haniel awakens psychic perception and unleashes emotional issues you might have buried deep within. She assists you with purging this while discovering hidden secrets about yourself or someone else. Perhaps you have found out that someone you are personally involved with on some level has not been operating with integrity. Before jumping to conclusions, it is important to address any issues with them by communicating peacefully about it. Remember that not all may be what it appears during a Full Moon transit. If you find that this person is repeatedly hostile or defensive when you attempt to have a healthy discussion, then this might be a sign to distance yourself from them if even temporarily.

The energy of the Full Moon is so intense and powerful that some souls cast important spells during this transit. Spells have two important ingredients: Energy and intention. Intention is feeling what you want in every cell of your body. When you put intention into a spell casting, then you are adding more energy into manifesting that which you are seeking. A spell merely enhances the energy of what you want. This is why it is important to be careful when working with energy. You are made up of energy and there can be repercussions with how you direct this energy. When in an angry mood about a situation, you'll find more negativity piles into your life. How many times has this happened and you have said, "Wow, it's just one thing after another today?" You create your reality with your emotions and thoughts.

You do not need to have a spell cast to work with intention. Meditate on the Full Moon and commune quietly with Archangel Haniel about what you desire. Create your own ambient sanctuary with candles, incense, and soft music playing. Write down a list of what you would like to release and then burn it or trash it. Let it go and follow this with what you do want. This does not have to be material items. This can be requesting that you have a more positive mindset. It can be that you do not hold grudges towards others so intensely and are able to forgive more readily. Since you manifest from within, fixing your inner self will assist you in bringing grand opportunities much more swiftly to you. Having an optimistic attitude, and being able to forgive and forge on, will keep your manifestations positive.

It is important to remain affirmative during this process. Recite positive statements to remind your soul of the good that is around you. Say what you want with intention, but say it as if you already have it and that it is here in your life now. List the things and people you want to release. *(i.e., thank you for releasing my anger, thank you for*

465

releasing my fears, etc.)

Check the calendar for the Full Moon dates of the year. Call in Archangel Haniel to work with you then in releasing toxic energy, people and substances. Be open to letting go of all that no longer serves your higher good, then be receptive to the blessings that will follow.

Archangel Azrael

Archangel Azrael is the "Angel of Death", but it is not as ominous as it sounds. He ushers and escorts the human souls that are crossing over to the other side gracefully. He heals those grieving over a death or loss. This can be any kind of pain you're feeling such as over someone's death or the hurt over a past relationship. If you are living a toxic life, he can help remove those negative vices and blocks by guiding you to change course towards a healthier minded path.

When my father passed away in November 2010, I found him in one of the rooms in his house on the floor. There were a couple of people frantically trying to revive him. Archangel Azrael was also there in the room when I walked in. I told them that my father had passed on already. Those around him were understandably in a panic shouting for him to wake up. It is difficult to speak to someone who is under stress as you have likely experienced at one time or another. I remained calm and firm, as I tend to be in most situations where others are not. I let everyone else react in ways that are typical when a death has happened. Archangel Azrael pointed to my father's heart. I nodded knowing that was the cause of his death. He had passed on in under a few minutes. It was a smooth transition process to the other side. My father was shown something profoundly incredible where the Light was. He experienced immense joy and serenity. It was enough for him to choose that peace instead of any discomfort and pain he was having in this life. The negatives he felt in this life such as stress and worry caused irreparable issues to his body, but his soul was always kept whole.

Archangel Azrael does not leave during this process. He comforts the grieving and those who have a tough time accepting someone's death. He is unlimited as all Heavenly benevolent beings are and therefore he can be everywhere at once. The death of someone you love is nothing to fear or be upset about. It is a natural part of life and is not truly a death. It is an ending of one particular life, but your soul is still alive. The body your soul inhabits has reached its maximum potential. The soul has fulfilled its purpose in this lifetime. Your soul can no longer reside in that body, but your soul itself never dies. Your body disintegrates back into the Earth's atmosphere. Your soul exits the body and travels onto the "other side", or whatever you equate Heaven to be. It is all the same regardless of the name human souls give it.

When you are experiencing difficulty over the end of certain friendships or relationships, then ask Archangel Azrael to be present for you. He will work with you in ending certain toxic lifestyle choices when you request it. At times, you are being forced to end circumstances that no longer work for you. The conditions you were living in only stalled and held you back. This can be a work related endeavor, to relationships, including love and friendships. Many suffer through some inner turmoil during this process. Archangel Azrael will assist you in easing your heart so that you can have a peaceful ending with whatever it is you are looking to eliminate and bring to a close. When you think of death or endings that cause any measure of upset, immediately think of Archangel Azrael and he will appear and get to work on you.

Some of these endings might be forced and not what you had initially wanted, but they are necessary for your growth. They are essential in order to bring in the magic you crave in your life. Out with the old and in with the new. Greater opportunities cannot enter the picture until people and circumstances that no longer serve your higher good exit your world. You might experience a roller coaster ride of emotions including anger, depression, and even forms of grieving when there is an ending of any kind in your life including a death. Call on Archangel Azrael to be with you and help if you are feeling distress or grieving over anything in your life. He can help you unburden the load of heavy emotions associated with this departing, while guiding you through this transition in your life so that you can be at peace much more quickly.

Messages from Archangel Azrael

Archangel Azrael is with those grieving, in distress, or experiencing loss. He helps you unburden the load of heavy emotions associated with any kind of ending that brings turmoil, especially the death of a loved one. He guides and assists the souls who cross over to the other side, as well as the human souls on Earth experiencing a major transition in their life. Azrael is present whenever there is a crucial soul transition in one's life. Major transitions and transformations can cause prolonged suffering when not attended to. Azrael eases your soul allowing the crossroads one is moving through to happen more efficiently than without his help.

Endings can be anything from friendships and relationships, to eliminating harmful lifestyle choices. They can be circumstances that no longer operate in your life. This can be work related endeavors or relationships. Many experience uncomfortable feelings on some level or inner turmoil during a transition or ending.

Your soul wakes up when faced with the death of a close loved one. You come to terms with your own mortality and see the rest of the world and its way of life as being trivial and superficial. Circumstances open up in profound ways after the death of a loved one, even though this might not be evident right away.

Some soul's crossing over fear the light and might avoid moving through it. They equate the light with judgment or eternal Hell. This is due to their upbringing on Earth with others hammering into their psyches that there is a wrath of judgment waiting for them. This is not based in the reality of what happens when you cross over. Your ego, feelings, and thoughts remain whole as you cross over. They are no longer confined and trapped within the heavy weight of the human body. If your soul stays on the Earth's plane instead of moving graciously into the light, then you will continue to cling to the negative traits you assumed while in a human body. However, if you let go of this control and move with the natural process of crossing over to the other side, you will gradually feel any pain lifted off your soul. You will retain this information in your subconscious and pull it out when it is your time to cross over.

Many human souls are battling intense energies and emotions as we move out of the final Dark Age. With this comes tons of purging and releasing of the old ways of living that no longer work for you. There are human souls rigidly stuck in the dark ages. Azrael helps you along as you move through an indefinite closure to a situation or way of life that must end. Closure or completion is a reason to celebrate as it moves you to the next plateau of your soul's growth. Enjoy the rewards that come with the effort or lessons you have gained through this completion. It is a transition into something far greater.

There comes a time in your life where you will experience an ending that you're unprepared for. This might have happened already at least once in your life. A door closes on a chapter that your ego does not want to end. You are moving down another path which feels unknown. This may conjure up something unpleasant within you. Call on Archangel Azrael to be your guide and protector to have with you on this important ride, such as an event that requires closure. Perhaps your love relationship has ended abruptly and you feel devastation and depression. Maybe you are experiencing wasted emotions in your relationship, such as plaguing thoughts of suspicion or jealousy. It is driving you mad, but you do not know how to stop it on your own. You feel like an unattached leaf blowing in the wind without the security you had come to know while in this relationship. Azrael is the powerful being you will want to invite into your life to help you through it much more quickly.

This can be any kind of ending beyond a relationship. It can be an actual death of a loved one, the ending of a job and the beginning of a new one. It can be a transition into another life, or if you're feeling stuck in limbo. Azrael is the Archangel Light who smoothes out the rough edges and helps ease any feelings of sadness, depression, or confusion. He will brighten up your world just when you need it most.

Azrael is there for a death or ending whether physical or metamorphic. Death is nothing to fear. The word has a negative connotation to it, but death is the opportunity to move into something more incredible beyond what you can imagine. It is the ending of one way of life and the ushering in of a newer more improved one. It feels like everything is over, but this is an illusion. What is happening is opportunity. What once existed has now run its course. The pain that endured on any level must be stopped. When it reaches its end, then you can be free. Call in Archangel Azrael to assist with any transition in your life. You will find that circumstances start working itself out. You will reach a happier and content space much more rapidly.

Archangel Metatron

Archangel Metatron and Archangel Sandalphon are the two Archangels who once lived in human form whereas the other Archangels have always been spirit. Metatron and Sandalphon ascended into an angel due to the profound work they did on Earth. In this section, I will touch on Archangel Metatron. He was the prophet Enoch in human form before he ascended into an Archangel in the spirit world.

As an evolving spiritual teacher throughout the course of my life, Archangel Metatron has been present making sure I stay on the right path. He does this with all spiritual teachers and healers of all kinds. He guides you in the direction of contributing to help this world be a more beautiful place. You do this through positive service.

He assists you in balancing your life through giving and receiving gestures. When you over give and receive little, then this creates imbalance in your world. Metatron taught me that giving out assistance and the free wisdom to others that I do on occasion qualifies as the same as giving. I would do this act of service as I am guided. I never put any additional thought into it, until he explained that it was something that Heaven was noticing. When no one else appreciates or notices what you do, he tells me it is all recorded in Heaven and with God. This is all that matters in the reality of it all.

Those who tend to over give are typically uncomfortable with receiving. This is likely due to elements in your upbringing where you were made to feel undeserving of anything good. You over give because you are indeed a beautiful and wonderful person, but sometimes it can be in the hopes that someone specific likes you.

Never give to others for false attention and know that the right people will love you regardless of your gifts.

If you feel undeserving of anything, ask Metatron to remove those feelings and thoughts from your aura. He can remove those blocks and help you to see and understand how you are a child of God who is just as worthy as anybody else to receive. Do not allow yourself to experience guilt or fall into the space of feeling unworthy of anything good handed to you. To deny receiving is to create an imbalance in your life. If one part of your life is lopsided, you block positive manifestations and good things that the Creator bestows on you.

Archangel Metatron can help you balance your giving and receiving energies and get your life on track. He will guide you to organize and prioritize what is important towards your higher purpose. He will lead those human souls who are ready to become a more evolved spiritual soul.

Archangel Metatron records your good and bad deeds in a book in Heaven that is devoted solely to you. Every human soul has one and it is filled up with your actions on Earth. This book is pulled out into the open when you cross over for your life review. This way you can experience all that you have done. Included in this are both the good and bad deeds or words and actions made toward yourself and others. You will feel all of this with great veracity.

Metatron is the Archangel who steps in to guide sensitive children by helping them to stay on path and become a spiritual warrior of light when they grow up. If you are a new spiritual teacher or healer, you likely have called in Archangel Metatron into your life without knowing it. Be open to receiving him and his wonderful gifts and knowledge. When you invite him into your life, he can do things such as stretch time and space if you are late for an event, to transforming you into a spiritual Warrior of Light.

Messages from Archangel Metatron

Archangel Metatron focuses his light on the new souls being born. These young people are entering a new phase in their soul's growth and he is here to assist them on their journey. Remain optimistic and open as you navigate the choppy waters that this life hands you at times. Children are born wide-eyed with a clean slate and not tampered with by the human ego of others. Do not allow others to influence you in a negative way. This is your life and you need to live it for you. Focus on all of the opportunities and possibilities that await you. This applies to anyone who is about to embark on a new chapter in their life. In this state, you are also open to whatever circumstances come your way. Be carefree and detached from all negativity, stresses, and worries. You have the entire world at your feet as you forge on a new path with no baggage. You have nothing to lose and are ready to seize fresh opportunities. Being in the right space is by feeling excitement and optimism. This can be the young adult heading off to college with immense anticipation, or it can be someone who moves into a new home with the intention of starting a healthy positive life. They all have a blank canvas to paint their newly gained knowledge onto.

I have been living several lifetimes rolled into this one particular lifetime. With that have come many forks in the roads. These have been transitions, awakenings, and spiritual evolutions. If you have reached at least one major transition in your life, then you can be sure that Archangel Metatron is present around you. The awakenings we speak of are the kind of transitions that propel you into something profoundly empowering. Metatron takes immediate note when he sees human souls with a clear road ahead of them. He sees that these souls are looking to improve themselves. He swoops in brightening up the way leading them out of any previous darkness. He assists those souls by helping them live in the moment and enjoy what their new life has to offer. Believe, trust, and have faith in the miracles that he bestows upon you as you forge down a sunnier road with a brighter outlook.

Move through life as if you have the world at your feet. This broadens your vision and the Heavenly guidance becomes clearer. You take chances on things that you ordinarily would not have done before you propelled forward with this new life. These chance circumstances are positive opportunities and not to be confused with experimenting with toxic ways of living that includes drugs, alcohol, and partying, etc. Those are escapism tendencies, which offer no positive benefit in the end. There is nothing wrong with having a drink once in awhile. Heaven says this only for your benefit. They know that the great high you crave is when you are operating from your higher self and free of toxic vices and addictions. Your mind is clearer and your perception is broader.

You cannot sit back and allow your dreams and opportunities to come to you without effort. You need enormous willpower and determination to reach the varying heights of success. Metatron guides these particular souls down these new roads. His focus is on those souls who put in the work. It is not enough to embark on a new journey with no point or destination in sight. The souls highlighted are the ones who have a spark ignited within them. They have a thirst for knowledge wanting to accomplish many positive things while here. They have strength of will and drive. They are good people and their resolve brings them to enormous heights. Even in the face of setbacks, they do not allow that to crush their spirit or depress them. They brush it off as if it is merely a little bit of dust on their shoulder. They continue smiling while remaining open as they proceed on to the next step. They do not see the disappointments as anything remotely strong enough to stop them on their quest. Instead, they are inspired and ready for the next challenge. There will be struggles, but this soul knows there are more victories that supersede that. In the end, the efforts are worth it. When you do the work in evolving your spirit, the wonders and triumphs gained in your life overpower any menial setbacks. Archangel Metatron plays an important part in this process for these particular souls.

Archangel Sandalphon

Archangel Sandalphon is the other Archangel who once lived as a human soul. He was the prophet Elijah. Archangel Sandalphon works with tender and gentle energies and souls. He is the angel of music who works with all artists. If you are a singer or musician, you would do well to invite Archangel Sandalphon into your life to assist you in making harmonious music. He is an inspiration for all human souls who love to work in the Arts. He personally aligns my clairaudience with the messages I hear over the notes and sounds of music.

Sandalphon bridges the gap linking the physical Earth with the spiritual heavens. He can help you remain connected and grounded while being linked to Spirit. He helps with your ascension in deciding whether you are ready to move to the next spiritual path or not. He is a super compassionate Archangel, which is why he tends to show up for the ultra-sensitive as to guide them gently out of heightened turmoil.

Archangel Sandalphon will often stretch his appearance to the point where he is taller than a human soul can comprehend. He stretches his appearance from Earth to Heaven bridging both worlds. He reminds you that all of your wishes, dreams, and hopes happen through Divine timing. You must first complete one-step, before the next one is shown. Call on Archangel Sandalphon if you have been using harsh words towards yourself and ask him to infuse gentleness into your life. If you are a singer losing confidence in your voice or your voice is wavering in general, ask him to pour his turquoise light energy into your throat chakra.

If you have prayers you feel are not being heard by God, ask

Archangel Sandalphon to step in. He delivers these great prayers to God for tending. Understand that sometimes there are delays on when a particular prayer will be answered. There are various reasons for this. You have some things you need to be enlightened about on your own. Heaven may be maneuvering certain pieces to the puzzle that allow your prayers to be answered. Your prayers may be answered, but you're not seeing how it is. Sometimes Heaven sends assistance in the form of steps that you might not be noticing. Ask for clarity when this happens from Archangel Sandalphon.

Messages from Archangel Sandalphon

Archangel Sandalphon says that there are divinely guided artists in front of all of us. These include singers, musicians, painters, photographers, comedians, entertainers, actors, writers, and anyone in the creative arts. He sends a reminder that if a human ego chooses to dislike an artist, then they must remember that the artist is a light of God. The artist has a purpose that benefits and attracts in specific human souls for a reason. Everyone is in various stages of awareness and development. Not all human souls love the same artist, but you must respect all of God's creation regardless. Those who are in the arts have varying purposes that inspire, uplift, or change someone's way of thinking into something more positive. They may not motivate or attract you, but they do attract in someone who needs their inspiration to be empowered. These artists, actors, musicians, and writers have a role in this lifetime that benefits others in a positive way. They are able to lift the vibrations of other human souls simply through their inspired creative work. This work is heavenly guided and Archangel Sandalphon is at the helms running the show like a conductor with an orchestra.

Archangel Sandalphon is the muse who channels God's light through the human souls that entertain and create. He also does this with healers and spiritual teachers as well. Archangel Sandalphon is a bit of a traditionalist. There are artists out there who entertain and bring joy to the masses. They should not be confused with the artists who shock for mere attention and ego gratifying purposes. The artists all have elements of divinely guided work within them. Mixed with this is the tug of war of the ego. This is due to the demands of promoting and selling your art as a business. In the end, they serve the purpose of entertainer and heavenly inspiration, even though on occasion their ego may run the show. The basic light and concept within each of their souls is profound.

Sandalphon was a holy man when he was a human soul and this energy magnified as an Archangel. Because he can be with as many as he wants to be, his role carries over to the spiritually wise. This is from those who work in the church to those who are spiritual healers on any level. His light is around the schools, learning institutions, and self-help organizations of all types. This is by acting as a holy teacher. He guides or inspires those in the teaching professions towards the right road where they can benefit the masses positively. Some human souls abuse their gifts and operate from massive ego, so it is important to note the difference between what is divinely inspired and what is not. The ego of a human soul never listens to the guidance and messages of any enlightened heavenly soul and spirit. When an artist or teacher is not operating from their higher self, they are experiencing their own lessons and repercussions as a human soul by their personal actions. This has nothing to do with the real work put out there when they function from their true self.

Archangel Raguel

Archangel Raguel is instrumental in harmonizing all relationships, whether it is friendships, love, or business connections. If any discord arises with your relationships with others, ask him to help you balance, elevate, smooth, and mend the connection. Fighting injustice, wanting harmony, and a fair resolution are other areas in which Archangel Raguel can assist you with. You cannot get away with treating others badly as Archangel Raguel will come in and correct your behavior.

One thing to note is that Archangel Raguel will not get rid of a love interest you are having trouble with, but rather will enter the situation to help you see it in a new light that benefits everyone involved. This is not the case if your significant other is abusive, but rather when misunderstandings arise with no hope for solution. He rushes in to infuse his light in the situation by merging both of your souls to a place of understanding and love.

Do you have to deal with difficult co-workers or a tiring parent? Ask Archangel Raguel to restore balance and harmony on this and other situations where you are experiencing discord.

Messages from Archangel Raguel

Archangel Raguel shifts your perspective towards one that is fair, balanced, and objective. This reduces friction, pain, or any other unpleasant emotion that rises during a rift with another party or person. Raguel is all about compromise. Hanging dangerously close to the middle is always best. It benefits all parties especially when experiencing a disagreement. Archangel Raguel points out that so many human souls have a detachment from God and spirit. This is evident in the way that souls have a hyper rigid view with no room for movement. If someone does not believe in the same things they do, then they attack them. In some instances, they kill them!

As any intelligent being can point out, having no room for compromise does not bring people together. This is evident in media, politics, and religion. Three circumstances which control and develop human souls. Your ego wants to dominate and it is stubborn, rigid, and bruised when slighted. It acts out in aggression or in upset when something does not go according to its plan. Your higher self and soul are too high up to be bothered with such pettiness. Your higher self is unaffected by slights done to it. It knows that others are acting out of ego and this warrants no attention. It stands strong like a lone reed in the wind. This applies to all connections when it reaches a place of tension or discord. This is when you should immediately call in Archangel Raguel to smooth out the rough edges and bring balance and fairness to all parties involved.

The problem is when confronted with antagonism by another, your ego immediately slams on the gas without thinking anything through. It runs over everything in its way like a car driving out of control. It knocks things out of the way with aggression only to find you've gained nothing in the end. The only thing gained is angry emotions, which cause further internal and external harm. Your ego has control and does not listen to the voice of God or your higher self. It becomes a naughty spoiled child throwing a tantrum. What happens when a child behaves this way? A proper parent trains the child by sending them away to their room. They withhold the activities the child enjoys. The child does not get any of the wonderful prizes. Taken away from them are the toys or video games they love. The parent sends them away ignoring them and leaving them left to sulk and pout. No one pays much attention to a child stomping their feet and acting out. In addition, neither does any adult when there is conflict. You are only thinking for

480

yourself in those instances. This is where Archangel Raguel comes in to dissolve those cords of strife. When you request his intervention he brings peace and harmony to all parties involved. If you do not wish the one you are angry with to receive harmony in a disagreement, then you will not receive it either.

Archangel Raguel is beneficial for couples who are distant and no longer connecting. He can lift the thorns of distance or disagreement and help the couple to find compromise and middle ground. What happens afterwards is the couple begins working together and meeting each other half way. Raguel nudges them to open up peacefully and lovingly with one another. Neither of them understands where the immediate camaraderie has come from, unless they work with Raguel firsthand. This also carries over to legal drama or issues with particular organizations where they are exerting their power and intimidation over you. Call in Archangel Raguel immediately to help the situation and bring a positive conclusion for all parties. Archangel Raguel would make an awesome right hand man for anyone who is an attorney or practices law. It cannot hurt you or your cases when you request that he works with you full time.

There is no doubt that many human souls are in relationships where there is no communication. They have built up tension, estrangement, or arguments. Speak your mind lovingly and work it out together in order to bring any misunderstandings to closure. Addressing issues allows you to start a new chapter in your life with this person. The illusions and deceptions going on within certain relationships are an interesting dichotomy. There will be secrets that pop up or new discoveries you wish you had not known about. Some of your thoughts may be deceptive by exaggerating a situation. This is where your relationship appears one way and you jump to conclusions about it only to discover it was not true. You say, "Oh was that all it was." Some of the thoughts you conjure up can be detrimental causing a potential break up or add hostility to your union. When you allow negative thoughts about what you think your partner is doing to overtake you, then it's time to bring in Archangel Raguel. He will infuse harmony within your relationship, or a peaceful separation if it has been abusive.

How Raguel works is he helps all parties involved have an eagle's eye view of how they are playing a part in the friction. If you are with a love partner that contributes nothing to the relationship, then Raguel can help bring in a love partner who is balanced and in the relationship with you. He will not do this without first nudging your partner to make significant changes in how they invest or contribute towards the relationship. Since you have free will, some souls will ignore his guidance. If this is the case where both parties are unwilling to bend from their innate values and put in an effort, then Raguel will dissolve the union and bring another soul mate potential into your life that is more aligned with your beliefs and ways of living. However, it is important to note that if you're someone who is inflexible to begin with, and you place excessive and outlandish demands on your partner, then you may end up alone. No high vibrational potential soul mate will put up with a controlling disciplinarian for a love partner, let alone be attracted to it to begin with. Give yourself a good hard objective look to see where you play a part in relationship friction. If you're unable to, then ask a close trusted one to be honest with you about your basic behavior in general and in relationships. Be prepared for the answer and work on those negative traits about you that need to be adjusted so that you can attract in a loving soul mate partner.

When you are with someone in a love relationship who does not know what they want, then this creates an imbalance between the both of you. This can be where you are more committed to the relationship than they are. This can also be relationships where neither party works on the connection together by opening up and communicating regularly. Both parties are affected negatively by the lopsided energy moving back and forth between you. You block abundance and great things in your life when there is an imbalance such as this. Call on Archangel Raguel to work with you on your relationship if this is the case. Ask him for guidance if you do not know what to do. Step out of the way and pay attention to any repeated signs he gives you.

You know you do not want to leave the love relationship, but you know it cannot continue in its current state. This is where Raguel can work his magic and help you both find a common ground using compromise. Compromise means both parties will need to let go of certain rigid beliefs so that you are on an equal level. Compromising is considering your partner's feelings. It is meeting them half way with issues so that you can both be happy. Both of you need to do this. This is not to say that you have to deny who you are, but you do need to be clear with each other. You have to be willing to work on the areas that cause unhappiness within the union. If one or the both of you is unable or unwilling to, then the relationship will either end or continue the way it is indefinitely.

If you are with someone who never knows what they want when it comes to your connection, then ask Archangel Raguel to intervene and help correct this indecisiveness. He will do this by bringing you together, or by bringing in someone aligned with your relationship values. This would be someone who wants to commit to you and knows this without a doubt. Raguel knows for sure that the person you are with will never want the things you want. Archangel Raguel, like all heavenly hosts, is profoundly psychic and knows what you and your mate desires even if neither of you says it to one another. Raguel clairvoyantly sees that your partner will be more committed to you years down the line. He may ask you to be patient as he avoids bringing you someone new, because he knows that all will be well with your current mate eventually.

Archangel Chamuel

Archangel Chamuel is referred to as, *'the finding angel'*. He can help you find anything from the right career, love partner, home, or your keys! I have had incidents where I am frantically looking for something I misplaced. I will say something like, *"Archangel Chamuel, please help me find...."* Almost immediately, I head straight to where the item I lost is. I will hear him through my clairaudience channel tell me where it is, or he will infuse the message claircognizantly, where I suddenly know exactly where the item I misplaced is.

If you are in the middle of a career or job transition, ask Archangel Chamuel to be by your side ushering this change. He will help make the transition effortless and smooth ensuring that you are moving into the right work position. He also works with the Romance Angels when someone longs for or wishes for a loving soul mate relationship, or new friendships that are more aligned with your higher values and beliefs. He will only bring you those that are positively beneficial to you. If your twin flame is living in this lifetime with you, he can assist you both in uniting while having the courage to speak to one another.

Chamuel sparks new passion and interest into current relationships. This also applies to married/committed couples who are having issues. Before you can attract in a new career or partnership, it is first important to love and believe in yourself. Archangel Chamuel is all about the love and can infuse God's love into a cold heart. He will awaken your heart chakra if it is blocked and help you to attract in love. Call upon Archangel Chamuel if you need help finding the right career, job, love partner, or friendships.

Messages from Archangel Chamuel

Everyone has more than one soul mate in their lifetime. Soul mates are not just love relationships. They can be friends, family members, business connections, lovers, animals, acquaintances, and even your own Children. It can be someone in passing that relays information to you that shifts your world towards something brighter. Soul mates challenge you and open you up. They help you face your baggage and learn from your mistakes. They help your spirit grow and enhance. This Earthly life is one big class after all. This is what it means when someone says that the person you're dating would be good for you.

Archangel Chamuel understands this human need for a love partner. Therefore, he works diligently to bring many human souls together in loving relationships when they request his help. He can also work on your current relationship connections, and with those relationships from the past that ended without closure. If you have found people popping up from your past to re-connect, know that they are appearing for a reason that benefits your soul. You might feel uncomfortable with that and throw your hands in the air, "Oh, I'm not talking to them!" The re-connection is to give you or them an opportunity to have closure. You need to make your peace with them. This is by forgiving them for what they might have done to hurt you. You do this when you allow them back into the picture to make amends and balance your connection out. You do not have to continue with a forged friendship or relationship with them, but there is previous Karma that needs working on between the two of you. Chamuel says that this is going back to make good with what was wronged in the past.

I have been with those who are all brains. They have little to no emotion, feeling, or love. Meanwhile, I am feeling drained with all of my giving stuff. I sensed the great imbalance in those connections. On top of that, my soul feels neglected on other levels since I crave a high quotient of romance and passion on a regular basis. Each of your relationship connections prep you to work on certain things pertaining to your soul. You have insight to gain while in them.

In this modern day world, it can be rare to see a couple go the distance. Part of this is due to the many contributing factors that exist today. The ego is powerful wanting to be free. It finds it difficult to merge comfortably and unconditionally with others. Chamuel can assist you in opening up your heart to love by stripping away your obsession with what your ego demands in a love relationship. He can bring you a new sense of self and help you love yourself more. When you love yourself, then you attract in a wonderful loving mate into your life that picks up on your high vibration. People are turned off and not attracted to someone who exudes a consistent dose of insecure feelings. I was involved with someone such as this. It ultimately ended at the hands of the insecure one who placed me on too high of a pedestal. They ultimately felt as if they could not measure up and also preferred to be free and unattached.

Chamuel will bring you a new partner or a renewed passionate feeling with your current partner if this is what you choose. He will help you experience a deeper connection with each other. In my particular case I understood that Chamuel was dealing with someone who governed their life primarily from free will and ego. Archangel Chamuel also prompts marriage proposals or stronger commitments between two souls. He will bring in a new beginning in your relationship where it feels you are starting a brand new relationship with the same person. This can be in a current relationship or just a renewed outlook on how you would want your relationship to be. These relationships always include love, friendships, neighbors, families, business colleagues...you name it. It all applies and Chamuel wants to assist to bring you more love and harmony in your life. This raises your vibration which ultimately helps the energy on the planet. When you have joyful and peaceful human souls, you have a high vibrational energy wave that affects the globe. This is why the Archangels work with you on the little things to get you happy!

Archangel Chamuel helps you examine the connections you have with others. The ties you make with other people whether they are a lover, friend, colleague, boss, sibling, parent, or child are no accident. You have bonds with certain souls where you feel like you are being tested at times. Perhaps every time you are with this person you feel uncomfortable or you feel forced to put on the face and be civil to avoid a disagreement. Chamuel asks that you look at the unions that cause you some form of upset or grief. Observe the underlying lessons within them. Make your peace with it and then let it go. This can also be a circumstance where you are drawn to the same type of wrong person repeatedly. You cannot seem to let them go even though you are perfectly aware they are damaging to you. There are a couple of reasons for this. One of them is that you both have unfinished lessons together. Each person needs the characteristics that the other has in order to fulfill a specific lesson. This will help in their spiritual growth while here. Once the lessons are learned and you have changed positively because of it, then the shift happens and you attract in healthier stronger people into your life.

An example of a scenario is a guy who came from an abusive household. With him is his girlfriend who is a successful, self-confident, and well-respected human soul in her career. They meet and are immediately attracted to one another and thus form a relationship. Over time, she loses herself in the relationship. Feeling the imbalance, she starts to assert herself, as this is how she used to be before the relationship. When she does this though, he cuts her down using the violence and bullying he learned from his upbringing. He continues to belittle and cut her down. She starts to believe it and ultimately leaves him. Yet, he comes around apologizing and begging for forgiveness. She is drawn right back to him again as she remembers all the good times and forgets about the violence. The lesson here for both of them to learn is that he needs to stop the cycle of violence in his family history, and she needs to learn to assert herself and not falter once in a relationship. Someone will love all of who she is without compromise.

There are lessons in all of your connections that you must learn in order for you to grow. If this does not happen, you will continue to attract in the same types of people who exude similar characteristics from one another. You are essentially attracted to these types of people without realizing it until you are knee deep in it.

How often do you hear someone say, "Why do I keep attracting the same types of people to me?" It is important to come to terms with the lesson you are meant to learn in how or why you are attracting in the same characters. These connections are not happening by chance. Once you have honed in on this, then it is time to enact an inner change. This is in order to start attracting in relationships at a higher level. It is common to be unaware that there is a lesson in these unions while you are in them. Your ego and lower self takes over and places blame on the other person. It looks at what the other person is doing to them. This is giving your power away to someone else. You need to take a step back to see the lesson you must learn in that particular relationship that will prompt you to grow and move to the next level. Once you have done that, you experience a release from that tie. You will attract in souls who are nothing like who you used to be attracting in. You will instead invite in new healthier relationships and connections.

Archangel Zadkiel

Archangel Zadkiel is the angel of knowledge who will walk by your side if you are a teacher, student of higher learning and spiritual pursuits. He can keep your ear chakras clear of debris so that you can clearly hear the voices of God, your angels and guides. He can assist with helping you remember things you need to know from grocery lists to speeches you need to make publicly. Writers can work with him if they are writing a book that contains tons of information that is easy to forget. Call on Archangel Zadkiel if you need help with unloading heavy toxic burdens and if you need to experience mercy, compassion, help with forgiveness, or letting go of past pain. He is the remembering angel and this is from recalling the smallest detail needed, to identifying who you are as a soul of God.

Messages from Archangel Zadkiel

Archangel Zadkiel restores balance in your life and helps you find peace. He brings your life to a place where you are giving and dispersing equal energy towards all that exists around you. This is from family, love, career, and home. He knows that when one area is lopsided that you feel out of sorts. You become distressed, worn, and agitated. To reach a place of peace is to accept that your needs happen on their own course and time. Zadkiel can help you be at peace with how your life is. He will guide you to live in the now by exercising patience with what is to come.

Zadkiel guides you away from excess. This includes whatever you are abusing or addicted to. If you have been consuming too much alcohol for example, then he can diminish this need when you ask for his intervention.

What is important is seeing all sides of an equation or argument with an objective view. Zadkiel helps you stay neutral because taking sides gets everyone nowhere. He helps you find the balance between opposing views and issues.

Unrequited is about anything that is not reciprocated. When there is no reciprocation in your life, then there is no balance. If you want to witness an investment, profit, or return in terms of your desires, then button down the hatches and drive full force into your passion. Put all of your energy into it knowing that the rewards will come out of it on its own time. You could be sitting idly around waiting for a hand out, but this will never happen. You have to get up and dive into what you want. When you do that, then you are met more than half way. Meditate on what you want. This is by being still and allowing ideas to come forth on your next step. Many meditate and connect with the other side in a myriad of ways. I enjoy jumping into physical activity. This is climbing, jogging, or walking through nature. This is where the big messages from spirit happen for me.

If you want to see something positive manifest out of your interests and passions, then you have to go after it. This can be a business venture or even a romantic partner. If you feel like something is not happening in your life in a particular area, or you are not seeing any sort of abundance or return coming in, then there may be an imbalance at play. Zadkiel asks that you question how much work you are putting into what you want. Perhaps you have been slacking a bit or taking some time off from it. He reminds you that some effort needs to happen on your part. Traits like patience, forgiveness, and cooperating with other people is vital in certain situations. Meeting others half way will take you far.

Ask Archangel Zadkiel to balance your life out in every way possible and in every area in all directions of time. He can bring you a renewed sense of self and positive feelings of well-being into your life. This brings in the great miracles you dream of. You have the power to be happy, to accomplish your dreams, and to do whatever it is that you seek to do as long as it is aligned with love. This power is at your fingertips and has been since birth into this lifetime, so go for it, access it and utilize it.

Forgiveness is one of the most difficult acts for human souls to do. Your ego can hold slights so close to your soul to the point where that toxic feeling festers and grows tampering with your psyche. Zadkiel can help you release this non-forgiveness. Holding onto it towards anyone is not healthy because the only person it hurts is you. It is understandable to have anger towards someone who has abused you or treated you unkindly; however, it is necessary to reach that place where you do forgive them. When you do not forgive someone and you hang onto that tightly, then you create blocks that prevent you from reaching a state of happiness. You are not saying what they did to you is okay, and nor are you letting them off the hook. You are forgiving them for yourself, and so that you can be freed of that pain. This is for you and your overall soul. You know how it feels to hold onto negative emotions like anger or sadness. This state feels horrible! It bogs you down and you are unable to focus clearly. You end up making mistakes and you alienate people who care about you in the process.

Make a list in a notebook of those that you harbor resentment towards and why. Go over each line and mentally or out loud forgive them for the sake of release. Feel the heavy weight of not forgiving you carry, and then allow Archangel Zadkiel to transport it away to Heaven. Take that sheet of paper out of your notebook and destroy it in the name of God. This will release it and the energy.

Archangel Zadkiel aligns my vibration with those in the higher realms when I'm in the zone or channel. At times I cut in and out of frequency when important information or guidance is being relayed. It is Zadkiel that comes in and restores the communication line ensuring that it is crystal clear and connected. He's not someone I had originally called in to work with, but this was how he first introduced himself to me. Instantly he went into work mode whenever I moved into the channel space. He voluntarily comes in to adjust my frequency so that I hear my Spirit team clearly. This is especially beneficial when attempting to reach God or those in a higher plane. The higher I need to reach, the more he shows up to bend these etheric light cords that appear much like a telephone wire. The only difference is these are various different sparkly colored lights that bend, curve, and distort depending on where my thoughts are. He is also brushing away dust, dirt, and dark particles that sometimes accumulate around this wire.

Zadkiel is not around much on day-to-day communications with my Spirit team, but when I'm writing Spirit messages for a book for example, he is present through the entire process. Without my request, he shows up almost as if he wants to. This is no surprise that he keeps me connected since he works with clearing out the ear chakras. Your ear chakras are connected to your clairaudience. If I break out of the connection when vital messages are in the process of being relayed, then I will say, "Zadkiel, please connect me. Thank you." Thirty seconds to one minute later the connection is strong again. This is a common occurrence when it comes to the spiritual work. The many that are not around me regularly band together around me whenever I'm in work mode.

Archangel Jeremiel

Archangel Jeremiel comes forward to do your life review with you when you cross over to the other side. Contrary to some beliefs of you being judged by God, you do go through a life review where you may find that you are judging yourself for your actions on Earth. This is why it is important to face what you have done in this lifetime. Look at what you have been through in the past and heal those wounds that others caused you or where you inflicted hurt on them. Make your peace with it now. Archangel Jeremiel will assist you with this when you let him know that you are ready.

In my book, "*Reaching for the Warrior Within*", Archangel Jeremiel was front and center guiding me through my past so that I could forgive and let go of what had happened to me. This was in keeping only the lessons and love that led me to where I am today. I did a serious evaluation of my life and the experiences I went through personally while writing that book. Doing this helped me remove former patterns and ways of living in order to move to the next spiritual plateau and see life through new eyes. The purpose of a life review with Archangel Jeremiel is so that you can correct your mistakes so that you do not continue making them. He prepares and ushers you through and toward positive transformations in your life. Ask Archangel Jeremiel to help heal and release past pain in your life while ushering you into a brighter new world.

Messages from Archangel Jeremiel

Martin Luther King Jr. was a warrior of light whose goal was peaceful activism in bringing people together. When he passed on into the next plane, it was intended that he be remembered on Earth for several things. One of them was to love and serve humanity. This is why all souls are here. See the innocence in someone's actions and release any harsh judgments that unknowingly plague you. Many are caught up in the past, worried about the future, and simultaneously trying to make huge transitions into a better life calmly. The ego is like a loud spoiled child and gets in the way by making you feel frustrated or confused. If you let it get a hold of you and run your life, then you will drown in its energy.

Jeremiel's message is to clear the clutter and space in and around you, from your mind, your place of work, and even your car. All souls on Earth are transforming globally. Even if they are not aware of it, it is happening and has been for centuries. You can move with it graciously or have an outburst, which is what you might be witnessing in others who partake in violence, hate, or cruel judgments. There is no going back to the past as it is outdated and no longer realistic. With this change comes seeing things in a new light. The way to transform into this new life is to start at the core individually. This is by organizing yourself, your surroundings, and your life one step at a time. Adopt healthy new ways of living and seeing circumstances. This includes releasing any feelings of guilt or sadness you carry around regarding someone or a past decision you made. Forgive yourself and others for previous mistakes you or they have made.

The colors of Archangel Jeremiel are a bright and vibrant violet color with indigo tinges. This light latches onto everything around you when he is present. The violet light is the light energy of physical and spiritual transformation. The way he works is by washing your soul as if it is experiencing a baptism. Allow his light to wash over you and clear away any debris which prevents you from moving forward. Get rid of all that senseless weight. Do not be afraid to get your feet wet as you release issues of the past. Call on Archangel Jeremiel who will work with you through this process using grace and willingness.

Clutter creates chaos and this is why it is important to do a routine stripping of any disorder in your surroundings. Archangel Jeremiel conducts a life review and part of this process is by removing things that no longer serve you once it's addressed. He has you examine your past with a fine toothcomb before you make your peace with it. You must make your peace with it before he releases it from your aura. Making your peace with it includes understanding why the situation happened to begin with. This will help you feel complete, whole, and ready for your next juncture.

Learn from your circumstances, choices, and experiences. If you are buried in heavy feelings in relation to what is not working in your life, then it is time to work through this to reach a place of contentment. It does not help you when you are focused on feeling yucky emotions. In order to work through them, you have to examine them and look for the underlying cause and message. What areas in your life are provoking you in a negative way? Those areas require a major change on your part. Ask Archangel Jeremiel for help with this and follow his guidance even if it is pushing you out of your element. Following his instructions will help you move to the next plateau. See only the love and lessons in your current experiences and make your peace with it.

The Mercury Retrograde cycle is a planetary transit that happens three times a year. It forces every individual human soul to pause, move within, and evaluate all areas of their life. Those who do not understand the Mercury Retrograde cycle tend to battle with anxiety and stress while making one error after another. They vent frustration and do not understand that the transit prompts you to pause whether you like it or not. Mercury Retrograde is not going to wait for a company or corporation to get with the program of the Universe. Mercury Retrograde is God created while corporations are man created. You cannot win a battle with the universe, God, and spirit, no matter how powerful your man made company is.

Look up the more in depth meaning of the Mercury Retrograde transit online. Knowing the dates of the Mercury Retrograde in any given year will help you prepare and plan important dates outside of that if possible. The Mercury Retrograde transit is a terrific time to do a life review with Archangel Jeremiel, since it is all about going back to examine the past. Of course, you can have a life review anytime you are ready. The Mercury Retrograde transit prompts you to go back and re-trace your steps. What better time to go back, review, and re-examine everything in your past than during the Mercury Retrograde transit. Re-evaluate your life, where you are at and see what needs changing or eliminating. When Mercury moves direct, use that time to take action steps to make the necessary improvements in your life that came to light during the Mercury Retrograde transit. Doing a thorough life review with Archangel Jeremiel can take some time, because if you are not owning up to the mistakes you made, then you do not move past the review. For some, this life review can take years or an entire lifetime.

Questions from Readers about Spirit Guides & Angels

Q: What is the best way to contact guides when you are having trouble connecting through meditation?

A: Spirit Guides and Angels are by your side the instant you call them. You do not need to do any special invocation or meditation to communicate with them. The reason why meditating is effective is because it puts you in a calm and relaxed state. You are more apt to receiving their messages clearly when you are in that space, rather than stressed or distracted.

Q: Can you explain blinks of light? I've been seeing them for years. Not sure if it is guides.

A: There are angel trails or lights that may show up in one's peripheral vision if their third eye is open. If this is the case, then you are seeing them clairvoyantly. They do appear as lights for some people.

Q: Do guides work through numbers to get your attention? When you see the same sequence of numbers, could it be your guide?

A: Angels and Spirit Guides communicate with you in many ways and yes through numbers and symbols is one way.

Q: With meditation, how do I know if I am connecting with my guide and it's not my imagination or wishes?

A: They will use the pronoun *"You"* while your own thoughts and ego use the pronoun *"I"*. Your higher self is 100% psychic while your lower self is not. Every human soul communicates with them in varying ways whether they are aware of it or not. They mainly communicate through their 'clair channels'. If you are receiving positive messages and nudges repeatedly, then it is likely them. These messages will come to you more than three times. Your ego or lower self will conjure up something once and discard it. If your ego is being repetitive or obsessing, it is prompting you to do something that you know is not good for you. The messages or guidance from Spirit will be urging you to do something that will positively benefit you or someone else.

Q: Could Children's imaginary friends be Spirit Guides?

A: Children are more adept at communicating with Spirit Guides. They don't hold lower self-judgments the way adults have learned to do. Children know more about acceptance and love than any adult. Adults are damaged children who were lured into a certain way of thinking due to their surroundings and upbringing. Children view things in a purer way and use less of their ego. The ego blows up to the size of a football field once adults get a hold of it.

Q: I'm new to this, what are guides?

A: A guide is a spirit on the other side who is assigned to you through the duration of your lifetime on Earth. Their purpose is to help, nudge, and guide you along the right path steering you away from poor choices if you pay attention to them. They do not make your decisions for you, but they intervene when you are going off course. They are essentially your right hand confidante who knows everything about you including your thoughts, feelings, and needs. They do not help you fulfill needs that are against your greater good such as hanging around the wrong people, doing drugs, and alcohol, or absorbing yourself in toxic addictions. In fact, they nudge you to steer clear of bad vices. Your ego is so powerful that it ignores the wisdom your guide has for you.

Q: When I meditate I see faces of people I do not know. Are these guides?

A: They may be your guide or an angel, but not always. You may be outwardly projecting your subconscious mind. This may prompt your mind to display shadows. This is a sign of an activated clairvoyance channel.

Q: How do you tell the difference between a Guide versus an Angel?

A: A guide is typically someone who had an Earthly life, but went through advanced training on the other side to be a pure Spirit Guide for a human soul during its Earth life. Guardian Angels were never human, but always a spirit. The exception is incarnated angels. They may temporarily appear human for a purpose or to avert you from danger or crises and then disappear.

Q: Can guides heal you with your body and mind?

A: Some guides have specific specialties that they work with you on like love, health, career, etc. They heal your body and mind so that you are operating from your higher self and more able to communicate with God.

Q: Are we able to call more than one Guide for help with different projects or problems? Is it always necessary to call them?

A: You can call on as many Guides and Angels as you like. When they have worked with you on a specific issue and there is no need for anymore assistance, then they move on to help other souls calling out for them. Your main Spirit Guide and Guardian Angel are always around you and never leave. They guide and help you along your life path. However, it is necessary to ask for their help, as they cannot intervene with your free will unless you have asked them to.

Q: How long do you experience meditation before you feel your guides' presence?

A: To feel them it can take anywhere from 5 to 15 minutes of meditation or by being still and relaxed. Breathing is important as it not only relaxes you, but delivers oxygen into every cell in your body allowing you to be a fine tuned receptive communication tool with them. It's like clearing the static of a telephone line.

Q: I get those voices that tell me what's going on. It's a voice, a feeling, and a twinge in my heart area all at once. They validate questions at times, sometimes they validate before I have the questions. Is that my Guide?

A: If the messages you are receiving this way end up coming true, then yes they are your guide or your angel.

500

Q: Do the deceased watch us do things like taking a shower?

A: They do not watch you shower, dress, or have sex. They do not have that kind of attraction or interest. They see your soul as light and feeling. If that gives you peace of mind to know you're not being watched every time you strip down. Those on the other side are not Peeping Toms. The only exception may be an Earth bound spirit who chose not to cross over and is basically hanging out in limbo mode. They get a rush out of re-enacting the same activity with a human soul indefinitely, or until they make the move into the light to be purified.

Q: How can I find out the name of my Spirit Guide and Guardian Angel?

A: Knowing their name varies from person to person. There are times where they do not go by any name, specifically your guardian angel who has never been in human form. Some may make up a name so that you feel more comfortable able to address them in some way. It doesn't matter how you address them. You can ask them to tell you their name. Ask them to continue to show you signs and confirmation of what it is. Then start paying attention to the signs and symbols in your surroundings. Perhaps in the following week or so you keep running into people with the name of "James" and you see that name out of nowhere on Billboards, signs, etc. That's one way they can communicate with you.

Q: How do I communicate with the Archangels?

A: Communicating with the Archangels happen the same way you communicate with the angels, guardian angels, ascended masters, spirit guides, and deceased loved ones. Being in a relaxed state helps since it brings your soul into a calmer and receptive place. When you are calm and feeling uplifting joy without any chemicals is the most efficient way. This is when your energy vibration is raised closer to Heaven and you receive clear divine communication more

501

effortlessly. When you are under stress, experiencing negative emotions, or on heavy alcohol, bad foods, or other toxic vices, then this creates restrictions, which form blocks that clog up these etheric phone cords that connect you to Spirit. Of course they are always communicating with you, but are you hearing them?

Q: Why do people who do bad things or hurt others have great success in life or seem to have it easier? How come those who do good get nowhere?

A: One of the things is that some of these perceived bad people know they are going to get what they want no matter what. Their intention to getting what they want is so great and they are so optimistic and sure of themselves about it that they manifest it. They are not going to get away with something bad. If they do, it will be short-lived. They will be stopped. The angels see the goodness in ALL people whether that person is good or bad. They do not place them into separate categories. There are guides and spirits who are not egoless and are doing different work in Heaven. They see the behavior of mankind and do not take it lightly. Each individual case would have to be examined to give you the reasons why as it's not that cut and dry. If a good person is not manifesting, but instead living in frustration over it, then that is what they are attracting to themselves.

Q: I am starting to open my heart and eyes to new vibrations and I am trying to have a connection with angels by sending them my love. The more I do this I seem to be getting small white feathers left in front of me. At work, at home, in the street, and even one in my hair. What's going on or am I starting to be weird? It's almost daily now. I'm not sure what to do so I feel happy to pick it up and say thank you. Should I be doing something? I think I have made myself look strange enough for now, but I had to ask someone and it's not something I can bring up around people I know.

A: You are opening yourself up more to the light and to the angels. When someone is making an attempt to communicate or connect with the angels sometimes they wonder if they are being heard. Some don't visually see the angels in front of them and so they may question whether or not they are being heard. The angels have connected with you the second you have put out the intention to communicate with them. They try various ways of making contact with you, either through your various senses or in other ways through numbers and symbols. This is how you communicate with Spirit.

We have various ways of communicating such as by phone, email, or texting. Since those on the other side can't just pick up the phone, they use creative ways of communicating as we will too when we cross over. We won't need things like phones or computers. One of the big ways that angels like to let you know that they are hearing you is they love to drop white feathers around. You suddenly start finding them in places where it doesn't seem feasible for it to suddenly show up. They tend to do it quite a bit with those who are fervently trying to connect with them. They will do it when someone is desperately needing an answer to something specific and wondering if they're being heard. You are. This is their way of telling you, *'We hear you loud and clear.'* There is nothing you need to do, but accept this love that they are showering upon you. You can even save the feather in a special place as a gift if you choose.

"Thy word is a lamp unto my feet
and a light unto my path." – Psalms

Let your Spirit team of God, Angels, and Spirit Guides be your companions on your life's journey.

Available in paperback and e-book by Kevin Hunter,
"REALM OF THE WISE ONE"

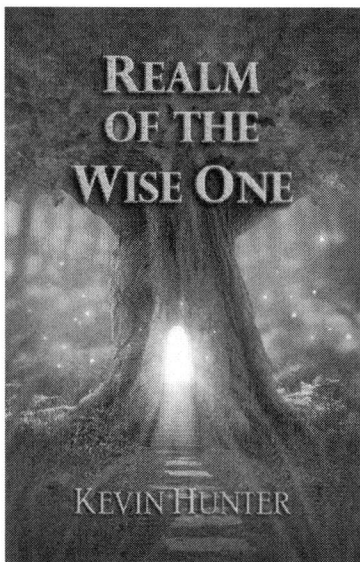

In the Spirit Worlds and the dimensions that exist, reside numerous kingdoms that house a plethora of Spirits that inhabit various forms. One of these tribes is called the Wise Ones, a darker breed in the spirit realm who often chooses to incarnate into a human body one lifetime after another for important purposes.

The *Realm of the Wise One* takes you on a magical journey to the spirit world where the Wise Ones dwell. This is followed with in-depth and detailed information on how to recognize a human soul who has incarnated from the Wise One Realm.

Author, Kevin Hunter, is a Wise One who uses the knowledge passed onto him by his Spirit team of Guides and Angels to relay the wisdom surrounding all things Wise One. He discusses the traits, purposes, gifts, roles, and personalities among other things that make up someone who is a Wise One.

Wise Ones have come in the guises of teachers, shaman, leaders, hunters, mediums, entertainers and others. *Realm of the Wise One* is an informational guide devoted to the tribe of the Wise Ones, both in human form and on the other side.

Reaching for the Warrior Within is the author's personal story recounting a volatile childhood. This led him to a path of addictions, anxiety and overindulgence in alcohol, drugs, cigarettes and destructive relationships. As a survival mechanism he split into different "selves". He credits turning his life around, not by therapy, but by simultaneously paying attention to the messages he has been receiving from his Spirit team in Heaven since birth. He explains how he was able to tell the difference between when his higher self was intervening and ruling the show, and when his lower self was running his life into the gutter.

Living several lifetimes in one, he did not let anything stop him from getting his life together, going after what he wanted and achieving it. He describes how he pulled himself up by his bootstraps and obtained every job he wanted without prior experience. This is from work in the entertainment industry with some of Hollywood's respected talent, to ridding himself of toxic addictions and living a healthier lifestyle clear-minded.

Kevin Hunter gains strength, healing and direction with the help of his own team of guides and angels. They navigate all of us through the treacherous waters in our lives. Living vicariously through this inspiring story will enable you to distinguish when you have been assisted on your own life path.

Reaching for the Warrior Within attests that anyone can change if they pay attention to their own inner guidance system and take action. This can be from being a victim of child abuse, or a drug and alcohol user, to going after the jobs and relationships you want. This powerful story is for those seeking motivation to change, alter and empower their life one day at a time.

Available in paperback and e-book by Kevin Hunter,

"IGNITE YOUR INNER LIFE FORCE"

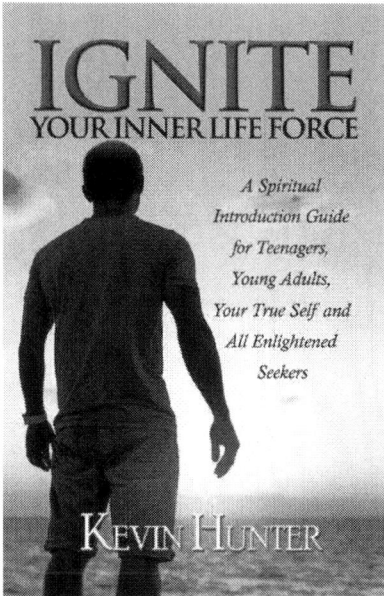

Ignite Your Inner Life Force is an introduction guide for teens, young adults, and anyone seeking answers, messages, and guidance and surrounding spiritual empowerment. This is from understanding what Heaven, the soul, and spiritual beings are to knowing when you are connecting with your Spirit team of Guides and Angels.

Some of the topics covered are communicating with Heaven, working with your Spirit team, what your higher self is, your life purpose and soul contract, what the ego is, love and relationships, your vibration energy, shifting your consciousness and thinking for yourself even when you stand alone. This is an in-depth primer manual offering you foundation as you find a higher purpose navigating through your personal journey in today's modern day practical world.

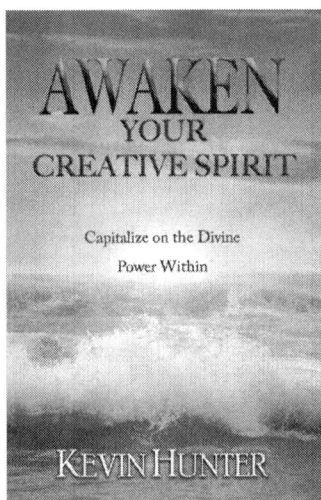

Your creative spirit is present when you experience positive energy flowing through you. This energy is ignited when you make a direct connection with God. This vibration state is where you have access to the true you, which is your higher self. Your higher self rules when you work to strip, reduce, or dissolve any negative tampering influenced by a domination of your physical surroundings. Make a connection with something greater than yourself and allow that energy Light to permeate your soul and cleanse it of toxic debris. This will assist in the process of awakening your creative spirit from slumber.

Your creative spirit is more than being artistic and getting involved in creativity pursuits, although this is a good part of it. When your creative spirit is activated by a high vibration state of being, then this is the space you create from. You can apply this to your dealings in life, your creative and artistic pursuits, and to having a greater communication line with your Spirit team on the Other Side.

Your creative spirit brings your soul into a high vibration state of being because coming from a place of creativity raises your vibration. This is the place where you create and manifest your visions at higher levels while moving you into the joy of your life. It is thinking like a kid, unleashing your inner artist, and realizing your soul's potential. When you claim your celestial power with the assistance of your heavenly helpers by your side on your Earthly life, then this assists in capitalizing the true divine power within you. *Awaken Your Creative Spirit* is an overview of what it means to have access to Divine assistance and how that plays a part in arousing the muse within you in order to bring your state of mind into a happier space.

Available in paperback and e-book by Kevin Hunter,

"THE SEVEN DEADLY SINS"

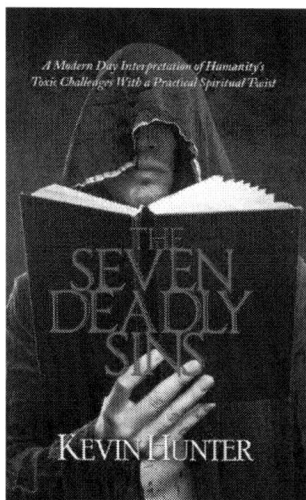

The Seven Deadly Sins is a mini-pocket book that takes a look at the traditional sins in a practical way. The Seven Deadly Sins in today's language would be the Seven Toxic Challenges. Being aware of these toxic challenges are helpful since falling into a deadly sin creates a block from achieving greatness, finding peace, and picking up on the messages and guidance coming in from Heaven. The messages and guidance are intended to help guide you along your path. You were born with an ego that expands as it enters the Earth's atmosphere. This ego causes you to struggle and have conflicts as it attempts to take over you and dominate your actions, thoughts, and feelings. When your ego runs recklessly it grows and expands into darkness. The dark ego is what prompts you to wrestle with challenges in this lifetime. These challenges were called *sin* during ancient times. The sins committed can delay you on your path and wreak havoc on your soul's innate system. This innate system is the higher self part of you that governs your life through a broader perspective.

The seven deadly sins were created in order to assist human souls in making sounder choices. They are challenges that all human souls wrestle with to one degree or another. When you're deeply absorbed in these toxic challenges, then it causes an array of issues and complications on your life path. These sins or challenges prevent the positive flow of energy and abundance in your life. They also play a hand at creating a block that stops up the communication line with your team on the Other Side. The sins or toxic challenges looked at include, Pride, Envy, Greed, Lust, Gluttony, Wrath and Sloth.

About Kevin Hunter

Kevin Hunter is an author, love expert, and channeler. His books tackle a variety of genres and tend to have a strong male protagonist. The messages and themes he weaves in his work surround Spirit's own communications of love and respect which he channels and infuses into his writing and stories.

His spiritually based books include *Warrior of Light, Empowering Spirit Wisdom, Realm of the Wise One, Darkness of Ego, Ignite Your Inner Life Force, Awaken Your Creative Spirit, Reaching for the Warrior Within* and *The Seven Deadly Sins*. He is also the author of the single's dating love relationship hand guide, *Love Party of One*, the horror, drama, *Paint the Silence*, and the modern day erotic love story, *Jagger's Revolution*.

Before writing books and stories, Kevin started out in the entertainment business in 1996 becoming actress Michelle Pfeiffer's personal development dude for her boutique production company, Via Rosa Productions. She dissolved her company after several years and he made a move into coordinating film productions for the big studios on such films as *One Fine Day, A Thousand Acres, The Deep End of the Ocean, Crazy in Alabama, The Perfect Storm, Original Sin, Harry Potter & the Sorcerer's Stone, Dr. Dolittle 2,* and *Carolina*. He considers himself a beach bum born and raised in Los Angeles, California.

For more information, www.kevin-hunter.com

21104817R00293

Printed in Great Britain
by Amazon